Henry Hart Milman D.D.

History of Latin Christianity

Including that of the Popes to the Pontificate of Nicolas 5.

Henry Hart Milman D.D.

History of Latin Christianity
Including that of the Popes to the Pontificate of Nicolas 5.

ISBN/EAN: 9783741181764

Manufactured in Europe, USA, Canada, Australia, Japa

Cover: Foto ©Lupo / pixelio.de

Manufactured and distributed by brebook publishing software (www.brebook.com)

Henry Hart Milman D.D.

History of Latin Christianity

HISTORY

OF

LATIN CHRISTIANITY;

INCLUDING THAT OF

THE POPES TO THE PONTIFICATE OF NICOLAS V.

BY HENRY HART MILMAN, D.D.,

DEAN OF ST. PAUL'S.

IN NINE VOLUMES.—Vol. VIII.

FOURTH AND REVISED EDITION.

LONDON:
JOHN MURRAY, ALBEMARLE STREET.
1867.

LONDON: PRINTED BY WILLIAM CLOWES AND SONS, STAMFORD STREET,
AND CHARING CROSS.

CONTENTS

OF

THE EIGHTH VOLUME.

BOOK XII.—*continued.*

CHAPTER XI.

INNOCENT VI.

A.D.		PAGE
1350-1-2	The Black Plague	1
1352	Innocent VI. Pope	4
	Emperor Charles IV.	6
	Cardinal Albornoz	7
1353-4	Rienzi in Italy—in Rome	9
	His death	11
1362	Death of Innocent	ib.

CHAPTER XII.

URBAN V.

	His character	13
	State of Europe	14
	of Italy	15
	The Visconti	ib.
	Determines on return to Italy	19
1367	Return to Italy	20
1368	The Emperor at Rome	21
1370	Return to Avignon	22
	Death	ib.

CONTENTS OF VOL. VIII.

CHAPTER XIII.
Gregory XI.

A.D.		PAGE
	His character	23
	State of Italy	ib.
1372	Free Companies	24
1376	Catherine of Sienna	26
	Gregory arrives in Italy	29
	His death	31

BOOK XIII.
CHAPTER I.
The Schism.

1378	The Conclave	34
	Tumults	35
	Election of Archbishop of Bari	38
	Coronation	40
	Character of Urban VI.	41
	Cardinals at Anagni	45
	Declaration against Urban VI.	ib.
	Clement VII.—Antipope	48
	Schism	49

CHAPTER II.
The Rival Popes.

	Acts of Urban—of Clement	51
1380	Successes of Urban	52
1381	Charles of Durazzo in Naples	53
1382	Death of Queen Joanna	55
	Louis of Anjou	56
1383	The Pope at Naples—Butillo Prignano	57
1384	Quarrel of Charles and Urban	59
	Arrest of Cardinals	60
1385–6	Urban flies to Genoa	63
1386	Death of Charles of Durazzo	64
1389	Death of Urban VI.—Clement VII. at Avignon	66

CONTENTS OF VOL. VIII.

CHAPTER III.

BONIFACE IX. — BENEDICT XIII.

A.D.		PAGE
	Accession of Boniface IX.	70
	Simony—Annates	73
	Nepotism	75
1394	Death of Clement VII.	76
	Benedict XIII.	77
1393	Boniface IX. in Perugia	78
1399	In Rome	79
1400	Jubilee	80
	Gian Galeazzo of Milan	81
1395	Benedict XIII.—Council at Paris	82
	Peter d'Ailly	86
1398	Benedict besieged in Avignon	88
1398-1403	Imprisonment and flight	90
1404	Death of Boniface IX.	92

CHAPTER IV.

INNOCENT VII. — GREGORY XII. — BENEDICT XIII.

	Election of Innocent—Insurrection in Rome	94
	Ladislaus of Naples	95
1405	Death of Innocent	97
	Gregory XII.	98
1407	Meeting appointed at Savona	100
1407-8	Ladislaus in Rome	103
	Cardinals at Pisa	105
1408	Benedict flies to Spain	106

CHAPTER V.

COUNCIL OF PISA.

GREGORY XII., BENEDICT XIII., ALEXANDER V., AND JOHN XXIII.

	Cardinals summon the Council	109
	Benedict's Council at Perpignan	111
	Gregory's Council	112
1409	Meeting of Council at Pisa	113
	Both Popes deposed	117

CONTENTS OF VOL. VIII.

A.D.		Page
	Election of Alexander V.	120
	Bull in favour of the Friars	123
1410	Death of Alexander—Election of John XXIII.	128
	Character of John XXIII.	ib.
	Balthasar Cossa	129
1411	Crusade against Ladislaus	134
	Pope submits and again quarrels with Ladislaus	136
	Flies from Rome	137
1413	The Emperor Sigismund	139
	The Council of Constance determined	141
1414	Death of Ladislaus	144

CHAPTER VI.

WYCLIFFE.

	Teutonic England	146
	Edward II.	148
	Wars of Edward III.	150
	Archbishop of Canterbury	152
1324	Birth of Wycliffe	155
	Wycliffe at Oxford	156
	Preferments	162
	Discussion on tribute to Rome	163
1371	Parliamentary Petition against Hierarchy	165
1376	Wycliffe Commissioner at Bruges	170
	The Good Parliament	173
	William of Wykeham	175
1377	Death of Edward III.	176
	Wycliffe at St. Paul's	ib.
	Proceedings against Wycliffe	179
	Wycliffite Teachers	182
	Translation of the Bible	183
1381	Insurrection of the Peasants	185
	Council at the Grey Friars, London	189
1382	Parliament at Oxford—Convocation	193
	Wycliffe at Lutterworth	195
	Crusade—Spencer Bishop of Norwich	196
1384	Death of Wycliffe	198

CHAPTER VII.

THE LOLLARDS.

A.D.		PAGE
	Queen Anne of Bohemia	205
	Petition of Lollards	207
1399	Accession of Henry IV.	208
1400	Statute de Hæretico Comburendo	210
	William Sautree Martyr	211
1409	Badbeo and Thorpe	215
	Oldcastle, Lord Cobham	217
1417	His death	225

CHAPTER VIII.

COUNCIL OF CONSTANCE.

1415	Assemblage	227
	Pope John XXIII.	230
	Frederick of Austria	ib.
	John Huss	233
	Huss at Constance	243
	Huss in prison	246
	Arrival of the Emperor	247
	Number and Members of the Council	248

CHAPTER IX.

COUNCIL OF CONSTANCE — JOHN XXIII. — JOHN HUSS.

1416	Threatening Signs against the Pope	253
	The Emperor abandons John Huss	ib.
	Deputies from Antipopes	256
	Charges against the Pope	258
	Pope John's renunciation	260
	Flight of the Pope	267
	Gerson	270
	The Pope at Schaffhausen	271
	Proceedings of Council	273
	Surrender and Imprisonment of the Pope	277
	John Huss	278
	Examination	284
	Huss refuses to recant	291

CONTENTS OF VOL. VIII.

A.D.		PAGE
1416	Sentence	294
	Execution	295
	Proceedings in Bohemia	297
	Jerome of Prague	299
	The three Johns—John XXIII., John Huss, Jean Petit	303

CHAPTER X.

CLOSE OF THE COUNCIL OF CONSTANCE — POPE MARTIN V.

	Death of Robert Hallam	309
	Election of Martin V.	310
	Struggles for Reform	315
	Concordats	317
	Dissolution of the Council	319
	Results	ib.
1419	Martin in Florence	322
1421	Martin in Rome—State of Rome	324
	Martin on Statute of Præmunire	327
1431	Death of Martin	332

CHAPTER XI.

EUGENIUS IV. — HUSSITE WAR.

	Election of Eugenius IV.	334
	Seizes Martin's Treasure	335
	Bohemian War	337
1419	Death of King Wenzel—Accession of Sigismund	340
1420-1	Ziska—Battles of Wyschebrad, Saaz, and Deutschbrod	341
1426	Procopius—Battle of Aussitz	343
1431	Invasion of Germany—Battle of Taus	345

CHAPTER XII.

COUNCIL OF BASLE.

The Legate Julian Cæsarini	348
State of Germany	350
Emperor Sigismund in Italy	352

CONTENTS OF VOL. VIII.   ix

A.D.		PAGE
1433	Coronation	355
	Council declared lawful	356
1434	Eugenius flies from Rome	359
1435	Bohemians at Basle	362

CHAPTER XIII.

COUNCIL OF FERRARA — THE GREEKS.

	Proposed Reconciliation of Greek Empire and Church	365
	Proceedings at Constantinople	369
1435	Council suspends the Pope	ib.
	The Emperor John Palæologus	370
	Fleets of the Pope and the Council	371
1437	The voyage	376
1438	Arrival at Venice	ib.
	Arrival at Ferrara	379
	Plague at Ferrara	383
	Journey to Florence	384
	France—Pragmatic Sanction	385
	Synod of Bourges	386

CHAPTER XIV.

COUNCIL OF FLORENCE.

1438-9	Procession of the Holy Ghost	390
	Terms of Treaty	395
	Close of the Session	399
	Return of the Greeks to Constantinople	ib.

CHAPTER XV.

CONTINUATION OF THE COUNCIL OF BASLE — POPE FELIX.

	Archbishop of Arles	403
1439	Deposition of Pope Eugenius	405
	Election of Pope Felix *Amadeus, a layman*	410
1440	Coronation	ib.
	Neutrality of Germany—Diets	412

VOL. VIII.   b

CONTENTS OF VOL. VIII.

CHAPTER XVI.

ÆNEAS SYLVIUS PICCOLOMINI—DISSOLUTION OF COUNCIL OF BASLE.

A.D.		PAGE
	Youth of Æneas	415
	Æneas in Scotland	417
	His morals	421
	Æneas at Basle	428
	Secretary to Pope Felix	429
	Secretary to the Emperor	430
	Æneas in Holy Orders	433
1444	Æneas Imperial Ambassador to Rome	437
	Æneas Secretary to the Pope	439
1446	Again at Rome	441
	Gregory of Heimburg	442
	Diet at Frankfort	443
1447	Death of Eugenius IV.	447

CHAPTER XVII.

NICOLAS V.

	Election of Nicolas V.	449
1449	Dissolution of Council of Basle	450
	Abdication of Pope Felix	451
	Æneas in Milan	453
	Character of Nicolas V.	454
1450	Jubilee	456
1452	Coronation of the Emperor Frederick III.	459
1453	Conspiracy of Stephen Porcaro	463
	Taking of Constantinople	467
1455	Death of Nicolas V.	468
	Nicolas patron of letters and arts	469
	His buildings	474

HISTORY OF LATIN CHRISTIANITY.

BOOK XII.—*continued.*

CHAPTER XI.

Innocent VI.

The terrible Black Plague had startled the voluptuous Court of Avignon to seriousness. The last act of Clement VI. was one of papal wisdom and of earnest religion. He had not set the example of Christian courage and devotion to the distresses of the more than decimated people (two-thirds, it was said, of the population in Languedoc and Provence had perished [a]), but he dared to admire that virtue in others which he displayed not in himself. The clergy, too, had mostly stood aloof during these dreary times in terror and in apathy. The Mendicant Friars alone were everywhere, braving con-

---

[a] Petrarch writes of it (it swept away his Laura)—

"Exempla caritura quidem, ignaraque nepotum
Vix habitura fidem: speramus si forte nepotes,
Nec finem modo fata parant imponere mundo."—*Ecloga* ix.

The "Epistola ad seipsum" is at once more true and throughout more poetical:—

"Funera crebra quidem, quocunque pervenit a flectis
Lumina, conturbant aciem: perplexa feretris
Templa gemunt, passimque simul sine honore cadaver
Nobile plebeiumque jacet."

See on the Black Plague Dr. Hecker's book on the Epidemics of the Middle Ages, translated by Dr. Babington. Third Edition, London, 1859.

tagion, by the sickbed, in the church, in the churchyard; praying with the people, praying for the people, praying over their bodies, which owed to them alone decent interment. The grateful people repaid them with all they could bestow. Alms, oblations, bequests, funeral dues, poured upon them, and upon them alone. The clergy took alarm; they found themselves everywhere supplanted in the affections of men, in their wills, in the offerings at the altar. The very dead seemed to reject them, and, as it were, to seek the churchyards of the Friars for their holy rest. They began to clamour, even more loudly than heretofore, against these invasions of their rights. The cardinals, many bishops, a multitude of the secular clergy, thronged to Avignon; they demanded the suppression of the Mendicants. By what authority did they preach, hear confessions, intercept the alms of the faithful, even the burial dues of their flocks? The Consistory sat, not one was present who dared to lift his voice in favour of the Friars. The Pope rose: the Pope might well know of what incalculable importance were the Mendicants to his own power, but he might also at this time have had more generous, more pious motives. He defended them with imposing eloquence against their adversaries. At the close of his speech he turned to the prelates: "And if the Friars were not to preach to the people, what would ye preach? Humility? you, the proudest, the most disdainful, the most magnificent among all the estates of men, who ride abroad in procession on your stately palfreys! Poverty? ye who are so greedy, so obstinate in the pursuit of gain, that all the prebends and benefices of the world will not satiate your avidity! Chastity? of this I say nothing! God knows your lives, how your bodies are pampered with pleasures. If you

Consistory of Avignon.

into the Begging Friars, and close your doors against them, it is that they may not see your lives; you had rather waste your wealth on pandars and ruffians than on Mendicants. Be not surprised that the Friars receive bequests made in the time of the fatal mortality, they who took the charge of parishes deserted by their pastors, out of which they drew converts to their houses of prayer, houses of prayer and of honour to the Church, not seats of voluptuousness and luxury." So went forth to the world the debate in the Consistory at Avignon.[b]

Yet Clement VI., not long before his death,[c] had filled up the conclave with French prelates; twelve were appointed at once in the interests of the King of France. The King of England, now, by the victory at Crecy and by conquest, master of great part of France, had in vain demanded one place.[d] The remains of the deceased

---

[b] Continuator of Nangis, sub ann.
[c] There are two terrible satires by Petrarch against Clement VI. The one an Eclogue (the sixth) between Pamphilus (St. Peter) and Micio (Pope Clement). Pamphilus, whom Micio in his unblushing effrontery insults by openly avowing his love of gold and pleasure, and by comparing himself with St. Peter, breaks out in these lines:
"Ex meritus post vincla crucem, post verbera ferrum,
Supplicium breve! quin potius sine fine dolores
Carceris æterni, vel si quid tristius æquum est.
Serve infide, fugax, Dominoque ingrate bralæna."
The other (Eclogue VII.) is between Micio (Pope Clement) and Epi, or Epicureanism, who in the warmest language declare their mutual, inseparable attachment.

[d] Vit. apud Baluz. The seventh Eclogue of Petrarch also contains the most bitter descriptions of the Cardinals who formed the Conclave on the death of Clement. De Sade (ill. pp. 149 and 276) boasted that he could furnish the key to the whole satire, and show the original of every one of the portraits drawn in such sharp and hateful lineaments, but he abstained, not perhaps without some recollection that they were French Cardinals. It dwells chiefly, in no modest terms, on their voluptuousness. Of one he says:
"Tamen omnis turbat
Septa furens, nullasque sinit dormire quietas
Somnifera sub nocte capros."
Of another :
"Liquitur hic luxu."

Pope were attended to their final resting-place at Chaise Dieu in Auvergne, by five cardinals, one his brother, three his nephews, one his kinsman. The Conclave looked at first to John Borelli, General of the Carthusian Order, a man of profound learning and piety. The Cardinal Talleyrand Perigord warned them, that under his austere rule their noble horses would in a few days be reduced to draw waggons or to toil before the plough. They passed a law by unanimous consent which would have raised the College of Cardinals to a dominant, self-elected aristocracy, superior to the Pope. The Pope could create no Cardinal till the number was reduced to sixteen, nor increase the number beyond twenty. Nor could he nominate these Cardinals without the consent of the whole, or at least two-thirds of the Conclave. Without their consent he could neither depose nor put under arrest any Cardinal, nor seize or confiscate their property. The Cardinals were to enjoy, according to the statute of Nicolas IV., one-half of all the revenues of the Papal See.* All swore to observe this statute; some with the reservation, if it was according to law.

The election fell on Stephen Aubert, a Limousin, a distinguished Canon lawyer, Bishop of Clermont. The first act of Innocent VI. was to release himself from his oath, to rescind, and declare null and illegal, this statute of the Conclave. He proceeded to redress some of the abuses under the rule of his predecessor. He was more severe and discriminating in his preferments; he compelled residence: he drove away a great part of the multitude of bishops and beneficed clergy who passed their time at Avignon in luxury

---

* Raynaldus, A.D. 1352, c. xlix.

and in the splendour of the papal court. One instance was recorded of his conduct. A favourite chaplain presented his nephew, quite a youth, for preferment. "One of the seven benefices which you hold," said the Pope, "will suit him well." The chaplain looked grave and melancholy. The Pope compelled him to choose the three best of his remaining benefices: "with the other three I shall be able to reward three of the poor and deserving clergy."[f] But for the nepotism, which seemed the inalienable infirmity of the whole succession, Innocent VI. had escaped that obloquy, which is so loud against almost all the Avignonese pontiffs. The times were favourable to his peaceful and dignified rule: his reign of nearly ten years was uneventful, or rather the great events disturbed not the temporal or religious tranquillity of the Pope. John, King of France, a prisoner after the battle of Poictiers, was too weak to exercise any degrading tyranny over the Pope, and though French at heart, by birth and by interest, Innocent was too prudent to attempt to enforce his offers of mediation by ecclesiastical censures against Edward or his son the Black Prince. Once, indeed, the course of victory brought the younger Edward to the foot of the bridge of Avignon (the Pope had taken the precaution of encircling the city with strong fortifications). The border districts of Aquitaine, which the King of France was required to surrender, would have included many of the southern bishoprics in the English province. England would have been in dangerous approximation to Avignon.[g] Bands of English adventurers burned St.

France and England.

---

[f] Vit. III. apud Baluz.
[g] During the pontificate of Innocent VI. there is scarcely a historical document in the Papal correspondence; it consists almost wholly of dispensations for holding pluralities, decisions

Esprit and Mondragon; and were only bought off by a large sum of money.[h]

Charles IV. was undisputed Emperor; his prudence or his want of ambition kept him in dutiful submission to the Pope.[i] He determined to observe nearly to the letter the humiliating agreement, by which he was to enter Rome only to be crowned, and to leave it the instant that ceremony was over. He descended into Italy with a small squadron of horse. Notwithstanding the urgent entreaties and tempting offers of the Ghibelline chieftains; notwithstanding a vigorous and eloquent remonstrance of Petrarch, whose poetic imagination would have raised him into a deliverer, a champion of the unity of Italy, as Dante Henry of Luxemburg; Charles pursued his inglorious course, and quietly retired beyond the Alps, virtually abandoning all the imperial rights in Italy.

The Emperor Charles IV.

Charles IV., despised by many for his ignominious subservience to the Pope, and his total withdrawal from

---

on convent property, dispensations for marriage. V. xxiv. p. 336: Is a letter to the Prince of Wales; his men had taken Robert de Veyrac, canon of Bourges, and plundered him. May 4, 1368: Safe-conduct is requested for his Legates, sent to entreat peace. P. 352: Is a curious letter to the Bishop of London; "The tongue offends trebly by a lie, God, our neighbour, and ourselves." The Pope was accused as though "non mediatoris partes assumpsimus sed turbationis egimus." The Bishop of London had not contradicted these wicked rumours.—Villeneuve, June 18, 1356. See following letters.

[h] The Pope (June 24, 1356) writes to his *Vicar* in the March of Ancona about *English* troops (condottieri?) making irruptions into the territory of St. Peter. English cruisers had seized a Neapolitan and a Genoese vessel with Papal effects on board. There is a letter (Oct. 1356) praising the noble conduct of the Black Prince to his prisoner, King John. See also other singularly meek letters to the Black Prince.—March, 1362.

[i] Ockham described Charles IV. as "mancipium Avinonensium sacrificulorum a quibus imperium emerat."— Quoted in Wolfii Lectiones, p. 498.

Italian politics, nevertheless, by one sagacious or fortunate measure, terminated the long strife between the Papacy and the Empire. The famous Golden Bull seemed only to fix the constitutional rights of the electors. It declared the electoral dignity to be attached for ever to certain hereditary and indivisible fiefs. Before this time the severance of those fiefs had split up the right among many competitors. It thus raised the electoral office to a peculiar and transcendant height. It gave to the Seven, the four lay fiefs, Bohemia, Saxony, Brandenberg, the Palatinate, and the three great archbishoprics, the full, absolute, unlimited power of election. It did not deny, but it did not acknowledge, any right of interposition in the Pope, either to control the election or to refuse his confirmation. Germany had the sole, unquestioned privilege of electing the King of the Romans (that appellation sunk into a mere title of honour); the King of the Romans became Emperor, but Emperor of Germany. On Italy, the great cause of contention between Popes and Emperors, the Golden Bull was silent. Innocent, whether he had the wisdom to discern the ultimate bearings of this great act, raised no protest. His acquiescence was tacit, but still it was acquiescence. A.D. 1355.

Innocent VI., by the prudent or happy choice of his legate, the martial Cardinal,—Ægidio Albornoz, Archbishop of Toledo, restored the papal influence, which had been almost lost, at least in Southern Italy. When Albornoz took the field, all Romagna was in the hands of the old Roman barons or fierce and lawless military adventurers. The papal banner hung only on the walls of two castles, Montefiascone and Montefalcone. Petty tyrants of either The Cardinal Albornoz.

class had seized the cities; Giovanni del Vico, nominally Prefect of Rome, occupied on his own account the greater part of the patrimony of St. Peter, even Viterbo. In a prison at Avignon Albornoz found perhaps his most useful ally, no less than the Tribune Rienzi.

A.D. 1352.

Who could have supposed that this man, hardly escaped from death as a dangerous usurper of the papal authority, and who had endeavoured to incite the Emperor to reduce the papal power within the strict limits of papal jurisdiction; that the writer of those stern and uncompromising invectives against the desertion of Italy by the Popes, the unsparing castigator of the vices of the clergy, the heaven-appointed reformer (as he asserted) of the Church, the harbinger of the new kingdom of the Holy Ghost; that Rienzi should emerge from his dungeon, to reappear in Italy as the follower of the papal Legate, and reassume the supreme government in Rome with the express sanction of the Pope. Such, however, were the unparalleled vicissitudes in the life of Rienzi. Since the fall of the Tribune Rome had returned to her miserable anarchy. For a time two Senators chosen out of the nobles, for another period a popular leader named Cerrone, held the government. A second Tribune had arisen, Baroncelli, who attempted to found a new republic on the model of that of Florence; but the fall of Baroncelli had been almost as rapid as his rise. Plague and earthquake had visited the city; and though the Jubilee had drawn thousands of pilgrims from all parts of the world, and poured wealth into her bosom, this wealth had been but a new object of strife, faction, and violence.

Rienzi.

Rome. Baroncelli.

Rienzi had been released from prison. The Papal court began to think that under the judicious guidance of Albornoz, Rienzi's advice and knowledge of Italy and of Rome might be of use to the Papal cause. The Vice-Legate in Rome, too, Hugo Harpagon, represented that his sufferings had no doubt taught Rienzi wisdom, that he had abandoned his old fantastic dreams of innovation; his name was still popular in Rome, he might be employed to counteract the dominant impiety and evil. The more immediate object appears to have been to use him as an opponent to Baroncelli, who had usurped the office and title of Tribune. Harpagon requested that he might be sent to Rome.

Rienzi, weary of his long incarceration and long inactivity, embraced the offer without reluctance. So was he now to share in that work, which he had said in one of his addresses to Charles IV., would be much more easy, more safe, and more congenial to his disposition; to reduce distracted Italy to unity and peace in the name of the Holy Mother the Church, rather than in the interests of the Empire.[k] Ere his arrival, Baroncelli had already fallen. Albornoz, who perhaps had formed a sounder estimate of Rienzi's character, retained him in his own camp. There Rienzi cast the spell of his eloquence over two distinguished youths, Arimbaldo, a lawyer, and Brettone, a knight, brothers of the celebrated and formidable Fra Moreale, the captain of the great Free Company.

On Moreale in some degree depended the fate of Romagna and of Rome. Out of the books of his

---

[k] See Papencordt, p. 232.

youthful studies, the companions of his dismal prison, Livy and the Bible, the Tribune filled his young partisans with his lofty notions of the greatness of Rome, and infatuated them by splendid promises of advancement. They lent him considerable sums of money, and enabled him to borrow more. He appeared, accompanied by these youths, and in a gorgeous dress, before the Legate, and demanded to be invested in the dignity of Senator of Rome. The Papal authority was yet acknowledged in Rome by the factious Nobles. It seemed a favourable opportunity, and worth the hazard. In the name of the Church Albornoz appointed Rienzi Senator of Rome. With a few troops the Senator advanced, and in a short time was once more master of the scene of his former power and glory.

But Rienzi had not learnt wisdom. He was again bewildered by the intoxication of power; he returned to his old pomp and his fatal luxury. He extorted the restoration of his confiscated property, and wasted it in idle expenditure. He was constantly encircled by his armed guard; he passed his time in noisy drunken banquets. His person became gross, hateful, and repulsive.* Again called on to show his

---

[1] The Roman biographer, who seems to have been an eye-witness, describes his splendid attire with minute particularity.

* The Roman biographer is again our authority. "Formerly he was sober, temperate, abstemious; he had now become an inordinate drunkard.. he was always eating confectionary and drinking. It was a terrible thing to be forced to see him (horribile cosa era potere patire di viderlo). They said that in person he was of old quite meagre, he had become enormously fat (grasso sterminatamente); he had a belly like a tun; jovial, like an Asiatic Abbot (habea una ventresca ioana, joviale, a modo de ano Abbate Asiano). (Another MS. reads Abbate Asinino.) He was full of shining flesh (carbuncles?), like a peacock—red, and with a long beard; his face was always

military prowess against the refractory Colonnas, he was again found wanting. The stern and equal vigour which had before given a commanding majesty to his wild justice, now seemed to turn to caprice and wantonness of power. His great measure by which he appeared determined this time at least, to escape the imputation of pusillanimity as shrinking from the extermination of his enemies, was sullied with ingratitude, as well as treachery. The execution of Fra Moreale, the brother of the youths to whom he had been so deeply indebted (Moreale he had perfidiously seized), revolted rather than awed the public mind. The second government of Rienzi was an unmitigated tyranny, and ended in his murder in a popular insurrection. With the cry of "Long live the people" was now mingled "Death to the Tribune, to the traitor Rienzi." His body was treated with the most shameful indignities. *Death of Rienzi. A.D. 1354.*

Cardinal Albornoz proceeded calmly, sternly, in his course. In a few years he had restored the Papal power in almost all the cities of Romagna, in Rome itself. Once he was rashly recalled; all fell back into its old confusion. On the return of Albornoz, who was equally formidable in the darkest intrigue and in the fiercest conflict of arms, the Papal authority resumed its predominance. *A.D. 1394.*

Just before his death, Innocent VI. received the grateful intelligence, that long-rebellious Rome had at last submitted to the dominion of a foreign Pope. The only condition was that the dreaded Cardinal Albornoz should not bear sway within the city. *Rome submits.*

---

changing; his eyes would suddenly kindle like fire; his understanding, too, kindled in fitful flashes like fire (così | se mutava suo intelletto come fooco).'—Apud Muratori, Ant. Ital. xii. p. 524.

The magnificent tomb of Innocent VI. in Villeneuve, the city on the right bank of the Rhone, remains to bear witness to the wealth and splendour of the most powerful and most prudent of the Avignonese Pontiffs; the fame of the most pious he must leave to his successor.

CHAPTER XII.

Urban V.

On the death of Innocent VI. twenty Cardinals met in Conclave. Mutual jealousies would not permit them to elect one of their own order; yet it seemed so strange that they should go beyond that circle, that the election of Urban V. was attributed to direct inspiration from God.[a] The choice fell on William Grimoard, Abbot of St. Victor in Marseilles, then on a mission in Italy, and yet unsuspected of Italian attachments. William heard the tidings of the death of Innocent at Florence. He exclaimed, that if a Pope were elected who should restore the seat of St. Peter to Italy, and crush the tyrants in Romagna, he should die content. Had this speech, bruited abroad in Italy, been heard in Avignon, William Grimoard had never ascended the Papal throne.

Oct. 28, 1362.

Urban V.

Urban V. (he took this name) excelled in the better qualities of a Benedictine monk. He enforced severe discipline upon the Conclave, the court, the clergy.[b] He discountenanced the pomp and luxury of the Cardinals, and would endure no factions. He

Character.

---

[a] Petrarch boldly asserts that the election was supernatural; that such men as the Cardinals could only have been overruled by the Holy Spirit to suspend their own jealousies and ambition; that the object of the Holy Spirit was the elevation of a Pope who should return to Rome.—Compare Vit. I.

[b] See authorities in the four lives in Baluzius.

introduced into the court the most rigid order, and impartial justice. He punished the abuses among the lawyers practising in these courts, and cut short their profitable delays. He set himself against concubinage in all orders, especially the clergy. He condemned usurers, and obliged certain of that craft to regorge 200,000 florins. He mulcted and expelled all who were guilty of simony from his court. He compelled those who had accumulated many benefices to surrender all which they could not serve in person. He was rigid in examining the attainments and morals of those whom he preferred. He was a munificent patron of learned men; maintained at his own expense one thousand scholars at different Universities; he was constantly supplying them with books. At Montpellier, the great school of medicine, he founded and endowed a noble college. He was not charged with avarice, he imposed no unusual subsidies; he was liberal to the poor.* With the exception of his brother, whom he made Bishop of Avignon, and, at the request of the Conclave, Cardinal, and one nephew, a man of merit, he advanced none of his kindred. He kept his lay relatives in their proper sphere; a nephew married the daughter of a merchant at Marseilles. He established a kind of secret moral and religious inspection throughout Christendom, and invited to his court devout and discreet men of different nations. From them he obtained knowledge of the life and morals of the more notable men in all realms.

Pope Urban V. might stand aloof in dignified seclusion from temporal affairs, except in Italy. The King of France was in too low a condition to enforce any unbecoming submission; the King

State of Europa.

---

* Vit. i. et iv.

of England too strong for the Pope even to resent the vigorous measures of the English Parliament in limitation of the Papal power. The Emperor Charles IV., after the Golden Bull, demeaned himself almost as a willing vassal of the Holy See. The old antagonists of the Popedom, the Viscontis, were almost alone in open hostility with the Pope. The head of that house had united in himself the spiritual and civil supremacy in Italy.[d] John, Archbishop of Milan, ruled as Sovereign, headed his armies as General, invaded his neighbours as an independent potentate. The warlike Legate, Albornoz, fully occupied in the South, respected the warlike Archbishop. The Archbishop found it politic to maintain peace with Albornoz. The death of the Archbishop left his territories to be divided between his three nephews. The elder, the voluptuous Matteo, soon died of debauchery, or poisoned by his two brothers, Bernabo and Galeazzo, who dreaded the effect of those debaucheries in thwarting their loftier ambition. Bernabo sought to advance his power by intrigue and arms. Galeazzo had bought the daughter of the King of France, Isabella of Valois, as a bride for his son. He afterwards wedded his daughter to Lionel, Duke of Clarence, son of Edward III. Bernabo had been expelled from Bologna by the Cardinal Albornoz; he had besieged the city in vain: he was thus in open war with the Church. Almost the first act of Urban V. was to fulminate a Bull against Bernabo;[e] summoning him to appear at Avignon in March to hear his sentence. The charges were sufficiently awful, debaucheries and cruelties, diabolic hatred of the Church.

Of Italy.

The Viscontí.

Oct. 6, 1354.

A.D. 1362.

---

[d] Sismondi, Républiques Italiennes, vi. c. 43. [e] The Bull in Raynaldus.

He had forced the Archbishop of Milan to kneel
him, and fiercely asked him whether he knew nc
Bernabo Visconti was Pope, Emperor, and Sovere;

Crimes of Bernabo. his own territories; that neither Emper
God could do anything against his will.
had cast the Archbishop into prison; he had pub
a prohibition to all his subjects, under pain of
burned, to seek any act of pardon from the Papal
or from the Pope's Legate, to make them any pay
or to take counsel with them. He would admit n
sentation of the Pope to bishopric or abbacy. H
contemptuously opened, publicly torn, and trampl
sundry writings and ordinances of the Holy See.
was not the worst: he had burned priests and 1
in iron cages; beheaded or tortured others to d
bored the ears of a pious Franciscan with a r(
iron; compelled a priest at Parma to mount a
tower and pronounce an anathema against Pope
cent VI. and his Cardinals; he had seized with inan
rapacity the goods of the Church.

Bernabo, as might be expected, appeared n
Avignon. The Pope declared him excommunicate
all who aided and abetted him involved in his e:
munication. He knelt and invoked Christ himse:
apostles St. Peter and St. Paul, and all the h'
heaven, that this bloody and misbelieving tyrant :
be punished in the world to come as in this world.
ordered a crusade to be preached throughout
against the Visconti.

But in Italy, even from an Italian Pope, these t
words had worn out all their magic; from a f(
Pope hated by the Italians as an alien, despis
the vassal of France, even of fallen France, they
utterly disregarded. Bernabo, this monster of w:

ness, found no difficulty in purchasing peace by abandoning his groundless claims on Bologna. Even Urban V. must close his eyes to the crimes of the Visconti. The state of Italy was doubtless among the motives which induced Pope Urban to meditate the restoration of the Papal See to Rome. The reign of each successive Pope in Avignon had widened the estrangement of Italy and of Rome from the Papal interests. The successes of the Cardinal Albornoz were but the invasions and conquests of a foreign power. Both awe and attachment must eventually, if slowly, die out altogether. The Ghibellines had long lost all awe; the Guelfs would become an anti-Ghibelline, no longer a Papal faction; they would neither fight nor intrigue for a Pope who had ceased to be Italian. Rome would not endure much longer (she had but partially endured) her baffled hopes of becoming again the metropolis of Papal dignity and Papal wealth, the heart of the world, the centre of religious business, the holy place of religious pilgrimage, of the simultaneous reverence and oblations of Christendom to the shrines of the apostles, and the shrines of their successors; she would not, she could not, much longer be deluded by specious but insincere promises, with the courteous mockery of her urgent ineffective invitations. It might be dangerous to reside among the feuds of the turbulent nobles at Rome and in the Roman territory, or the no less turbulent people; but the danger of alienating Italy altogether was still greater.

If a Transalpine Pontiff might thus insensibly lose all authority in Italy—if throughout Christendom the illusion of Apostolic Majesty, which invested the successor of St. Peter in what was believed to have been his actual throne at Rome, would gradually but inevitably have melted away, should he entirely desert that throne—

besides this the position of the Pope at Avignon had become insecure. The King of France, a prisoner in England, had ceased to tyrannise, but he had also ceased to protect. The leaders of the English conquests had approached to a dangerous proximity. England openly resisted the Papal grant to France of the tenths to maintain the war.[f] The Black Prince could not be ignorant of the inclinations, the more than inclinations, the secret subsidies and aids, of the Pope to his enemies. Urban was a Frenchman: what Frenchman had not deeply commiserated the state of his native land? England (since the Papal power had reached its height within the realm, in the time after Becket and that of King John) had been gradually assuming the tone of ecclesiastical independence. The civil and spiritual liberties had grown up together: the Commons showed as great reluctance to submit to Papal as to Royal exactions. Under Edward III., the nation, proud of his victories, was entirely on the King's side. The subservient attachment of the Pope to the King of France had no doubt considerable influence on the bold measures of the English Legislature. They had infinitely less reverence for a French Pope. All this will require further development.

Rumours began to spread of Urban's design to return to Italy. Perhaps his speech at Florence, before his election, had now transpired in Avignon. The Conclave, almost entirely French, heard with dismay the

---

[f] See the curious Eclogue of Petrarch (the twelfth), written after the battle of Poitiers. Pan is France, Faustula the Papacy, Articus England.

"Tot deerant alimenta viris, nisi Pana virili Faustula solicitum curarum parte levasset.

Nam grege de magno decimas largissima quantitae Obtulit, atque famem ardavit pinguibus hædis. Ah meretrix ! (obliqua tuens ait Articus illi) Immemorem sponsi, cupidus quem mangit adulter. Hæc tibi sola fides? sic sic alienas minitaris?"

urgent and reiterated representations from Rome, to which the Pope lent too willing an ear. Petrarch, who in his youth had appealed to Benedict XII., in his manhood to Clement VI., now in his old age addressed a more grave and solemn expostulation to Urban V. The poet described, perhaps with some poetic licence, the state of widowed Rome:—"While ye are sleeping on the shores of the Rhône, under a gilded roof, the Lateran is a ruin, the Mother of Churches open to the wind and rain; the churches of the Apostles are shapeless heaps of stones." The tremendous appeal which closed his prolix argument demanded of Urban, "whether, on the great day of judgement, he had rather rise again among the famous sinners of Avignon, than with Peter and Paul, Stephen and Laurence, Silvester, Gregory, Jerome, Agnes, and Cecilia?"[g]

The determination of the Pope was doubtless confirmed during a visit of the Emperor to Avignon. He resolved to break through the thraldom of the Conclave. He had himself never been a Cardinal, he belonged not to their factions. He had deprived their houses of the right of asylum: in those houses the most infamous in that infamous population had found refuge. By one account he created two new Cardinals, and contemptuously declared that he had as many Cardinals as he chose under the hood of his cowl.[h] The Cardinals heard the summons to accompany the Pope to Italy as a sentence of exile. They were strangely ignorant of Italy: supposed the climate, country, food, wretched and unwholesome.[i] They trembled for their lives in turbulent Rome; they would not quit their sumptuous and luxurious palaces.

---

[g] Petrarch, Senilis, lib. vii.   [h] Vit. iii.   [i] Vit. ii.

Five only, it is said, followed him to Marseilles. As they left the port they shrieked aloud as in torture, "Oh wicked Pope! Oh godless brother! whither is he dragging his sons?" as though they were to be transported to the dungeons of the Saracens in Ctesiphon or Memphis, not to the capital city of Christendom.[k]

The Pope set sail from Marseilles. The galleys of Joanna of Naples, of Venice, of Genoa, and of Pisa, crowded to escort the successor of St. Peter back to Italy. He landed at Genoa, was received in great state by the Doge and the Seignory. He celebrated Ascension Day in the cathedral church. He embarked and reached the shore near Corneto. He was received by Albornoz, the Legate; silken tents were pitched upon the sands, amid arches of green foliage. He said Mass, mounted a horse, and rode into Corneto: there he stayed during the Feast of Pentecost. The ambassadors of the Roman people presented themselves to acknowledge his full sovereignty, and to offer the keys of St. Angelo.

Embarks for Italy, April 20, 1367.

May 4.
June 4.

His arrival in Viterbo was saddened by the death of Albornoz, a Prelato who, though highly skilled and expert in deeds of arms, never forgot his pontifical decency.[m] A riot in Viterbo was suppressed; the ringleaders hanged by the people themselves.

Aug. 24.

After some delay Urban made his public entry into Rome. He was greeted by the clergy and people with a tumult of joy. He celebrated Mass at the altar of St. Peter, the first Pope since the days of Boniface VIII. The Papal palace was in ruins; Urban

At Rome.

---

[k] Petrarch, Senilis, ix. 2, p. 857.
[m] "In factis armorum, non omissâ pontificali decentiâ, valde doctus et expertus."—Vit. i. 379.

commenced extensive repairs; but his chosen residence was not Rome, but Montefiascone, whose pleasant and quiet situation filled him with delight. While he lived in a noble palace built there, the affairs of his Court were conducted at Viterbo. The next year the Emperor, who in an assembly of his Estates at Vienna had proclaimed himself the loyal protector of the Pope, and confirmed him in the possession of all his territories, set out for Rome at the head of a powerful force. In Rome he led the Pope's horse from the Castle of St. Angelo to St. Peter's, and served him as a Deacon during the high service. The Empress received the crown from the Pope. The Emperor named an ecclesiastic, the Cardinal du Porto, his Vicar in Italy. To some this was a most magnificent, to others a contemptible spectacle. The clergy were in raptures of joy at the honours paid to the Pope; the Roman people were delighted at the unwonted amity between these old implacable antagonists, the Emperor and the Pope; but the cold Ghibellines either looked with scorn at the humiliation of the Emperor, or treated it as base hypocrisy. The enemies of the Church laughed at it as a theatric show. "I," says a devout eye-witness, "was drunk with delight, I could not command myself, beholding a sight which my forefathers had never seen, and that we had never hoped to see—the Papacy and the Empire at unity, the flesh obedient to the spirit, the kingdom of the earth subject to the kingdom of heaven."[a]

But neither the pomps of Rome nor the pleasant seclusion of Montefiascone could retain a French Prelate, though that Prelate was Urban V. He had not

---

[a] Coluccio Salutati (he was present), quoted by Pelzel.

firmness to resist the incessant murmurs, the urgent entreaties, of the Cardinals. From the vast buildings which were still going on at his cost at Avignon, he must have contemplated a return, if but for a time, to that city. Only two years after the interview with the Emperor at Rome, Pope Urban embarked again near Corneto, after a prosperous voyage arrived at Marseilles, and re-established himself at Avignon. The excuse alleged in public was his parental desire to reconcile the Kings of France and England, but no one believed that he himself believed in this excuse. He went there, however, only to die: two months had hardly passed when he expired. His weakness may have been a secret inward longing for his native land. Petrarch, notwithstanding this last act of infirmity, honoured his memory, and wrote in fervent language of his virtues.*

Sept. 5, 1370.

Dec. 19.

---

* Petrarch, Senil, iii. Epist, 13.

CHAPTER XIII.

Gregory XI.

THE Conclave, in raising the nephew of Clement VI. to the Pontificate, might think themselves secure against any compulsory return to Italy. Peter Roger had become a Cardinal before he was eighteen years old. Among those dissolute youths whose promotion by Clement VI. gave offence, the young Cardinal Peter alone vindicated this flagrant act of nepotism by his severe theological studies, and by his mastery over the canon law. His morals were blameless; he was singularly apt, easy, and agreeable in the despatch of business, popular in the Conclave. He assumed the Popedom with sincere reluctance. Gregory XI. inherited the weakness of his uncle—immoderate love of his kindred, with whom he crowded all offices, ecclesiastical as well as civil. This was his one infirmity. Gregory XI. was in the prime of life, but he suffered under a painful disease.

Dec. 30, 1370.

The first years of Gregory's Pontificate were one long period of disasters. His offers of mediation between England and France were rejected with indifference approaching to contempt.[a] Italy,

State of Italy.

---

[a] MS., B. M. Instructions and powers to two Nuncios, the Cardinals S. Sisto and IV. Coronarum. There is a tone of serious and commanding earnestness in the admonitions to peace: this continues, if possible with deepening solemnity, perhaps because so ineffective, during the whole seven years from the accession of Gregory, 1370, to the death of Edward III., 1377.

abandoned by the Popes, except to be tyrannised over and burthened with inordinate exactions by weak and venal Legates, unworthy successors of the able and vigorous Albornoz, seemed determined altogether to revolt from allegiance to the Pope. Bernabo Visconti aimed at absolute dominion; he laughed to scorn the excommunications repeated from time to time, if possible, with accumulated maledictions. One of these contained a prohibition against intermarriages with the females of that house—an invention of Papal presumption reserved for this late period, but an idle protest against the splendid and royal connexions already formed by that aspiring family. The Free Companies—that more especially of the Englishman, John Hawkwood, taking service with the highest bidder, or, if unhired, plundering and wasting under their own banner — inflicted impartial misery on Guelf and Ghibelline.[b]

Dec. 17, 1372.

In the north the Viscontis were all-powerful; the

There is a striking letter to the Black Prince (who must have received it when perhaps under his slow mortal illness, near his end), dwelling on all the horrors of war. Did the Black Prince think of the massacre of Limoges? June 2, 1374 (vol. xxvii.). Among other powers the Nuncios have that of consecrating or ordering consecration of churches, and of purifying cemeteries polluted by the burial of excommunicated persons; having first exhumed and cast out their bodies, if they could be discerned. March 9, 1371. They have very large powers of granting benefices, of visiting monasteries, described as, in England, in great need of visitation. One hundred women, of *high birth and rank*, to be named by the Nuncios; some of them, with four "honest matrons," were to enter and visit any convent of females, but not to eat or sleep therein. The Nuncios have power to absolve thirty persons who have committed homicide or mutilation on deacons or archdeacons, with a form of penance, scourging in the church. There are several of these powers of absolution; one for the homicide of priests. The clergy should seem to have fared ill, or to have exposed themselves to these wars.

[b] There is a curious history of the Free Companies by Illicotti, which, with some other recent works, does credit to the modern Italian school of history.

wretched government of the Papal Legates raised the whole south in one wide revolt.° Even in Florence, Ghibellinism was in the ascendant. A league was formed, after some years, which comprehended the Viscontis, Joanna of Naples, Florence, Pisa, Sienna, Lucca, Arezzo, against the iniquitous ecclesiastical rule. Viterbo, Montefiascone, Narni, raised the banner of liberty; in the next month, Perugia, Assisi, Spoleto, Gubbio, Urbino, Cagli, Fermo. Though the Cardinal Legate let loose John Hawkwood, now in the pay of the Church, in a few days eighty cities, castles, and fortresses had thrown off the Papal rule. Early in the next year followed Ascoli, Civita Vecchia, Ravenna, and other cities. Bologna drove out the Cardinal, who fled in disguise. Forlì raised the standard of the Ordelaffi. Hawkwood, now receiving no pay, paid himself by the sack of Faenza. Imola, Camerino, Macerata, fell under the dominion of the Alidori and Rodolf di Vacano.

The Pope had no resources but in the wealth at his command. The tenths were levied in all the remote kingdoms of Christendom—in Poland, Hungary, Denmark, Sweden, Norway, even in the British Isles ᵈ—to subjugate the immediate subjects of the patrimony of St. Peter.ᵉ Wealth could raise

Tenths levied for war in Italy.

ᶜ 1375. Muratori, Ann. sub ann.
ᵈ March 10, 1372, Gregory XI. writes to the Archbishop and Bishops of England, describing the enormous expenses of the Roman See in Italy, the usurpation of the Papal rights and territories. He has obtained subsidies from the prelates and clergy of France, Spain, Germany, and almost all the faithful in Christ, except the kingdom of England. He urges a subsidy, seemingly a voluntary one, in England. —MS., B. M., March 10, 1372.

ᵉ Throughout it is the war urged by the Viscontis, Bernabo, and Galeazzo, those sons of iniquity, which enforces and justifies his exactions on the English Church. At one time he demands 100,000 gold florins (July 1, 1372), at another 60,000. It is a

armies: in those calamitous times there were soldiers to be hired for any cause. A formidable force of wild and barbarous Bretons was levied: the fears of Italy magnified them to fourteen thousand, they were at the least four thousand men. Under the command of the Cardinal Robert of Geneva, unopposed by the Visconti (the Pope, by the surrender of Vercelli and other cities, had bought off Galeazzo Visconti), they were let loose on wretched Romagna. They achieved no conquests: but by their excesses they made the Papal sway only more profoundly odious.

A.D. 1376.

None but the Pope himself could restore the Papal power. He must himself rule in Italy, or cease to rule. The mind of Gregory XI. was already shaken:[f] he had rebuked a non-resident prelate. "Why do you not betake yourself to your diocese?" "Why do you not betake yourself to yours?" was the taunting reply. An ambassador of a singular character accepted a mission from Florence to reconcile that city with the Pope. Catherine of Sienna was at the height of her fame for sanctity.[g] Already she had sent to the

Catherine of Sienna.

---

case when, according to the Constitutions of the Council of Vienne, they might pawn their chalices, books, the ornaments of churches and altars. The Pope implores the King not to impede the collection, as he is a Catholic prince of Catholic parents (the King's officers (gentes) had been guilty of this), nor to favour the contumacious clergy who will not pay. The letter to Edward is submissively urgent; no menace of censure. Afterwards the Bishop of Lincoln and the King's justiciaries are cited to Avignon for impeding the collection.

[f] Above two years before his return

he writes to King Edward III. (Jan. 9, 1375): "Etsi debitum honestatis exposcat ut sacram urbem, in quâ, principalis sedes nostra consistit, personaliter visitemus .... ut quam cito commode fieri poterit accedamus." He adds that further he is distant, the more the Church in England requires the support of the King; he commends it to the care of Edward. He positively states his intention of being in Rome the autumn of that year, 1375.

[g] One most extraordinary letter of S. Catherine of Sienna may illustrate the times, the woman, the religion: it is addressed to her confessor, Raymond

Pope a solemn admonition to name worthy Cardinals. She appeared at Avignon; she urged, she implored the Pope to return to Italy. The visions of another saint, S. Brigitta of Sweden, had been long full of the same heaven-inspired remonstrances; Christ had spoken by that holy virgin.[b]

---

of Capua, who was at Rome. When she wrote it she can hardly have been more than 32. She urges Raymond in the most rapturous phrases to hide himself in the wounded side of the Son of God. (S. Catherine herself, says her biographer, was permitted constantly to approach her lips to the side of the Lord, and to quaff his blood.) "It is a dwelling full of delicious odours; even sin takes a sweet perfume." "Oh blood! oh fire! oh ineffable love!" But the object of the letter is to relate the execution of a man, young or old does not appear, nor for what crime he suffered, but there can be little doubt that it was political, not religious. The day before his death she conducted him to the Mass; he received the Eucharist, from which he had before kept aloof. The rest of the day was passed in ineffable spiritual transports. "Remain with me," he said, "and I shall die content." His head reposed on her bosom. She awaited him next morning on the scaffold; she laid her head down on the block; she obtained not what she ardently desired. He came at length, suffered his fate with the gentleness of a lamb, uttering the name of the Saviour. She received his head in her hands. At that moment appeared to her the God-Man with the brightness of the sun. She was assured of her friend's salvation. She would not wash off the stain of the rich smelling blood from her garments. Yet, though she must remain on earth, the first stone of her tomb was laid. "Sweet Jesus! Jesus' Love!" My attention was directed to this remarkable letter (the 97th in Gigli's edition) by a translation in the Annales Archéologiques, vol. xi. p. 65. S. Catherine had the stigmata. And this woman interposed between Popes, Princes, and Republics!

[b] Revelationum S. Brigittæ, L. iv. c. cxxxvii. *et seqq.* The Saint is especially denunciatory of the Curia of Gregory XI. at Avignon. "Quid feci tibi, Gregori. Ego enim patienter permisi te ascendere ad Summum Pontificatum, et prædixi tibi voluntatem meam, per literas de Roma, illâ divinâ revelatione transmissas . . . . . Quid ergo pro tantis beneficiis rependis mihi? Et cur facis hoc, videlicet quod in Curiâ tuâ regnat superbia maxima, cupiditas insatiabilis, et luxuria mihi execrabilis, ac etiam vorago pessima horribilis symoniæ? Insuper etiam rapis et deprædaris a me innumerabiles animas. . . . Et ideo culpa tua est. . . ." She prophesies his speedy death, if he thinks of returning to Avignon. These two huge volumes, 'Revelationes S. Brigittæ' are for the most part mystic rhapsodies, visions of the Saviour, and the Virgin, full of strange pious

The commission, however, entrusted to S. Catherine of Sienna for the reconciliation of contumacious Florence failed till, after the accession of Urban VI., her words wrought with irresistible influence on the more than wavering Pope. Gregory XI., notwithstanding the opposition of the Cardinals, though six of them remained at Avignon, embarked, like his predecessor, at Marseilles,[i] put in at Genoa, and then landed near Corneto. His voyage was not so prosperous, many ships were lost, the Bishop of Lucca was drowned. The Pope passed the Feast of the Nativity at Corneto. On the seventeenth day after, he arrived by sea, and sailed up the Tiber to Rome. All was outward splendour and rejoicing in Rome, processions through decorated streets, banquets, a jubilant people, every one prostrate before the successor of St. Peter.[k] But before long the Bannerets of the Regions, who had cast down their ensigns of authority at the feet

---

allegory: and frequent free and bold censures of the clergy, cardinals, even the Pope. See L. i. c. 41. After describing the guilt of Lucifer, Pilate, Judas, the Jews, she adds of the Pope, "Similis est Lucifero, injustior Pilato, Immitior Judâ, abhominabilior Judæis." L. iii. c. 27. She contrasts the Papacy from the days of S. Peter to Cœlestine V. with the Papacy after "sedem ascendit superbia." L. vii. c. 7.

[j] "Multi summi Pontifices fuerunt ante Joannem Papam (John XXI.) qui sunt in Inferno." In all these female Revelations there is a prompter and guide behind, and he is always a Friar.—See Prologus D. Alphonsi, c. 2.

[i] He was at Marseilles, Sept. 29; at Genoa, Oct. 23-4; St. Peter's,

Rome, April, 1377.—Documents in MS., B. M.

[k] Compare the account in rude verse by Peter, Bishop of Senigaglia:—

"Egredients summo Pontifice S. Pauli palatium affuerunt mille histriones...
Verè non crediderim in præsenti sæculo videre tantam gloriam oculis propriis.
Diro falligator Prævul prolixitate itineris cum suis servulis...
Membra fatigata debilitatæque magnifice gemmatis ferculis refocillavimus."
Apud Raynald. 1377, 1.

The whole dreary but curious poem, which describes minutely the journey from Avignon to Marseilles, the voyage from Marseilles to Corneto, from Corneto to Rome, the retirement to Anagni, may be read, if it can be read, in Ciacconius and in Muratori.

of the Pontiff, resumed their independent rule. De
Vico, the Prefect of the city, held Viterbo and Montefiascone; not a city returned to its allegiance. The
sack of Faenza and Cesena by the sanguinary Cardinal
Robert and his Bretons, and by the soldiers of Hawkwood, whom he called to his aid, deepened, if it could
be deepened, the aversion; scenes of rape and bloodshed,
which even shocked those times, were perpetrated under
the Papal banner.[m]

Gregory had the barren consolation, that beyond the
Alps he had still some power. The Emperor Charles IV.
humbly sought his influence to obtain the succession for
his son Wenceslaus. Even in Italy, wherever his authority was acceptable, it was admitted. Sicily was erected
into an independent kingdom, that of Trinacria.

But neither the awe of his spiritual authority, though
he launched excommunication and interdict with un-

---

[m] On the massacre of Cesena read the passage from a very remarkable Canzone of F. Sacchetti, the writer of loose novels and powerful sermons, as well as poet. He was a contemporary. The Poet writes of the frightful carnage:

"Per ingrassare i porci di Brettagna."

The Breton soldiers of Cardinal Robert. He charges the guilt on the Pope himself:—

"E tu, che sei pel dei vicario in terra,
Non pensi che a lui ne venga il tenzo,
Che per lo tuo difetto erate, e vede
Il popol tuo errar l' altrui merrede."

After two other frightful charges,

"La terza, micidial, crudele e fera,
Fu l' innocente sangue di Cesena,
Sparto da lupi tuoi con tanta rabbia;
Gravide e vecchie morte in grande schiera,
Tagliando membri, e segando ogni vena;
Fuisile prese; e dir: Chi l' ha, se l' abbia.
E altre rifuggite in nuova gabbia,
Alcune co' fanciulli per più exempi
Seguite a morte su l' altar de' templi.

O terra, o lago rosso dei lor sangue,
O Pontifice."

Gigli, Vita di F. Sacchetti, prefixed to Works, p. xxvii, Firenze, 1858.

I will add the judgement of Sacchetti as a theologian, on the validity of a Papal excommunication: "Un' altra opinione tengono molti uomeni grossi, e dicono che chi muore scomunicato è dannato. *Sententia Pastoris justa vel injusta timenda est.* E si dee temere la sentenzia del pastore o giusta o in-giusta; ma l'ingiusta non mi danna, ma farommi meritare s' io la porto pa-zientemente. Se la sentenzia ingiusta mi dannasse, dunque potrebbe il papa e il vescovo più che la justizia divina, se la loro injustizia annullasse la justizia di Dio; e questo non può essere; adunque la scomunica ingiusta non danna, ma più tosto salva chi paziente-mente la porta."—Sermone xiv. p. 45.

wearied hand, nor his gentler virtues, could allay the evils which seventy years absence of the Popes from Rome had allowed to grow up. During the retreat of Gregory from the heats of the summer to Anagni were made some approaches to pacification with the Prefect de Vico and with Florence. The Pope despatched the holy Catherine of Sienna to Florence as a mediator of peace. But the delays of the Saint, and her intercourse with some of the Guelfic leaders in somewhat of a worldly and political spirit, inflamed the fury of the adverse factions.[a] They threatened to seize and burn the wicked woman. She hardly escaped political martyrdom.

A.D. 1377.

---

[a] "Cum haec sacra virgo me teste (her biographer and confessor) de mandato felicis memoriæ D. Gregorii hujus nominis Papæ XI. accessisset Florentiam (quæ pro tunc rebellis erat et contumax in conspectu Ecclesiæ) pro pace tractandâ inter Pastorem et oves, ibique multas persecutiones injustas fuisset passa... nullo modo voluit recedere, quousque defuncto Gregorio, Urbanus VI., successor ejus pacem fecit cum Florentinis prædictis." It will reconcile this with the text, if it is supposed that she went to Avignon before on a mission from one of the parties in Florence. Urban VI. afterwards sent for her to Rome, through her confessor. She went unwillingly, but went.—Vit. apud Bolland. c. i. p. 111. Alban Butler has told well, though not quite fully, the Life of Catherine of Sienna.—April 30. S. Catherine of Sienna learned to read at once by spiritual inspiration of the Saviour. She learned by the same all-powerful influence to write, while she was asleep; but in this latter acquirement she was aided by S. John the Evangelist and S. Thomas Aquinas. I have, since the second edition, read a Life of Catherine, by M. Malan. No book ever so sorely tried my disposition to believe men to be in earnest, when they think themselves to be so. But the life of S. Catherine, as related by M. Malan, is a curious physical as well as religious study; a singular display of an intensely hysterical temperament, wrought up by the circumstances and superstitions of the times. The man named in the extract above was, according to M. Malan, Nicolas Toldo of Perugia, who suffered under the cruel Terrorism of the Monte del Reformatori, at Sienna. M. Malan will hardly suppose how disgustingly profane, too profane to be ludicrous, is much on what he enlarges with rapture, to others of more sensitive, and assuredly not less sincere piety. Read too on Catherine of Sienna an Article in the Archivio Storico Italiano, by Tommaseo, vol. xii. 3. pp. 21, 45.

But these negotiations dragged heavily on. A great congress was held at Sarzana. The main difficulty was a demand by the Pope for the reimbursement of 800,000 florins expended in the war through the contumacy of the Florentines. The Florentines retorted that the war was caused by the maladministration of the Cardinal Legates.

Negotiations with Florence.

Pope Gregory, worn out with disease and disappointment, and meditating his return to Avignon, died, leaving all in irreparable confusion, confusion to be still aggravated by the consequences of his death.[o]

Death of Gregory XI. March 21 or 28, 1378.

With Gregory XI. terminated the Babylonish captivity of the Popedom, succeeded by the great schism which threatened to divide Latin Christendom in perpetuity between two lines of successors of St. Peter, and finally to establish a Transalpine and a Cisalpine Pope.[p]

---

[o] Muratori, sub ann.

[p] The will of Pope Gregory XI. may be read in D'Achery, iii. p. 738. The whole gives a high notion of his character as a man of conscience and piety. There is this singular passage: "Quod si in Consistorio aut in publicis consiliis ex lapsu linguæ, vel etiam lætitiâ inordinatâ, aut præsentiâ magnatum ad eorum forsan complacentiam, seu ex aliquali distemperantiâ aut superfluitate aliquâ dixerimus errores contra Catholicam fidem . . . seu forsitan adhærendo aliquorum opinionibus contrariis fidei Catholicæ, scienter, quod non credimus, vel etiam ignoranter, aut dando favorem aliquibus contra Catholicam religionem obloquentibus, illa expressè et specialiter revocamus, detestamur et habere volumus pro non dictis." Is not this to be taken as illustrating the free conversation at the court of Avignon? See also the very curious account of the interview of Gregory XI. with two of the German Friends of God, Nicolas of Basle (see Book xiv. c. 7), the friend of Tauler— the anger of the Pope at being rebuked by two such plain-spoken men, his gentleness and meekness, and friendliness, when he discovered their deep and earnest piety.—Karl Schmidt, Der Gottesfreund in XIV. Jahrhundert.

BOOK XIII.
CONTEMPORARY CHRONOLOGY.

POPES.	EMPERORS OF GERMANY.	KINGS OF FRANCE.	KINGS OF ENGLAND.
A.D. 1378 Urban VI. 1389 1378 Clement VII. (Antipope) 1394 1389 Boniface IX. 1404 1394 Benedict XIII. (Antipope) 1423 1404 Innocent VII. 1406 1406 Gregory XII. 1415 1409 (Council of Pisa) Alexander V. 1410 1410 John XXIII. 1415 1417 Martin V. 1431 1431 Eugenius IV. 1447 1439 Felix V. (Antipope) 1448 1447 Nicolas V. 1454	A.D. 1378 Wenceslaus 1400 1400 Rupert 1410 1410 Sigismund 1438 1438 Albert II. (of Austria) 1440 1440 Frederick III. (of Austria)	A.D. Charles V. 1380 1380 Charles VI. 1422 1422 Charles VII.	A.D. Richard II. 1399 1399 Henry IV. 1413 1413 Henry V. 1422 1422 Henry VI. *Archbishops of Canterbury.* Simon Sudbury 1381 1381 William Courtenay. 1397 Thomas Arundel. 1398 Roger Walden (substitute). 1308 Arundel 1414 1414 Henry Chichely 1443 1443 John Stafford 1452 1452 John Kemp.

KINGS OF SCOTLAND.	KINGS OF NAPLES.	KINGS OF SPAIN.		EMPERORS OF THE EAST.
A.D. Robert II. 1390 1390 Robert III. 1406 1406 James I. 1436 1436 James II.	A.D. Joanna 1343 1343 Charles III. (of Durazzo) 1386 1386 Ladislaus 1414 1414 Joanna 1434 1434 Alfonso (of Arragon).	A.D. *Castile.* Henry II. 1379 1379 John I. 1390 1390 Henry III. 1406 1406 John II. 1452 *Arragon.* Peter IV. 1387 1387 John I. 1395 1395 Martin 1410 1410 Ferdinand 1415 1416 Alphonso V. KINGS OF PORTUGAL. A.D. Ferdinand 1383 1383 John I. 1433 1433 Edward. 1438 Alphonso V.		A.D. John V. Palæologus 1391 1391 Manuel 1424 1424 John VI. 1448 1448 Constantine. OTTOMAN EMPERORS. A.D. Amurath I. 1389 1389 Bajazet I. 1403 1403 Soliman 1409 1410 Musa 1413 1413 Mahomet I. 1421 1421 Amurath II. 1450 1450 Mahomet II.

BOOK XIII.

CHAPTER I.

The Schism.

GREGORY XI. had hardly expired when Rome burst out into a furious tumult. A Roman Pope, at least an Italian Pope, was the universal outcry. [March 27, 1378.] The Conclave must be overawed; the hateful domination of a foreign, a French Pontiff must be broken up, and for ever. This was not unforeseen. Before his death Gregory XI. had issued a Bull,[*] conferring the amplest powers on the Cardinals to choose, according to their wisdom, the time and the place for the election. It manifestly contemplated their retreat from the turbulent streets of Rome to some place where their deliberations would not be overborne, and the predominant French interest would maintain its superiority. On the other hand there were serious and not groundless apprehensions that the fierce Breton and Gascon bands, at the command of the French Cardinals, might dictate to the Conclave. The Romans not only armed their civic troops, but sent to Tivoli, Velletri, and the neighbouring cities; a strong force was mustered to keep the foreigners in check. Throughout the interval between the funeral of Gregory and the opening of

---

[*] The Bull in Raynald. 1378.

the Conclave, the Cardinals were either too jealously watched, or thought it imprudent to attempt flight. Sixteen Cardinals were present at Rome,[b] one Spaniard, eleven French, four Italians.[c] The ordinary measures were taken for opening the Conclave in the palace near St. Peter's. Five Romans, two ecclesiastics and three laymen, and three Frenchmen were appointed to wait upon and to guard the Conclave. The Bishop of Marseilles represented the great Chamberlain, who holds the supreme authority during the vacancy of the Popedom. The Chamberlain the Archbishop of Arles, brother of the Cardinal of Limoges, had withdrawn into the Castle of St. Angelo, to secure his own person, and to occupy that important fortress.

The Conclave.
April 7.

The nine solemn days fully elapsed, on the 7th of April they assembled for the Conclave. At that instant (inauspicious omen!) a terrible flash of lightning, followed by a stunning peal of thunder, struck through the hall, burning and splitting some of the furniture. The Hall of Conclave was crowded by a fierce rabble, who refused to retire. After about an hour's strife, the Bishop of Marseilles, by threats, by persuasion, or by entreaty, had expelled all but about forty wild men, armed to the teeth. These ruffians rudely and insolently searched the whole building; they looked under the beds, they examined the places of retreat. They would satisfy themselves whether any armed men were

---

[b] See in Sismondi Répub. Ital. vii. p. 107 (or in Ciacconius), the list of the Cardinals, and their titles. Sismondi throughout has followed Thomas di Acerno. But perhaps Acerno's account is rather suspicious, as his object was to prove the legitimacy of the election of Urban VI. This was supposed to depend on the election not having been compulsory; but if one thing be clear, it is that the majority would have preferred a French Pope. —Baluz. in Not. p. 1065.

[c] Orsini, Florence, Milan, St. Peter's.

concealed, whether there was any hole, or even drain through which the Cardinals could escape. All the time they shouted, "A Roman Pope! we will have a Roman Pope!" Those without echoed back the savage yell.[4] Before long appeared two ecclesiastics, announcing themselves as delegated by the commonalty of Rome; they demanded to speak with the Cardinals. The Cardinals dared not refuse. The Romans represented, in firm but not disrespectful language, that for seventy years the holy Roman people had been without their pastor, the supreme head of Christendom. In Rome were many noble and wise ecclesiastics equal to govern the Church: if not in Rome, there were such men in Italy. They intimated that so great was the fury and determination of the people, that if the Conclave should resist, there might be a general massacre, in which probably they themselves, assuredly the Cardinals, would perish. The Cardinals might hear from every quarter around them the cry, "A Roman Pope! if not a Roman, an Italian!" The Cardinals replied, that such aged and reverend men must know the rules of the Conclave; that no election could be by requisition, favour, fear, or tumult, but by the interposition of the Holy Ghost. To reiterated persuasions and menaces they only said, "We are in your power; you may kill us, but we must act according to God's ordinance. To-morrow we celebrate the Mass for the descent of the Holy Ghost; as the Holy Ghost directs, so shall we do." Some of the

---

[4] The accounts of this remarkable transaction are perhaps less contradictory than at first appears. Some are from eye-witnesses, or from persons in the confidence of one or other of the Cardinals. That in the second Life of Gregory XI. (apud Baluzium) has to me strong internal marks of truth in its minuteness and graphic reality.

French uttered words which sounded like defiance. The populace cried, "If ye persist to do despite to Christ, if we have not a Roman Pope, we will hew these Cardinals and Frenchmen in pieces." At length the Bishop of Marseilles was able entirely to clear the hall. The Cardinals sat down to a plentiful repast; the doors were finally closed. But all the night through they heard in the streets the unceasing clamour, "A Roman Pope, a Roman Pope!" Towards the morning the tumult became more fierce and dense. Strange men had burst into the belfry of St. Peter's; the clanging bells tolled as if all Rome was on fire.

Within the Conclave the tumult, if less loud and clamorous, was hardly less general. The confusion without and terror within did not allay the angry rivalry, or suspend that subtle play of policy peculiar to the form of election. The French interest was divided; within this circle there was another circle. The single diocese of Limoges, favoured as it had been by more than one Pope, had almost strength to dictate to the Conclave. The Limousins put forward the Cardinal de S. Eustache. Against these the leader was the Cardinal Robert of Geneva, whose fierce and haughty demeanour and sanguinary acts as Legate had brought so much of its unpopularity on the administration of Gregory XI. With Robert were the four Italians and three French Cardinals.[*] Rather than a Limousin, Robert would even consent to an Italian. They on the one side, the Limousins on the other, had met secretly before the Conclave: the eight had sworn

---

[*] There were five,—Limoges, Aigrefeuille, Poitou, Majoris Monasterii (St. Martin in Tours), and De Verny.

not on any account to submit to the election of a traitorous Limousin.[1]

All the sleepless night the Cardinals might hear the din at the gate, the yells of the people, the tolling of the bells. There was constant passing and repassing from each other's chambers, intrigues, altercations, manœuvres, proposals advanced and rejected, promises of support given and withdrawn. Many names were put up. Of the Romans within the Conclave two only were named, the old Cardinal of St. Peter's and the Cardinal Jacobo Orsini. The Limousins advanced in turn almost every one of their faction; no one but himself thought of Robert of Geneva.

In the morning the disturbance without waxed more terrible. A vain attempt was made to address the populace by the three Cardinal Priors; they were driven from the windows with loud derisive shouts, "A Roman! a Roman!" For now the alternative of an Italian had been abandoned; a Roman, none but a Roman, would content the people. The madness of intoxication was added to the madness of popular fury. The rabble had broken open the Pope's cellar, and drunk his rich wines.[2] In the Conclave the wildest projects were started. The Cardinal Orsini's was to dress up a Minorite Friar (probably a Spiritual) in the Papal robes, to show him to the people, and so for themselves to effect their escape to some safe place, and proceed to a legitimate election. The Cardinals, from honour or from fear, shrunk from this trick.

---

[1] See in Raynaldus the statement of the Bishop of Casanno, the confidential friend of Robert of Geneva.

[2] "Sitibundi et altientes, volentes bibere de bono vino Papali, aperuerunt cellarium Domini Papæ, in quo erant vina Græca, Garnaria, Malvobia, et diversa alia vina bona."—Thomas di Acerno, apud Muratur. iii.

At length both parties seemed to concur. Each claimed credit for first advancing the name, which most afterwards repudiated, of the Archbishop of Bari, a man of repute for theologic and legal erudition, an Italian, but a subject of the Queen of Naples, who was also the Countess of Provence. They came to the nomination. The Cardinal of Florence proposed the Cardinal of St. Peter's. The Cardinal of Limoges arose, "The Cardinal of St. Peter's is too old. The Cardinal of Florence is of a city at war with the Holy See. I reject the Cardinal of Milan as the subject of the Visconti, the most deadly enemy of the Church. The Cardinal Orsini is too young, and we must not yield to the clamour of the Romans. I vote for Bartholomew Prignani, Archbishop of Bari."[b] All was acclamation; Orsini alone stood out: he aspired to be the Pope of the Romans.

Archbishop of Bari.

But it was too late; the mob was thundering at the gates, menacing death to the Cardinals, if they had not immediately a Roman Pontiff. The feeble defences sounded as if they were shattering down; the tramp of the populace was almost heard within the Hall. They forced or persuaded the aged Cardinal of St. Peter's to make a desperate effort to save their lives. He appeared at the window, hastily attired in what either was or seemed to be the Papal stole and mitre. There was a jubilant and triumphant cry, "We have a Roman Pope, the Cardinal of St. Peter's. Long live Rome! long live St. Peter!" The populace became even more frantic with joy than before with wrath. One band hastened to the Cardinal's palace, and, according to the strange

---

[b] A Niem says, "Per electionem uniformem scilicet nemine eorum discrepante."—De Schism. c. 11.

usage, broke in, threw the furniture into the streets, and sacked it from top to bottom. Those around the Hall of Conclave, aided by the connivance of some of the Cardinal's servants within, or by more violent efforts of their own, burst in in all quarters. The supposed Pope was surrounded by eager adorers; they were at his feet; they pressed his swollen, gouty hands till he shrieked from pain, and began to protest, in the strongest language, that he was not the Pope.

The indignation of the populace at this disappointment was aggravated by an unlucky confusion of names. The Archbishop was mistaken for John of Bari, of the bed-chamber of the late Pope, a man of harsh manners and dissolute life, an object of general hatred.[1] Five of the Cardinals, Robert of Geneva, Acquasparta, Viviers, Poitou, and De Verny, were seized in their attempt to steal away, and driven back, amid contemptuous hootings, by personal violence. Night came on again; the populace, having pillaged all the provisions in the Conclave, grew weary of their own excesses. The Cardinals fled on all sides. Four left the city; Orsini and S. Eustache escaped to Vicovaro, Robert of Geneva to Zagarolo, St. Angelo to Guardia; six, Limoges, D'Aigrefeuille, Poitou, Viviers, Brittany, and Marmontiers, to the Castle of St. Angelo; Florence, Milan, Montmayeur, Glandève, and Luna, to their own strong fortresses.

The Pope lay concealed in the Vatican. In the morning the five Cardinals in Rome assembled round him. A message was sent to the Bannerets of Rome, announcing his election. The six Cardinals in St. Angelo were summoned; they were hardly

Election confirmed.

---

[1] "Jo. de Bari vulgariter nuncupatum, Gallicum seu de terrâ Lemovicensi oriendum, satis, ut fama erat, superbum, pariter et lascivum."—A Niem, c. 11.

persuaded to leave their place of security; but without
their presence the Archbishop would not declare his
assent to his elevation. The Cardinal of Florence, as
Dean, presented the Pope Elect to the Sacred College,
and discoursed on the text, "Such ought he to be, an
undefiled High Priest." The Archbishop began a long
harangue, "Fear and trembling have come
upon me, the horror of great darkness." The
Cardinal of Florence cut short the ill-timed sermon,
demanding whether he accepted the Pontificate. The
Archbishop gave his assent; he took the name of
Urban VI. Te Deum was intoned; he was lifted to
the throne. The fugitives returned to Rome.
Urban VI. was crowned on Easter Day, in
the Church of St. John Lateran. All the Cardinals
were present at the august ceremony. They announced
the election of Urban VI. to their brethren who had remained in Avignon.[k] Urban himself addressed the
usual encyclic letters, proclaiming his elevation, to all
the Prelates in Christendom.

None but He who could read the hearts of men could
determine how far the nomination of the Archbishop of
Bari was free and uncontrolled by the terrors of the
raging populace; but the acknowledgment of Urban VI.
by all the Cardinals, at his inauguration in the holy
office—their assistance at his coronation without protest,
when some at least might have been safe beyond the
walls of Rome—their acceptance of honours, as by the
Cardinals of Limoges, Poitou, and Aigrefeuille—the
homage of all[m]—might seem to annul all possible irre-

---

[k] See in Raynaldus the letter and signatures.

[m] The Cardinal of Amiens, absent as Legate in Tuscany, came to Rome to do homage to the Pope.—Raynald. sub ann. No. xx.

Thus writes S. Catherine of Sienna, a resolute Partisan of Pope Urban VI.:

gularity in the election, to confirm irrefragably the legitimacy of his title.

Not many days had passed, when the Cardinals began to look with dismay and bitter repentance on their own work. "In Urban VI.," said a writer of these times^a (on the side of Urban as rightful Pontiff), "was verified the proverb—None is so insolent as a low man suddenly raised to power." The high-born, haughty, luxurious Prelates, both French and Italian, found that they had set over themselves a master resolved not only to redress the flagrant and inveterate abuses of the College and of the Hierarchy, but also to force on his reforms in the most hasty and insulting way. He did the harshest things in the harshest manner.

The Archbishop of Bari, of mean birth, had risen by the virtues of a monk. He was studious, austere, humble,[c] a diligent reader of the Bible, master of the canon law, rigid in his fasts; he wore haircloth next his skin. His time was divided between study, prayer, and business, for which he had

Character of Urban VI.

---

[a] Questo annunciarono a noi e a voi, e a li altri signori del mondo, manifestando per opera quello che ci dicevano con parole; cioè facendoli reverentia, e adorandolo come Christo in terra e coronandolo con tanta solennità, rifacendo di novo la elezione con grande concordia, a lui come sommo Pontefice chiesero le grazie e usaronle. E se non fusse vero che Papa Urbano fusse Papa, e che l' havessero eleito per paura, non sarebbero essi degni eternalmente di confusione; che le colonne de la sancta Chiesa posta per dilatare la fede per timore de la morte corporale volessero dare a loro e a noi morte eternale . . . . e non sarebbero essi idolatri,

adorando per Christo in terra, quel che non fusse."—Al Rè di Francia, Epist. cxcvi.

[a] Theodore à Niem, De Schism. l. i. c. 7.

[c] "Ante Papatum homo humilis et devotus, et retrahens manus suas ab omni munere, inimicus et persecutor symoniarum, zelator caritatis et justitiæ, sed nimis suæ prudentiæ innitendo et credens adulatoribus," &c.

[p] In person he was " brevis staturæ et spissus, coloris lividi sive fusci."— A Niem, liv. i. ch. i. He often before his papacy made à Niem read the Bible to him till he fell asleep.

great aptitude. From the poor bishopric of Acherontia he had been promoted to the archbishopric of Bari, and had presided over the Papal Chancery in Avignon. The Monk broke out at once on his elevation in the utmost rudeness and rigour, but the humility changed to the most offensive haughtiness. Almost his first act was a public rebuke in his chapel to all the Bishops present for their desertion of their dioceses. He called them perjured traitors.[q] The Bishop of Pampeluna boldly repelled the charge; he was at Rome, he said, on the affairs of his see. In the full Consistory Urban preached on the text "I am the good Shepherd," and inveighed in a manner not to be mistaken against the wealth and luxury of the Cardinals. Their voluptuous banquets were notorious (Petrarch had declaimed against them). The Pope threatened a sumptuary law, that they should have but one dish at their table: it was the rule of his own Order. He was determined to extirpate simony. A Cardinal who should receive presents he menaced with excommunication. He affected to despise wealth. "Thy money perish with thee!" he said to a collector of the Papal revenue. He disdained to conceal the most unpopular schemes; he declared his intention not to leave Rome. To the petition of the Bannerets of Rome for a promotion of Cardinals, he openly avowed his design to make so large a nomination that the Italians should resume their ascendancy over the Ultramontanes. The Cardinal of Geneva turned pale, and left the Consistory. Urban declared himself determined to do equal justice between man and man, between the Kings of France and England. The French Cardinals, and those in the pay of France, heard this with great indignation.[r]

---

[q] "Me præsente," writes à Niem, c. 111.   [r] Reynaldus, sub ann.

The manners of Urban were even more offensive than his acts. "Hold your tongue!" "You have talked long enough!" were his common phrases to his mitred counsellors. He called the Cardinal Orsini a fool. He charged the Cardinal of S. Marcellus (of Amiens), on his return from his legation in Tuscany, with having robbed the treasures of the Church. The charge was not less insulting for its justice. The Cardinal of Amiens, instead of allaying the feuds of France and England, which it was his holy mission to allay, had inflamed them in order to glut his own insatiable avarice by draining the wealth of both countries in the Pope's name.[a] "As Archbishop of Bari, you lie," was the reply of the highborn Frenchman. On one occasion such high words passed with the Cardinal of Limoges, that but for the interposition of another Cardinal the Pope would have rushed on him, and there had been a personal conflict.[b]

Such were among the stories of the time. Friends and foes agree in attributing the schism, at least the immediate schism, to the imprudent zeal, the imperiousness, the ungovernable temper of Pope Urban.[c] The

---

[a] So writes Walsingham :—"Cum sæpius missus fuisset a Papâ Gregorio prædecessore suo, ut quoquomodo pacem inter Angliæ et Franciæ regna firmaret, et ipse inæstimabiles auri et argenti summas, pro labore sui itineris Jussu Papæ de utroque regno cepisset, omisso suæ legationis officio non curavit paci providere regnorum, sed potius elaboravit, ut dissentiones et odia continuarentur inter reges diutius, et dum ipse descenderet taliter sub umbrâ firmandæ concordiæ, rediretque multoties infecto negotio, suo providarat uberius nefando marsupio de male quæsitâ pecuniâ relevatâ de Christi patrimonio, utroque regno sophistice spoliato."—Walsingham, p. 216.

[b] Baluz., note, p. 1067.

[c] "Talis fuit Dominus noster post coronationem suam asper et rigorosus, nescitur tamen, utrum ex divinâ voluntate, quam certè ante creationem suam fuerit multum humilis, amabilis et benignus."—A. Niem. Catherine of Sienna remonstrates with the Pope on his bursts of passion: "Mitigate un poco, per l' amore di Christo crocifisso

Cardinals among themselves talked of him as mad;[a] they began to murmur that it was a compulsory, therefore invalid, election.[f]

The French Cardinals were now at Anagni: they were joined by the Cardinal of Amiens, who had taken no part in the election, but who was burning under the insulting words of the Pope, perhaps not too eager to render an account of his legation. The Pope retired to Tivoli; he summoned the Cardinals to that city. They answered that they had gone to large expenses in laying in provisions and making preparations for their residence in Anagni; they had no means to supply a second sojourn in Tivoli. The Pope, with his four Italian Cardinals, passed two important acts as Sovereign Pontiff. He confirmed the election of Wenceslaus, son of Charles IV., to the Empire; he completed the treaty with Florence by which the Republic paid a large sum to the See of Rome. The amount was 70,000 florins in the course of the year, 180,000 in four years, for the expenses of the war. They were relieved from ecclesiastical censures, under which this enlightened Republic, though Italian, trembled, even from a Pope of doubtful title. Their awe showed perhaps the weakness and dissensions in Florence rather than the Papal power.

---

quelli movimenti subiti—dato il bozzo a natura come Dio v'ha dato il core grande naturalmente." These sudden passions were to him "vituperio e danno de l'anime."—Epist. xlx. Compare the following Epistle.

[a] This account of Thomas di Acerno, Bishop of Luceria, is as it were the official statement of Urban's party, which accompanied the letter to the King of Castile.

[f] Thomas di Acerno gives six causes for the alienation of the Cardinals: I. The sumptuary limitation of their meals. II. The prohibition of almony of all kinds under pain of excommunication: this included the Cardinals. III. His projected promotion of Cardinals. IV. The determination to remain at Rome. V. His insulting demeanour and language to the Cardinals. VI. His refusal to go to Anagni, and his summons to Tivoli.

The Cardinals at Anagni sent a summons to their brethren inviting them to share in their counsels concerning the compulsory election of the successor to Gregory XI. Already the opinions of great logists had been taken; some of them, that of the famous Baldus,* may still be read. He was in favour of the validity of the election.

July 20.

But grave legal arguments and ecclesiastical logic were not to decide a contest which had stirred so deeply the passions and interests of two great factions. France and Italy were at strife for the Popedom. The Ultramontane Cardinals would not tamely abandon a power which had given them rank, wealth, luxury, virtually the spiritual supremacy of the world, for seventy years. Italy, Rome, would not forego the golden opportunity of resuming the long-lost authority. On the 9th August the Cardinals at Anagni publicly declared, they announced in encyclic letters addressed to the faithful in all Christendom, that the election of Urban VI. was carried by force and the fear of death; that through the same force and fear he had been inaugurated, enthroned, and crowned; that he was an apostate, an accursed Antichrist. They pronounced him a tyrannical usurper of the Popedom, a wolf that had stolen into the fold. They called upon him to descend at once from the throne which he occupied without canonical title; if repentant, he might find mercy; if he persisted, he would provoke the indignation of God, of the Apostles St. Peter and St. Paul, and all the Saints, for his violation of the Spouse of Christ, the common Mother of the Faithful.* It was

Declaration of Cardinals at Anagni.

---

* Opera Baldi, vol. vi., and summarily in Raynaldus, sub ann. 1738, c. xxxvi.   * Document in Raynaldus, and in the Gersoniana.

signed by thirteen Cardinals. The more pious and devout were shocked at this avowal of cowardice; Cardinals who would not be martyrs in the cause of truth and of spiritual freedom condemned themselves. But letters and appeals to the judgement of the world, and awful maledictions, were not their only resources. The fierce Breton bands were used to march and to be indulged in their worst excesses under the banner of the Cardinal of Geneva. As Ultramontanists it was their interest, their inclination, to espouse the Ultramontane cause. They arrayed themselves to advance and join the Cardinals at Anagni. The Romans rose to oppose them; a fight took place near the Ponte Salario, three hundred Romans lay dead on the field.

Urban VI. was as blind to cautious temporal as to cautious ecclesiastical policy. Every act of the Pope raised him up new enemies. Joanna, Queen of Naples, had hailed the elevation of her subject the Archbishop of Bari. Naples had been brilliantly illuminated. Shiploads of fruit and wines, and the more solid gift of 20,000 florins, had been her oblations to the Pope. Her husband, Otho of Brunswick, had gone to Rome to pay his personal homage. His object was to determine in his own favour the succession to the realm. The reception of Otho was cold and repulsive; he returned in disgust.[b] The Queen eagerly listened to suspicions, skilfully awakened, that Urban meditated the resumption of the fief of Naples, and its grant to the rival house of Hungary. She became the sworn ally of the Cardinals at Anagni. Honorato Gaetani, Count of Fondi, one of the most turbulent barons of the land,

---

[b] A Niem, l. c. vi. Compare letters of Catherine of Sienna to the Queen of Naples.

demanded of the Pontiff 20,000 florins advanced on loan to Gregory XI. Urban not only rejected the claim, declaring it a personal debt of the late Pope, not of the Holy See, he also deprived Gaetani of his fief, and granted it to his mortal enemy, the Count San Severino. Gaetani began immediately to seize the adjacent castles in Campania, and invited the Cardinals to his stronghold at Fondi. The Archbishop of Arles, Chamberlain of the late Pope, leaving the Castle of St. Angelo under the guard of a commander who long refused all orders from Pope Urban, brought to Anagni the jewels and ornaments of the Papacy, which had been carried for security to St. Angelo. The Prefect of the city, De Vico, Lord of Viterbo, had been won over by the Cardinal of Amiens.

The four Italian Cardinals still adhered to Pope Urban. They laboured hard to mediate between the conflicting parties. Conferences were held at Zagarolo and other places; when the French Cardinals had retired to Fondi, the Italians took up their quarters at Subiaco. The Cardinal of St. Peter's, worn out with age and trouble, withdrew to Rome, and soon after died. He left a testamentary document declaring the validity of the election of Urban. The French Cardinals had declared the election void; they were debating the next step. Some suggested the appointment of a coadjutor. They were now sure of the support of the King of France, who would not easily surrender his influence over a Pope at Avignon, and of the Queen of Naples, estranged by the pride of Urban, and secretly stimulated by the Cardinal Orsini, who had not forgiven his own loss of the tiara. Yet even now they seemed to shrink from the creation of an Antipope. Urban precipitated and made inevitable this

Aug. 20.

disastrous event. He was now alone;[a] the Cardinal of St. Peter's was dead; Florence, Milan, and the Orsini stood aloof; they seemed only to wait to be thrown off by Urban, to join the adverse faction. Urban at first declared his intention to create nine Cardinals; he proceeded at once, and without warning, to create twenty-six.[d] By this step the French and Italian Cardinals together were now but an insignificant minority. They were instantly one. All must be risked, or all lost.

On September 20, at Fondi, Robert of Geneva was elected Pope in the presence of all the Cardinals (except St. Peter's) who had chosen, inaugurated, enthroned, and for a time obeyed Urban VI. The Italians refused to give their suffrages, but entered no protest. They retired into their castles, and remained aloof from the schism. Orsini died before long at Tagliacozzo. The qualifications which, according to his partial biographer, recommended the Cardinal of Geneva, were rather those of a successor to John Hawkwood or to a Duke of Milan, than of the Apostles. Extraordinary activity of body and endurance of fatigue, courage which would hazard his life to put down the intrusive Pope, sagacity and experience in the temporal affairs of the Church; high birth, through which he was allied with most of the royal and princely houses of Europe: of austerity, devotion, learning, holiness, charity, not a word.[e] He took the name of Clement VII.: the Italians bitterly taunted the mockery of this name, assumed by the Captain of the Breton Free Companies

Or Quatuor Tempora, Sept. 18. Clement VII.

---

[a] Like a sparrow on the house-top. —A Niem, L. xi.
[d] Some authorities give twenty-nine.
[e] Vit. I. apud Baluzium. A Niem agrees, and adds: "Unde potest elici,
quod illa electio a Spiritu Sancto et puris conscientiis non processit."— Read Catherine of Sienna's letter to the Count of Fondi. Epist. cxclv. another hint of the furious passion of Urban VI

—by the author, it was believed, of the massacre at Cesena.[f] So began the Schism which divided Western Christendom for thirty-eight years. Italy, excepting Schism the kingdom of Joanna of Naples, adhered to [1378-1418.] her native Pontiff; Germany and Bohemia to the Pontiff who had recognised King Wenceslaus as Emperor; England to the Pontiff hostile to France;[g] Hungary to the Pontiff who might support her pretensions to Naples; Poland and the Northern kingdoms, with Portugal, espoused the same cause. France at first stood almost alone in support of her subject, of a Pope at Avignon instead of at Rome. Scotland only was with Clement, because England was with Urban. So Flanders was with Urban because France was with Clement.[h] The uncommon abilities of Peter di Luna, the Spanish Cardinal (afterwards better known under a higher title), detached successively the Spanish kingdoms, Castile, Arragon, and Navarre, from allegiance to Pope Urban.

[f] Collatius Pierius, apud Raynald. No. lvi.

[g] Seldon, in his Table Talk, says: "There was once, I am sure, a Parliamentary Pope. Pope Urban was made Pope in England by Act of Parliament, against Pope Clement: the Act is not in the Book of Statutes, either because he that compiled the book would not have the name of the Pope there, or else he would not let it appear that they meddled with any such thing; but it is upon the Rolls."—Artic. "Pope." Compare Walsingham. Ambassadors for both were in England. "Domino Deo favente repulsi sunt apostolici, admissi Papales."—P. 215.

[h] "Exinde quanto plus divisi principes patronos sibi dilectos grato venerabantur aspectu, in eis plus excrescebat superbia et pertinacia dominandi, dum unus Alemanniam, Hungariam, Angliam et Hispaniam, sibi subditas cerneret, alter in Galliæ dulcissimo sinu foveretur, ditaretur, et ejus defenderetur viribus."—Relig. de St. Denys, i. p. 80.

CHAPTER II.

The Rival Popes.

NEITHER of these Popes were men whom religious enthusiasm could raise into an idol; they were men rather from whom profound devotional feeling could not but turn away abashed and confused. If the hard and arrogant demeanour of Urban might be excused when displayed only to the insolent and overbearing French Cardinals, or even justified as the severity of a Reformer of the Church, his subsequent acts of most revolting cruelty to his own partisans showed a type of that craft, treachery, and utter inhumanity which were hereafter to attaint the bad Italian Popes. He might seem almost to confirm the charge of madness. On the other hand, the highest praise of Clement was that he was a sagacious and experienced politician, a valiant Captain of a Free Company.

The French Cardinals, the King of France, all parties at times spoke loudly of an Œcumenic Council. But who was to summon that Council? how was it to be composed? under whose auspices was it to sit, so that Christendom might have faith in the wisdom or justice of its determinations? So long as the sole question was the validity of Urban's election, the Cardinals declared for a Council; but no sooner had the Antipope been chosen, and the rival claims must be disputed before this uncertain yet authoritative tribunal, than the Cardinals became averse to the measure, and

General Council.

started all possible difficulties. As Clement's party drew back, the Urbanists took up the cry, and clamorously defied their antagonists to meet them before an ecclesiastical Senate of Christendom.

The rival Popes had first recourse to their spiritual arms. Urban at the close of the year issued a long Brief, declaring four especially of the French Cardinals, among them the Archbishop of Arles, who had carried off the Papal crown and jewels, the Count of Fondi, and many other of the Romagnese and Campanian nobles, guilty of heresy, schism, treason, and apostasy. All were excommunicated; the Cardinals deposed; the nobles were degraded from their haughty order, their estates confiscated; all who had sworn fealty to them were released from their oaths: the usurping Pope was denominated Antichrist. <small>Acts of Urban.</small>

Clement VII. was not less authoritative or maledictory in his denunciations. The Roman Pope was called upon to lay down his ill-gotten power. He, too, was an Antichrist, as opposing the College of Cardinals in their full right of electing a Pontiff, unawed by popular clamour or fear of death. From Fondi Clement went to Naples. Nothing could equal the magnificence of his reception. The Queen, her husband Otho of Brunswick, many of the nobles and great ecclesiastics kissed his feet. <small>Of Clement.</small>

But Urban in his first creation of twenty-six Cardinals in one day[*] had included many Neapolitans of the highest families and dignities in the kingdom, and had thus secured himself a strong interest. He had degraded Bernard di Montoro, the Archbishop of Naples, and appointed Bozzato, a man of influence and powerful

---

[*] A Niem, l. xii.

connexions in the city. The people had been somewhat jealously excluded from the splendid spectacle of Pope Clement's reception: they rose in their resentment; they declared that they would not desert a Neapolitan for a foreign Pope.[b] Urban's Archbishop set himself at their head. The Queen with great difficulty subdued the insurrection. Clement was so alarmed for his own safety that he fled rapidly to Fondi; and, not daring to rest there, embarked in all speed for Provence. He landed at Marseilles; and from that time became the Pope of Avignon and France.

Flight of Clement from Naples.

Urban's great difficulty was the disorder and poverty of his finances. The usual wealth which flowed to the Papal Court was interrupted by the confusion of the times. The Papal estates were wasted by war, occupied by his enemies, or by independent princes. Not only did he seize to his own use the revenues of all vacant benefices, and sell to the citizens of Rome property and rights of the churches and monasteries (from this traffic he got 40,000 florins); not only did he barter away the treasures of the churches, the gold and silver statues, crosses, images of saints, and all the splendid furniture; he had recourse to the extraordinary measure of issuing a commission to two of his new Cardinals to sell, empawn, and alienate the estates and property of the Church, even without the consent of the Bishops, Beneficed Clergy, or Monasteries.[c] Thus having

A.D. 1380. Successors of Urban.

---

[b] Giannone, xxiii. 4.

[c] Muratori, Ann. sub ann. 1380. Urban appointed Cosmo Gentili, Chancellor of Capua, his Nuncio in England. All other commissions were annulled. He was to collect "omnes et singulos fructus, redditus et proventus beneficiorum ecclesiasticorum dicti regni vacantium, per nos seu Aplicâ auctoritate collatorum et conferendorum in antea, census quoque annuos, et alia omnia et singula res et bona nobis et cameræ prædictæ quæcunque ratione vel causâ debita." He specifies Peter's Pence.—MS., B. M., Aug. 27, 1379. The Archbishop of York is ordered to

hardly collected sufficient funds, the Pope hired the
services of Alberic Barbiano, Captain of one of the Free
Companies, and prepared for open war. The Romans
undertook the siege of the Castle of St. Angelo, which
still held out for the Cardinals and continued to bombard
the city. It was at length taken; but the Romans,
instead of surrendering it to the Pope, razed the fortress,
so long hostile to their liberties, nearly to the ground.
The Romans, if they loved not the Pope, had the most
cordial detestation of the French. The Pope's courtiers
of ultramontane birth or opinions, all indeed except a
few Germans and English, were insulted, robbed, treated
with every contumely. "I have seen," writes one present,
"Roman matrons, to excite the mob against them, spit
in the faces of the courtiers."[4] Before the close of the
year, Pope Urban could announce to Christendom the
total discomfiture of the Gascon and Breton bands by
Alberic Barbiano, the capture of St. Angelo, the flight
of the Antipope, the submission of the Queen of Naples.[5]

Pope Urban and Queen Joanna were equally insincere:
the Queen in her submission, the Pope in his
acceptance of it. Joanna had been the child-
less wife of four husbands; the heir to the realm of
Naples by both lines was Charles of Durazzo, nephew
of the King of Hungary. The King of Hungary still
cherished the deep purpose of revenge for the murder
of his brother. Charles of Durazzo had been already
invited during the hostilities of the Pope with Joanna

---

sequester all goods of adherents of Robert, "that son of iniquity." March 14, 1381. All sums, "ratione communium servitiorum" (the ordinary phrase) on the translation of William (Courtenay), Bishop of London, to the Archbishopric of Canterbury, to be sent to Rome. Nov. 3, 1382.

[4] Curiales, Theodoric & Niem, I, 14.
[5] Apud Raynald, 1379, n. xxxi.

not to wait the tardy succession, but to seize at once the crown of Naples.

All the passions least becoming a pontiff combined to influence Urban VI., policy, vengeance, family ambition, interest, pride; policy, for he could not depend on the hollow friendship of Joanna; vengeance, for without Joanna's aid and instigation the Cardinals at Fondi had not dared to elect the Antipope; family ambition, for the nepotism of Urban, like that of his successors, was not content with benefices and cardinalates, it soared to principalities. One of his nephews, Francis Prignano, had been among the new Cardinals; another, Butillo Prignano, he aspired to invest in the princedom of Capua, Amalfi, and other wealthy fiefs. Interest and pride urged the advantage of a King of Naples, indebted to him for his crown, over whose power and treasures he might rule, as he afterwards endeavoured to rule, with the almost undisputed despotism of a Protectorate.[f]

Charles of Durazzo came to Rome: he was invested by the Pope in the Sovereignty of Naples, as forfeited to its liege lord the Pontiff by the iniquities of Queen Joanna; he was crowned by the hand of the Pope.

Charles of Durazzo. June 1, 1381.

Joanna was hardly less undisguised in her hostility to Pope Urban. In evil hour for herself, in worse for Naples, she determined to adopt as her heir Louis of Anjou, nephew of the King of France, thus again inflicting on her unhappy realm all the miseries of a French invasion. The French Pope hastened to invest the French Prince in the rights which, as Pope, he claimed with the same title as his rival in Rome.

---

[f] According to Gobelinus Persona, Urban had adherents in Naples. The parties met in strife in the streets: i. p. 297. "Vivat Papa di Roma!" "Vivat Papa di Fundis!"—Apud Meibomium,

Charles of Durazzo was first in the field. The unpopularity of Joanna with her subjects was heightened by their hatred of the French, and the long tradition of their tyranny. The churchmen were for Pope Urban; their inclination had been skilfully increased by the distribution of benefices and dignities. The Hungarian and Papal forces met scarcely any resistance. Treacherous Naples opened its gates. Otho *July 16.* of Brunswick, the husband of Joanna, hastily summoned from Germany, was betrayed by his own bravery into the power of his enemies: Joanna was besieged in the Castel-Nuovo. She looked in vain for *Aug. 25.* the Provençal fleets and the French armament. Famine compelled her to capitulate; she was sent prisoner to a castle in the Basilicata. The inexorable King of Hungary demanded the death of the murderess, though acquitted of the crime by one Pope, and in close alliance with successive Popes. Pope Urban was silent; the unhappy daughter of a line of kings was put *May 72, 1382.* to death, either strangled while at her prayers,[f] or smothered, according to another account, under a pillow of feathers. Thus died Joanna II. of Naples, leaving her fame an historic problem. To some she was a monster of lust and cruelty, the assassin of her husband; to others a wise, even a most religious princess, who governed her kingdom during peace with firm and impartial rule, promulgated excellent laws, established the most equitable tribunals. Her repeated marriages were only from the patriotic desire of bearing an heir to the throne of her fathers.[h]

Louis of Anjou, in the mean time, had been crowned

[f] A Niem says: "Cum quâdam die oraret, ut fertur, ardens ante altare genuflexo, de mandato Ipsius Caroli, per quatuor satellites Hungaros fuerat strangulata."   [h] Compare Giannone on the character of Joanna.

King of Naples by Clement VII. But Clement, prodigal of all which might embarrass the hostile Pope, not only as liege lord granted away Naples, he created for his French ally a new kingdom, that of Adria. It comprised all the Papal territories, the March of Ancona, Romagna, the Duchy of Spoleto, Massa Trabaria, the cities of Bologna, Ferrara, Ravenna, Perugia, Todi, the whole region except the City of Rome, with her domain, the Patrimony of St. Peter in Tuscany, the Maritima, and Sabina. These were reserved for the Pope and his successors.[1]

Louis of Anjou.

The Provençal fleet of Louis (Provence received him at once as her lord) was too late to rescue the Queen. His powerful land army encountered no resistance till it reached the frontiers of the kingdom.[b] Among the followers of Louis was Peter, Count of Geneva, the brother of Pope Clement. Many of the highest Neapolitan nobles, the great Constable Thomas di San Severino, the Tricarici, the Counts of Conversano, Caserta, S. Agata, Altanella, fell off from Charles, and joined the invading ranks. Louis had passed Benevento and occupied Caserta; Charles stood on the defensive.

The embarrassment of Charles was increased by tidings that the Pope was marching towards Naples:[m] he mistrusted his friend almost as much as his enemy. He hastened to meet Urban at Capua, from thence, by Aversa,[n] conducted him to

A.D. 1383.

---

[1] Leibnitz, Cod. Jur. Gent. l. 206, quoted by Muratori, Ann., sub ann. 1382.

[b] The army of Louis is stated at 40,000, 45,000, even 60,000 men.—Note of Mansi, in Raynald., A.D. 1382.

[m] Urban set out in May to Tivoli; then to a small castle, Vellemonte, in Campania. He was at Ferentino in Sept. till Michaelmas Day.

[n] At Aversa à Niem (then with Urban) was in a great fright "quod aliquid sinistrum contra nos dispositum esset, quia sicut in sacco tenebamur inclusi." Compare Gobelinus Persona,

Naples, under the cover of anxiety for his personal safety. He would not permit the Pope to take up his residence in the archiepiscopal palace; he escorted him, under a strong guard of honour, to the Castel Nuovo. Charles had eluded the condition of his elevation to the throne, the erection of the principality of Capua for Butillo, the Pope's nephew. Urban seized the opportunity of his distress to demand, not only Capua, with its adjacent towns, Cagnazzo and Caruta, but also the Duchy of Amalfi, Nocera, and other towns and castles. On these terms, and these alone, the Pope would aid the King against the invading French, and grant the plenary dominion over the rest of the realm. Charles was compelled to yield; the compact was celebrated with great rejoicings; the Pope was permitted to occupy the archiepiscopal palace; the marriage of two of his nieces with two Neapolitan nobles was celebrated with high festivity. In the midst was a tumult in the city. The Pope's nephew had broken into a convent and ravished a nun of high birth and celebrated beauty. Loud complaints were made to the Pope; he laughed it off as a venial outburst of youth: his nephew Butillo was forty years old. But the King's justice would not or dared not endure the crime. A capital sentence was passed against Butillo. The Pope, as Suzerain of the realm, annulled the sentence of the King's Justiciary and of the King. After some contest Butillo was, if not rewarded, bought off from the indulgence of his lusts, by a wife, the daughter of the Justiciary, and of the King's kindred, with a dowry of 70,000 florins a year,* and the noble castle of Nocera.

---
apud Meibomium. By his account, Naples. Charles was compelled to use much courteous force to bring Urban to then in the Pope's retinue.
* All this from Theodoric à Niem

Spiritual censures were reserved for offenders of another kind. The Pope celebrated high mass, and declared Louis, Count of Anjou, heretic, excommunicated, accursed, published a crusade against him, and offered plenary indulgence to all who should take up arms. Charles of Durazzo was proclaimed Gonfalonier of the Church.* During all this time there was a violent persecution of all the Neapolitan clergy, as before of the Sicilian, suspected of inclinations to the Antipope. The Cardinal di Sangro was the chief agent to the Pope in these measures of destitution, confiscation, and torture. The basest of the clergy were substituted for the ejected Prelates or Abbots.¶

Charles protracted the war with skill; it is difficult to account for the inactivity of the French. Charles was suddenly relieved by the death of his enemy. Louis of Anjou died at Bariglio. The French army, already wasted by the plague of which Amadeo, Duke of Savoy, perhaps Louis of Anjou himself, had died,' broke up, and retired beyond the Alps.

Death of Louis of Anjou.

Charles had now no open adversary. He had still eluded the surrender of the great city of Capua to the Pope's nephew. He had ceded

Oct. 10, 1384.

---

* MS., B. M. There is a commission appointing John, Duke of Lancaster, Gonfalonier of the Church in the crusade against John, calling himself King of Castile and Leon. March 21, 1383. Privileges are granted to all crusaders against Robert, Antipope, and the King of Castile. About the same time Thomas, Archbishop of York, who owed 2000 florins under the title "communium servitiorum," is called on to pay. Aug. 6, 1383.

¶ "De Sangro credidit sacrificium offerre se Deo, sic omnes ipsos miseros perturbando ... adeo miser et iners Neapolitanorum clericus eâ vice vis reperiebatur, qui non fieret Archepiscopus vel Episcopus aut Abbas vel Prælatus per eundem Urbanum, dummodo talis vellet esse."—Theod. à Niem, l. c. xxvi. Compare, on the persecutions, Vit. I. Clement, p. 502.

' The plague may have been the cause of the previous inactivity. Charles himself had the plague, but recovered.

CHAP. II. CHARLES AND POPE URBAN. 50

Nocera, and in that fortress the Pope and some of his Cardinals had taken up their dwelling. The Cardinals had once fled, but were recalled. Amidst the rejoicings of the capital Charles summoned the Pope to meet him to deliberate on important affairs. "Kings have been wont to wait on Popes, not Popes on Kings," was the mistrustful and haughty reply of the Pope. He added, to ingratiate himself with the people, "If Charles would have me for his friend, let him repeal the taxes imposed on his kingdom." Charles sent back for answer, "that if he came he would come like a king, at the head of his army; he wondered that priests should presume to interfere with his kingdom—his by force of arms, and as the inheritance of his wife: to the Pope he owed but the four words in the investiture." "The kingdom," rejoined Urban, "belongs to the Church—a fief granted to a king who shall rule with moderation, not flay his subjects to the quick: the Church may resume her gift, and grant it to a more loyal liegeman." Charles made no further answer. Alberic Barbiano, the Constable of the kingdom, with a strong force, laid siege to Nocera. But this old stronghold of the last Mohammedans in the kingdom defied the insufficient engines and battering trains of the times. Daily might the old Pope be seen on the walls, with lighted torches, and with bells sounding, pronouncing his malediction against the besiegers.*

Quarrel of Charles and Pope Urban. May, 1384.

Nov. 1384.

Feb. 1385.

Some of the Cardinals whom Urban had created, and who had followed him, though reluctantly, to Naples

---
* Urban at least gave ground for the suspicion that he contemplated the resumption of the kingdom, the depusal of Charles. Did his extravagant nepotism look even higher than the priestdom of Capua?

(many of them were with him still more reluctantly in Nocera),[1] endeavoured to soften the furious Pope, and to induce him not to provoke too far the victorious Hungarian, now elated with success. They urged him at least to return to Rome. Urban suspected treachery. No doubt some secret consultations were held about his conduct. Bartolino of Piacenza, a bold, shrewd, unscrupulous lawyer, had framed answers to twelve questions, abstract in their form, but significant enough in their intent.[2] " Whether, if the Pope were notoriously negligent or incompetent, or so headstrong and obstinate as to endanger the whole Church—if he should act entirely according to his arbitrary will in contempt of the Council of the Cardinals—it might be lawful for the Cardinals to appoint one or more guardians, according to whose advice he would be bound to regulate his actions." One of the Cardinals, an Orsini by birth, betrayed the secret to the Pope, and declared certain of his brethren privy to the agitation of these perilous questions. The Pope inveigled such as were not there, to Nocera, as though to hold a consistory. Six of them, the most learned and of best repute, were seized and cast into a close and fetid dungeon, an old tank or cistern. Of the names given are the Cardinal di Sangro, John, Archbishop of Corfu (C. S. Sabina), Ludovico Donati, Archbishop of Tarento (S. Marco), Adam, Bishop of London (C. S. Cecilia), Eleazar, Bishop of Rieti.[a] There Theodoric à Niem (whose relation is extant), appointed with other of the Pope's ministers to take their examination, found them in the most pitiable state. The Cardinal di Sangro, a

<small>Arrest of Cardinals.</small>

---

[1] In Ferentino he had threatened to deprive some.—A Niem, xxviii.

[2] Theodoric à Niem had seen the questions, with the opinions of some learned theologians.

[a] Compare Balusius, ii. 985.

tall and corpulent man, had not room to stretch out his feet. They were all loaded with chains. The Pope's ministers questioned them, adjured them in vain to confession. The inquisitors returned to the Pope; two of them burst into tears. Urban sternly taunted their womanish weakness. Theodoric, by his own account, ventured to urge the Pope to mercy.^r Urban became only more furious; his face reddened like a lamp; his voice was choked with passion. He produced a confession, wrung forth the day before by torture from the Bishop of Aquila, which inculpated the Cardinals. The conspiracy, indeed, with which they were charged by the suspicion of Urban, or by their enemies who had gained the ear of Urban, was terrible enough. They had determined to seize the Pope, to declare him a heretic, and to burn him.^s They were brought before the public consistory; if they had confessed, it was believed that they would have been made over to the executioner and the stake. They persisted in their denial; they were thrust back into their noisome dungeon, to suffer from hunger, thirst, cold, and reptiles.

Three days after the Cardinals were submitted to the torture: that of two is described with horrible minuteness by the unwilling witness. The Cardinal di Sangro

---

^r Theodoric & Niem.

^s "Tanquam hæreticus condemnaretur paniendus ... et statim sententiâ per ipsos Cardinales tanquam per Collegium sic lata, executio ejusdem per ignem fieret ibidem."—A Niem. Gobelinus (of Benevento), a contemporary, apud Meihomium, I. 301, says: "Prout postea quibusdam officialibus Papæ revelatum est unde ad me notitia hujus facti devenit, quis de familiâ Cameræ Apostolicæ tunc extiti." This version of the affair is even worse for the character of Urban. His harshness and pride had driven above half the Cardinals to invite an Antipope; now the same harshness and pride, with nepotism, had driven five more Cardinals to conspire to seize the Pope and burn him as a heretic. Gobelinus confirms the torture; he speaks of the nephew as Prince of Capua, who seized the Cardinals.

was stripped almost naked, and hoisted by the pulley. Butillo, the Pope's nephew, stood laughing at his agonies. Thrice he was hoisted. Theodoric, unable to endure the sight, entreated him to make some confession. The Cardinal bitterly reproached himself with the tortures which he himself had inflicted on archbishops, bishops, and abbots, the partisans of the Antipope, for the cause of Urban. The executioner was a fierce ruffian, who had been a pirate, and was now Prior of the Hospitallers. The Cardinal of Venice, an old, feeble, and infirm man, had not to suffer the same bitter self-reproach as Di Sangro: yet he was racked with even worse cruelty from morning to dinner-time. He only uttered, "Christ has suffered for us." The Pope was heard below in the garden, reciting aloud his breviary, that the executioner might be encouraged by his presence.*

Urban was besieged in Nocera; among his fiercest enemies was the Abbot of Monte Casino;[b] but he had still active partisans in Italy. The Pope was the head of a great interest. Raimondello Orsini made a bold diversion in his favour. A Genoese fleet hovered on the coast. Pope Urban made a sudden sally from

---

* "Idemque Urbanus interim in horto inferius ambulabat, altâ legendo officium, ita quod eum legentem nos in aulâ audiebamus, volens dictum Basilium per hoc reddere sollicitum quod mandatum de diligenter torquendo Cardinalem non negligeret."—A Niem, c. lii. p. 44.

[b] They were horrible times. Peter Tartarus, the Abbot of Monte Casino, watched all the outlets from Nocera, seized and put to the torture the partisans of the Pope. "Eos idem Abbas variis tormentis affecit."—Gobelinus, p. 303. A messenger with secret letters to the Pope was taken and slung like a stone from the machines into the castle; he was dashed to pieces. Gobelinus describes the siege at length. He was then at Benevento; he saw a placard offering indulgences to all who would succour the Pope, the same as for a crusade to the Holy Land. See also the flight in Gobelinus, who was in the Pope's train.

Nocera, aided by some troops raised by Sanseverino and the Orsini, reached first friendly Benevento, then got on board the galleys between Barletta and Trani. He dragged with him the wretched Cardinals. During the flight to the galleys, the Bishop of Aquila, enfeebled by torture, could not keep his sorry horse to his speed. Urban, suspecting that he sought to escape, in his fury ordered him to be killed; his body was left unburied on the road. With the rest he started across to Sicily; thence to Genoa. The Cardinals, if they reached Genoa alive, survived not long. By some accounts they were tied in sacks and cast into the sea, or secretly despatched in their prisons.[c] One only, the Englishman, was spared: it was said, out of respect for, or at the intervention of, King Richard II. Nocera fell; the Pope's nephew, Butillo, was the prisoner of King Charles.

Escape of the Pope to Genoa.

A.D. 1384.

Urban remained in Genoa almost alone. Some of his Cardinals had perished under his hand; others, Pileus Cardinal of Ravenna, Galeotto of Pietra Mala, fled, after a vain effort to save the lives of their colleagues. They might indeed dread the wrath of the Pontiff: they too had written letters to the Roman clergy, on the means of coercing the proud and cruel Pope, whom they not obscurely declared to be mad, though his madness excused not his horrible wickedness.[d] But Genoa would not endure the barbarous

---

[c] Muratori, sub ann. 1385. A Niem says, "Utique ipsi quinque Cardinales postea non videlantur." There was a report that their bodies were thrown into a pit in a stable and consumed with quicklime. Gobelinus (who wrote a poem in praise of Urban) says, "Quinque Cardinale quos usque tunc in carceribus detinuit ibidem mortuos reliquit, sed quomodo aut quali modo vitam finierint, non planè mihi constat." Eleven years after he heard that they had been murdered in prison, and buried in a stable.—P. 310.

[d] Literæ apud Dalusium, ii. No.226. "Ut videbatur insano similis et furenti.

inhumanities of the Pope; not only did the inhabitants treat him with cold disrespect, the magistrates seized and punished some of the satellites of his cruelties: the indignant Pope left the city and proceeded to Lucca.* Before this he had shown some disposition to forgive, not, indeed, his own enemies. Gian Galeazzo Visconti had surprised his uncle Bernabo by the basest treachery, and poisoned him. Gian Galeazzo had no difficulty (his power and wealth were boundless) in obtaining absolution.*

The wounded pride of Urban was not the sole motive for his journey to Lucca. Charles, King of Naples, now his deadly foe, had gone to Hungary to claim the crown of that realm. There he had been murdered. His enemies refused him burial, as under excommunication.* The Pope remorseless as ever warred against the unburied body, against his widow and his orphans. Queen Margaret and her blameless children were loaded with malediction. Margaret claimed the crown of Naples for her son Ladislaus; the Angevin party for the son of Louis of Anjou. The Pope maintained a haughty and mysterious silence as to their conflicting pretensions.* He levied troops; he set himself at their head in Perugia. No one could penetrate his design. It was surmised that he aspired to

---

... Multasque iniquitates et detestabilia scelera committit et cottidie committit." They allege the imprisonment, torture, starvation of the Cardinals at Nocera.

* Walsingham asserts that Urban did not get away from Genoa "donec inestimabilem auri summam pro suâ ereptione persolvisset januensibus, qui plus propter summam quam propter Deum ejus ereptioni pretenderent, sicut patet."—P. 320.

f A Niem, c. lvi.

g Mailath, Geschichte der Magyaren, ii. 110.

h " Dimorava intanto Papa Urbano in Lucca, mirando con dispetto le rivoluzioni di Napoli, tutte contrarie a suoi interessi."—Muratori, Ann. sub ann.

assume the kingdom himself as Pope, or to raise his nephew to the throne. He issued a furious manifesto to the whole of Christendom, calling on all clerks and laymen to take up arms and join the Papal forces against the Antichrist, the Pope of Avignon, alleging the example of the Levites who slew in one day 23,000 idolaters without regard to kindred or consanguinity, and against the contumacious kingdom of Naples.[1] Of the rights of Ladislaus not one word, though Queen Margaret had attempted to propitiate him, by sending his nephew, a prisoner since the capture of Nocera by King Charles, to Genoa.

This nephew, Butillo, was at once the madness, the constant disgrace, danger, and distress of the weak, imperious, unforgiving Pontiff. At Perugia the ruffian stole into the house of a noble lady, for whom he had a violent passion; he was waylaid by her brothers, and well scourged. The Pope withdrew from the insolent city, but he did not suspend his martial preparations. He had determined to provide for his financial wants, and to confirm his waning popularity with the burghers of Rome, by a Jubilee, of which he himself might reap the immediate fruits. The period of this great festival had been contracted by Clement VI. to fifty years. An ingenious calculation discovered, that if the time of the Saviour's life were reckoned, thirty-three years, the Jubilee would fall during the year next ensuing.[k] This holy pretext was eagerly seized; Christendom was summoned to avail itself of the incalculable blessings of

---

[1] This manifesto is dated Lucca, Aug. 29, 1397. It contains this extraordinary passage about the Virgin Mary (the army was to assemble on the feast of the Nativity of the Virgin) : "Quæ est Impiis terribilis, velut castrorum acies ordinata, et cunctas hæreses sola interemit in toto mundo."—Apud Raynald. 1387, No. 6.

[k] Gobelinus, p. 310.

a pilgrimage to Rome, with all the benefits of indulgences. The treasury of the Holy See was prepared to receive the tribute of the world.

But Urban sowed for another to reap.[a] A fall from his mule shook the enfeebled frame of the Pontiff. He could not return to Perugia, distant about ten miles: he was carried in a litter to Ferentino, on his way to the kingdom of Naples. At the approach of winter he was compelled, by the failure of funds for the payment of his soldiers, to return to Rome. He was coldly received.[b] He lingered for a year, giving directions to regulate and eagerly awaiting the coming Jubilee, which he never saw. He died in the autumn.

Aug. 1389.

Death of Urban VI. Oct. 15, 1389.

Charity might almost admit for the manners and the acts of this Pontiff the excuse of insanity (some of the Cardinals manifestly entertained this belief); but whether more than the insanity of ungoverned passions, pride, ambition, cruelty, and blind nepotism, must be left to wiser judgement than that of man.[c]

Clement VII. reigned at Avignon in comparative peace and dignity. The fiercer parts of his character, which had been so darkly shown during his wars as Legate, at the massacre of Cesena, in which perished 30,000 human beings, were no longer called into action. His war against his adversary was waged by the more innocuous arms of encountering

Clement VII.

---

[a] The words of Theodoric à Niem.
[b] Gobelinus adorns his return to Rome with miracles, and says, "Romam cum honore magno regressus est."
[c] "Hic obiit Romæ et dicitur quod fuerit intoxicatus propter nimiam suam duritiam."—Chron. Ratisbon. Eccard, i. 2118. Walsingham sums up the character of Urban VI.: "Rigidus erat sibi, sed suis multò rigidior, Ita ot delinquentibus nunquam ignosceret, aut eorum ærumnis aliquatenus compateretur: probat hæc pœna suorum Cardinalium ferociter indicta et æterna damnatio carceris subsecuta."—P. 340.

ecclesiastical censures, and by the investiture of Louis of Anjou in the kingdom of Naples. The clergy in all the great kingdoms followed or led their rulers. No doubt there were partisans of Clement in the realms which espoused the cause of Urban—of Urban in those which sided with Clement. Schism, when it was a stern acknowledged duty to hate, punish, exterminate schismatics, could not but produce persecution and victims of persecution. Everywhere might be found divisions, spoliations, even bloodshed; ejected and usurping clergy, dispossessed and intrusive abbots and bishops; feuds, battles for churches and monasteries. Among all other causes of discord, arose this the most discordant; to the demoralising and unchristianizing tendencies of the times was added a question on which the best might differ, which to the bad would be an excuse for every act of violence, fraud, or rapacity. Clement and his Cardinals are charged with great atrocities against the adherents of Urban.[p] The Italian partisans of Clement, who escaped the cruelty of Urban, crowded to the court of Clement; but that court, at first extremely poor, gave but cold entertainment to these faithful strangers: they had to suffer the martyrdom of want for their loyalty. When this became known, others suppressed their opinions, showed outward obedience to the dominant power, and so preserved their benefices.[q] France at times bitterly lamented her indulgence of her pride and extravagance, in adhering to her separate Pontiff. If France would have her own Pope, she must be at the expense of

---

[p] "Multum enim atrociter contra obedientes dicto Urbano præfatus Clemens et sui Cardinales ac eorum complices, in principio dicti schismatis, se habuerunt."—See the rest of the passage, Theodoric à Niem, i. xix.

[q] Vit. Clement. p. 497. Evils of the Schism, ibid. Compare with à Niem.

maintaining that Pope and his Conclave. While the Transalpine kingdoms in the obedience of Urban rendered but barren allegiance, paid no tenths to the Papal See, took quiet possession of the appointment to vacant benefices; in France the liberties of the Church were perpetually invaded. The clergy were crushed with demands of tenths or subsidies; their estates were loaded with debts to enrich the Apostolic Chamber. The six-and-thirty Cardinals had proctors in ambush in all parts of the realm, armed with Papal Bulls, to give notice if any large benefice fell vacant in cathedral or collegiate churches, or the priories of wealthy abbeys. They were immediately grasped as Papal reserves, to reward or to secure the fidelity of the hungry Cardinals.' They handed these down in succession to each other, sometimes condescending to disguise the accumulation of pluralities by only charging the benefices with large payments to themselves. "So," says an ecclesiastic of the day, "the generous intentions of kings and royal families were frustrated, the service of God was neglected, the devotion of the faithful grew cold, the realm was drained; many ecclesiastics were in the lowest state of penury; the flourishing schools of the realm were reduced to nothing; the University of Paris mourned for want of scholars."* Clement had the satisfaction of receiving some important partisans, who were alienated by the rude manners or repulsive acts of Urban. The two surviving Italian Cardinals of the old Conclave, Milan and Florence, joined him early.

* Compare the Monk of S. Denys: "Omnes ecclesiasticas dignitates quascunque, post episcopalem, majores indifferenter suæ dispositioni reservavit." P. 82. See also p. 398, and the regulations adopted by the King, at the instance of the University of Paris, to check the Papal exactions.

* Relig. S. Denys, ut supra. Documents Inedits.

The Cardinal of Prato and the Cardinal of Pietra Mala[1] had revolted from Urban at Genoa. Da Prato publicly burned his red hat, and received another from Clement. But on the accession of Boniface IX. he fell back again to the Italian Pontiff: he was called in derision the triple-hatted.[2] The kingdoms of Spain, after an ostentatiously laborious examination of the titles of the two Pontiffs, were won, by the dexterous diplomacy of the Cardinal of Luna, to Clement. Clement was generous, affable, accomplished, perhaps with more of the French noble than the Pope. He was splendid and liberal, and therefore could not be too scrupulous as to the sources of his revenue. The creation of Cardinals was chiefly in the French interest, as those of his predecessors, to perpetuate the see at Avignon, though he did not lose sight of the advantage of maintaining some Italian supporters. His nepotism tempted him not to the daring courses of Urban; his kindred were content with ecclesiastical dignities or Church estates, which Clement did not hesitate to alienate to the lay nobility. By the death of his brother, Clement became Count of Geneva, but in him expired the line. He survived his rival Urban VI. about five years.[3]

---

[1] Ciacconius, p. 637.
[2] The indignant biographer of Clement charitably wishes him a fourth of red-hot brass or steel.—Apud Balus. p. 524.
[3] He died Sept. 16, 1394. See on his death next chapter.

CHAPTER III.

Boniface IX. Benedict XIII.

THE Avignonese Pontiff, Clement VII., and his Cardinals had some vague hope that on the death of Urban Christendom would recognise his claims. Those hopes were speedily dissipated. The Italian Cardinals proceeded at once to the election of Peter Tomacelli, a Neapolitan.[a] He took the name of Boniface IX. Would he be the worthy successor of the last true Italian Pope, Boniface VIII.? He was a man of ability;[b] though by one account not above thirty years old, he had mastered the passions of youth. After the turbulent and restless reign of Urban, that of Boniface might seem to promise at least comparative repose. The charge against his fame is insatiable avarice, flagrant and shameless simony. But Boniface was pressed with more than common necessities.[c] The schism imposed upon Christendom the maintenance of two Papal Courts; the more peaceful magnificence of Avignon; that of Rome less secure, involved in almost inevitable wars, and in the

Boniface IX.

State of Italy.

---

[a] On this election the Monk of St. Denys observes: "Infidelibus quoque sanctæ religio et Catholicæ fidei habebatur ludibrio, dum Bonifacius Romæ, Clemens vero Avinione sibi Apostolicam auctoritatem vindicabant."—xi. 9, p. 692.

[b] He was not skilled in chanting or in writing, not eminently instructed in any science but grammar, fluent in speech. Theodoric à Niem, one of his secretaries, had a contemptuous opinion of his capacity for business.

[c] "Per lo Papa manteneva lo stato suo con molta paw, e dovisin."—Infessura, apud Muratori, p. 1175.

perplexed politics of Italy. The ordinary revenues of the Roman Pontiff were cut off. France, once the wealthiest and most prodigal of the kingdoms, and Spain, acknowledged the Antipope. In England the King and the Parliament had become extremely jealous of the wealth of their own Clergy, still more of the subsidies levied by Rome. The statutes of the realm began to speak a defiant and economic language; that of Provisors under Edward III., the fuller statute of Mortmain under Richard II., showed a determination to set a limit to the boundless exactions of the hierarchy. The Clergy were not unwilling to restrict the tribute paid to the Papal Chamber. The progress of Wycliffite opinions strengthened the reluctance of the people. The Pope was reduced to implore a charitable subsidy of the Archbishop and Clergy;[d] and could not but betray how he writhed under the stern restrictions of the statutes of Provisors, and the refusal to permit the revenues of English benefices to enrich the Cardinals of Rome.[e] The northern kingdoms, as well as Poland and Hungary, were poor. Germany had to

---

[d] MS., B. M. He writes to the Archbishop of Canterbury to obtain "certum caritativum subsidium."— Jan. 2, 1390.

[e] See the very curious document, MS., B. M., in which Boniface rehearses at length all the main articles of the three Statutes of Provisors passed by Edward III. and Richard: his utter amazement that the last came from such a Catholic King, one so zealous for the orthodox faith (with almost a page of laudatory titles). "The King ought to have seen, what is clearer than noonday, that laymen can have no right to dispose of ecclesiastical things." He pronounces all the statutes "cassa et irrita." Feb. 4, 1391. He writes of the great Council of the realm, "Quia nonnulli avaro cupiditatis vicio." Certain persons had intruded into benefices held in York by Adam, Cardinal of S. Cecilia. He urges redress to the Cardinal. March 15, 1391. A month after he makes a pathetic appeal to the whole clergy of England for a subvention. They coldly refused it. April 14, 1391. We have one account of his modest receipts, amounting to but 1515 florins, reckoned equal to 252*l*. 12s. 6d.

maintain her own splendid and princely Prelates, and those Prelates to keep up their own state. In Italy the Patrimony of St. Peter had been invaded by the Duke of Milan, Gian Galeazzo Visconti, who seemed to aspire to the kingdom of Italy. On his death the Duke bequeathed to his sons, among his territories, Bologna, Perugia, Sienna. Even in the immediate domain of the See most of the towns and cities were in the power of petty independent tyrants or of the old nobles. Naples was distracted by civil war. The sons of Charles of Durazzo and Louis of Anjou were fighting for the throne.

At the same time there were imperious demands on the Papal exchequer. The Pope could not stand aloof from the affairs of Naples. The nepotism of Boniface was more humble than the audacious family ambition of Urban. He espoused at once the cause of Ladislaus. Queen Margaret was relieved from ecclesiastical censures, and the house of Hungary declared the rightful heirs. But the award of the Holy See must be enforced; aid in money and in troops must be afforded to expel the French usurper, whose title was his grant from the Pope of Avignon. In Rome, where at first Boniface took up his abode, all was ruin. The churches were in miserable dilapidation; the Capitol was falling; the Castle of St. Angelo had been almost razed to the ground. The Jubilee of 1390, to which pilgrims came from Germany, England, Poland, Hungary, enriched the Papal coffers for a time. Boniface raised 600 horse under Alberic Barbiano, in aid of Naples. He ordered extensive repairs in the churches. The treasures in hand were soon exhausted. The one resource of the Papal Chamber was the wealth of the Clergy, and that wealth could hardly be reached by direct taxation. The

Pope was reduced to that which was branded by the odious name of Simony, and, as the system was organised by Boniface IX., was Simony in its worst form. At first, and even for seven years of his Pontificate, Boniface stood in some awe of the more rigid Cardinals. He did not publicly take money for the higher promotions; he took it only in secret, and through trustworthy agents; but he had always reasons to allege to the Cardinals against the advancement of those who were unable or refused to pay. As these Cardinals to his joy dropped off, he gave free rein to his cupidity.¹ At length, after ten years, at once to indulge, palliate, and to establish this simony, he substituted as a permanent tax the Annates, or First-fruits of every bishopric and rich abbey, calculated on a new scale, triple that at which they stood before in the Papal books.⸵ This was to be paid in advance by the candidates for promotion, some of whom never got possession of the benefice. That was matter of supreme indifference to Boniface, as he could sell it again. But as these candidates rarely came to the court with money equal to the demand, usurers, with whom the Pope was in unholy league, advanced the sum on exorbitant interest. The debt was sometimes sued for in the Pope's court.

The smaller benefices were sold from the day of his appointment with shameless and scandalous notoriety. Men wandered about Lombardy and other parts of

---

¹ By a regulation in his Chancery of the seventh year of his Papacy, the Archbishop, Bishop, or Abbot who did not exhibit letters from the Pope himself in the Papal Exchequer, and had not fully discharged all the claims upon him, forfeited his preferment.

⸵ Mansi has proved against Raynaldus, that Boniface, if not the inventor of the annates, first made them a perpetual burthen.—Note on Raynald. sub ann.

Italy, searching out the age of hoary incumbents, and watching their diseases and infirmities. For this service they were well paid by the greedy aspirants at Rome. On their report the tariff rose or fell. Benefices were sold over and over again. Graces were granted to the last purchaser, with the magic word "Preference,"[h] which cost twenty-five florins. That was superseded by a more authoritative phrase (at fifty florins), a prerogative of precedence.[i] Petitions already granted were sometimes cancelled in favour of a higher bidder: the Pope treated the lower offer as an attempt to defraud him. In the same year the secretary Theodoric à Niem had known the same benefice sold in the course of one week to several successive claimants. The benefices were so openly sold that if money was not at hand the Pope would receive the price in kind, in swine, sheep, oxen, horses, or grain. The officers were as skilful in these arts as himself. His auditors would hold twenty expectatives, and receive the first-fruits. The Argus-eyed Pope, however, watched the deathbed of all his officers. Their books, robes, furniture, money, escheated to the Pope. No grace of any kind, even to the poorest, was signed without its florin fee. The Pope, even during Mass, was seen to be consulting with his secretaries on these worldly affairs.[k] The accumulation of pluralities on unworthy men was scandalous even in those times.[m]

---

[h] Anteferre.
[i] Prærogativa antelationis.
[k] Compare à Niem, ii. c. 7 to 12.
[m] "Vidi etiam tunc unius auditorum causarum dicti Bonifacii hominis inutilis et solo nomine Decretorum Doctoris literas super expectativâ gratiâ in diversis provinciis Germaniæ fabricatas, in quibus dispensabatur inter alia secum, qand sex incompatiblia beneficia recipere et simul retinere, illaque totiens, quotiens sibi placeret, simpliciter vel ex causâ pronunciationis dimittere et loco dimissorum totidem similia et dissimilia beneficia recipere et retinere posset etiam si essent digni-

The rapacity of Boniface was more odious from the unpopularity of his mother and his brothers; the mother the most avaricious of women, his brothers and their sons, in whose favour the nepotism of Boniface, in general sordid, yet in one instance was ostentatiously prodigal. He bought the principality of Sora for one of them at an enormous price from Ladislaus of Naples.

Nepotism of Boniface.

Boniface, on his accession, had proclaimed to Christendom his earnest anxiety to extinguish the schism. The means he proposed were not well chosen to promote the end. He addressed Clement VII. as the son of Belial. "Some perverse men, trusting in the arm of flesh against the Lord, cry out for a Council. O damned and damnable impiety!"[a] Two years after he sent a milder letter by two Carthusian monks. They were imprisoned by Clement, and only released on the intervention of the King of France.

The death of Clement VII. might seem a providential summons to close the schism. The University of Paris,

---

tales majores post Pontificales," &c. &c.—A Niem, ii. xl. Compare Gobelinus, who is almost as strong on the abuses of the Papal Chancery under Boniface IX. as à Niem, pp. 316, 318. "In this tyme cam oute a bulle fro the Court (Curia) which revoked alle the graces that he had granted many zeres before: of which ros much slaunder and obliqui agayne the Cherch; for thei swide playnly that it was no more trust to the Pope's writing than to a dogge tail, for as ofte as he wolde gader mony, so often would he annullen eld graces and graunt newe."—Capgrave's Chronicle of England, p. 281. Capgrave was no Lollard; he hated Wycliffe with a Monk's hatred, and has many passages very hostile to the Lollards.

[a] " Sed dicunt impii perversores, in carnali brachio contra potentiam Domini confidentes, fiat Concilium, ut schisma sedetur. O damnosa, et damnanda impietas!" He accuses the Cardinals of having gained the consent of the King of France to the creation of Clement, by accusing Urban VI. of a design to deprive him of his kingdom. It was the aim of the King of France to unite the French and Papal crowns. —Apud D'Achery, vol. i. p. 770. The Monk of St. Denys gives this letter, l. xiii. 14. The second, xiv. 12.

now the first learned body in Christendom, had already taken the lead, denouncing the diabolical schism.* They had urged the King to take affairs into his own hands, and to compel the conflicting Popes to accede to one of three schemes for the termination of the contest—Cession, Arbitration, or a General Council. Clement had received this memorial in a fury of passion: he denounced it as an insolent and defamatory libel. "Dost thou understand this Latin?" he said to the bearer. "Sufficiently!" the officer replied; but when the Pope withdrew into his chamber in such manifest wrath, he thought it prudent to leave Avignon. The Pope would see no one, speak to no one. The Cardinals met and agreed to press on the Pope the measures proposed by the University. He assembled them, and bitterly reproached them with their traitorous cowardice. They replied by urging calmly the necessity of the measure. Clement retired and never more left his chamber. Three days after he was struck with apoplexy: his death was attributed to his grief.[p] So soon as his death was known the University wrote again to the King, adjuring him to prohibit the Cardinals at Avignon from proceeding to a new election.[q] The wary Cardinals, lest they should

Sept. 16, 1394.

Sept. 16, 1394.

Oct. 12, 1394.

---

* See for the proceedings of the University, during the lifetime of Clement, the Monk of St. Denys, xiv. 10. Read too (in the Gersoniana) the address of the University to the King —Quare hoc? They ask of the consequences of the schism. Because unworthy men are promoted to the highest rank in the Church. "Quibus nihil sancti est, nihil pensi nihil honesti curæ sit; exhauriunt ecclesias, religiones dissipant, monasteria spoliant."

The churches are in ruins; the lower priesthood oppressed, reduced to mendicancy; the treasures of the churches sold. "Exactiones gravissimæ, maximas, intolerabiles panperibus Ecclesiæ ministris imponunt, impiissimos homines, atque inhumanissimos ad colligendum eligunt," &c. &c.

[p] Rel. de St. Denys, xv. v.

[q] There are 24 names of Cardinals in Ciacconius.

seem to despise the King's counsel, hurried over the election, and then opened the royal letter. The Cardinals swore to do all in their power to end the Schism now they had put it out of their power. No act could be more certain to perpetuate it than the election of the Spaniard, the crafty, able, ambitious, unprincipled Cardinal of Luna. Before the election their solemn oath had been taken to each other that whoever was chosen should at once resign the Papacy at the requisition of the Cardinals, if Boniface would likewise resign. The Cardinal of Luna had been the loudest to condemn the Schism; he had openly and repeatedly declared that if he were Pope he would put an end to it at once.

Benedict XIII. (such was his title) communicated his election to the King of France. "The importunity of the Cardinals had compelled him to accept the unwelcome office, but he was prepared by all means which should be advisable to promote the union of the Church."[1] The University sent an address, eloquent and almost adulatory; it was received with the most gracious urbanity. "I am as ready to resign the office as to take off this cap." He took it off and saluted them. Each of the Popes was fully prepared to heal the Schism provided he himself remained Pope; but neither could show such disrespect to the Cardinals to whom he owed his elevation as to invalidate their privilege of election: neither would acknowledge himself an intrusive and usurping Pontiff.

Benedict XIII. Oct. 23.

In Italy Boniface IX., notwithstanding his rapacity (perhaps through his rapacity, which extorted ecclesiastical wealth for the secular purposes of his government), by ability, moderation, and firmness,

Boniface IX.

---

[1] Dupuy, Hist. du Schisme, p. 39.

had made some progress towards the reinstatement of the Papacy in respect and authority.* That respect it had almost lost, when the Roman dominions of the Pope were treated as the province of a foreign prelate, oppressed rather than governed by a Cardinal Legate: that authority the fierce and desultory ambition of Urban VI. had shaken rather than confirmed. The noble city of Perugia was weary of her factions, Guelf and Ghibelline. The Beccarini (the nobles and their partisans), the Raspanti (the burghers with their adherents) offered to receive the Pope as a resident and as sovereign within their walls. Boniface knew that nothing promoted the popularity of the Pope in Rome so much as his absence. No sooner had the Romans lost the Pope than they were eager for his return. He moved to Perugia. Ancona and some of the other cities made advances towards submission. But the unhappy parsimony of Boniface did not permit him to environ himself with a strong well-paid body of guards, which might keep down the still adverse factions in Perugia. At midnight, during the following summer, he was awakened by a wild tumult.¹ The exiled Guelfs, who had re-entered the city through his mediation, had risen, not without provocation, and were perpetrating frightful carnage on the Ghibellines. Pandolfo Baglioni, the head of the Ghibelline nobles, his brother, eighty nobles, a hundred of their followers, the Beccarini, were slain. The Pope fled in horror and disgust to Assisi. Biordo, a chief of Condottieri, in league with the Guelf Raspanti, was

In Perugia. Oct. 17, 1392.

July 30, 1393.

---

* "Nec fuit ante eum quisquam Romanorum pontificum, qui talem potestatem temporalem Romæ et in patrimonio S. Petri exercuisse legatur."—Gobelinus, p. 346.

¹ Theodoric à Niem, II. xv. He was with the Pope. See also Sismondi, Républiques Italiennes, t. vii. p. 350.

under the walls with 1500 adventurers. He entered the city and became its lord. Biordo's power lasted not long; he was excommunicated by the Pope. The Pope with bolder nepotism had now created his brother Marquis of the March of Ancona. The Marquis was besieged in Macerata by Biordo, taken prisoner, and released for a large ransom. Biordo even became master of Assisi by treachery, but himself, having made peace with the Pope,* was murdered in Perugia by the Abbot of St. Peter's, who aspired by this good deed to the Cardinalate. "Perugia will not endure a tyrant," was the watchword of the new insurrection. The Abbot was received by Boniface, but died a short time after unrewarded. The Pope had long before the fall of Biordo determined no more to honour the fickle and perilous city of Perugia with his residence. He had returned by urgent invitation to Rome; he made the Capitol a strong fortress. But Rome would neither be without the Pope, nor when he was within her walls leave him in peace. The Romans took umbrage at the fortification of the Capitol; the life of Boniface was endangered in an insurrection, instigated by the Bannerets of the city. He was saved by the fortunate presence of King Ladislaus with some troops. Not two years after broke out another revolt. The Pope met it with firmness. Thirteen persons were executed.ˣ

But the Pope had other means to reduce the contu-

---

* According to Theodoric à Niem the Pope was concerned in the murder of Biordo, returned to Perugia, and fled again to Assisi. I am not quite confident that I have rightly unravelled this intricate affair, which lasted several years.

ˣ "Egli, che non era figliuolo della paura fece prendere i delinquenti," &c. —Muratori, sub ann. 1397.

macious city. The year of Jubilee was at hand. He treated that which had been interpolated by his predecessor but ten years before, and of which himself had enjoyed the gains, as an irregular breach in the solemn order of the Ritual. To Rome the Jubilee was of as inestimable value as to the Pope. Without the Pope it was a vain unprofitable ceremony. They sent an embassy to entreat him to vouchsafe his presence. Boniface yielded, but enforced his own conditions. His partisan, the Malatesta, was to be created Senator of Rome. The magistracy of the Bannerets, the democratic leaders of the Regions of the city, was to be abrogated for ever. Boniface entered, and assumed for the first time the full sovereignty of Rome.[?] He had already, it has been said, fortified the Capitol: the Castle of St. Angelo rose again from its ruins in more than its ancient strength.

Jan. 1400. But this was not without a fierce struggle. Two of the Colonnas, lords of Palestrina, in league with the deposed Bannerets, broke into the city, and reached the foot of the Capitol with shouts, "Death to the Pope; long live the Roman people!" They were repulsed; thirty-one hung up alive.[s]

The Jubilee was held in all its pomp and all its prodigality of pardon. Pilgrims from all Christendom flocked to Rome, even from France, notwithstanding the inhibition of the King. To the French the Pope who bestowed indulgences was the legitimate Pope. The King himself, by besieging the Antipope Benedict XIII. in Avignon, and by taking him into captivity, had destroyed the awe which belonged to the holy office. Many of the wealthier pilgrims, however, brought not

---

[?] Sozomen. Hist. S. R. L. xvi. Raynaldus, sub ann. 1400.
[s] Theodoric à Niem, II. c. xxvii. A youth was compelled by promise of pardon to hang the rest; among them were his own father and brother.

their rich offerings to the shrines of the Apostles in Rome. They were plundered in every part of the neighbourhood, noble matrons and damsels ravished. The plague broke out in the crowded city. The Pope thought of withdrawing to a place of security, but he dared not risk the loss of Rome, the loss of the oblations. His bitter adversary taunts him with refusing alms to the plundered and dying pilgrims.ᵃ

But a more formidable enemy to the Popedom seemed to be advancing with irresistible force. The first time for centuries, Italy seemed likely to fall under the dominion of a native King. Gian Galeazzo Visconti had cast off the ignoble name of Count of Virtù;ᵇ by the sanction of the Emperor Wenceslaus he was Duke of Milan. By his success in arms, by his more successful intrigues, he had obtained the power, he meditated the assumption of the title, of "King of Italy." All the great cities of Lombardy owned his dominion; Bologna, Perugia, Sienna were his. He threatened at once Florence and Rome. All the great Free Companies, all the distinguished generals, marched under the standard of the Serpent. What had a Pope, with a contested title, a Pope even with the ability of Boniface, to oppose to such puissance? and, against a King of Italy with such vast territories, wealth, ambition, what had been the Pope?

Gian Galeazzo of Milan.

The death of Gian Galeazzo from the plague relieved the Republic of Florence and the Pope. His last willᶜ divided his great dominions among his sons. All the great warlike Lombard Republics, the

Sept. 8, 1402.

ᵃ "Solitus enim erat rapere, nec rapta indigentibus communicare."—A Niem, li. 28.
ᵇ Muratori, Ann., sub ann. 1395.
ᶜ See the will and the magnificent obsequies in Corio, Storia di Milano, L. lv. p. 286.

cities of Tuscany and Romagna, were recited in that will as passing to his descendants. The Pope, with prompt ability, took advantage of the occasion. He detached the famous Alberic Barbiano, the Great Constable, from the service of Milan. Barbiano with his bands began the reconquest of the cities in the ecclesiastical territories. His avarice and extortions gave Boniface the command of wealth, wealth the command of all the mercenary soldiery in Italy, and all the soldiery were mercenary.[d] Had not Boniface been compelled by the failure of his health and a painful disease to retire to the warm baths of Pozzuoli, he might have witnessed the restoration of the whole patrimony of St. Peter to his rule.

During all this period the Ultramontane Kings had been labouring to extinguish the Schism. So long as the Pope at Avignon was a Frenchman, so long the King of France and the French Cardinals adhered to his cause. Their sympathy with a Spaniard was much less strong,[e] the evils of the Schism became more glaringly manifest. Immediately after the accession of Benedict XIII. the King (Charles VI.) summoned a Council of the higher Clergy of Paris. Simon de Cramault, Patriarch of Alexandria, Bishop of Carcassonne, presided in the Council over nine Archbishops, forty-six Bishops, Abbots and Doctors innumerable. The Council threw aside at once the proposition of compelling all the Christian kingdoms

Benedict XIII.

A.D. 1395.

---

[d] "Verbis conflatis in aurum, auroque verso in arma, terras ecclesiae alienatas rebellibus subactis, verbis, auro, armis potenter recuperavit."—Gobelinus, p. 323.

[e] "Ferunt quidem Dominos Cardinales Gallicos odio habentes Dominum Benedictum pro eo quod erat alterius nationis quam Gallicae, et quoniam inter se de uno Gallico post mortem Clementis VII. non potuerunt concordare, propterea in istum convenerunt."—Contin. Chronic. Theodor. à Niem, apud Eccard. i. p. 1534.

who supported the Italian Pontiff to submit to Benedict XIII.[r] It was an avowed impossibility. Three courses remained:—1. A General Council; 2. Compromise by the appointment of arbiters; but who was to choose the arbiters, or enforce their award? 3. The renunciation of both into the hands of the College of Cardinals—either the two Colleges united in one, or each to his own College. The voices were in overwhelming number for the renunciation. A stately embassy was determined of three Princes of the blood, the Dukes of Berry and Burgundy *Ambassadors to Avignon.* the King's uncles, the Duke of Orleans his brother, three Bishops, Senlis, Poitiers, and Arras, with eight nobles. The University of Paris addressed letters to all the Cathedral chapters of France, urging them to make processions, and offer prayers for the success of this embassy. The Ambassadors arrived at Avignon. The Pope at first entrenched himself behind forms; but he was at length obliged to admit them to an audience.[s] Gilles de Champs communicated to the Pope that the King and the Church having duly *June 1, 1395.* considered all other courses had determined on that of the renunciation of the two Popes. Benedict sought delay; he was Vicar of Christ, answerable to Christ in an affair of this solemn import; it must not be driven on with unseemly speed. The Ambassadors returned; they summoned the Cardinals in the King's name to Villeneuve (on the right bank of the Rhone). Of the twenty Cardinals nineteen approved the project of the King; the Spanish Cardinal of Pampeluna alone declared that it was injustice to place the legitimate Pope on a level with the intruder Boniface. Benedict attempted

---

[r] This was called the "via facti."   [s] Dupuy, Hist. du Schisme, p. 43.

to propitiate the Ambassadors by courtesy and hospitality. They dined with him, he gave them the blandest promises. At length he delivered a schedule with a counter-project. The two Popes and the two Colleges of Cardinals were to meet in some place bordering on France, under the King's protection. No one could discern more clearly than Benedict himself the insuperable difficulties of this scheme: it was rejected by the ambassadors of the King, by those of the University, and by the Cardinals. Their prayers, remonstrances, admonitions were vain. Benedict took a lofty tone; he commanded them under the penalties of contumacy, disobedience, unbelief, under threats of the severest procedures, to adopt his scheme and no other. Some fell on their knees, and conjured him with tears to assent to the counsels of the high and mighty Prince. Benedict replied, "They were his subjects; he was their sovereign; he was lord not only over them, but over all who were living in death;[b] he had to render account to God alone." The negotiations lingered on, but at length the Ambassadors returned to Paris. It was determined to enter into communication with the other great powers of Christendom. Two Abbots were sent into Germany; the Patriarch of Alexandria, the Admiral of France, and other nobles into England. Benedict attempted to win the King of France by the grant of a tenth. This alienated the Clergy; the King dared not levy the subsidy. The University of Paris entered an appeal against all acts of Benedict to a future one, true, and universal Pope. Benedict in a Bull annulled this defamatory libel.[i] The next year the University replied

Benedict's counter-project

A.D. 1396.

A.D. 1394.

---

[b] "Mortement vivants."—Dupuy, p. 51.   [i] Gersoniana, p. iii.

to the Bull by a new appeal, in which they declared that many Popes had been repudiated for their wickedness.

Two years passed. In 1398 the Assembly of the States and Clergy of France met again. There were present the Dukes of Berry, Burgundy, Orleans, the King of Navarre, eight Archbishops, thirty-two Bishops, Abbots without number, deputies from five Universities. It was announced not only that the King and the Church of France had determined the renunciation by both Popes, the Kings of Hungary, Bohemia, England,[k] Arragon, Castile, Navarre, and Sicily concurred in this measure as the only way to end the Schism. After long, grave, learned debate, a vast majority had resolved on the unconditional subtraction of allegiance from Benedict XIII. This act of renunciation was solemnly published with processions and prayers on a Sunday, and promulgated by letters with the King's signature throughout the realm.[m] No sooner was it published at Avignon than the Cardinals, except Pampeluna and Tarascon, disclaimed Pope Benedict; he thundered invectives against them; they withdrew across the Rhône to Villeneuve in the dominions of the King.

July 27.

---

[k] In 1398 Benedict seems to have entertained some hope of moving the King of France against the Antipope Boniface. He writes to Richard II. of England to interpose in his behalf with the King of France, whom Richard called Father (Richard had married Isabella of France), but who had long strayed from the bosom of Mother Church and the way of truth.—MS., B.M., Dec. 21, 1398.

[m] See the Document in the monk of S. Denys, xix. c. 5. He enters at length into the conduct of Pope Benedict. Among other charges is the following:—"Successive idem Benedictus, ad suam ambitionem hujusmodi palliandam, quoadam per diversa mundi climata mandavit falsidicos, qui non erubuerunt contra veritatem seminare quod idem Illustris ducis legati, solum et adeo apperuerunt viam cessionis simplicis parte nostræ, ut illico cederet, et onus Gallicus eligeretur in Papam."

Peter d'Ailly, Bishop of Cambray, the most learned theologian of the age, had held the singular office of enforcing on both Popes the duty of renouncing their dignity, and submitting to a just award. At a Council at Rheims, the Bishop of Cambray received his commission from the Emperor and the King of France, and the Clergy of both realms. He had set out for Rome. He found Pope Boniface at Fondi, having subdued the turbulent and marauding Count, the author or abettor of the Schism, and who had boldly alleged his refusal to acknowledge the Roman Pontiff as an excuse for plundering his dominions. The Commissioner of the Ultramontane Sovereigns returned to Rome with the Pontiff. Boniface entertained him with the utmost courtesy, and with vague but promising protestations of his earnest desire to close the Schism. The Pope's avaricious and ambitious brothers took alarm at the extent of his concessions. Throughout Rome were murmurs of doubt and apprehension. They feared lest they should lose their Pope, their dignity, their profit, the general pardon of the Jubilee.* A great deputation addressed the Pope, exhorting him to assert himself to be the true Pope, not to abandon the privilege and patrimony of St. Peter. They would hazard their lives in defence of his right. "My good children," returned Boniface, "Pope I am, Pope will I remain, despite all treaty between the Kings of France and Germany."

---

* "Se doutèrent fort les Romains, qu'ils ne perdissent le siège du Pape qui par an trop leur valoit, et portoit grand profit, et en tous les pardons généraux, qui devoient âtre dedans deux ans à venir, dont tout profit devoit rélonder en la cité de Rome et là environ."—Froissart, iv. 67. This mission was in 1398, before the Jubilee. Dupin, in his Life of Peter d'Ailly (Gersoni Opera, vol. i.), has omitted this journey to Rome, so vividly described by Froissart.

Peter d'Ailly had returned to France; he was now joined in a second Commission to Avignon with the Marshal Boucicaut. If the eloquence of the Bishop should not prevail, the Marshal was to employ the force of arms. Peter d'Ailly arrived in the Court of Benedict. He had first an interview with Pope Benedict. All the answer which he could obtain was, "Let the King of France issue what ordinances he will, I will hold my title and my Popedom till I die." D'Ailly entreated him to consult his Cardinals.* In a full Consistory he delivered a long and persuasive Latin harangue. He then withdrew. The Cardinal of Amiens urged the inevitable necessity of submission to the determination of the Kings of France and Germany. Pope Benedict steadily refused; "he had been invested by God in his Papacy; he would not renounce it for Count, or Duke, or King." The Consistory was in tumult; almost all the Cardinals clamoured against him. The Bishop of Cambray entered again; he demanded an answer. "Pope I have written myself; Pope I have been acknowledged by all my subjects; Pope I will remain to the end of my days. And tell my son, the King of France, that I had thought him till now a good Catholic; he will repent of his errors. Warn him in my name not to bring trouble on his conscience." Such at Rome and at Avignon was the reply to overtures of peace.

The Marshal Boucicaut in the mean time was gathering his forces around Avignon. The Provençal gentlemen, with Raymond de Turenne at their head, crowded to his banner. Expectation of the pillage of Avignon,

---

* See the picturesque description in Froissart, iv. 67, compared with other accounts.

with the Papal treasures, and the plunder of the luxurious villas of the Cardinals, drew together men accustomed to fight in the Free Bands. The citizens of Avignon would have compelled the stubborn Pontiff to yield; the old man answered with dauntless courage, "I will summon the Gonfalonier of the Church, the King of Arragon, to my aid. I will raise troops along the Riviera as far as Genoa. What fear ye? Guard ye your city, I will guard my palace." But Avignon and the Cardinals capitulated at the first summons.

Pope beleaguered in his palace. The Pope shut himself up in his palace, and prepared for a resolute defence. He had laid in great store of provisions, grain, oil, wine: his fuel was burned by an accidental fire; he pulled down part of the buildings to cook the food. Boucicaut from awe, or in confident expectation that the Pontiff must soon submit, would not lead his soldiers to storm the strong Papal Palace. The Cardinals had fled again to Villeneuve; Pampeluna and Tarascon alone were still faithful to Benedict.

The Cardinals sent an embassy, three of their body, *Cardinals at Paris.* to the King. They urged the seizure of Pope Benedict, and that Boniface should be compelled by the same withdrawal of obedience to submit to the decree of a Council. They suggested their apprehensions lest Benedict should escape into the dominions of the King of Arragon, with whom he was connected by marriage. They neglected not their own interests; they stipulated that their own privileges, emoluments, expectatives should be religiously respected. None of the great benefices, bishoprics, or abbacies were to be filled till the union of the Church, the proceeds to be set apart to advance that object. The insolence, violence, and avarice of the Cardinals retarded rather than promoted peace. They were insulted in the streets of Paris.[a] The King began to waver. Instructions were sent to Boucicaut not to proceed against Benedict by force of arms, only to prevent his escape with the Papal treasures. The palace was closely blockaded; Benedict's two Cardinals in an attempt to fly were seized and thrown into prison.

Benedict had in vain entreated succour from the King of Arragon. He had offered to make Barcelona or Perpignan the seat of the Papacy. "Does the priest think that for him I will plunge into a war with the King of France?" Such was the reply of Martin of Arragon. Benedict was constrained to capitulate. The harshest part of the terms was that they were to be enforced by the hostile Cardinals and by the wealthier burghers of Avignon. The Cardinals and the burghers pledged themselves to keep strict guard, that Benedict should not leave his palace: he was their prisoner.

Benedict capitulates.

It was remarked that throughout this contest Benedict employed not the spiritual sword. The Pope endured the siege without hurling anathemas on his foes.[b] His malediction could only have struck in general at the King and all his nobles; the interdict, had he dared to issue it, would have smitten the whole realm. But he knew the state of the Court of France, the insanity of the King, the implacable feud between the houses of Burgundy and Orleans. The withdrawal

---

[a] "Et inde vulgares sumpserunt audaciam, ut cum issent ad palacia dominorum cum pomposo equitatu, eis conviciabantur, verba ignominiosa proferentes quæ cum maximâ indignatione audiebant."—Relig. de S. Denys, xix. p. 680.

[b] "Nec aliqualiter usus fuit contra quemquam gladio spirituali, nam sciebat non a cunctis lilia deferentibus istas iniquitates procedere, cum multi illos dampnarent, sibi favorabiliter adhærentes."—Chronic. S. Denys, xix. 8.

from his allegiance by one of the furious factions which divided the Court and Kingdom ensured the sympathy of the other. The Armagnacs and Burgundians, the rival Dukes, could not join in hatred or persecution of the same object. Who would know, in those superstitious times, whether the constant paroxysms of derangement which seized the King might not be attributed to the Papal excommunication? The two Augustinian Monks who had undertaken to cure the King's malady, having utterly failed in their mission, were arraigned for the impious magic, in which the kingdom had put its full faith, by the Bishop of Paris and the Clergy. They were beheaded at the Place de Grève as sorcerers, not as impostors; their quarters exposed to the insult and abhorrence of the furious populace.[r]

For five years Benedict XIII. endured this humiliating imprisonment. The Cardinals kept jealous ward, their vigilance was unwearied, unrelaxed. Yet Benedict could not be ignorant that the Duke of Orleans now publicly espoused his cause against the Dukes of Burgundy and Berry. The University of Toulouse had entered the lists against the University of Paris, and boldly arraigned the sacrilegious revolt from the one true Pope.[s] Louis, King of Sicily, forced his way to the presence of the Pope. His title to his throne depended on the Papal grant. Louis tendered his full and loyal allegiance to the successor of St. Peter. Benedict knew that his time was come. On a still evening, with the aid of a Norman gentleman, Robert de Braque-

A.D. 1398-1403.

March 12, 1403.

---

[r] Chron. de St. Denys. Sismondi, Hist. des Français.
[s] Dupuy, Hist. du Schisme.

mont, he stole in disguise out of the palace, unquestioned and unsearched by the guards. He passed the night in Avignon. The next morning he dropped down the Rhône to Château Rénaud, a strong fortress held by 500 soldiers of King Louis. His first act was to send for a barber; ever since he had been a prisoner he had let his beard grow.

Never was revulsion more rapid or complete. The abject prisoner of his own Cardinals, from whom half Christendom, the loyal half, had withdrawn their allegiance, was again the Pope of France and Spain. His two faithful Cardinals were at his side, the rest in trembling submission at his feet. They dared not disobey his summons. He entertained them at a sumptuous repast. In the midst of the festivity was heard the clang of arms; soldiers were seen with their gleaming halberds taking their stations in silence. The Cardinals sat in speechless terror. But Benedict desired only to show his power: at a sign they withdrew. The feast went on; but if a dark tradition be true, his mercy confined itself to churchmen. Two centuries and a half afterwards the ruins of a hall were shown, in which the Pope had given a banquet of reconciliation to some of the principal burghers of Avignon, and then set fire to the building and burned them all alive.[1] Be this but an ancient legend, he compelled the citizens to rebuild the battered walls of the Papal palace: he garrisoned it with Arragonese soldiers. The *May 14.* clergy of France had been again convoked in Paris. The Cardinals of Poitiers and of Saluces appeared to plead the cause of Benedict (the last time they had

---

[1] Bouché, Hist. de Provence, li. 432. Sismondi, Hist. des Français, xii p. 380.

been his bitter adversaries). The Dukes of Burgundy, Berry, and Bourbon still held with the University of Paris, but the University of Paris was now divided. On a sudden appeared the Duke of Orleans, leading the King. It was a lucid interval in the melancholy state of the prince. Charles faltered out, at the suggestion of his brother, a declaration of his high opinion of the learning and virtue of Benedict. The Duke of Orleans took the Cross from the altar; the King laid his hands upon it, and declared that he restored to Benedict the allegiance of the realm of France: "so long as he lived he would acknowledge him alone as the Vicar of Christ." The faint gleam of doubtful reason in a madman was to determine who was the representative of God's Almightiness on earth! The Bishops burst into the chant of the Te Deum, the bells rang out. Paris knew by those pealing sounds that Benedict was again the successor of St. Peter.[a] The King's letters announced these glad tidings to the provinces. Benedict still, to the King, to the Duke of Orleans, to the whole kingdom, professed his eager desire to extinguish the Schism. In proof of his sincerity he sent an embassy to his rival at Rome. Boniface refused to receive the ambassadors but as Pope. The Bishop of S. Pons, Benedict's Legate, and his colleagues had the prudence to yield. They were received in full Consistory. They urged a free conference, at some appointed place, to discuss the rival claims. Boniface, perhaps suffering under his painful malady, the stone, answered with bitter pride, "that he alone was Pope, Peter di Luna an Antipope." "At least," rejoined the

Feast of St. Michael. Sept. 29, 1404.

---

[a] Compare Gersoniana, p. xvi. Dupin's abstract of these proceedings is full and fair.

offended ambassadors, " our master is guiltless of simony.'
The insult struck to the heart of Boniface. He
retired to his chamber, and ere two days was
dead.*

Oct. 1.

* Dupuy, p. 90. Theodoric à Niem, ii. 23. We read in Ciacconius: "Fuit Bonifacius unus Insigniorum et prudentissimorum Pontificum, quos unquam Roma vidit, et qui plus timoris, observantiæ et obedientiæ apud Romanos cives obtinuit." Of his avarice and rapacity, and other faults, or of Christian virtues he says nothing. See also his epitaph. Boniface had a complication of fearful maladies, of which the stone was the fatal one. This extraordinary story of a proposed cure of this malady rests on the authority of the Archbishop of Florence: ' Multis vulgatum est quod cum secundum medicinam carnalem diceretur albi, quod per coitum cum muliere liberaretur a calculo, ex quo decrevit, minime acquiescere voluit tanto sacrilegio contra divinam legem, eligens potius mori quam impudicè vivere."—S. Antonin. Chronicon, sub ann. Compare, on the other hand, Gobelinus Persona, who hates Boniface as cordially as he flattered Urban VI. Gobelinus, now in Germany, saw the workings of the avarice and rapacity of Boniface. Boniface absolutely annulled all and every one of his own acts, grants, indulgences, and dispensations, and those of his predecessors (read the whole 87th chapter). It should seem, to regrant for five years with new fees. Of his death he says, " Et sic quamvis tormentibus intolerabilibus cotidie quatitur, tamen sanum sitire non desinit."—P. 323.

CHAPTER IV.

Innocent VII. Gregory XII. Benedict XIII.

SUBMISSION to a foreign Pontiff was the last thought of the Italian Cardinals. There were only eight[a] in Rome. They solemnly swore that whosoever of them should be chosen would abdicate the Popedom so soon as Benedict should do the same. This oath was taken by Cosmo Megliorotto, who was elected, and assumed the name of Innocent VII. The ambassadors of Benedict demanded their safe-conduct as accredited only to Pope Boniface. They had been seized; they were forced to buy their release from the Commander in the Castle of St. Angelo.[b]

Innocent VII. had too much virtue, gentleness, and humanity for these tumultuous times.[c] His first year was a year of purgatory in the Conclave. The Cardinals, headed by the Cardinal of Montpellier, would not abandon the good old profitable usages of simony. But he had to encounter more terrible enemies. Nothing can redound more to the praise at least of the firm and resolute policy of Boniface than the fierce outbreak immediately after his death. The Guelfs and Ghibellines, awed by his stern conduct, had crouched in sullen repose. Innocent had hardly time

---

[a] Severa, Ciaconius; nine, Oldoin. I make out eight. Gobelinus gives seven names.
[b] Dupuy, p. 90.
[c] Theodoric à Niem, ii. 34. He writes to the Archbishop of York, announcing his election, and hopes that the "desiderabilis unionis tranquillitas" may ensue on his accession.—MS., B. M., Dec. 27, 1404.

to return to the safe Vatican Palace from his coronation in the Lateran, when Rome rose in tumult to demand the restoration of the Bannerets, and the surrender of the city to their rule. Two Colonnas, one Savelli, hastened from the fortresses in the neighbourhood to inflame the insurrection against the Papal Government.[4] The Orsini were the hereditary defenders of the ecclesiastical authority. There were all the evils and miseries of a Roman insurrection — palaces pillaged, matrons and virgins violated.

Ladislaus King of Naples was in the city at the accession of Innocent; he was leagued with the Ghibellines, but the champion of liberty brooded over designs fatal to liberty. He was now almost undisputed sovereign of the realm of Naples. He aspired to include Rome within his dominions. The yielding Pope endeavoured to purchase the friendship, he averted the open hostility of Ladislaus, by the cession, for a certain number of years, of the Maremma. The King of Naples interposed his mediation between the Pope and the people. But the terms betrayed at once his power and his inclinations. 20,000 florins from the tax on salt, which belonged to the Papal exchequer, were awarded to the people. The Pope held the Castle of St. Angelo (Murchardon, a famous condottiere, commanded the garrison), the Capitol was surrendered to the people. The Tiber flowed between the city of the Church and the city of the people. The Senator was to be named by the Pope out of three prescribed by the people. Ten magistrates, called the Ten of Liberty, were to be renewed every two months.[e]

Ladislaus of Naples.

---
[4] "Quod urbicola per ecclesiam non per cives regerentur."—A Niem.
[e] Sozomen, apud Muratori, S. R. I. t. xvi. Raynaldus has the treaty sub ann. 1404.

The Pope still endeavoured to maintain a popular policy. In a creation of Cardinals, five were Romans; but the emissaries of Ladislaus were still active. A dispute arose, which led to armed strife, about the fort which commanded the Ponte Molle, and so all the northern approaches to Rome. A deputation of the people, among which were some of the most audacious and most popular leaders, two of the captains of the regions,[f] entered the Castle of St. Angelo. Ludovico Megliorotto, the nephew of the Pope, a bold, fiery man, an intimate associate of Murchardon the commander of the Papal troops, would not endure their plebeian insolence. As they departed, he fell on them, eleven were killed.[g] Their bodies were left till night reeking on the pavement. There they were seen by Leonardo Aretino (the historian), who made his way with difficulty to the presence of the Pope. He found the old man, who was entirely guiltless of all connivance in the act, in the deepest depression and horror. He lifted his eyes to heaven, as though to call God to witness his innocence.[h]

Sept. 8, 1485.

The bell of the Capitol tolled out; the people rose to vengeance: all the palaces of the Cardinals and courtiers were pillaged. The Pope and Cardinals with difficulty fled to Viterbo. The Pope had almost perished of thirst. The Abbot of St. Peter's was murdered in his sight, as also another of his Court; their bodies were cast in the highway. John of Colonna took possession of the Vatican; the arms of the

Flight of the Pope.

---

[f] Capi di Rioni.
[g] The murder was committed in a house, "ubi habitabat mater Bonifacii." The bodies were thrown out of the window, and lay near the Amilia, where the Veronica was commonly shown.—Diarium Anton. Petri. Morat. R. I. S. xxiv. p. 917.
[h] Leonard. Aretin. Comm. xxi. p. 922.

Pope were defaced or covered with mud. The Colonna was ironically called John XXIII.

Ladislaus thought that his hour was come. His troops were under the walls; he hoped to hear himself welcomed as Lord of Rome. The Colonnas, the Savellis, some other Barons were prepared to raise the cry. His troops found their way into the city, and began to sack the houses.[a] But the turbulent people had not cast out the Pope to submit to a king and a stranger.[b] The whole city was a great battle-field. The soldiers of Ladislaus set fire to it in four quarters; but at length, after great slaughter, the King abandoned his desperate enterprise, his discomfited troops withdrew. With more than her usual versatility, Rome had her ambassadors at Viterbo imploring the return of Pope Innocent,[m] offering to recognise his plenary dominion,[n] and laying at his feet the keys of the city. Innocent was again Lord of Rome. He waited about two months, he was received in triumph. Three months after, he issued his Bull of Excommunication against King Ladislaus and the Colonnas. Ambassadors from King Ladislaus were at his footstool. Peace was made; the Castle of St. Angelo surrendered. In the same month, in the year after he had fled from Rome, Innocent departed from this dismal world to the quiet grave.[o]

Return to Rome.

Death.

---

[a] "Posuit ad sacchum totam Romam."—Diarium Petri. He was master of three Rioni.

[b] "E benchè li Colonnesi, e li Savelli, e alcuni altri Baroni el volessero, tutto il popolo no'l voleva."—Piero Minorbetto, apud Tartini, sub ann. 1405.

[m] Theodoric à Niem, ll. 38.

[n] "Dominium totius Romæ."

[o] The dates seem to be :—Dominion offered to the Pope, Jan. 14 (1406). Return of the Pope, March 13. Anathemas on Ladislaus and the Colonnas, June 18. Ambassadors from Ladislaus, July 17. Peace, Aug. 6. Castle of St. Angelo surrendered, Aug. 9. Death of Innocent, Nov. 13.

The Schism could not terminate with the death of
either Pope. The Roman Cardinals could not acknowledge Benedict unconditionally without condemning
their own obstinate resistance, or without vitiating their
succession, and imperilling their title to the Cardinalate.
An ecclesiastical head was necessary for the assertion of
the ecclesiastical dominion in Rome:[p] it would have
been wrested at once, perhaps for ever, by the turbulent
people from the feeble and disunited grasp of the Cardinals. Fifteen Cardinals met in Conclave.

Nov. 30.

Again they administered, and all took, an
oath of unusual rigour,[q] that whoever might be elected
Pope would at once renounce the Papacy, directly his
rival at Avignon would consent to the same abjuration.
Of all the fifteen, none seemed to take this oath with
more promptitude and sincerity, none had for years so
deeply deplored the Schism, or urged all measures for
its termination so earnestly, as Angelo Corario, a Venetian by birth, now verging on eighty years of age. On
his election as Gregory XII., in public and in

Gregory XII.

private Corario seized every opportunity of
expressing, in the strongest words, the same determination.[r] "His only fear was lest he should not live to
accomplish the holy work." At his coronation he was
seen to weep when he renewed this protestation; it was
the one subject of his grave sermon. In private he
declared, that for the union of the Church, if he had

---

[p] Theodoric à Niem, iii. See in the Stimmen aus Rom (on this book more hereafter) the curious account by the ambassador of the Teutonic Order of the turbulent state of Rome. His house was seized by some of the mercenary soldiers; he could not get them out, and was obliged to share it with them. He was summoned to do homage to the new Pope, but was afraid to venture through the streets.

[q] The oath is in Oldoin. Addit. ad Ciacconium, p. 755; and in à Niem, iii. 2.

[r] "Me præsente," says à Niem.

not a galley, he would embark in the smallest boat; if without a horse, he would set out on foot with his staff. He refused to grant expectatives. His first act was a letter, of which the superscription might seem offensive, "to Peter di Luna, whom some nations during this miserable schism call Benedict XIII." The rest was respectful, earnest: no sacrifice could be too great for the reunion of the Church. "The mother before King Solomon was their example; to save her son's life she had ceased to be a mother. This they should do for the Church." Benedict, from Marseilles, replied with the same superscription, "to Angelo Corario, whom some in this pernicious schism name Gregory XII." The Spaniard vied with his rival in Rome in the fervour of his words: he offered to receive ambassadors with the utmost respect. "Haste, delay not, consider our age, the shortness of life, embrace at once the way of salvation and peace, that we may appear with our united flock before the Great Shepherd." Each pledged himself to create no new Cardinals, unless to keep up their equal numbers. Gregory's pacific letters to the King of France were read with joy and admiration; he was held to be an angel of light.[t]

Savona, on the Riviera of Genoa,[a] was named as the

---

[s] See the letter addressed to Christendom by the Cardinals at Pisa.—A Klem, Nemus Unionis, vi. 11.

[t] In the MS., B. M., is a letter addressed to the clergy and nobility of the whole Christian world, in which he describes himself as "ad extirpationem inveterati ac lugubris et pestiferi schismatis paternis et sollicitis studiis intendentes."

[a] He writes to Henry IV. of England, as one "quem unionis hujusmodi accipimus ardentissimum zelatorem," announces the agreement for meeting at Savona, and solicits a subsidy, without which he cannot move; he urges Henry "subventionis munus extendere de tuâ regali munificentiâ." Rome, June 1, 1407. He writes, too, to the Archbishop of Canterbury, soliciting a subsidy.

place where the rival Popes were to meet, each to depose himself, and to remit the election of the one supreme Pontiff to the united College of Cardinals. Ambassadors from Genoa arrived at Rome in May, offering safe-conduct, protection, the temporary cession of the city of Savona, to be occupied half by each Pope. Ambassadors arrived also from the King of France and the University of Paris.

A.D. 1407. Meeting appointed at Savona.

But already to the jealous ears of some about his Court the language of Gregory had become suspicious.* He spoke, not perhaps without some ground, of the insecurity of Savona, which, as the French King now ruled in Genoa, was subject to him as its temporal lord, and in spiritual affairs owned the sway of Benedict. The advancement of one of his three nephews—ambitious, unpopular men—to the office of President of the Papal Chamber,[1] and the reception of magnificent presents from Ladislaus of Naples, threw darkening doubts on his sincerity. The confessor of King Ladislaus, a Franciscan of great worldly ability, was admitted to the confidence, and never quitted the person of the Pope. The ambiguous movements of the King and of the Pope increased the perplexity. The King's troops suddenly appeared within the walls of Rome. John of Colonna joined them. The Pope, whom some supposed to be in secret league with the King, retired, it was given out, in fear, but in slow pomp, into the Castle of St. Angelo. But the soldiers of Colonna committed some brutal outrages in a nunnery, and plundered some shops. The people rose, headed by Paolo

Doubtful conduct of the Pope.

---

* Theodoric à Niem, lii. The cause of à Niem's rancorous hatred of Gregory may possibly have been personal, but his writings have a character of honesty, though full of passion. They are in general supported by other documents. Gregorius he calls throughout "Errarius." [1] Camerarius.

Orsini, who commanded the Papal troops. The assailants fell into an ambush; Nicolas Colonna and other leaders were taken and beheaded in the Capitol. Gregory put on the appearance of great joy at the discomfiture of Ladislaus; but men mistrusted his joy. June 17.

The month had not elapsed before Pope Gregory set off from Rome in state—in pontifical state, it seemed—on the holy mission of restoring peace to the distracted Church. He remained two months at Viterbo: in September he moved to Sienna. Michaelmas was the appointed time for the meeting at Savona. Vigil of St. Laurence. Aug. 9. Viterbo. Sept. Sienna.

Then began the long and weary tergiversation, the subtle excuse, the suggestion of difficulty after difficulty, the utter neglect and abandonment of all his lofty protestations, the tampering with, the breach of, the most solemn oaths. His more inveterate enemies taunt him as a hoary hypocrite:[a] he is exculpated only as a weak old man, wrought upon by his rapacious and ambitious kindred.[b] His first act, the alienation of some great estates of the Church for the endowment of his three nephews, might pass as only a prudent provision in case the Papacy should be adjudged away from him.[b] There may have been ground for some other of his manifold excuses: that Venice did not furnish the galleys which alone could make him a match for the fleets of Genoa at the command of Benedict; that the land journey through Lombardy, to the friendly territory of the Marquis of

---

[a] Theodoric à Niem.
[b] Leonard. Aretin. "Nos de Pontifice nullo modo credimus, de propinquis non dubitamus." The acts are certain.
[b] One was to have Fanum, another Forli, a third Volteto, in Tuscany; they were also to have the noble city and port of Cornelo: the grants for these alienations were made, but not fulfilled.—A Niem, c. xxl.

Montferrat, was perilous on account of the wars raging in that district; that he was in want of money to meet his rival in equal magnificence.° A large sum was borrowed from Florence, to be forcibly reimbursed by the clergy of that city; the clergy of Rome were wrung by the unrelenting exactions of Paolo Orsini; sacred furniture and vessels were sold. All this embittered and exasperated the clergy. But deeper and more powerful influences were at work. The kindred of the Pope would not hazard his supremacy. With King Ladislaus his title to Naples hung on the perpetuation of the Schism, at least on the maintenance of the Italian Pontiff. If there was a French Pope, a French King of Naples was inevitable.ᵈ Gregory, while he seemed to anathematise, was ruled by Ladislaus. He still professed the profoundest solicitude for the conference, but he still raised new impediments. Monks and friars preached openly against his cowardly abandonment of his incontestable rights. If Gregory and his Cardinals went to Savona, they would be murdered, such was the notorious determination of the odious Benedict. Those who urged the immediate accomplishment of his vows were coldly heard, or put to silence. The negotiations dragged on. Gregory, in a long statement, raised twenty-two objections to Savona;

Delays.

° See in the Summen aus Rom the difficulty of dealing with Gregory XII. He refused to confirm the ordinary decrees and compacts of his predecessor. He is unmanageable on such litigated points, for he is unlearned in the canon law, and always thinks that he is being cheated. Yet he will do everything himself, even the business usually despatched by the Cardinals. He grants no graces; all must depart with their affairs unsettled. In one week he had 2000 supplications, all of which were crammed into a bag, hardly ten of them were ever got out and signed.— P. 152.

ᵈ "Veretur nunc ut abdicatione factâ, et utroque collegio ad electionem coeunte, Gallicus forte aliquis ad pontificatum sumatur, qui favorem in regno obtinendo in Ludovicum convertat."— Leonard. Aretin. Epist.

he insisted on some town in the occupation of a neutral power. Carrara was named, Lucca, Pisa, Leghorn. Benedict saw the advantage of advancing on his tardier rival; he moved to Porto Venere, afterwards to Spezia. Gregory to Lucca. They were not more than fifteen leagues asunder; but the one, like a water animal, would not leave the sea-shore—the other, like a land animal, would not approach the sea.*

So closed one year; another began. Towards the spring Ladislaus advanced on Rome with 15,000 men. He was admitted into the city by the secret connivance of Paolo Orsini.¹ He gave out that he came to protect Rome from a descent meditated by the fleet at the command of Benedict. Of this descent Gregory had more than once declared his apprehension. He almost avowed his joy at this aggressive act of Ladislaus; the design of Benedict, which he assumed as unquestionable, justified all his caution. Marshal Boucicaut had, in truth, thirteen galleys, destined for the mouth of the Tiber, to protect the city of Rome from the King of Naples; but they were kept in port by stress of weather. Ladislaus was not content with Rome; he still advanced; Perugia, Orta, Amelia, Todi, Rieti, submitted to his sway.ᵍ

1407, 1408. Ladislaus in Rome.

April 25.

The weary negotiations had gone languishing on. Gregory offered at one time to abdicate the Papacy, if he might retain his old titular dignity of Patriarch of Constantinople, two bishoprics in his native territory

---

* Leonard. Aretin. p. 926.
¹ See the account of the entrance of Ladislaus into Rome (April 25), the public joy, the peace, abundance, and cheapness of provisions. — Nemus Unionis, vi. c. 9. "Ita quod in genere omnes contentantur de domino regis, exceptis forsan aliquibus Romanis habentibus gravamen." All the armed men on the other side were repelled from the city.
ᵍ Muratori, Ann. sub ann. 1408. Nemus Unionis, vi. c. 27.

Venice, with the English archbishopric of York, then expected to fall vacant.[h] But there was now a sudden and total rupture. Gregory reassumed the unlimited Pontifical power. He declared his determination, in direct violation of the compact, to create four new Cardinals—two of his nephews, his Protonotary, and Brother John the Dominican, Bishop elect of Ragusa, a man odious on all accounts,[i] now especially so, as having not only secretly urged, but openly preached the sole indefeasible Popedom of Gregory.[k] The old Cardinals were summoned to his presence. They sat in mournful stillness; they heard the Pope condescend to communicate his purpose. One broke out, "Let us die first." Another fell at his feet. Defiance, protest, entreaty, moved not the impenetrable old man. He heard that they were meditating flight to Pisa. At the same time came forth a Bull for the creation of the four Cardinals, and an inhibition to the rest to leave Lucca. Paolo Guinigi, Lord of Lucca, interposed; he refused to permit any violence to be used against the Cardinals. They withdrew to Pisa: there they published an appeal to a General

---

[h] A Niem, c. xxi.

[i] See the letter from Satan to this Fra Joanne Dominico, wishing him "salutem et superbiam sempiternam." A. Niem, Nemus Unionis, vi. 29. This Nemus Unionis is a very curious collection of documents made by Theodoric k Niem, selected perhaps in hostility to Gregory XII., but neither invented nor falsified. "In hoc nemore laborantibus hypocrisis Veneta (of Gregory XII.) argutia Cathalonica (Benedict XIII.) versutia Sicula (Ladislaus) fallacia Genuensis, elegantia Gallica, sinceritas Theutonica, et æquitas Portugallica obviabunt."—In Præf.

[k] See Nemus Unionis, tract. iv. c. 4, for the arguments against the cession of Gregory. "XV. Quia sic privarentur Italici injuste tanto honore Sedis Apostolicæ et Ecclesia transferretur ad Gallicos, ad Avinionenses. XVI. Quia Italici post renunciationem divulgabuntur per universum orbem terrarum insensati, recordes, ignari, quia tantam gloriam Papatus perdiderunt: et Gallici prædicabuntur sensati, animosi, sapientes, quia licet falsum Papam habuissent tamen viceruut." It was a strife of Italy and France for the Popedom. Compare iv. 8.

Council. Their taunting address^m reminded the Pope of his vow to go on foot with his staff to accomplish the union of the Church. They asserted that they had been in danger, if not of their lives, of imprisonment in noisome dungeons: manacles and fetters had been prepared in the Pope's palace." Gregory could not be silent. He haughtily declared them unworthy of reply, but he did reply. He accused them of secret and suspicious conversations with the French ambassador and those of Peter di Luna. He utterly denied all designs against their lives and liberties. They alleged, he said, that they had sworn to go to Pisa, but not to go without the Pope.°

Cardinals at Pisa.

Christendom had beheld with indignation this miserable game of chicanery, stratagem, falsehood, perjury, played by two hoary men, each above seventy years old. But the great European kingdoms were too much divided, too much agitated by intestine disunion, to act together in this momentous common cause. Benedict XIII., taking courage from the more tardy movements and more glaring violation of faith in his adversary, seemed resolved to assert his Papal title by an act of Papal arrogance. France had threatened to stand neutral and to withdraw her allegiance from both Popes. Benedict presumed no doubt on the state of affairs, the hopeless derangement of the King, the deadly feud still raging between the houses of Bur-

Indignation of Christendom.

---

^m Dated May 14.
ⁿ Apud Raynald. sub ann.
^o Read the letter of the University of Paris to the Cardinals at Pisa: " Superfluum potamus referre, quoties requisitæ fuerunt dilationes, refutationes, et illusiones quibus jam orbem fatigaverunt. . . . Credimus neminem tam improbum, tam perditum, tamque eorum similem inveniri posse, qui posthac eos defendendos arbitraretur, nisi forsitan is fuerit, quem eadem infausti schismatis cognatio in damnatam hæresim demerserit." — Nemus Unionis, vi. 15.

gundy and Orleans. A Christian preacher had startled even the low morality of that age, by vindicating the assassination of the Duke of Orleans. Benedict prepared two Bulls: one, the more violent, had been drawn up in the year 1407; one during the present year, in a more mitigated tone. Both, however, arraigned the King of France, more or less directly, as under the seduction of the devil, and as inflaming the Schism in the Church. All who were guilty of this crime, even though clothed in the highest temporal or spiritual dignity, he pronounced under excommunication—excommunication from which they could be absolved only by the Pope himself, and on the bed of death. Their kingdoms were threatened with interdict. The milder Bull, more distinctly addressed to the King of France, expostulated with him as a father with a disobedient son, but warned him against those awful censures.*

<small>Benedict's letter of excommunication.</small>

The Pope's messengers were instructed to deliver these Bulls into the King's hands, and to return with all speed. They were apprehended and thrown into prison. The King was sane enough to assemble nobles, prelates, some members of the parliament, and deputies from the University of Paris. John Courtecuisse, a distinguished theologian, delivered a sermon on the text, "His iniquity shall fall on his own head." He exhibited thirteen articles against Peter di Luna, called Benedict XIII. He charged him with perjury for not fulfilling his vow of abdication; with heresy, as having asserted that the Pope would be guilty of a deadly sin, if he should renounce the Pope-

<small>Monday, May 21, 1408.</small>

---

* The superscription was "Domino Regi et omnibus Domini de sanguine et concilio."—Gersoniana, xxii.

dom, even to restore unity in the Church of God.⁴ The Bulls were declared illegal, treasonable, injurious to the King's majesty. The King gave his assent to the prayer, and commanded the Chancellor, the famous Gerson, to "do what was right." Gerson tore the Bulls in two; one half he gave to the nobles, one to the prelates and the delegates of the University; they rent them into shreds.⁵ The Pope's messengers, some days after, were brought forth in black linen dresses, on which, on one side, were painted themselves presenting the Bulls to the King; on the other the Pope's arms reversed. They had paper crowns on their heads, with the inscription, "Traitors to the Church and to the King." They were placed on a high scaffold, and exhibited to the scorn and derision of the people. They were sent back to perpetual imprisonment; one got away after three years.⁶

The inexorable University pursued its triumph; some of the highest and most learned prelates of the realm were assailed as being favourable to Peter di Luna. The King's proclamation was published in Italy, announcing the neutrality of France, asserting the perjury, treachery, heresy of both Popes. All churches were called on to abandon Angelo Corario and Peter di Luna. The Marshal Boucicaut had orders to seize the person of Benedict XIII., but Benedict had his galleys ready; he set sail, and arrived safe at Perpignan. Gregory took refuge in the territories of his native Venice.

---

⁴ See the account of John de Courtecuisse (Breviscoxa) in Dupin's Gersoniana, p. xl. There is a long treatise of Courtecuisse on the Pope and General Councils in the first volume of Gerson's works. Courtecuisse was Bishop of Paris, A.D. 1420.
⁵ Dupuy, p. 146.
⁶ Dupuy, 137.

CHAPTER V.

COUNCIL OF PISA.

Gregory XII., Benedict XIII., Alexander V., and John XXIII.

THE mutual fear and mistrust of the rival Popes was
their severest self-condemnation. These grey-
headed Prelates, each claiming to be the representative of Christ upon earth, did not attempt
to disguise from the world that neither had the least
reliance on the truth, honour, justice, religion of his
adversary. Neither would scruple to take any advantage of the other; neither would hesitate at any fraud,
or violence, or crime; neither would venture within the
grasp of the other, from the avowed apprehension for
his liberty or his life. The forces at the command of
each must be exactly balanced; the cities or sovereigns
in whose territories they were to meet must guarantee,
or give hostages for their personal security. They
deliberately charged each other with the most nefarious
secret designs, as well as with equivocation, evasion,
tampering with sacred oaths, perjury.

The College of Cardinals, not only by their great
public act, the summoning on their own authority a full independent Council, but even
more offensively by the language of their addresses
to the Popes, from whom they had severally revolted, and those to the Kings and nations of Christendom, condemned both. Each arraigned the Pope

whom he had till now honoured as the successor of St. Peter, as guilty of the most odious and contemptible conduct, falsehood, perjury, obstinate adherence to a fatal and damnable Schism. The two parties met at Leghorn; the four Cardinals, who either of their own free will, or under compulsion, had accompanied Benedict to Perpignan, had found their way to Italy; the eight who had abandoned Gregory at Lucca—Naples, Aquileia, Colonna, Orsini, Brancaccio, Ravenna, Lucca, St. Angelo.[a] There they determined to assume, as the senate of Christendom, a dictatorial power over their Sovereign; and to call on their own authority, without the sanction of the Pope or the Emperor, the famous Council of Pisa. Strong measures must be justified by strong asseverations of their necessity. The Popes, thus superseded in the highest branch of their authority, and made amenable to a new tribunal, must first be surrendered to general aversion and scorn. The Cardinals in the *obedience* of Benedict XIII.[b] (new terms were required to express new relations) maintained in their

[a] H. Miontelo, a Neapolitan, Cardinal of Tusculum.
Antonio Gaetani, a Roman, C. Præneste.
Odo Colonna, Roman, C. S. George in Velabro.
Odo Orsini, Roman, C. S. Silvester and S. Martin.
Raynold Brancaccio, Neapolitan, S. Vitus and Modestus.
John de Migliorotto, of Sulmona, C. S. Cross.
Angelo Somaripa, of Lodi, C. S. Pudentiana.
Peter Stefaneschi, Roman, C. of St. Angelo.
[b] Guy de Malesico, a Poitavin, C. of Præneste.

Nicolas Brancaccio, Neapolitan, C. Albano.
John de Brogniæ, Frenchman, C. of Ostia.
Peter G. Dupuy, Frenchman, C. of Tusculum.
Peter de Thurey, Frenchman, C. S. Susanna.
Amadeo of Saluzzo, Piedmontese, C. S. Maria Nuova.
Angelo di S. Anna, Neapolitan.
The Cardinals of Milan, Peter Philargi of Candia, afterwards Pope Alexander V., and De Baro, a Spaniard, Cardinal of S. Agatha, soon appeared. Then the Cardinals of Bordeaux, of Urbino, and De Friss, Cardinal of Spain.

summons to their Pope some words of respect. They addressed him as Pope; they spoke of his rival as Angelo Corario. But in their letter to the King of France and to the Universities, and in the circulars addressed to Christendom, he was, as the author and maintainer of the Schism, wicked as the Jews and the heathen soldiers who would rend the seamless robe of Christ. His utter insincerity, his artifices, his obstinacy, his contempt of his oaths, were exposed in unambiguous words.[c] The Cardinals in the obedience of Gregory were more unmeasured in their reproaches. On the instant of their secession or escape from Lucca, the city walls were lined with a fierce satire against Gregory, in which invective and ridicule vied in bitterness.[d] It purported to be a summons not only from the Cardinals, but from all the officers of the Papal Court down to the grooms of the kitchen and stable; it summoned Gregory to appear in Lucca on a certain day, to be degraded not only as a man of blood, without honour, the slave of his carnal affections, but as a drunkard, a madman, a proclaimed heretic, a subverter of the Church of God, an accursed hypocrite. It deposed all his adherents, especially his four new Cardinals.[e]

Their avowed proclamations were hardly more seemly in language. They darkly described and attributed to

---

[c] D'Achery, Spicilegium, i. 818.

[d] This placard is in the work of à Niem. It is entitled Epistola Delusoria. L'Enfant supposes that it was really the work of the Cardinals. It is manifestly a furious satire against all parties, perhaps by à Niem himself.—L'Enfant, Concile de Pise, i. p. 235.

[e] Compare in the Nemus Unionis à Niem's correspondence with one of the Cardinals; his address to the Pope (was it delivered ?), and his description of the perplexity of the courtiers, who held fat benefices: "plerique eorum remanent nobiscum et non nobiscum, timore perditionis dictorum beneficiorum non amore." A Niem had no benefice, and could speak boldly and freely. He quotes, "Cantabit vacuus coram latrone viator," vi. c. 23.

him and to his adversary all the evils of the Schism. They had chosen him as the best and most holy of their order; he had sworn deeply, repeatedly, solemnly, to extinguish the Schism by renunciation; he had afterwards declared such renunciation diabolic and damnable, as though he had taken the keys of St. Peter only to acquire the power of perjuring himself, and of giving free licence of perjury to others.[f]

The rival Popes were too well aware of the authority which a General Council would exercise over the mind of Christendom not to make a desperate effort to secure that authority in their own favour. They made all haste to anticipate the Council of Pisa, which the Cardinals with more dignified tardiness, had summoned for the Lady-day in the following year. Benedict collected a hasty but somewhat imposing assembly at Perpignan.[g] It was said to have been attended by nine Cardinals, by four Prelates, invested for the occasion with the venerable titles of the four Patriarchs of the East. There were the Archbishops of Toledo, Saragossa, Tarragona; many Bishops from Arragon, Castile, and the other kingdoms of Spain, Savoy, Lorraine, still in the obedience of Benedict XIII. The Scotch Bishops had not time, or were prevented from attendance. There were even some Prelates from France, notwithstanding the declaration of the King and Parliament of their absolute neutrality, and although the Archbishop of Auch had been deposed, and the Archbishop of Rheims himself had fallen into disgrace for his obstinate resistance to the will of the King and of the nation. The assembly at Perpignan assumed all

<small>Benedict's Council at Perpignan. Nov. 1, 1408.</small>

---

[f] Raynaldus, A.D. 1408, No. xxiii.
[g] L'Enfant, Concile de Pise, i. 221. Martene, Anecdot. II. 1476. A Niem, De Schismate, iii. 37. Aguirre, Concil. Hispan.

the formalities of an Œcumenic Council; but the event answered neither these lofty pretensions, nor the bold hopes of Benedict. Violent disputes arose as to the course which they should counsel the Pope to pursue. The higher dignitaries gradually shrunk away, till the Pope was left with but eighteen Prelates. The final deliberations of this remnant of a Council, with their results, are among the irreconcileable contradictions of this period. By most accounts Benedict consented to send ambassadors with certain powers and instructions to Pisa. Some of them were arrested at Nismes by order of the King of France; the Archbishop of Tarragona with others hardly escaped stoning by the populace at Pisa. On their application for passports the Cardinal Legate of Bologna declared that if he found them in the city with or without passports he would burn them alive. Yet among the charges presented against Benedict in the Council of Constance, he is affirmed to have treated his own Council with contemptuous harshness, and to have repelled them from his presence. He certainly retired to the strong fortress of Peniscola, and there in sullen dignity awaited the event.

Gregory's proposed Council was even more inglorious: it had not where to hold its humble state.[b] No one great city was open to the poor old Pontiff. Rome was in the possession of King Ladislaus, who in outward friendship with Gregory, was making suspicious advances to the Council of Pisa. Florence held a synod of her own, condemnatory of both Popes.

Gregory's Council.

---

[b] See MS., B. M. Summons to the Irish Church to send the Bishops of Waterford and Lismore to the General Council. Sienna, Aug. 13, 1408. Gregory XII. sends the Cardinal Bishop of Porto, Legate to England and Ireland. He could be ill spared from the College of Cardinals. But the mission was of paramount importance. Jan. 17, 1409.

The Council of Pisa was in her territories, under her protection. The Cardinal Legate, that Legate Balthasar Cossa, was Tyrant of Bologna: he looked to rule for his own ends the Council of Pisa. The learned University of Bologna declared against both Popes; his native Venice would not embark in the desperate cause of her countryman Angelo Corario; her grave ambassadors gave cold counsel to the Pope to submit and renounce his dignity. Ravenna, Aquileia, Capua, even Ephesus, then for a brief time in the occupation of the Christians, were named. At length in an obscure corner of the Venetian territory, at Ciudad in the Friuli, a few Prelates were gathered to assert the indefeasible right of the old deserted Gregory XII.; to hear his feeble murmurs of anathema against his antagonists. But this was after the Council of Pisa had held her sittings.[1]

That Council of Pisa rose in imposing superiority above these secluded and fugitive conciliabules, as they were tauntingly called. Under the stately nave of the Cathedral in that city, where the aspiring Lombard or rather Italian architecture had lifted the roof to a majestic height yet unequalled in Italy, even by Gothic Assisi, and supported it on tall harmonious pillars (even now the noblest model of the Italian Basilica, expanded into the Latin cross); where over the altar hovered the vast and solemn picture of our Lord with the Virgin on one side, St. John on the other, in which Cimabue made the last and most splendid effort of the old rigid Byzantine art to retain its imperilled supremacy; and thus Latin Christianity seemed to assert its rights against Teutonic independence before their final severance: beneath these auspices met the most august assembly

[1] Labbe, Concilia. A Niem, De Schismate. L'Enfant, L. p. 295.

as to the numbers and rank of the Prelates, and the Ambassadors of Christian Kings, which for centuries had assumed the functions of a representative Senate of Christendom. At first fourteen Cardinals, seven in each obedience, took their seats; the number grew to twenty-one or two, and finally, on the arrival of the Legate of Bologna with three others, to twenty-six; four Patriarchs — Alexandria, Antioch, Jerusalem, Grado. Twelve Archbishops, eighty Bishops appeared in person; fourteen Archbishops and a hundred and two Bishops by their procurators.[b] Eighty-seven Abbots, among the Cistercians those of Clairvaux, Grammont, Camaldoli, represented each his order; there were the Procurators of two hundred more; those of the Præmonstratensians and of St. Antony in Vienne appeared for all their Order with forty-one Priors; the Generals of the Franciscans, Dominicans, Carmelites, Augustinians, the Grand Master of Rhodes, the Prior of the Knights of the Holy Sepulchre, the Proctor General of the Teutonic Knights. The Universities sent their delegates—Paris, Toulouse, Orleans, Angers, Montpellier, Bologna, Florence, Cracow, Vienna, Prague, Cologne, Oxford, Cambridge; as did the Chapters of a hundred Metropolitan and Collegiate churches. There were three hundred Doctors of Theology and of Canon Law. The hierarchy of France were in the largest numbers; but Italy, Germany represented by the Procurators of the Archbishops of Mentz, Cologne, Saltzburg, and Magdeburg, and England by those of Canterbury, York, London, Winchester, and many others, by the Bishops of Salisbury (the famous Robert Hallam), St. David's, Carlisle, perhaps Chichester

---

[b] There are considerable variations in the lists, as published in D'Achery, in Raynaldus, and by L'Enfant. Compare L'Enfant, i. pp. 239, 240.

—added their weight, as did Poland and Hungary. Even Spain had one or two Bishops. There were also ambassadors from the Kings of France, England, Portugal, Bohemia, Sicily, Poland, Cyprus; from the Dukes of Burgundy, Brabant, Pomerania, the Margrave of Brandenburg, the Landgrave of Thuringia, and many other German Princes. The Kings of Spain alone stood aloof as not having renounced the allegiance of Benedict, to whom also the Kings of Hungary, Scotland, Sweden, Norway, and Denmark gave a doubtful support. Ladislaus of Naples alone adhered to Gregory, from enmity to Florence rather than from friendship to the Pope. The Emperor Robert—or rather the claimant of the empire, elected on the deposition of Wenceslaus, whose indefeasible title was still acknowledged in some parts of Germany—alone of sovereign princes by his ambassadors contested the legality of the Council, its self-constituted authority, and its right of adjudication in the cause of two Popes, one of whom must be the legitimate Pontiff.

The Council conducted its proceedings with grave regularity, or rather (there were rare excep- *Proceedings* tions) with dispassionate dignity. It seemed *of the Council.* profoundly impressed with the sense of its own unprecedented position, and the extraordinary and dictatorial power which it had been compelled to assume, contrary to the usage of the last centuries. The assertion of the supremacy of a General Council, of a Council unsummoned by the Pope, was a doctrine which needed the boldness, authority, learning, and weight of such men as Gerson, the Chancellor of Paris,[a] to vindicate. The

---

[a] John Gerson was born 14th Dec. 1363, of a family devoted to the Church. His three brothers were monks. He studied at Paris under Peter d'Ailly in 1392 or 1393, succeeded Peter d'Ailly as Chancellor of

Treatise of that all-honoured man was acknowledged as the one work which contained and summed up with irrefragable force and erudition the arguments in favour of the Council.ⁿ

The Council met on Lady-day; but, in the commencement of the fifteenth century, that almost holiest of days must not be profaned by business even of that solemn importance. At the close of the first formal session on the next day, proclamation was made at the gates of the Cathedral, demanding whether Peter di Luna or Angelo Corario were present, either by themselves, their Cardinals, or Procurators. Three times on successive days this citation was repeated; at the close, neither Peter di Luna nor Angelo Corario making answer, they were pronounced in contumacy. The prelates and ambassadors from the more distant lands arrived but slowly; the Council occupied its time with sermons and the discussion of preliminary matters, the hearing and dismissing the ambassadors of the Emperor. The more solemn business commenced with the arrival of the French and English ambassadors (France had at first been represented only by the Bishop of Meaux), Simon de Cramault Patriarch of Alexandria, Giles de Champs Bishop of Coutances, and two doctors, Robert Hallam Bishop of Salisbury, Henry Bishop of St. David's, the

March 26.

---

the University. He had been the delegate of the University to both Popes.—Dupin, Vita Gersoni.

^a Gersoni Opera, ii. p. 114. His doctrine was this: "Unitas Ecclesiæ semper manet ad Christum sponsum suum... Et si non habet vicarium, dum scilicet mortuus est corporaliter vel civiliter vel quis non est probabiliter expectandum quod unquam sibi vel successoribus ejus obedientia præstetur a Christianis, tunc Ecclesia, tam divino quam naturali jure, potest ad procurandum sibi vicarium unum et certum semet congregare ad Concilium Generale repræsentans eam, et hoc non solum auctoritate Dominorum Cardinalium, sed etiam adjumento et auxilio cujuscunque Principis, vel alterius Christiani."

Prior of the Benedictines in Canterbury, Thomas Abbot of St. Mary Jervaulx, the Earl of Suffolk, and several doctors. They rode into Pisa in great pomp with two hundred horses in their train.[o]

One month had almost fully elapsed, when the Advocate Fiscal, the Secretary of the Council, read certain resolutions framed by the promoters of the cause: among these, that the Holy Council was canonically called and constituted by the two Colleges of Cardinals now blended into one; that to them it belonged to take cognisance of the two competitors for the Papacy. The Advocate read a long and elaborate report on the origin and progress of the Schism. He concluded with this proposition: "Seeing that the contending Prelates had been duly cited, and, not appearing, declared contumacious, they were deprived of their pontifical dignity, and their partisans of their honours, offices, and benefices; if they contravened this sentence of deposition, they might be punished and chastised by secular judges; all kings, princes, and persons of every rank or quality were absolved from their oaths, and released from allegiance to the two rival claimants of the Popedom."[p] The promoters demanded the hearing of witnesses to the facts deposed. The hearing of witnesses proceeded; but before many days the Council found that this hearing would draw out to an interminable length. They declared the main facts matters of public notoriety. All went on in slow form. One Prelate alone departed from the grave dignity of the assembly, the Bishop of Sisteron in Provence, an Arragonese, up to this time a strong partisan of Benedict XIII. In his sermon, on "Purge away your old

April 2L

Two Popes declared to be deposed.

---

[o] L'Enfant, p. 269.　　[p] Concilia, sub ann.

leaven," he caused astonishment among the audience by asserting that they were no more Popes than his old shoes; he called them worse than Annas and Caiaphas, and compared them to the devils in hell.[q] First was pronounced the general subtraction of obedience from both Popes. On the 5th June, proclamation having been again made for their appearance and no answer heard, the gates of the Cathedral were thrown open, and the definitive sentence read by the Patriarch of Alexandria. "The Holy Universal Council, representing the Catholic Church of God, to whom belongs the judgement in this cause, assembled by the grace of the Holy Ghost in the Cathedral of Pisa, having duly heard the promoters of the cause for the extirpation of the detestable and inveterate Schism, and the union and re-establishment of our Holy Mother Church, against Peter di Luna and Angelo Corario, called by some Benedict XIII. and Gregory XII., declares the crimes and excesses, adduced before the Council, to be true, and of public fame. The two competitors, Peter di Luna and Angelo Corario, have been and are notorious schismatics, obstinate partisans, abettors, defenders, approvers of this long schism; notorious heretics as having departed from the faith; involved in the crimes of perjury and breach of their oaths; openly scandalising the Church by their manifest obstinacy, and utterly incorrigible; by their enormous iniquities and excesses they have made themselves unworthy of all honour and dignity, especially of the Supreme Pontificate; and though by the canons they are actually[r] rejected of God, deprived and cut off from the Church, nevertheless the Church, by this definitive sentence, deposes, rejects and cuts them off, prohibiting

Sentence.

---

[q] L'Enfant, p. 273, from the Abbot of Saint Marzant.   [r] Ipso facto.

both and each from assuming any longer the Sovereign Pontificate, declaring for further security* the Papacy to be vacant." The rest of the sentence pronounced Christians of all ranks absolved from all vows and engagements towards them, uttered excommunication and other canonical penalties against all who should succour, abet, or harbour either of them. Whosoever should refuse obedience to this decree, the competitors or their abettors, were to be repressed by the secular arm. All censures, excommunications, interdicts, issued by the two pretendants, were annulled; all promotions since May, 1408, declared void.†

Such was the first solemn, deliberate, authoritative act, by which a General Council assumed a power superior to the Papacy, which broke the long tradition of the indefeasible, irresponsible autocracy of the Pope throughout Christendom. It assumed a dictatorial right in a representative body of the Church to sit, as a judicial tribunal, with cognisance of the title by which Papal authority was exercised, of offences committed by Prelates claiming to be Popes, and to pronounce in the last instance on the validity of their acts. It was much beyond a decision on a contested election; it was the cashiering of both, and that not on account of irregularity or invalidity of title, but of crimes and excesses subject to ecclesiastical censure; it was a sentence of deposition and deprivation, not of uncanonical election. Each party of Cardinals had concurred in the election of one or other of the Popes; they could not take that ground without impugning their own authority. If the Schism imperceptibly undermined the Papal power in

---

* Ad cautelam.
† The decree may be read in à Niem, c. 44, L'Enfant, and the Concilia.

public estimation, the General Council might seem to
shake it to its base.

The Council had a harder task than the deposal of
the two contesting Popes, of whom Christendom was
weary, and who were abandoned by most of their own
partisans. The election of a new Pope, who should
command universal respect, and awe back the world
into its old reverence for the Supreme Pontiff, was the
necessary but far more difficult function of the Council.
The Conclave could not be charged with precipitation.
During eleven days[a] the twenty-six Cardinals
were occupied in their momentous consultation.
The secrets of the Conclave were religiously kept. No
one knew whether these days were occupied by grave
and impartial deliberation or by the struggle of conflicting interests. The Cardinals must have gone beyond
their own pale to have found a Prelate whose name for
ability, learning, piety, would have extorted universal
admiration. Most of them had been promoted during
the Schism, as zealous partisans of either Pope, rather
than as distinguished Churchmen. One alone, Balthasar
Cossa, afterwards John XXIII., was known for his consummate power and energy, though certainly for no
other hierarchical qualifications. But his time was not
come. The warlike Legate, who had crushed the liberties
of Bologna, had doubtless the sagacity not yet to aspire
to the supreme dignity, probably had no chance of commanding the suffrages of the French Cardinals, to whom
he was unknown, or the Italian, by whom he was too
well known and feared.

The choice fell on Peter Philargi, of Candia, of the
Order of Friar Minors, commonly called Cardinal of

---

[a] From June 15 to June 26.

Milan, rightly Cardinal of the Twelve Apostles. This choice may have been the final determination to set up an irreproachable man, of some fame for eloquence and learning, or a compromise between the unyielding Cisalpine and Transalpine parties. Whenever such compromise takes place, it is usually in favour of an aged Prelate; and the Cardinal of Milan was above seventy years old. Alexander V. (the name he assumed) was of such obscure origin, that it is disputed whether the Candia from which he was named was the Island of Crete, or a small village in the Milanese. Cast parentless and friendless on the world, he had become a Mendicant Friar. Beggary was not his choice only, it was his lot. His life had been blameless, studious, holy. He had studied theology at Oxford and Paris; and had been raised by the discernment of Gian Galeazzo Visconti to the tutorship of his sons. By the same influence he became Bishop of Vicenza, of Novara, and Archbishop of Milan. Alexander V. was superior to the two vices which had loaded with reproach the fame and memory of most of his predecessors—avarice and nepotism. His weakness was prodigality. He lavished what under the existing circumstances must have been the limited and precarious resources of the Papacy with such generous profusion, that he said of himself, he had been rich as a Bishop, as a Cardinal poor, as Pope he was a beggar. On the day of his enthronement his grants were so lavish as to justify, if not to give rise to, the rumour, that the Cardinals, on entering into the Conclave, had made a vow that whosoever should be elected would grant to the households of his brother Cardinals the utmost of their demands. From nepotism Alexander V. was safe, for he was without kindred or relatives. But there was another, perhaps more fatal, nepotism which turned the tide of popularity against him—the nepotism of his Order. It was more than the accumulation of all the offices of his Court on his beloved brethren, more than the lavish grant of bishoprics and dignities—it was the undue elevation of the Franciscans [a] above all the Secular, all the Regular Clergy. Two hundred years had not allayed the strife of the Mendicants and the Clergy. From the highest seats of learning to the most obscure country parish, there was rivalry, strife, jealousy, hatred. Still the theory of the Church, her whole discipline, depended on the sole and exclusive authority of the lawful pastors in their parishes, and on their exclusive right to perform the services of the Church, to hear confession, to grant absolution. Some highminded and far-seeing among the Prelates or the Clergy might welcome the Friars as active and zealous coadjutors in the task of Christianising mankind; they might keep on terms of mutual respect and harmony. The Mendicants might even, by their noble exertions under terrible exigencies, as declared in the Consistory of Avignon after the great plague, command the unwilling approbation of Cardinals and Popes.[f] But in general they were still hated with unmitigated hatred by the Clergy: by some of the better, as unjustly interfering between them and their beloved flocks, and as alienating and seducing away their people's affections; by the worse, as a standing reproach on their negligence and ignorance, and as drawing off to themselves the emoluments which the Clergy deemed their sole right—the oblations, the gifts,

---

[a] "Aliquos etiam Fratres Minores sibi charos et sociales publicis officiis et lucrativis quæ prius consueverant regi per seculares personas habiles et expertas in eisdem suâ curiâ præfecit, et miro modo constabat plerosque Fratres Minores Cathedralibus Ecclesiis præficere ut pastores."—A Niem, iii. c. 51.

[f] See vol. viii. pp. 1, 2.

the bequests. The inevitable degeneracy of the Friars would no doubt aggravate the strife. The Mendicant Orders had spread their net too wide not to comprehend multitudes of men with no other qualification than beggary. So soon as they became, if not rich, with the advantages of riches, with splendid convents, ample endowments, or even the privilege of subsisting at the cost of others, they would become little better than what they had been long called by their adversaries in England—sturdy beggars. Up to this time the Popes (as has appeared in our history)* had left some restraint on the Friars. They were too useful partisans, too much under the Papal control, not to find as much favour as could be granted without absolutely estranging the Clergy; yet the Bishops retained some power over them; and the Popes had refused absolutely to abrogate the exclusive privileges of the secular clergy. The relations of the two rival bodies were still kept in a kind of politic balance, and rested on vague and contradictory decrees.

The Bull of Alexander V., issued but a few months after his accession, rudely struck down the barrier.* It invested the Friar Preachers, the Friar Minors, the Augustinians, and the Carmelites, in the full, uncontrolled power of hearing confession and granting absolution in every part of Christendom. It rescinded, and declared null, if not heretical, seven propositions advanced or sanctioned by other Popes, chiefly John XXII. One of these it averred, with unnecessary insult and disparagement of the Papal infallibility, to have been issued by that Pope, when

^{Bull of Alexander in favour of the Friars. Oct. 12.}

---

* Compare Book xi. c. 2. L'Enfant has given the substance of the former Bulls, p. 309, &c.

* Relig. de St. Denys. Labourear's translation of the Bull may be read in L'Enfant, p. 314.

under condemnation for heresy. These propositions had enacted that without the consent of the parish priest, or at least of the Bishop, no Friar could hear confession. This Bull was not only the absolute annihilation of the exclusive prerogatives and pretensions of the Clergy, but it was ordered to be read by the Clergy themselves in all the churches in Christendom. They were to publish before their own flocks the triumph of their enemies, the complete independence of their parishioners on their authority, their own condemnation for insufficiency, their disfranchisement from their ancient immemorial rights. Henceforth there was a divided dominion in every diocese; in every parish there were two or more conflicting claimants on the obedience, the love, and the liberality of the flock. Still further, all who dared to maintain the propositions annulled by the Bull were to be proceeded against as contumacious and obstinate heretics. Thus the Pope, who was to reconcile and command or win distracted Christendom to peace and unity—a narrow-minded Friar, thinking only of his own Order—had flung a more fatal apple of discord into the world, and stirred up a new civil war among the more immediate adherents of the Papacy, among those who ought to have been knit together in more close and intimate confederacy.

The reception of this Bull in Paris, though its injurious workings were more openly and indignantly resented in Paris than elsewhere, may show its effect throughout Christendom. The old war of the University with the Dominicans and Franciscans, which had ended in the humiliation of their champion William of St. Amour, and the triumphant participation by their intrusive rivals in their ancient privileges (perhaps not mitigated by the assumption of the mastery

University of Paris.

over her schools by the great Dominican and Franciscan teachers, Albert the Great, Aquinas, Bonaventura, Duns Scotus), was not beyond the scope of their recollection. The tradition of academic jealousy and rivalry is endowed with pertinacious vitality. The schools rose in almost unanimous insurrection. The University of Paris had hailed with acclamations the accession of Pope Alexander. No sooner had this Bull arrived in the city, than, with contemptuous doubts of its authenticity, they sent delegates to Pisa to inquire whether it was genuine. The delegates would not be satisfied without seeing the leaden seal attached to the Bull.[b] The Bull professed to have been framed with the advice and consent of the Cardinals; the delegates visited and inquired separately of the Cardinals whether they had given such advice and consent, thus tacitly accusing the Pope of falsehood or forgery. The Cardinals disclaimed all participation in the decree; they did not deny that it was injurious to all who had the cure of souls.

The University, on the report of her delegates, proceeded to expel all Mendicant Friars from her walls, and to prohibit their preaching in Paris till they had produced and renounced the original Bull. The Preachers (Dominicans) and the Carmelites declared that they had no knowledge of the Bull, that they were content with the privileges possessed before the time of Alexander V. But the Franciscans, proud of a Pope from their own Order, went about defying all authority, and boasting that to them alone it belonged to preach,

---

[b] "A Pope's Bull and a Pope's Brief differ very much, as with us the great seal and the privy seal: the Bull being the highest authority the Pope can give, the Brief is of less. The Bull has a leaden seal upon silk, hanging upon the instrument; the Brief has *sub annulo Piscatoris* upon the side." I quote this from Selden's Table Talk, on account of the illustration.

to hear confession, and even to levy tithes.ᶜ The King interposed; on their convent gates was affixed a royal proclamation, forbidding Priests and Curates to permit the Franciscans or Augustinians to preach or hear confession in their churches.ᵈ The Chancellor Gerson, the Oracle of the Council, denounced the act of the Pope in no measured language.ᵉ

Whatever tended to destroy the popularity of Alexander threw discredit on the Council of Pisa. Murmurs were heard in many quarters that the Council, instead of extinguishing the Schism, had but added a third Pope. Benedict from his fastness at Peniscola issued his anathemas against the Council and against his rivals. *Gregory and Ladislaus in Rome.* Gregory had been obliged to take ignominious flight from the territories of Venice; he found refuge with Ladislaus. As the price of his security, and for 25,000 gold florins, he was reported at least to have sacrilegiously alienated the patrimony of the Church, to have sold Rome, the March, Bologna, Faenza, Forli, and all the lands of St. Peter to that ambitious King. Ladislaus unfurled his standard, which bore the menacing inscription, "Cæsar or Nothing." He occupied Rome with a

---

ᶜ A Niem describes the joy of the Franciscans at the elevation of Alexander V.: " Mirabiliter lætificati sunt; discurrebant enim per vicos et plateas civitatis catervatim valde multi eorum per singulos dies, velut essent mente capti."—iii. c. 53.

ᵈ Relig. de St. Denys.

ᵉ Relig. de St. Denys. " Dedisti nobis unum et verum Ecclesiæ Pastorem, quem recepimus magno cum gaudio, reverentiâ et exultatione. Et ecce malignum spiritum prœlii et divisionis, qui visus est suscitare turbationem novam, malam nimis, nimis expertam et fraudulentam sub umbrâ boni et religionis." The Christian hierarchy, writes Gerson, consists of the Pope, Cardinals, Archbishops, Bishops, successors of the Apostles; of curates, successors of the 70 disciples. Gerson asserts in the strongest terms the exclusive and perpetual rights of the curates to all the offices and emoluments of their function. They are more perfect than simple monks. " Sequitur statum curatorum perfectiorem esse statu simplicium religiosorum." This was new doctrine.—Gersoni Opera, ii. p. 433.

large force;' he had made terms with Paolo Orsini, the Guelfic condottiere; he was advancing on Tuscany. Alexander, Pope without a rood of the Papal dominions, fulminated his Bulls against the ally of the deposed Gregory, the usurper of the dominions of the See of Rome. But the Pope, recognised by France, and by most of the Italian States, had more formidable forces than spiritual censures. Louis of Anjou, in whom centered the hereditary pretensions of his house to the kingdoms of Naples and Sicily, appeared at Pisa with five hundred lances. Florence, who feared and hated Ladislaus, and the Cardinal Legate with his bands at Bologna, formed with Louis a strong league. Their armament moved towards Rome; Paolo Orsini advanced against Louis.⁸ But the religion and loyalty of the captain of a Free Company depended on the highest bidder. He had no scruples in changing his service and his Pope. He marched back with Louis of Anjou to reduce Rome, which he had gone forth to protect. At first the Leonine City, the Vatican, and St. Peter's, Oct. 1. then the Castle of St. Angelo, at length the Cisteverine region, and the Capitol submitted to the conqueror. Rome acknowledged Pope Alexander V.

' The occupation of Rome by Ladislaus is afterwards described by Pope John XXIII. as "optentu nephario atque velamine maledictionis filii Angeli Corarii, heretici et schismatici, per generale Pisan* Concilium justo Dei judicio sententialiter condemnati."— MS., B. M., Oct. 23, 1411. There is in the Diary of Antonius Petri (Muratori, t. xxiv.) a very curious account of the transactions in Rome day by day, of the hangings and decapitations, daily occurrences, of many of which Antonius was eye-witness. But on great events he is provokingly silent. He gives this strange inscription on one of the banners of Ladislaus, which be unfurled with the Papal banner:—
" Io son un povero Rè, amico della Sacco-manni,
Amatore delle popoli, e distruttore della Tyranni."—p. 979.

⁸ Antonius Petri describes the entrance of King Louis and the Orsini, with the Cardinal S. Eustachio (Balthasar Cossa), into Rome, Oct. 1.

Alexander had been driven by the plague from Pisa to Prato; from Prato he removed to Pistoia.[h] Instead of taking possession of Rome he crossed the cold snowy Apennines to put himself under the protection, or to deliver himself into the hands, of the Cardinal Legate. In Bologna he died in peace after a Pontificate not much exceeding ten months. Rumours of course that he died by poison spread abroad, and his successor bore also of course the guilt of his untimely end.[i]

May 3, 1410.

The Conclave had followed the Pope. After a very short interval it was announced to Christendom that twenty-four Cardinals had given their unanimous suffrages;[k] that Balthasar Cossa was chosen Supreme Pontiff, and had taken the name of John XXIII.[m]

Sunday, May 25, 1410.

John XXIII. is another of those Popes the record of whose life, by its contradictions, moral anomalies, almost impossibilities, perplexes and baffles the just and candid historian. That such, even in those times, should be the life even of an Italian Churchman, and that after such life he should ascend

John XXIII.

---

[h] The appointment of Marcello Strozzi Nuncio and Collector in England is dated Pistoia, 30th Dec. 1409.—MS., B. M.

[i] "Idem dominus Alexander Papa in lecto ægritudinis constitutus Bononiæ coram suis Cardinalibus pulchrum sermonem Latinum fecit." He died four days after, May 3, 1410. In the Chronicon attributed to À Niem is the text of this sermon, "Pacem meam do vobis, pacem relinquo vobis."—Apud Eccard, p. 1536. S. Antoninus, Chronic., h. Dugloss, Hist. Polon., attribute his death to a poisoned clyster. Monstrelet speaks more generally of poison. The sixth article against John XXIII. at Constance accuses John, and his physician, Daniel de S. Sophia, of the crime.—Ap. Von der Hardt. iv. 1, 3. But see in Monstrelet the pompous funeral.

[k] The list in Ciacconius, p. 780. It was not certain how many were actually present at the election.

[m] Read in Monstrelet the account of his election and splendid inauguration, l. i. c. lxviii.

to the Papacy, shocks belief; yet the record of that life not merely rests on the concurrent testimony of all the historians of the time, two of them secretaries to the Roman Court, but is avouched by the deliberate sanction of the Council of Constance to articles which, as will hereafter appear, contained all the darkest charges of the historians, and to some of which John himself had pleaded guilty.

Balthasar Cossa was a Neapolitan of noble birth;[a] as a simple clerk he served in the piratical warfare carried on by the hostile fleets of the rival Provençal and Hungarian Kings of Naples. He retained through life the pirates' habit of sleeping by day, and waking by night. At a later period two of his brothers, who had not like himself abandoned in time that perilous vocation, were taken by King Ladislaus, and notwithstanding the influence of Balthasar with the Pope, and the Pope's strenuous exertions in their behalf, hanged without mercy. Balthasar cherished from that time an implacable hatred to Ladislaus. He retired to Bologna and studied the Canon Law, it was said without much success. He was raised by Boniface IX. to the dignity of Archdeacon of Bologna. But his ambition had higher views. He returned to Rome, and was appointed one of the Pope's chamberlains.[o] He became one of the dexterous and unscrupulous agents of the Pope's insatiable avarice and of his own. He was the most daring and skilful vendor of preferments, the most artful of usurers. By secret, and as they demeaned themselves to their victims, friendly messengers, he

His youth.

---

[a] De Vitâ Joannis XXIII., à Theodoric à Niem, apud Meibomium, I. This work must be compared with the charges entertained and confirmed by the Council of Constance, and at length admitted by John himself.
[o] Cubicularius.

warned rich Prelates, that the Pope, ill-disposed towards them, designed to remove them from their wealthy and peaceful benefices to preferments in barbarous countries, in remote islands, or lands held by the Saracens. He received vast bribes to propitiate the unfriendly Pontiff. To him was attributed the enormous abuse of Indulgences. Already Priests and Friars loaded with these lucrative commodities, travelled through Germany, by Thuringia, Swabia, Saxony, into the Northern kingdoms, Denmark and Sweden. On their arrival in a city they exhibited a banner with the Papal arms, the keys of St. Peter, from the windows of their inn. They entered the principal church, took their seat before the altar, the floor strewed with rich carpets, and, under awnings of silk to keep off the flies, exhibited to the wondering people, notwithstanding the remonstrances of Priests or Bishops, their precious wares. "I have heard them," writes the biographer of John XXIII., "declare that St. Peter himself had not greater power to remit sins than themselves." One of the wealthiest of these Papal merchants, on his return from his journey, was seized at Bologna. Balthasar Cossa, perhaps his former patron, but now Legate, plundered him of 100,000 florins. The poor victim hanged himself in prison.*

Pope Boniface had formed so high an estimate of the abilities of Balthasar Cossa, that he was raised to the Cardinalate, and appointed Legate to wrest the city of Bologna from the domination of the Visconti.ᵠ The Legate fulfilled his mission; the poor student of law, the Archdeacon of Bologna, became the

---

* A Niem, p. 7.
ᵠ There was another notorious, it was said, but unavowed reason for his foreign mission, his separation from his brother's wife, the sister of a Cardinal, with whom he was living in incestuous, and, even for Rome, scandalous concubinage.

lord of that city with as absolute and unlimited dominion as the tyrant of any other of the Lombard or Romagnese commonwealths. Balthasar Cossa, if hardly surpassed in extortion and cruelty by the famous Eccelino, by his debaucheries might have put to shame the most shameless of the Viscontis. Under his iron rule day after day such multitudes of persons of both sexes, strangers as well as Bolognese, were put to death on charges of treason, sedition, or other crimes, that the population of Bologna seemed dwindling down to that of a small city. He used to send to the executioners to despatch their victims with greater celerity. Neither person nor possession was exempt from his remorseless taxation. Grain could not be ground, nor bread made, nor wine sold, without his licence. From all ranks, from the noble to the peasant, he exacted the most laborious services. He laid taxes on prostitutes, gaming-houses, usurers. His licentiousness was even more wide and promiscuous. Two hundred maids, wives, and widows, with many nuns, are set down as victims of his lust. Many were put to death by their jealous and indignant husbands and kindred. The historian wonders that in so rich and populous a city no husband's, or father's, or brother's dagger found its way to the heart of the tyrant.'

So is Balthasar Cossa described by Theodoric à Niem, his secretary. Leonardo Aretino, another secretary, in pregnant and significant words, represents him as a

---

' Yet the Chronicle, or rather the Continuation attributed to à Niem, speaks thus of his nearly nine years' administration of Bologna: "Floruit multum civitas et adaucta est longâ pace." But the author, who passes over Cossa's early life, admits that before the Council of Constance above forty charges were proved, some against his life, some against his doctrine; and that John XXIII. admitted their truth. —Apud Eccard, p. 1537.

great man, of consummate ability in worldly affairs, nothing or worse than nothing in spiritual.

At the death of Alexander V. the Conclave, of sixteen Cardinals at least,* in Bologna, were entirely in the power of this ambitious and unscrupulous man. They may have discarded the suspicions awakened by the opportune death of Alexander, though, as has been said, among the crimes afterwards not only murmured in secret, but alleged against John XXIII., was that of having poisoned his predecessor: no man whose death was important could be suffered to die in the course of nature.

The election, though without actual violence, may have been compulsory; yet at Constance, though almost all the Cardinals bear testimony against John, this does not seem to have been among the charges.† But the awe, the terror of his character and of their perilous situation may not have been less real. They may have wilfully closed their eyes (dastardly or almost impossible as it may seem) against his crimes and vices, allowing themselves to be dazzled by his higher qualities, his energy, courage, military skill, success. He was the Pope to restore the Papal interests in Romagna, in Italy, in Christendom. Already Cardinal Cossa had won back Rome to the dominion of his predecessor. He had his own powerful forces; he had bought over Paolo Orsini; with his close confederate, Louis of Anjou, he had made Ladislaus of Naples tremble on his throne. The ambassadors of Louis were in Bologna, strongly urging the election of their King's useful, indispensable ally.

No wonder if the secrets of that Conclave were

---

* The number present varies. See above.
† This charge had been a condemnation of their own weakness and want of Christian courage.

betrayed; it is still less wonderful that the accounts are contradictory; none would wish, none would dare to speak the truth. Each as his own exculpation might require, or his hatred predominate, would colour the facts. Cossa, it is said, appalled the Conclave with his threats; he scornfully rejected each name proposed; in their fear and discord they left him to name the Pope. He demanded the stole of St. Peter to array the worthiest, put it on his own shoulders—" I am Pope."[*] By another account he proposed the Cardinal Caracciolo, an unlearned, rude, and most unfit man. On his rejection Cossa himself was chosen.[x] The same writer in another place speaks of unmeasured bribery. Perhaps the simple phrase of a third may be most true—he owed his election to the troops at his command.[y] But whatever their motives, fear, deception, corruption, foreign influence—whether affrighted, cajoled, bribed, dazzled —the Conclave refused to remember the enormities of the life of Balthasar Cossa; the pirate, tyrant, adulterer, violator of nuns, became the successor of St. Peter, the Vicegerent of Christ upon earth.[z] Cossa was Pope; Louis of Anjou hastened to kiss the feet of his brother-in-arms; fourteen ecclesiastics, some of the wisest and ablest Prelates of Italy, accepted the title and rank of Cardinal at his hands. He fulminated his sentence of excommunication against the deprived Antipopes Gregory and Benedict; against King Ladislaus, whom he deposed from his throne.

---

[*] Philip of Bergamo. Supplem. Chronic. L'Enfant, il. p. 4.

[x] Theodoric à Niem, Vit. Johan. XXIII. In his Invectiva, à Niem accuses Cossa of having broken up the threshold with a golden axe, and given a sop to the Molossian hounds.

[y] Platina.

[z] " In cujus electione multi scandalizati sunt, quia ut tyrannus regime Bononiam, vitæ mundanæ deditus dicebatur."—Gobelinus, p. 330. This is at the least less passionate authority

At first the united forces of the Pope and Louis of Anjou met with some reverses; but during the next year, at the battle of Rocca Secca, Ladislaus suffered a total defeat. But Louis of Anjou, with his French impetuosity, knew not how to profit by his victory. "On the first day," said Ladislaus, "my person and my realm were at the mercy of the enemy; on the second my person was safe, but my realm was lost; on the third hope arose for my realm as well as my person."[a] Pope John had already advanced to Rome. No sooner had he left Bologna than the whole city rose with cries of Long live the people! Long live the Arts![b] The Cardinal Legate fled to the citadel, from whence he looked down on the plunder of the palace; in a few days he was compelled to surrender at discretion. The Pope at Rome received with exultation the tidings of the battle of Rocca Secca. The standards of the vanquished Ladislaus were dragged ignominiously through the miry streets. But the triumph was short; Louis had in vain attempted to force the passes which led into the kingdom of Naples; he returned baffled and discomfited to Rome, and after a few weeks embarked for Provence.

The Pope was left alone to the vengeance of Ladislaus. Florence had abandoned the League; he renewed his idle maledictions against a King who laughed them to scorn. He published a Crusade throughout Christendom in Italy, France, Germany, England,[c] Denmark, Norway, Prussia, Poland, Lithuania,

---

[a] S. Antoninus, p. 156.
[b] The guilds of the city.
[c] MS., B. M. Not merely was the Crusade to be preached with all the privileges of a Crusade to the Holy Land, but a subsidy implored, and a tenth demanded of the clergy, by the Legates, Antonio da Pinerio, General of the Minorites, and Paul de Sulmona, Archdeacon of Ravenna. Oct. 23,

Hungary, even in Cyprus and the East.[d] He summoned and held a Council at Rome, but few prelates would venture their lives in the unapproachable and insecure city. The Council was only memorable for an incident, in itself ludicrous, which nevertheless struck deep fear into many hearts as a dismal omen. Immediately after the opening Mass for the descent of the Holy Spirit, a huge owl flew out, screeching and fixing its eyes on the Pope. Those who dared to laugh laughed; some whispered, "A strange shape for the Holy Ghost!" The Pope broke up the assembly. On the next day there sat the owl, with its large eyes full on the Pope. The Cardinals with difficulty drove it out with sticks and stones.[e] These Papal acts, the excommunication and the Crusade, which displayed the dauntlessness and energy of the Pope, had been but feeble security against the King of Naples at his gates, if the crafty Ladislaus had not found it his interest to incline to peace. King and Pope had too many enemies, too few, and those but hollow friends. The Pope would purchase, at the highest price, not only peace but the recognition of his title.[f] Pope Gregory still lived under the protection of the King, in undisturbed retirement at Gaeta. Ladislaus was seized with qualms of religious conscience. He summoned the Prelates and theologians of his

---

1411. The Legates had power to absolve fifty persons excommunicated for trading with Alexandria in Egypt, and all the other ordinary powers. He hoped to make an agreement with Thomas of Lancaster, the King's second son, to head an English crusade. Nov. 9, 1411.

[d] The preaching of this Crusade and the Indulgences in Bohemia was a great cause of the Hussite disturbances.

[e] See Clemangis, Tract, p. 75, from an eye-witness. A Niem, apud Von der Hardt, II. 375.

[f] A Niem had heard from a partisan of Gregory XII. that John XXIII. paid, and that Ladislaus received by the hands of a certain Florentine, 100,000 florins for his abandonment of Gregory.—p. 17.

realm, and imparted to them his grave doubts whether he was not guilty of sin in maintaining a Pope rejected by all Christendom. He paid a cold civil visit to express his profound respect and sorrow to him whom he had so long honoured as Pope. Gregory had no ungrounded apprehensions lest he might be surrendered to his rival. Two Venetian merchant-ships were in the harbour; the inhabitants of Gaeta loved the poor old Pope; they bought a passage for him and his Court. The vessels sailed all round Calabria, and though pursued by the galleys of John XXIII. reached Rimini. Gregory was received by the Malatestas, the deadly enemies of Pope John.[a]

Ladislaus dictated the terms of the treaty with the Pope; at least no Pope not under hard necessity had submitted to such terms. Ladislaus was acknowledged not only as King of Naples, but also as King of Sicily. The Arragonese King of Sicily adhered to Benedict XIII. Ladislaus was named Gonfalonier of the Church. The Pope consented to pay 120,000 florins of gold; he surrendered as security the cities of Ascoli, Viterbo, Perugia, and Benevento. He absolved Ladislaus from a debt of 40,000 florins, the accumulated tribute to the Papacy. The Pope was to maintain 1000 horse for the subjugation of Sicily. The Pope obtained at this vast and dishonourable sacrifice only peace and the recognition of his own title; the dismissal not the surrender of the rival Pope.[b]

Oct. 1412.

Yet this peace did not last many months. The Pope had but time to exasperate Rome with his exactions. Though, as it should seem, himself possessed of great resources, he determined that Rome

New quarrel with Ladislaus.

---

[a] Raynald. sub ann.   [b] A Niem, p. 16.

should pay for her own security. His prothonotaries and referendaries wrung subsidies from the Cardinals and the clergy; the Senators from the people. A heavy duty on wine drove the populace to fury. The measure of wine usually sold at one florin rose to nine. He taxed the artisans and shopkeepers, and issued a debased coinage. The Pope was compelled to post up the abolition of the obnoxious wine-duty on all the corners of the streets.

The causes of the breach with the King of Naples are obscure, if any cause was wanting beyond the treachery and ambition of the King, the utter insincerity and avarice of the Pope. John hoped to reap a rich harvest by deposing all the Bishops and rich beneficiaries of the kingdom of Naples who had sworn allegiance to Gregory, or by extorting heavy mulcts for their confirmation. The wines of Naples were loaded with a prohibitory duty. Ladislaus had already troops moving in the March of Ancona, urging the cities to revolt; rumours spread of his designs on Rome; his troops were at the gates, within the city. The Romans swore that they would eat their children rather than submit to the dominion of that dragon Ladislaus.[1] The Pope went through the solemn mockery of committing the defence of the city to the patriotic heroism of the citizens; he himself fled in haste, first to Sutri, then to Viterbo, then to Montefiascone. The Cardinals and the Court followed as they might; some fell into the hands of the relentless enemy. The city, perhaps in secret intelligence with Ladislaus, made no resistance.[k] The Neapolitan soldiers plundered

---

[1] "Nos Romani primò volumus comedere filios nostros antequam volumus habere dominium istius Draconis."— Antonius Petri.

[k] According to à Niem, who describes the rupture, John XXIII. did not fly

all the palaces of the Pope and Cardinals, and did not
even spare the sacred buildings; they stabled their
horses in the churches. They pillaged all the wealthy
clergy; some lost their lives. The Pope fled by Sienna
to Florence, which opened her hospitable gates to
receive him, more from jealousy or dread of Ladislaus,
than from respect for the Pontiff. Ladislaus had summoned Sutri, Viterbo, Montefiascone to surrender him.
From Florence he withdrew to Bologna, now again
submitted to the Papal rule.

In John XXIII. it might almost seem that the weight
of his vices had crushed the stronger faculties of his
mind. This consummate master of Italian craft had
been overreached, baffled, put to shame, driven from
Rome, by the superior treachery as well as the superior
force of Ladislaus. He was now betrayed into a step
more fatal to his power, his fame, his memory, by the
overbearing energy and resolution, if it may be so said,
the single-minded cunning, of Sigismund, Emperor of
Germany. The Council of Constance, from which
John XXIII. hoped to emerge the undisputed Vicar of
Christ, the one all-honoured Pope, cast him out as a
condemned, degraded, unpitied captive, even more
utterly forsaken, scorned, and downtrodden than his two
old rivals deposed by the Council of Pisa.

Yet it was hard necessity which drove Pope John

---

till the soldiers of Ladislaus were in
the city. The Pope showed equal
want of courage and ability.—p. 21.
The city was weary of the taxation of
the Pope. Ladislaus had many of the
Romans in his pay. "Aliqui etiam
eorundem Romanorum secretè partem
dicti regis tennernot, stipendiati per
ipsum more veteri Romanorum." A

Niem fled with him. He was in Rome,
March, 1413. Ladislaus encamped in
the Roman Campagna the beginning of
May; the Pope fled in June. He was
in Florence Oct. 7 to the beginning of
November. He was at Bologna
Nov. 12; in the end of that month in
Lombardy. He returned to Bologna
about Easter in the ensuing year.

into close alliance with the Emperor Sigismund; and the character of Sigismund had not yet disclosed its obstinate firmness and determination to enforce submission even from Popes to the deliberate desires of Christendom. He might, as far as had yet appeared, be overawed by the vigour or circumvented by the astuteness, of a subtle Italian. At all events Sigismund was now the only safeguard against the irresistible Ladislaus. Already the Neapolitan troops had possession of the Roman territory as far as Sienna. Bologna, if strong in her citadel, disaffected in her city, might at any time be besieged. Sigismund might be expected to cherish profound revenge against Ladislaus for his attempt on the kingdom of Hungary.

The Emperor Sigismund.

Sigismund was now sole and uncontested Emperor. The schism in the empire had been extinguished, first by the death of the Emperor Rupert, then by that of Jodoc of Moravia, the competitor of Sigismund.[a] He was the most powerful Emperor who for many years had worn the crown of Germany, and the one unoccupied sovereign in Europe. France and England were involved in ruinous war. Henry V., by the battle of Agincourt, had hopes of the conquest at least of half France. France, depressed by the melancholy lunacy of the King, by the long implacable feuds of the Armagnacs and Burgundians, by the English victories, had sunk far below her usual station in Christendom. Sigismund, as Emperor, had redeemed the follies, vices, tyrannies of his youth. During that youth, as Margrave of Brandenburg, his wasteful prodigality had compelled him to pawn his Margravate; he had lost the kingdom of Poland by his harsh despotism; at times passionately

---

[a] Aschbach, Kaiser Sigmund, gives a full and good view of all these revolutions.

cruel, at times passionately merciful, his revenge on his enemies had no appearance of justice, his mercy no magnanimity. He had endangered his rightful kingdom of Hungary, by provoking the fiery Magyars to rebellion. He had attempted wrongfully to expel his brother from the kingdom of Bohemia. His immoderate love of women shocked an age accustomed to royal licence. As Emperor he seemed almost at once transformed into the greatest sovereign whom the famous house of Luxemburg had ever offered to wear the Imperial crown. On his accession Sigismund declared that he should devote himself to the welfare of his subjects, as well in his own dominions as in the Empire. His conduct justified his declaration. He enacted and put in execution wise laws. He made peace by just mediation between the conflicting principalities. He was averse to war, but not from timidity. His stately person, his knightly manners, his accomplishments, his activity which bordered on restlessness, his magnificence, which struggled, sometimes to his humiliation, with his scanty means, had cast an unwonted and imposing grandeur, which might recall the great days of the Othos, the Henrys, the Fredericks, around the Imperial throne.

But nothing so raised and confirmed the influence of Sigismund, as his avowed and steadfast resolution to terminate the Schism in the Church, and to compel the reformation of the clergy so imperiously demanded by all Christendom. This could be accomplished only by a General Council, a council of greater authority and more fully representing all the kingdoms and the whole hierarchy of Christendom than that of Pisa.

John XXIII. could not but know that the price of the alliance of Sigismund, now his only refuge, was the summoning a General Council. His own title rested on the authority of that of Pisa. The Council of Pisa had decreed that the same or another Council should meet after three years. If such Council were but a continuation of that of Pisa, he was the only Pope whom it could recognise; if summoned in his name, its obedience to that summons was an acknowledgment of his lawful authority. However dangerous so grave and solemn an assembly to a Pope whose election was by no means absolutely above the suspicion of force, bribery, or treachery; still more to a Pope burthened by the consciousness of a life so utterly unpapal; yet his confidence in his own subtlety and skill in intrigue; the authority of his position as actual and acknowledged Pontiff; the strong Italian interest which would rally round an Italian Pope; the great wealth, however obtained, at his command; the gratitude, if such virtue were known, of many Cardinals of high name for learning and virtue, whom he had promoted to that dignity; his power of impeding, protracting, postponing, perplexing, averting embarrassing questions; his personal presidency; a thousand fortuitous circumstances might mitigate the unavoidable danger, and enable him to involve in inextricable disputes a divided assembly: and what Council was ever without such divisions?

The Pope therefore determined to submit with a good grace to the inevitable Council. His ambassadors to the Emperor had full power to cede this momentous point.[a] To his secretary, Leonardo

The Pope consents to the Council.

---

[a] See summons to Archbishops of Canterbury, York, and Dublin to the Council. Pope John carefully asserts the *Presidency* of Alexander V. in the Council of Pisa. The Council of Rome, he acknowledged, was too thinly attended. The place of the Council was not named. MS., B.M., March 3, 1413. In another document it is said, "in loco decreti et ydoneo." Rome, May 15,

Aretino, he betrayed his secret policy. "All depends on the place appointed for the Council: I will not trust myself within the dominions of the Emperor. My ambassadors, for the sake of appearances, shall have liberal instructions, and the fullest powers to display in public: in private I will limit them to certain cities."* These cities he named, and adhered for some days to his resolution. But on the day on which those ambassadors, the Cardinal Challant, and Zabarella Cardinal of Florence, took leave, he seemed seized with a sudden access of courage and confidence. He had intended to restrict their powers, yet he had such reliance on their discretion, that he tore in pieces their secret instructions and threw them aside.

The interview between the Emperor and the Cardinals took place at Como. Whether the Cardinals deliberately preferred the interests of Christendom to the interests of the Pope, or were overawed or persuaded by the Emperor, the Pope was thunderstruck when he heard that in his name they had agreed on Constance, an Imperial city on the German side of the Alps.

Constance, but that it was an Imperial city, was admirably adapted for the seat of a Council—at the foot of the Alps, accessible from Italy and from all parts of the world, with its spacious lake, from whose shores provisions might be furnished, with a salubrious air, and a well-ordered population. The Pope was perplexed to find ostensible objections; his true ones he dared not avow. He had recourse to a personal conference with the Emperor, to try how far, by his blandishments or subtle arguments, he might move the stubborn German. They met at Lodi, with ostentatious display of mutual

---

* Leonard. Aretin. apud Muratori, S. R. I. Raynald. sub ann. 1413.

respect. The Pope celebrated Mass in his most magnificent attire; the Emperor condescended to officiate as deacon. But if the Emperor took the lower office in ecclesiastical rank, he made the Pope feel his superior moral dignity. He gravely admonished the Pope to amend his own irregular life, to correct the notorious simony of his court. The Pope was too politic to take offence. The Emperor and the Pontiff went together in seeming amity to Cremona. There an incident had nearly taken place, which, by preventing the Council of Constance, might have changed the fortunes of the world. Gabrino Fondoli from Podestà had become tyrant of Cremona. He entertained his distinguished guests with sumptuous hospitality. He led them up a lofty tower to survey the rich and spacious plains of Lombardy. On his deathbed Fondoli confessed the sin, of which he deeply repented that he resisted the temptation, and had not hurled Pope and Emperor down, and so secured himself an immortal name.[p]

Nov. 1413.

The irrevocable step was now taken: John had wasted his arts, his eloquence, on the impassive Sigismund. The Imperial letters and the Papal Bull were almost simultaneously issued to summon the General Council of Christendom to meet at Constance towards the close of the ensuing year. The Imperial edict addressed to all Christendom cited all whom it might concern to the Council at Constance. Sigismund declared his own intention to be present; he guaranteed his full protection as Emperor, to all who should attend the Council. To the Pope and to the Cardinals he guaranteed all their ecclesiastical privileges, their im-

---

[p] Muratori, Ann. sub ann. 1413, with his authorities.

munities to all prelates and clerks, to the Pope his plenary authority, jurisdiction, and power. At the same time he summoned Gregory XII., not as by name Pope, under the assurance of a full safe-conduct. Benedict XIII. was summoned through the King of Arragon.[q]

The Pope having passed some months at Mantua, under the protection of the Marquis Gonzaga, withdrew to Bologna. He had not calculated on his unlooked-for deliverance from his most dangerous and implacable foe. Ladislaus of Naples was master of Romagna almost to the gates of Bologna, and Bologna was awaiting every month an attack from his irresistible arms. He had compelled a hollow, unwilling treaty with Florence. But Ladislaus was suddenly seized at Perugia with a mortal malady, the effect of his immoderate debaucheries. He was conveyed in a litter to Rome, thence by sea to Naples, and died.[r]

<small>About Easter, 1414.</small>

<small>Death of Ladislaus. Aug. 6, 1414.</small>

The Pope might breathe freely. He had time, short time indeed, to repent of the haste and precipitancy with which he had committed himself (was he irretrievably committed?) to the dangerous, if not fatal Council. His kindred gathered round him, the friends of his power and fortune, if not of his person. They urged

---

[q] Cæsar. Sigismund. Edictum Universale, Von der Hardt, vi. p. 5 et seqq. Raynald. sub ann. 1413. L'Enfant, 191. It is dated Oct. 30. The Pope's Brief, Dec. 1413.

[r] Antonius Petri (p. 1045) of the death of Ladislaus: " De quâ novâ totâ Româ videlicet pro majori parte gavisa est." Afterwards: " Obiit de unâ morte in litore maris dominus Rex Venceslaus, cujus anima *benedicatur per contrarium*"—a delicate phrase for damnation—"quia multa mala operatus fuit in hoc mundo, specialiter in totâ Româ, ac etiam in Ecclesiâ Urbis, videlicet in Ecclesiâ S. Petri et ejus Burgo, ut apparuit." Neither party respected the churches. Orsini's troops with their horses were stabled in S. Paolo fuori delle mura.

the grave, ominous admonition, "You may set forth as Pope to the Council, return a private man." But the Cardinals—and it is among the inexplicable problems of his life, that some of the Cardinals whom he promoted were men of profound piety, as well as learning and character—if less true to his interests, were more faithful to his honour and truth. They pressed on him, that he was solemnly pledged to the Emperor—to Christendom: there was no retreat. Their urgency might seem a guarantee for their loyalty.* If they counselled his departure, they were under a strong obligation to adhere to his cause: they could not in honour, or in regard to Italian interests, forsake him. In all councils, according to the ordinary form of suffrage, the Pope and the Cardinals had maintained commanding authority. So with heavy heart, with dark and ominous misgivings, but, on the other hand, in impressive pomp and with a treasure of vast magnitude, hoarded for this end, a treasure in itself the best security for the fidelity of his adherents, John XXIII. set forth from the gates of Bologna to open the Council of Constance.

Oct. 1, 1414.

---

* Raynaldus, Bzovius, sub ann. 1414.

CHAPTER VI.

Wycliffe.

DURING the secession of the Popes for seventy years to Avignon, and the Schism which ensued on their return to Italy, not only grew up the strong league of the hierarchy against the autocracy of the Pope, which had already in the Council of Pisa asserted, and in that of Constance was about to assume, a power superior to the Supreme Pontiff, with the right of deposing him, and reforming the Church in its head as well as its members: in England also had appeared the first powerful adversary of the whole hierarchical system, and sowed deep in the popular mind thoughts, opinions, passions, which eventually led to the emancipation of mankind from sacerdotal and from Latin Christianity. The first teacher who shook with any lasting effect the dominion of the hierarchy—the harbinger, at least, if not the first apostle of Teutonic Christianity—was John Wycliffe.

The Teutonic constitution of England had slowly and steadily developed itself, encroaching at once on the Norman despotism of the Crown, and the Latin despotism of the Church. The privileges of the Clergy had fallen away, had been annulled, or sunk into desuetude, without resistance, with sullen but unregarded remonstrance.

Teutonic England.

The immunity of the whole order from the civil courts, and from the royal jurisdiction—their absolute right of being judged in all causes and for all crimes in the first instance, and therefore exclusively, in their own courts—that immunity for which Becket had begun his quarrel, lived in exile and died a martyr—had been abandoned in its extreme extent, or surrendered with no violent struggle. The strong hand of the law would no longer scruple to arrest and put on his trial a priest accused of treason, murder, or other felony. Some sanctity still adhered to his person; but his property was confiscated to the Crown, though himself might be delivered up to the Ordinary. The singular plea, the Benefit of Clergy, lingered till recent times in our law, a feeble memorial of the times when no one dared lay unconsecrated hands on the "anointed of the Lord."[a] But even archbishops appear before long in rude but vain encounter with the civil courts, in exile without public sympathy, one laying his head on the block for treason.[b]

Immunity of clergy from civil courts.

The second absolute immunity, from taxation, had been wrested from the Clergy, notwithstanding the obsti-

---

[a] See b. xii. c. viii.

[b] There is in Wilkins a curious instrument of Archbishop Langham (Primate, 1367). He complained in Parliament that the civil authorities had not scrupled to arrest, indict, even to condemn to public execution (morti turpissimae et insolitae condempnare), clerks and regulars in holy orders. The King and the magistrates, on the other side, complained that when such persons, so found guilty of the most flagitious crimes (such cases seem to have been very common), were given up on demand to their Bishops, they were negligently guarded, and so pampered in prison, that it was a place of comfort and enjoyment rather than of penance (quod carcer pro eorum flagitio non credit ad poenam, sed magis ad solatium et refocillationem eorum corporum). Some were allowed to escape, some discharged on slight evidence. They returned to their old courses, and were of bad example to unoffending clergymen. The Primate orders that the prisons be kept more strictly; these notorious malefactors and felons watched more closely and kept to hard diet.—Wilkins, iii. pp. 13, 14. In another document it is complained that priests and secular clerks are persons "pendus par agard des justices séculiers, en prejudice des franchises." King and Parliament grant benefit of clergy. In another, many clerks are found guilty of forging the King's coin.—P. 28.

nate and passionate resistance of Boniface VIII., by the vigour of Edward I. The Clergy who would not respect the king's law, being put out of the protection of the law, had found their old defence against the Crown, spiritual censures, so unavailing, the superstitious terror, or the grateful reverence of the people, so utterly gone, that they were compelled to yield.[c] They now hardly asserted more than their right to tax themselves for secular purposes in their separate Houses of Parliament, the Convocation, and to grant, assess, and levy the subsidies which they dared no longer to refuse.

Immunity from taxation.

Under the reign of the feeble Edward II. there is some resumption of the Papal power. We have heard Clement V. command the arrestation and persecution of the Templars: he was obeyed not without some reluctance, but obeyed. The avaricious John XXII. would not abandon the claims of the See of Rome on the yet wealthy, not yet exhausted land. The mediation of Pope John between England and Scotland was accepted with the eager willingness of conscious weakness by Edward II., in his conscious strength sullenly, coldly submitted to by Robert Bruce.[d] Bruce laughed to scorn the Pope's excommunication.[e] But Pope John would not espouse the cause of England without his reward. He peremptorily demanded the full arrears of the tribute of 1000 marks, fallen behind under Edward I.; still more under Edward II., whose

Edward II.

---

[c] See vol. vii. p. 61.
[d] See the apology of Pope John to Edward for addressing Robert Bruce by the title of King, without which Bruce would not receive his letters.—MS., B. M., Oct. 21, 1316; March 29, 1317.

[e] The Pope's Nuncios were waylaid and plundered near Durham by partisans of Bruce. The monks of Durham were concerned in this. It is a curious passage.—MS., B. M., vol. xvi., dated Avignon, April 28.

poverty, not his courage, resisted the Papal requisitions. The Pope recites the surrender of the island by King John. King Edward is admonished that the neglect is offensive to God, that on this payment depends his salvation.[f] In a letter to the Primate all the disasters of the land are traced to the sacrilegious withholding of the 1000 marks.[g] The Pope indeed gave good counsel to the young king.[h] He took his part, even by excommunication and interdict against the Barons, but at the same time warned him against his foolish and criminal favouritism.[i] Throughout the frequent correspondence appears the shrewd worldly wisdom of Pope John, too sagacious not to see and despise the weakness of the King; yet John is on the King's side, in order to secure the tribute of the land, the Peter's Pence, and other convenient emoluments of the See of Rome. He does not refuse to the King grants of subsidies from Church property.[k]

---

[f] "Et quorum præstatio divinam tibi gratiam poterit sequestrare."—Ad Reg. Edward. Sept. 18, 1317.

[g] Ad Episcop. Cantuaren.

[h] See the curious letter of advice, "cum juvenibus et imprudentibus tractus negotia ao consilium maturitatis abjiciens per viam Roboam, consilia (o?) juvenum incedis. Totius bona regni tui immoderatè distribuis."—Oct. 21, 1317. Compare p. 510: "Bona tua a garsionibus et gulosis hominibus aut aliis personis turpibus consumi contingunt."

[i] In 1322, Jan. 19, he exhorts Edward to peace with the Barons; he had not kept faith as to the sentence against the Despencers.—P. 431.

[k] There is one strange story, characteristic of the times and the men. Edward II., besides his ambassador, the Bishop of Hereford, sent a Franciscan friar to communicate most privately to the Pope ("nobis solis," writes John) a divine vision, and to take the advice of his Holiness. The Virgin appeared to S. Thomas when an exile in France, foretold his martyrdom, and that the *fifth* King after Henry II. would be "vir benignus ac Ecclesiæ Dei pugil." She gave the Saint an ampulla of most holy oil. The King anointed by that oil would recover the Holy Land. S. Thomas gave the oil to a monk of the Convent of S. Cyprian in Poitiers. The same monk also received a plate with an inscription which he only could read. (The oil was as that revealed to Pope Leo, with which Archbishop Turpin

The wars of England and France under Edward III. had found the Pope no longer, even in theory, as of old, the impartial and independent Pontiff of Christendom, residing in his own capital, lord of his own territory, usually an Italian and chosen by Italian Cardinals. He was now a Frenchman, elected by a French Conclave, almost nominated by the King of France; if not within the realm, in a city on the borders of, and surrounded by France; a vassal, in truth, and often an instrument in the hands of that King. The Pope had indeed appeared to assume a lofty neutrality, had pretended to impose his imperious mediation; and the weaker the King of France had become by his humiliating defeats, the less servile became the Pope. Yet this neutrality, though not violated, was held in just suspicion by England; the mediation was hardly so far respected as to be declined. The conqueror of Crecy and of Poitiers was not likely to submit to the arbitration of a French Pope.

---

anointed Charlemagne.) When the King of the Pagans heard that this oil was concealed at Poitiers, he sent a Christian and a Pagan to get it. The Pagan died; the Christian bought it with the Pagan's money, and carried to Germany, where it came into the possession of the Duke of Brabant. Edward might have been anointed with it at his coronation through his kinsman the Duke of Brabant, but, content with his usual anointing, had refused. Its virtue had now been proved by a miracle wrought on the Duchess of Brabant. Edward now gravely attributes all his misfortunes to his refusal of this oil. Still he would not be a second time anointed without the sanction of the Pope. Pope John treats the matter with solemn seriousness. He consults with a Cardinal. He decides that as "no observation of days or hours is enjoined," it is not superstitious to believe in the oil; it would not interfere with the former unction. The Pope, however, refuses to authorise any prelate to do it: the King may get it done, but secretly (clam), for fear of raising too much astonishment. The Pope in conclusion suddenly turns round, and wisely says "that a virtuous life will be more efficacious: it will be of more real value to the King to protect the Church of Rome and her liberties"—the Papal notion of virtue! All this is from the Pope's own letter.—MS., B. M., June 2, 1318.

CHAP. VI.   ALIENATION OF THE CLERGY.   151

More than once, it has been seen, the victorious bands of the Black Prince approached, alarmed, if they did not threaten, Avignon. The splendid palaces of the Cardinals at Villeneuve, on the right bank of the Rhône, might at any time fall a defenceless prey to the Gascon marauders.

In England the war had become popular, national.[m] The clergy did not dare or did not desire to withhold their contributions; but the heavier taxation of the Crown made them more impatient of the taxation of the See of Rome by first-fruits, annates, reservations, and direct burthens, carried to an unprecedented height by the need or the avarice of the Avignonese Pontiff;[n] and they had been almost entirely alienated from Rome by their hostility to the foreign prelates intruded into the richest benefices of the kingdom.[o] Throughout this long reign

---

[m] The Cardinal Legates, in 1346, about June, instead of being received with honour, were received "plerumque convicils, contemptibus, et injuriis;" they are in peril of being "pro bono opere lapidati." The Pope instructs them not to expose themselves to danger, to have guards against popular riot, to take care that everything is written.—MS., B. M., Aug. 28, vol. xxii. p. 194.

[n] In MS., B. M. Clement VI. complains to Queen Isabella and Queen Philippa, and to the King's Council (Aug. 28, 1343), that certain proctors of his Cardinals, in England on business, had been ignominiously expelled the realm. He claims (July 7, 1344) reservations of all vacant benefices for two years, on account of the poverty of the Roman See (vol. xxi. p. 190). He writes to the King complaining of Acts of Parliament against Reservations and Provisions. He asserts himself "ecclesiarum omnium tanquam Pastor Universalis." The King's interference is impious. The Acts are "in derogationem et enervationem prædictæ libertatis ecclesiasticæ, Primatus ejusdem Romanæ ecclesiæ et auctoritatis et potestatis ipsius sedis Aplicæ." Persons had been sacrilegiously imprisoned for disobedience to these Acts. He threatens divine vengeance. Jan. 30, 1345. Clement protests that he had not sent his Legates to fulminate censures or excommunications: they were only sent peaceably to endeavour to persuade the King to give up the obnoxious statutes (p. 472). The Bishopric of Ely is a reservation. "Thomas de Insula, penitentiarius noster," but ("oriundus") of English race, recommended to the King.

[o] The King had taken, or borrowed

M 2

England was becoming less hierarchical, the hierarchy more English.

Nothing shows more clearly the change in the national opinion and in the times than the relation of the King and the Primate of the realm. One Archbishop of Canterbury, Stratford, a few years after Edward III.'s accession,* is arraigned of high treason; he declares himself in danger of capital punishment, though the King disclaims such intention. The crime of which the Primate is, probably without justice, accused, is a secular offence—the malversation of subsidies levied for the French war. The Archbishop flies from Lambeth (two other bishops, Lichfield and Chichester, the King's treasurers, had been sent to the Tower). At Canterbury he ventures to excommunicate his accusers, the King's counsellors, with bell, book, and candle. He returns to London, but shrouds himself under the privileges of Parliament rather than under his ecclesiastical immunity. He forces his way, himself bearing his cross, into the House of Peers, as his place of security, his one safe sanctuary. He is at last obliged to submit, ere he can be admitted to com-

---

"sub obligatione congruâ," all the "proventus et redditus" of benefices held by foreigners (alienigenas) for the support and necessities of the realm, deducting the burthens on them. The Pope (Clement) wonders at his audacity. It was not by the advice of "periti," but "imperiti," that he occupied "bona Ecclesiastica, in quibus, sicut nosti, nulla laicis est attributa potestas." The "color quæsitus crediti non excusat." Let the King's counsellors observe "quod multi ex fratribus nostris Sanctæ Romanæ Ecclesiæ Cardinalibus in Regno tuo prædicto beneficia obtinentes, qui circa non universali Ecclesiæ serviendo singularum Ecclesiarum commoditatibus utiliter se impendunt." Those not resident in "obsequio nostro," or for other just causes, were to be considered resident. Clement entreats the King, for the good of his soul, to give up his sacrilegious design. April 24, 1346. Compare letter, April 29, 1347.

* Stratford, Archbishop, 1333. Edward III., viii.

purgation, to an investigation before a jury of twelve of his peers—four prelates and eight nobles. The quarrel is settled by amicable intervention, but the King grants rather than condescends to accept pardon.⁴ This arraignment of Becket's successor without a general insurrection of the Church, with no Papal remonstrance, though Stratford himself held the loftiest doctrines on the superiority of the priest to the layman, is an ominous sign. A second Primate, Simon Langham, having accepted a Cardinal's hat, lives in exile. A third (under Richard II.), Simon Sudbury, is cruelly murdered by the peasants of Kent; yet the land is darkened with no interdict; the martyr is canonised neither by the fear of the people nor the reverence of the clergy. A fourth, Arundel, is arraigned of high treason, sees his brother the Earl of Arundel executed before his face for a conspiracy in which himself is concerned, flees for safety to the continent, returns only under the protection of Henry Bolingbroke. That usurper (Henry IV.) hesitates not to strike off the head of the Archbishop of York for capital treason; and so sunken is the Pope through the Schism, that there is but a feeble shadow of remonstrance at this sacrilegious violation of the canon law. He vindicates the conduct of the King with an elaborate apology, and hastens to bestow his absolution on all concerned in the execution.ʳ

---

⁴ Godwin de Præsulibus. Vit. Stratford.

ʳ See MS., B. M. Gregory XII. to the Bishops of Durham and Lincoln. He dwells on the undoubted treason of Scrope, by which his life was forfeited to the laws of the land, " licet Archiepiscopus præfatus deliquerit, correctio tamen et punitio secundum canonum instituta ecclesiastico judici fuerit relinquenda." Yet the danger to the King and the urgency of his friends, fully justify the act. The interdict issued by the more virtuous and bolder Innocent VII. is annulled; all processes declared void; the Bishops

It was not indeed till the reign of Richard II. that the three great limitary Statutes—of Mortmain, of Provisors, and of Præmunire (the two first less stringently enacted before) took their perfect form—together the Great Charter, as it were, of English liberties against the Church. One had risen above the other. The first, Mortmain, set an impassable bound to the all-absorbing acquisitions of the Church, and the severance of the land into one sacred and one common territory—the sacred slowly encroaching till it threatened to swallow up the other.[a] The second, Provisors, wrested away the Papal power of disposing at least of all the benefices in the patronage of spiritual persons.[b] The third, Præmunire, boldly and openly vindicated the right of the State of England to prohibit the admission or the execution of all Papal Bulls or Briefs within the realm; a virtual prophetic, premonitory declaration of the King's supremacy.[c]

The three great Statutes.

---

have plenary authority to reconcile every one who had any hand in the affair.—Lucm, April 13, 1408. See the curious account of the death of Scrope. Wharton, 'Anglia Sacra,' II. 369. On the horror excited in good Churchmen and rigid monks, compare Capgrave, p. 291. "Where the Bishop dyed were many miracles; pilgrims crowded to the spot till forbidden by the King. The King was so struck with remorse that he became a leper, ever fouler and fouler; his body shrunk before his death to the height of a cubit. Archbishop Arundel took it so to heart (he was at dinner with the King), that he fell into a tertian fever, and in that state was carried home." See also Wright, 'Political Poems,' II. 114. "Ast Thomam (Becket) militum sudax atrocitas, Symonem (Sudbury) plebium furens feraclitas, Ricardum (Scrope) callidò sæva crudelitas, obtruncant *Christos Domini.*"

[b] Compare on the successive statutes and final law of Mortmain, Blackstone, c. 18.

[c] On Provisors, consult a book of greater merit than fame, 'England under the House of Lancaster' (London, 1852), p. 396. The abandonment of those in lay patronage was a prudent concession of the Pope. See Lingard, vol. iii. p. 108.

[d] On Præmunire, 16 Richd. II. c. 5. Hallam, Middle Ages, ii. p. 48.

About three years [a] before the accession of Edward III., was born of humble parentage in a village near Richmond in Yorkshire, John Wycliffe, who was to give lasting celebrity to the name of his obscure birthplace.[b] His destination, either from his own choice or the wise providence of his parents, was that of a scholar, to which the humblest could in those days aspire. England was almost a land of schools; every Cathedral, almost every Monastery, had its own; but youths of more ambition, self-confidence, supposed capacity, and of better opportunities, thronged to Oxford and Cambridge, now in their highest repute. In England, as throughout Christendom, that wonderful rush, as it were, of a vast part of the population towards knowledge, thronged the Universities with thousands of students, instead of the few hundreds who have now the privilege of entering those seats of instruction. This silent, regular, peaceful, and as yet inexhaustible crusade for the conquest of University learning, for the worship of the Schoolmen and the Doctors, for the adoration of the reliques of ancient religious and even philosophical wisdom, for the discovery of the Aristotelian or Arabian Dialectics, arose in great degree out of the state of society. There were in truth but two professions, Arms and the Church. But Arms—though the English yeomen, her archers, crossbow-men, and bill-men had now begun to make their importance felt in the continental wars—was, as to distinction at least, an aristocratic profession. The demand for foot-soldiers, though on the increase, was limited and precarious. They were

Birth of Wycliffe.

Movement to the Universities.

---

[a] 1324-1327. On the place of his birth, see Mr. Shirley's preface to Fascicull, Rolls Publications.

[b] This seems clearly proved by Lewis and Vaughan, the biographers of Wycliffe.

mostly raised for a short and hasty campaign, and dismissed again by their suzerain. The regular troops, and even the Free Bands, formed but a small part of the population. But the Church was constantly needing, constantly drawing from all quarters, recruits for her service; and that not only for her own special functions, most lawyers, physicians, even statesmen, were ecclesiastics. The Monastic establishments, the Friars in their various Orders, absorbed undiminished multitudes. The Church had no succession in herself. Not that married clergy were unknown or unfrequent, or that the canonical proscription could exclude the sons of the clergy, though held illegitimate, from holy orders, or the inheritance of patrimonial benefices.* Still these were few in proportion to the inexhaustible demand. The vast mass of the secular clergy, all those in the inferior Orders (the noble, even royal, families furnished some prelates and rich beneficiaries) as well as the Monks and Friars, came from below. It was the great strength, as among the great blessings of the hierarchy, that the meanest might themselves aspire to be, or might see their kindred become, the most learned, wealthy, powerful in the realm — Bishops, Chancellors, Archbishops, Cardinals, even Popes.

John Wycliffe found his way to Oxford; he was admitted into Queen's College, then just founded by Philippa of Hainault, Queen of Edward III. He removed to Merton, the older, wealthier, and more famous of the Oxford foundations.

Wycliffe at Oxford.

The English Universities had already begun to take their peculiar character, a league, as it were, of separate, independent Colleges, each a distinct republic, with its

---

* Compare vol. vi. p. 382.

endowments, statutes, internal government; though the University was still paramount, and the Chancellor, with his inferior officers, held the supreme, all-embracing authority. These colleges were founded for the maintenance of poor scholars by Statesmen, Prelates, Princes, Kings, Queens. There were now six of these colleges in Oxford, as distinguished from the halls or hostels, where the other scholars dwelt and studied only under the ordinary academic discipline.* Walter de Merton, Chancellor of Henry III., was the founder of the first of those noble institutions. De Merton, though he introduced, according to the habits of his time, much of the monastic discipline, the common diet, seclusion within the walls, regular service and study: perhaps as a churchman, possibly with even more widely-prophetic view, was singularly jealous lest his college should degenerate into a narrow monastic community. Whoever became a monk was expelled from his fellowship. Merton, among her older students, might offer famous names to excite the pride and emulation of her scholars. She boasted the venerable tradition of Duns Scotus, the rival of the most renowned of the Schoolmen, of Aquinas himself. Roger Bacon probably was an object as much of awe as of admiration, as little comprehended by Wycliffe as by the most supercilious churchman or narrow-minded monk. But if only the name of William of Ockham, the Locke of the Middle Ages in his common-sense philosophy, and in the single-minded worship of truth, was held in reverence; if his works were studied, it could be no wonder if the scholars of Merton indulged in speculations perilous

Famous men of Merton.

---

* All this has been well wrought out in the Report of the Oxford University Commission. See also the Histories of Oxford.

to the Pope, to the hierarchy, even to the imaginative creed of the Middle Ages. The bold and rigid nominalism of Ockham struck at the root of all the mystic allegoric theology; it endangered some of the Church doctrines. His high imperialist Apologies shattered the foundations of the Papal Supremacy, and reduced the hierarchy below the Throne. The last renowned teacher of divinity at Merton had been the profound Bradwardine, whose great learning (he was celebrated as a geometer as well as a theologian), his lowliness, and admirable piety, had made a strong impression on his age. He had just lived to be Archbishop of Canterbury.[b] Bradwardine may have left his influence on the mind of Wycliffe in his severe Augustinian Predestinarianism, a doctrine in which the more austere churchmen and all the first Reformers (or they would hardly have dared to be Reformers) met, as to its theory, if not its application.

Wycliffe's fame in Oxford, his promotion to offices of high trust and honour, and his writings, are the only testimonies to the extent and depth of his academic studies; his logic, his scholastic subtlety, some rhetorical art, his power of reading the Latin Scriptures, his various erudition, may be due to Oxford; but the vigour and energy of his genius, his perspicacity, the force of his language, his mastery over the vernacular English, the high supremacy which he vindicated for the Scriptures, which by immense toil he promulgated in the vulgar tongue—these were his own, to be learned in no school, to be attained by none of the ordinary courses of study. As with his contemporary and most

---

[b] Collier, I. 552. Godwin de Præsulibus. Bradwardine survived his consecration only five weeks and four days.

congenial spirit, Chaucer, rose English Poetry, in its strong homely breadth and humour, in the wonderful delineation of character with its finest shades, in its plain, manly good sense and kindly feeling (some of its richness and fancifulness it might owe to Italy and France): so was Wycliffe the Father of English Prose, rude but idiomatic, biblical in much of its picturesque phraseology, at once highly coloured by and colouring the Translation of the Scriptures.

Great obscurity hangs over the earliest publications of Wycliffe, obscurity further darkened by the publication of the tract called "The Last Age of the Church."[c] If this be genuine, Wycliffe must have been in danger of sinking into a wild follower of the Fraticelli, the believers in the visions of the Abbot Joachim. A profoundly religious mind like Wycliffe's may have brooded over the awful plague which a few years before had devastated Europe,[d] and might be accepted as a sign of the Last Days by devout men. The treatise may have been composed at that period, or the darkness then impressed upon his mind may have dispersed but slowly. The denunciations of the Tract are against the Clergy, the Simoniacs, and holders of great benefices;[e] no word against his future enemies, the Mendicants.

It was by his fearless and unsparing attack on the

---

[c] We are indebted for this publication, from the library of Trinity College, to the learned Dr. Todd of Dublin. Dr. Todd appears to me more completely sceptical as to its authenticity than he admits himself to be. The only authority for its genuineness is, that it appears in a volume which contains other tracts by Wycliffe; and that a Tract under this name is recounted among his works by the inaccurate Bishop Bale, and on his authority received by Lewis, who had not seen it.

[d] A.D. 1347-8-9. Ann. ætat. Wycliffe, 23-4-5.

[e] "Both vengeance of swerde and myschiefe unknown before, by which men then daies should be punished, shall fall for synne of prestis," &c. &c. —p. xxxiv.

Mendicant Friars that Wycliffe rose into fame, honour, and popularity at Oxford. The Mendicants in England, as everywhere else (now four Orders), had swarmed in their irresistible numbers. Here, too, they had invaded every stronghold of the clergy, the University, the city, the village parish. Here, too, the Clergy clamoured, and with unrelaxing clamour, that these intruders entered into their cures, withdrew their flocks from the discipline of the Church, intercepted their offerings, estranged their affections, heard confessions with more indulgent ears, granted absolution on easier terms. Fitz Ralph, Archbishop of Armagh, who before his Irish Primacy had been Chancellor of Oxford, a man of high character, had denounced them as utterly destructive of true religion. The Mendicants strove hard in Oxford, as heretofore in Paris and all the other Universities, to obtain the ascendancy, either from their ambition, their conscious pride in their great theologians, or as foreseeing the brooding rebellion of more free inquiry and a bolder speculative philosophy, which themselves had unknowingly fostered by some of their sons. They were accused of trepanning the youth who were sent up to the Universities.[f] Parents were afraid to risk their sons, who without their consent were enlisted into the Mendicant Orders. The number of scholars is said to have sunk from 30,000 to 6000. The Friars were at the same time ambitious of the honours of the University. They claimed degrees on their own terms, and demanded that the Statutes of the University which limited the age at which youths might become Friars should yield to their own.[g] Appeal was made

---

[f] The University, the Chancellor and Regents, passed a Statute, that none should be received into the Orders of the Friars under fifteen years old.—Lewis, p. 5, 6.

[g] Ibid.

to Rome. Urban V. condemned the Statutes in the strongest terms. Cambridge was equally guilty with Oxford in vigorous resistance to all encroachments on the University. And it appears not that the Universities obeyed the mandate to repeal their Statutes.[h]

Wycliffe struck boldly at the root of the evil: he denounced Mendicancy in itself. He denied, with vigour of argument which might have won the favour of John XXII., that Christ was a Mendicant; he dwelt on their blasphemy in likening their institutes to the Gospel, their founder to the Saviour. He treated all the Orders and both the classes among the Franciscans with the same asperity. He branded the higher as hypocrites, who, professing mendicancy, had stately houses, rode on noble horses, had all the pride and luxury of wealth with the ostentation of poverty. The humbler he denounced with all his indignation as common able-bodied beggars, who ought not to be permitted to infest the land.[i]

So far Wycliffe was the champion of a great party in the University and in the Church. Honours, dignities

---

[h] MS., B. M. The Pope Urban V. declares that the statute "canonicis obviat institutis." The Archbishop of Canterbury and the Bishops are to order the Chancellor, "summariè et de plano, ac sine strepitu et figurâ judicii," to repeal the statute, and this without appeal, June 1, 1365. The second letter condemns Cambridge as Oxford. The regulations are "dilectioni Dei dissona, proximis noxia et sacris traditionibus inimica." The Archbishop, the Bishops of Llandaff (London?) and Bangor, are to cite the Universities to show cause why they have enacted such statutes. In the mean time the Pope suspends their execution. July 19, 1365.

[i] The opinions of the austerer Franciscans that Christ and his Apostles were absolutely without property had been publicly taught in London by Roger Conway, a Minorite; opposed by Richard Kilmyngton, Dean of St. Paul's, and by Fitz Ralph, Archbishop of Armagh, who was born in London. In Oxford they were preached in 1360, opposed by Wycliffe, Thoresby Archbishop of York, and others.

crowded upon him. He was Warden of Baliol Hall, on the presentation of Baliol College,[k] Rector of Fylingham, Warden of Canterbury Hall. His last appointment plunged Wycliffe into litigation, and into an appeal to the Court of Rome.

[sidenote: 1361-1365. Preferments. Canterbury Hall.]

Simon Islip, Archbishop of Canterbury, had endeavoured in his foundation of Canterbury Hall to blend together the Monastic and Secular Clergy. Of twelve fellows the Warden and three were monks from Christ Church in Canterbury, eight secular Clergy. The Hall was endowed with the Rectory of Pagenham in Sussex, and a manor, Wingford, in Northamptonshire. One Wodehull was named Warden. Wodehull is described as a turbulent and violent man:[m] the scheme of amicable union broke up. Just before his death Islip dispossessed Wodehull and the monks; the Hall was surrendered altogether to the Seculars; Wycliffe was named Warden. Simon Langham became Archbishop; Langham was a monk by education and character.[n] It was alleged that the act of his predecessor Islip was extorted from him in a state of imbecility. Langham annulled the proceeding, and reinstated Wodehull; Wycliffe resisted; the Archbishop endeavoured to compel submission by the sequestration of the Pagenham Rectory; Wycliffe appealed to the Pope. This was his only resource; it implies no confidence in

---

[k] Doubt has been thrown on his Baliol preferment by Mr. Courthope. See 'England under Henry of Lancaster,' note iv. p. 356. On the other hand, Mr. Shirley (note, p. 513) attributes the whole of the affair of Canterbury Hall to another John Wyclyffe, Vicar of Mayfield. His reasons to me are strong, but not conclusive.

[m] Wodehull was unpopular in the University; it was with great difficulty that he was admitted to his degree.—Lewis.

[n] Simon Langham was hated by a large party in the Church, as appears from the well-known verses—

"Exultant cœli quia Simon venit ab Ely
Cujus ad adventum flent in Kent millia centum."

the justice of the Papal Court; it is consistent with serious misgivings as to his own chance of obtaining impartial justice; it was but the common order of things. Wycliffe's fame was not confined to Oxford; his opinion was demanded by the Crown on a subject of grave importance. The Pope Urban V. had been so unwise at this juncture as to demand the arrears of the 1000 marks, of which so much has been heard, the tribute and acknowledgment of fealty to the Roman See. That ignominious burthen had now been allowed to accumulate for thirty-three years. Urban was urged to the demand by his poverty, covetousness, or desire of embarrassing King Edward. Wycliffe was commanded to answer some bold Doctor who maintained the right of the Pope. As royal chaplain he was present at a solemn debate in the King's Council; he recites the opinions delivered by seven of the barons, singularly curious and characteristic. To these Wycliffe, as a humble and obedient son of the Roman Church, protesting that he held nothing injurious to that Church or offensive to pious ears, refers his own adversary before he begins his argument. The first was a frank, warlike Peer, of few, plain words:—"Our ancestors won this realm and held it against all foes by the sword. Julius Cæsar exacted tribute by force; force gives no perpetual right. Let the Pope come and take it by force; I am ready to stand up and resist him." The second was more argumentative:—"The Pope is incapable of such feudal supremacy. He should follow the example of Christ, who refused all civil dominion; the foxes have holes, and the birds of the air their nests, he had not where to lay his head. Let us rigidly hold the Pope to his spiritual duties, boldly oppose all his claims to civil power." The third said:—"The Pope calls himself the Servant of the Servants of the Most High; his only claim to tribute from this realm is for some service done; but what is his service to this realm? Not spiritual edification, but draining away money to enrich himself and his Court, showing favour and counsel to our enemies." The fourth:—"The Pope claims to be the suzerain of all estates held by the Church; these estates held in mortmain amount to one-third of the realm. There cannot be two suzerains; the Pope, therefore, for these estates is the King's vassal; he has not done homage for them; he may have incurred forfeiture." The fifth was more subtle:—"If the Pope demands this money as the price of King John's absolution, it is flagrant simony: it is an irreligious act to say, 'I will absolve you on payment of a certain annual tribute;' but the King pays not this tax; it is wrung from the poor of the realm; to exact it is an act of avarice rather than salutary punishment. If the Pope be lord of the realm, he may at any time declare it forfeited, and grant away the forfeiture." The sixth was even more vigorous in his retort:—"If the realm be the Pope's, what right had he to alienate it? He has fraudulently sold it for not a fifth part of its value. Moreover, Christ alone is the suzerain; the Pope being fallible may be in mortal sin. It is better, as of old, to hold the realm immediately of Christ." The seventh boldly denied the right of John to surrender the realm: —"He could not grant it away in his folly; the whole, the Royal Charter, signature, seal, is an absolute nullity." Wycliffe in his own resolute vindication of resistance to the Pope's claim had alluded to the peril which himself incurred lest he should be defamed at the court of Rome, and incur ecclesiastical censure and loss of benefices.° It cannot be known how far this act or the character of Wycliffe influenced the decision of the Court of Rome in his appeal; but after some delay Canterbury Hall was adjudged to the monks of Christ Church; Wodehull was again appointed Master.ᵖ

Just at this juncture appeared a clearer sign and an omen that the popular mind had begun to look with jealousy on the power of hierarchy. In the Parliament of 1371 the Commons addressed the Crown with a remonstrance against the appointment of Churchmen to all great dignities of the State, and a petition that laymen might be chosen for those secular offices. The King answered that he would consult with his Council on the matter. The connexion of Wycliffe or Wycliffe's opinions with this movement does not appear, or how far Wycliffe had as yet urged those principles which at a later time he expressed so strongly. The movement was generally attributed to John of Gaunt,—to John of Gaunt, the patron of Chaucer, the protector, as will soon appear, of Wycliffe against the hierarchy. The blow was aimed principally at William of Wykeham, that magnificent Prelate, who from the surveyor and architect of the King (Windsor owes its royal splendour to King Edward), had become Bishop of Winchester, Chancellor, and at the head of all affairs of State. The blow was not without effect. Wykeham ceased to be Chancellor the Bishop of Exeter resigned the treasurership. In writings of which the date is doubtful, Wycliffe directly

---

° "Primo ut personæ men sic ad Romanam curiam diffamata, et aggravatis censuris ab ecclesiasticis beneficiis sit privata."— Apud Lewis, p. 351, where the whole may be read at length.

ᵖ Richard Benger, who ought to have stood as proctor for Wycliffe, did not appear: he was declared contumacious. Judgement seems to have gone by default.

inveighs against this abuse:—"Neither prelates nor doctors, priests nor deacons, should hold secular offices, that is those of chancery, treasury, privy-seal, and other such temporal offices in the exchequer; neither be stewards of lands, nor stewards of the hall, nor clerks of the kitchen, nor clerks of accounts; neither be occupied in any secular office in lords' courts, more especially while secular men are sufficient to do such offices." In another passage there is a bitter and manifest allusion to Wykeham:—"Benefices, instead of being bestowed on poor clerks, are heaped on a kitchen clerk, or one wise in building castles, or in worldly business."ᵃ

Wycliffe's position in Oxford was not lowered by his expulsion from the Wardenship of Canterbury Hall. He became Doctor, Professor of Divinity; that is, as Doctor he had the right of delivering lectures on theology. From the public chair he had full opportunity of promulgating his own views; we know not how far as yet from the intrepid antagonist of the Mendicants he had become the open adversary of the wealthier hierarchy; how far he had departed from the established creed. We know not whether Wycliffe had now advanced beyond Oxford, or Oxford advanced as far as Wycliffe. From a man of unimpeachable morals, profound devotion, undoubted sincerity, vigour, and original eloquence, much denunciation against the abuses of the time, the enormous pride, wealth, luxury, loose morals, secular pursuits of the higher Clergy,

Wycliffe Professor at Oxford.

ᵃ Apud Vaughan, i. 312. See another striking passage on the incompatibility of such offices with thoughtfulness about heavenly things. Piers Ploughman is strong on this grievance; he says of the higher Clergy:

"Some serven the kinge, and his silver tellen,
In the Checkkere and the Chauncerie,
chalengynge his dettes,
Of Wardes and of Wardemotes, wayves and strayes."
—Whitaker's Edition, p. 5.

might be at once so popular and so true, that on the one hand a formidable host of partisans might form themselves around the dauntless Professor, while on the other he might give no hold for specific charges either of hostility to the Church or of heretical pravity. There was a wide field for safe freedom; his enemies in condemning Wycliffe would be pleading guilty to his charges.

The nomination of Wycliffe by the Crown as second in a commission to treat with the Papal Legate at Bruges, in the great questions at issue between the King of England and the Pope, shows his growing importance, his high esteem with some person powerful in Parliament and at Court, probably John of Gaunt, and strong confidence in his courage and ability.[r] That the Pope, a Pope of the high character and rigour of Gregory XI., should condescend to negotiations on such subjects, which he was wont to decide by fulminating censures, was in itself a sign of change. John, Bishop of Bangor and two others, a Benedictine monk and a knight, appeared as Edward's ambassadors at Avignon. They complained in no measured terms of the Papal interference with royal patronage, of provisors and reservations, and the citations of the King's subjects in the Court of Rome.[s] The Pope, on his side, appealed to the notorious fact, that the Apostolic Briefs were not permitted to be published in England; that his Nuncios were not admitted into the realm, as in every other king-

---

[r] Did Edward consider Wycliffe to come up to the Pope's description of the ambassadors? The King ought to send men "clarus scientiā ac laudandæ virtutis, et cunctā prudentiā præditos, cultores justitiæ, sedulosque pacis et concordiæ zelatores."—MS.,

B. M., May 1, 1374.

[s] The Bishop of Lincoln had been cited to Avignon to answer for impeding the collection of the Pope's subsidy from the Clergy. On this subject the Pope was forced to be bold.

dom of the faithful. The meeting at Bruges was to settle those differences by amicable concession; the Pope appointed the Bishops of Pampeluna and Sinigaglia as his ambassadors.[1]

During these disputes between the Crown of England and the Pope throughout the reign of the Edwards, a third party had begun to intervene, and with increasing weight. The Parliament were determined and obstinate in their resistance to the burthens imposed on the kingdom and on the Clergy by the Papal Court; and they were strong, as representing the will of the nation, and sure that their resistance was not disapproved by the King. It was not perhaps the taxation of the Clergy to which they were so resolutely opposed, so much as the continual drain of specie, which was considered as the impoverishment of the realm, and was as yet but imperfectly prevented by the bills of exchange, brought into use chiefly by the Lombard and Italian bankers.[2] The old grievance, too, still offended the whole realm, the Clergy as well as the people—the possession of so many of the most wealthy benefices by foreigners, some of whom had never entered the kingdom, some but for a short time; most were unacquainted with the language of the country. These revenues in hard money were transmitted to Rome or to Avignon, to be spent on the luxuries of Cardinals or Papal favourites. Parliament with one indignant voice declared the surrender of the realm by John null and void, as without the consent of

---

[1] There are many papers of Instructions to the Papal Commissioners. The meeting was appointed for St. John Baptist's Day, 1374, by different adjournments postponed to Easter, 1375. It took place in July. All suits in the mean time were suspended in the Papal as in the King's courts.

[2] From the Papal Letters (MS., B. M.) may be gleaned many curious particulars about the agency of these bankers, Siennese and Florentines.

Parliament, and contrary to the King's coronation oath. Both estates, Lords and Commons, asserted their determination to stand by the King against the usurpations of the Pope.[x] Parliament was as resolute against the other abuse. The first Statute of Provisors had been passed in the reign of Edward I.[y] Twice already in the reign of Edward III. was this law re-enacted with penalties rising one above another in severity. It was declared that the Court of Rome could present to no bishopric or benefice in England. Whoever disturbed a patron in the presentation to a living suffered fine and ransom to the King, and was imprisoned till he renounced the provision. To cite the King to appear in the Court of Rome was highly penal.[a] Yet ten years after arose new complaints, embodied in an address of the Commons to the King on the subject of provisions and first-fruits. The King answered, that negotiations were proceeding with the Pope for the amicable adjustment of these claims, that a commission of the Bishop of Bangor had been already sent to Gregory XI.—a Pope whose character commanded respect—in Avignon.[b] The new commission, in which

A.D. 1373.

---

[x] 40th Edw. III. Blackstone, iv. c. 8, from Selden.
[y] 35th Edw. I.
[a] 25th Edw. III. (1351); 27th Edw. III. (1353); 38th Edw. III. (1363); Blackstone, iv. c. viii.
[b] The milder, it might almost be said the meek, tone of Gregory XI. singularly contrasts with that of his predecessors. The Archbishopric of York was a Papal reservation. On the vacancy the Chapter (forsan ignari of this) elected Alexander Neville. The Pope has the judgement to cede the point, though he still asserts his right. He annuls the proceedings of the Chapter, but nominates Alexander (April 14, 1374). He presents his nephew, Adhemar de Rupe, Provost of S. Saviour's in Utrecht, to the much-coveted Archdeaconry of Canterbury as a reserve. But his letter to the King is no stern dictate; it is a prayer for the royal favour, which is most powerful in such affairs (1374). A year after he writes to the Bishop of Winchester to instal his nephew (Sept. 20, 1375). There is a very curious letter addressed to William de Lucumer (qu. Lord Latimer) on the

Wycliffe was named, proceeded in the next year to meet the Papal Legates at Bruges.

Wycliffe was at Bruges not quite two months.[b] The result of the conference was reported to Avignon. If the discussion at Bruges had any effect on the course of the negotiation, nothing could be finally determined but by the Pope himself. A kind of compact was at length made, rather a suspension of arms than a definitive peace. The Pope revoked all the reservations made by Urban V., his predecessor, which had not taken effect. He confirmed the nomination of all presented by the King without first-fruits. The benefices held by the Cardinals were made liable to the repairs of the Church and the buildings belonging thereunto. He quashed all the causes pending in his courts on the subject of Provisors. On his side the King remitted all the fines incurred under the three Statutes of Provisors. Thus each might seem to await better times to renew his claim. The Pope surrendered no right of future reservation or provision.[c] The prohibitory Statutes, with all their formidable penalties, remained unrepealed.[d]

Wycliffe Commissioner at Bruges

A.D. 1374.

Imprisonment of Roger de Beaufort and another nephew of his own, John de Rupe. He does not peremptorily order their release, but complains that they are ignominiously treated, "præter morem erga nobiles," and only implores more gentle usage in their behalf.—May, 1375.

[b] The accounts in the Exchequer show that Wycliffe was absent from July 27 to Sept. 14, 1375. He received 60*l*. for his expenses at 20*s*. a day: for passage 50*s*., for re-passage 42*s*. 3*d*., quoted in Preface to Wycliffe's Bible, Oxford, p. vii.

[c] Yet both the archbishoprics, the bishoprics, and rich abbeys continued frequently to be nominated to by the Pope. He ceased only in general to promote foreigners, *i. e.* "eodem anno Papa transtulit dominum Thomas Arundel, Episc. Ellen. ad Archiepiscop. Eboracc. Alexandro Nevillo præditore et susurrone translato ad Episcop. S. Andreæ in Scotiâ."—Walsingham, 336.

[d] In the year 1390 (Rich. II. 15) the Commons extorted the renewal

Whatever were Wycliffe's services at Bruges, or his actions, they did not pass unrewarded. He had already exchanged the Rectory of Fylingham (in the Archdeaconry of Stowe, Diocese of Lincoln) for that of Ludgershall, nearer to Oxford. He now received from the Crown the Prebend of Aust in Worcester, and the Rectory, which he occupied till his death, of Lutterworth.

During the last two years of Edward III.'s reign, the sad and gloomy close of that reign of splendour and glory,* there is a strange collision and confusion of religious and political interests, from which John Wycliffe emerges, now a dangerous and dreaded heresiarch. The Good Parliament is ejecting from the administration John of Gaunt, the favourer of the new opinions, and filling the council of the King with High Churchmen; at the same time it is presenting petitions against the abuse of the Papal power, such as might have been drawn by Wycliffe himself. Wycliffe is arraigned for perilous doctrines before the Bishop of London, openly protected by John of Gaunt. John of Gaunt is almost the victim of popular fury, which in a short time after appears as violently espousing the cause of Wycliffe. It may not be impossible to find the clue to guide us through this intricate labyrinth. The nation, now for the first time in the history of the constitution represented by the House of Commons, was under the influence of two strong passions. The strongest and the predominant was that of deep attachment and veneration for the Black Prince, the chivalrous hero of the French wars. The only blot on his fame was his cruelty†

---

of the Statute of Provisors in the strongest terms. Mr. Shirley, p. xxlii., says that the Statute of Provisors was repealed by royal authority?

* "And Sorrow's faded form, and Solitude behind."—GRAY.

† The barbarous massacre at Limoges.

in those wars, to them no way odious. The Black Prince had led a King captive through the streets of London; he had not only glutted the English pride with glory, he had won all hearts by his affability, his generous, gracious and noble demeanour. He was the model of perfect chivalry. The love of the Black Prince became jealousy, almost hatred, of John of Gaunt, supposed to be his rival. The Duke of Lancaster, while they were trembling with too well-grounded apprehensions for the waning life of their idol, was thought to be brooding over more sinister schemes of ambition. Their second passion was the old steady determination to emancipate the realm from the abuses of the Papal power, with some growing jealousy of the native hierarchy.

Edward III. was almost in his dotage, absolutely governed, it was believed, by John of Gaunt, by Latimer his partisan, the Lord Chancellor, and by Alice Perrers, who had not only infatuated the old man as a mistress, but was accused of having bewitched him by forbidden sorceries. Dark rumours were abroad that John of Gaunt designed to supplant the young Richard of Bordeaux on the demise of his father. So much was he hated that credence was given to a wild story (attributed, falsely no doubt, to William of Wykeham) that John of Gaunt was but a suppositious child, the son of a Flemish woman, substituted in the place of a dead daughter of the King. The Black Prince, sinking into mortal languor, seemed to rally with a father's energy to maintain the imperilled rights of his infant son. On his party were the powerful Churchmen, Courtenay Bishop of London, and Wykeham of Winchester. But the most intrepid and useful partisan was Peter de la Mare, Speaker of the House of Commons. De la Mare was steward of the Earl of March, who had married the daughter of Lionel Duke of Clarence, the second (deceased) son of Edward III. From the Earl of March sprang the House of York, hereafter to wrest the crown from the Lancastrian lineage of John of Gaunt. Parliament, for the first time led by the Commons, demanded the dismissal of the King's advisers (against whose maladministration of the realm they presented grievous complaints), and that ten or twelve Prelates and Peers should be called to the royal Council. At the head of this Council were the Churchmen, the Archbishop of Canterbury, the Bishops of London and Winchester. The new Council assumed its powers.[a] Latimer, John Lord Neville, Sir Richard Stafford, were ignominiously dismissed; Alice Perrers was prohibited, under pain of forfeiture and banishment, from approaching the Court. Popular sympathy denominated this Parliament "the Good Parliament." But these political measures were not their only acts. A petition was presented from which it might seem that in their view the Statutes of Provisors had been altogether inefficient. The taxes paid to the Church of Rome amounted, they averred, to "five times as much as those levied by the King; the Pope disposed of the same bishoprics by reservations four or five times, and received each time the first-fruits."[b] "The brokers of the sinful city of Rome promoted for money unlearned and unworthy caitiffs to benefices of the value of a thousand marks, while the poor and learned hardly obtain one of twenty. So decays sound learning. They present aliens, who neither see nor care to see their parishioners, despise

[a] See in Lowth's "William of Wykeham" the names of the Council.
[b] See the petition in the Parliamentary History. Compare it with Wycliffe's views.

God's service, convey away the treasure of the realm, and are worse than Jews or Saracens. God gave his sheep to the Pope to be pastured, not shorn and shaven; lay patrons are by his example urged to sell their benefices to mere brutes, as Christ was sold to the Jews. The Pope's revenue from England alone is larger than that of any prince in Christendom. The Pope's collector and other strangers have an office in London, from whence are betrayed the secrets of the realm; the collector remits yearly to the Pope 20,000 marks, sometimes more." The Commons insist on the immediate discharge of these traitorous and dangerous strangers. They appear to adopt a return made of the Crown Benefices held by aliens. The Cardinal of S. Sabina held the Deanery of Lichfield with annexed Prebends, worth 580 marks and 20l.; the Cardinal of S. Prassede had for twenty-six years held the Deanery of Salisbury, which he never saw, worth 254l., and many valuable benefices annexed to it; the Cardinal of S. Angelo the Deanery of York, worth 400l., with many other Prebends; others were Archdeacons of Canterbury (the richest benefice in England after the Bishoprics), of Suffolk, of York, of Durham; others possessed Prebends and various preferments. They received besides that the 20,000 marks a year.[1]

The remedies the Commons proposed were the re-enactment and enforcement of the Statute of Provisors with the utmost rigour. They demanded that no foreign proctor or collector of the Pope should be permitted to remain in England under pain of life and limb; any Englishman residing at Rome in such office to be liable to the same penalty.

[1] The report, which is very curious and interesting to ecclesiastical antiquaries, is in Fox, l. p. 560.

The Good Parliament was dissolved; before its dissolution the Black Prince had died. John of Gaunt resumed the administration. The Council was ignominiously dismissed. Alice Perrers was by the bedside of the King, now worn out with age, infirmity, and sorrow. The Earl of March was ordered to Calais, under the honourable pretext of surveying the castle and town. He surrendered the office of Earl Marshal, by which John of Gaunt bought the support of the Lord Percy, one of the Council. Peter de la Mare was committed prisoner to Nottingham Castle. William of Wykeham, Bishop of Winchester, was impeached on eight articles of maladministration, amounting to treason, or misprision of treason.[k] The temporalities of the see were seized into the hands of the King. The Bishop of Winchester was excepted from an act of grace issued on account of the Jubilee, the fiftieth year of the reign of King Edward. At a meeting of the new Parliament, as a further indignity (his temporalities being escheated), no writ was issued to Wykeham as a peer. But he was summoned to Convocation. In Convocation, William Courtenay, Bishop of London, rose and moved that no subsidy should be granted till justice was done to the Bishop of Winchester. The Convocation took the affair up with a high hand. It was an infringement on the jurisdiction of Holy Church. The King, or rather the King's Court, treated remonstrance and petition with contempt. The timid Archbishop, Whittlesey, tried in vain to mediate. The Bishop of Winchester came to his palace in Southwark, and took his seat in Convocation with loud applause. Parliament was dissolved, as

marginal notes: July, 1376. William of Wykeham. Feb. 23. About March 2.

---

[k] Lowth, p. 113.

well as Convocation, without any reconciliation. The
King, under the influence of John of Gaunt, attempted
to divert the popular mind by granting the temporalities
of Winchester to Richard of Bordeaux, now Prince of
Wales and proclaimed heir-apparent to the Crown.

But before the death of Edward, almost his last act,[a]
whether to propitiate Heaven, or still but as a
passive instrument in the hands of others, was
the restitution of these temporalities to the Bishop of
Winchester.[b] It was under a condition which shows the
vast opulence of that Prelate. He was to furnish three
ships of war, with fifty men-at-arms and fifty archers for
a quarter of a year, at the wages paid by the King; if
the expedition was not undertaken, the amount which
this army would cost.[c]

Death of Edward

Wycliffe, exactly at this time, between the dissolution
of the last Parliament and the death of the
King, appears summoned to answer at St.
Paul's before the Archbishop of Canterbury and the
Bishop of London, for opinions deserving ecclesiastical
censure. Of the specific charges on this occasion nothing
is known; though they may be conjectured from those
submitted to the Pope, and afterwards brought against
him by the Papal mandate. Wycliffe stood before the
tribunal, but not alone. He was accompanied by John
of Gaunt and the Lord Percy, now Earl Marshal.
There was an immense throng to witness this exciting
spectacle; Wycliffe could not make his way through.
The Earl Marshal assumed the authority of his office to
compel the crowd to recede. The Bishop of London, no
doubt indignant at the unlooked for appearance of the

Wycliffe at St. Paul's

---

[a] June 18. King Edward died June 21.
[b] Dr. Lingard says (note) that he made a valuable present to Alice Perrers.
[c] Lowth, p. 146.

Nobles, resented this exercise of the Earl Marshal's power in his church. He haughtily declared that if he had known how Percy would act, he would have inhibited his entrance into the Cathedral. The Duke of Lancaster in his pride rejoined that, despite the Bishop, the Earl Marshal would use the authority necessary to maintain order. They reached with difficulty the Court in the Lady Chapel. The Earl Marshal demanded a seat for Wycliffe. "He had many things to answer, he needed a soft seat." "It is contrary," answered Courtenay, "to law and reason that one cited before his Ordinary should be seated." Fierce words ensued between the Earl Marshal and the Bishop. The Duke of Lancaster taunted the family pride of Courtenay. The Bishop replied with specious humility, "that he trusted not in man, but in God alone, who would give him boldness to speak the truth." Lancaster was overheard, or thought to be overheard, as if he threatened to drag the Bishop out of the church by the hair of his head. The populace were inflamed by the insult to the Bishop, the insult to the City of London. The privileges of the City were supposed to be menaced by the Earl Marshal's assumption of authority within the jurisdiction of the Lord Mayor.[p] A wild tumult began. The proceedings were broken up: Wycliffe, who all along had stood silent, retired. Lancaster and the Earl Marshal had doubtless sufficient force to protect their persons. But throughout the City the populace arose; they attacked John of Gaunt's magnificent palace, the Savoy; his arms were reversed like those of a traitor. The palace, but for the Bishop

---

[p] Lancaster was afterwards accused of a design to abolish the Lord Mayor, and to appoint a captain under the Crown; and that the Earl Marshal's power should be current in the City as in other parts of the kingdom. Lancaster did turn out the Lord Mayor and Aldermen and appoint others.

of London, would have been burned down. A luckless clergyman, mistaken for the Earl Marshal, was brutally murdered. The Duke fled to Kennington, where the Princess of Wales was residing with her young son. The rioters were appeased by a message from the Princess: but they demanded that the Bishop of Winchester and Peter de la Mare should have their fair and immediate inquest before their peers, according to the laws of the land. It is difficult not to trace some latent though obscure connexion between the persecution of William of Wykeham and the proceedings against John Wycliffe.* It was the inevitable collision between the old and the new opinions. Wykeham, the splendid, munificent, in character blameless Prelate, was wise enough to devote his vast riches to the promotion of learning, and by the foundation of noble colleges, was striving to continue the spell of the hierarchical power over the human mind. Wycliffe, seeing the more common abuse of that wealth by Prelates of baser and more sordid worldliness, sought the interests of Christ's religion in the depression, in the abrogation, of the mediæval hierarchy. The religious annals of England may well be proud of both.

The accession of Richard II. shook the overweening power of John of Gaunt. The first act under the new reign was the full and ample pardon of Wykeham, hurried through, under the Privy Seal, with the utmost despatch. Peter de la Mare was released from Nottingham Castle; Lancaster condescended to pay humble court to the City of London. Henceforth, John of Gaunt is the less avowed and open supporter of Wycliffe. If, indeed, John of Gaunt had any real love of Christian

---

* Lewis, p. 81. Stowe's Chronicle.

liberty and truth, he had greater love of power. Yet on the accession of Richard appears the same conflict of opinions as under the Good Parliament. The King's Ministers and his Parliament looked with greedy eyes on a considerable treasure levied on the realm, which they knew to be in the hands of the Pope's agents or bankers. They determined to seize it and appropriate it to the public service. But they were desirous to obtain legal sanction for this course. It is probable that among the authorities to which they appealed was the University of Oxford. It was either the function, or imposed on Wycliffe by the University, or he was chosen at the suggestion of the Crown, well knowing the bias of his opinions, to frame the answer. In that answer, as might be expected, he declared boldly that the necessities of the nation have the first and paramount claim to all moneys raised within the realm. He sheltered himself with much ingenuity under the all-venerated name of St. Bernard, and was not sorry to have the opportunity of publicly proclaiming the opinion of that Saint, that Eugenius III. could pretend to no secular dominion as the successor of St. Peter.'

Information during this interval had been laid at Avignon against the opinions of Wycliffe. The Pope, Gregory XI., despatched his Bulls to England: three addressed to the Archbishop of Canterbury Simon of Sudbury and other

Pope orders proceedings against Wycliffe.

Fox, I. 384. Compare the whole very curious paper in Fasciculi Zizaniorum, p. 258 *et seqq.* The possessions of the Church of England were given to the Church of England alone; men may give alms to the Pope when in want. "Non autem ad fastum secularem aut voluptatem carnalem continuandum, nec ad gentes aliquas pro suo seculari dominio expugnandum."

Bishops; one to the King; one to the University of Oxford, commanding inquiry into the erroneous doctrines of Wycliffe. The Prelates are to investigate the truth of the allegations; if true to commit to gaol and obtain the confession of Wycliffe, and to transmit the same to Rome. Should they not be able to apprehend him, they are to cite him to appear before the Pope. The King is exhorted to render all assistance to the aforesaid Prelates. The University of Oxford is commanded to prohibit the teaching any of the doctrines promulgated by Wycliffe in his detestable madness, to apprehend him and to deliver him to the Archbishop of Canterbury and the Bishop of London. The University treated the Bull hardly with cold respect; they debated whether they should receive it: so far they condescended, but for the execution of its mandate they took no measures whatever. The opinions charged against Wycliffe were entirely against the ecclesiastical power, as yet he is not accused of departing from the creed of the Church: they are the opinions of Marsilius of Padua and John of Gandun, the defenders of the temporal monarchy against the Pope; they are denounced as subversive of civil as of ecclesiastical authority.*

The Archbishop, Sudbury, wrote to the Chancellor of Oxford to cite John Wycliffe to appear in the Church of St. Paul to answer for his errors. Wycliffe appeared not at St. Paul's, but at Lambeth. He had no longer Lancaster and the Earl Marshal at his side, but a more formidable array of partisans, the populace. Among these were citizens of London, now that their privileges were not threatened, on the side of

Wycliffe at Lambeth.

---

* Copy of Bull. Fasciculi Zizaniorum.

the Reformer.¹ They forced their way into the chapel; their menacing looks and gestures affrighted the Prelates. In the midst of their alarm arrived Sir Lewis Clifford, in the name of the Princess of Wales, now at the head of the administration, prohibiting the Bishops from any further proceeding against Wycliffe. The indignant historian is bitter upon their weakness. "They were as reeds shaken by the wind, became soft as oil in their speech, to the discredit of their own dignity and the degradation of the Church. Panic-stricken they were, as men that hear not, as those in whose mouth is no reproof."²

Eighteen articles had been exhibited, probably sent from England to the Pope, by the Pope back to England, as the definite charges against the Reformer. Wycliffe drew up three replies to these articles. One he delivered to the Papal Delegates; one more brief was intended, it should seem, for general circulation. The third was in Latin, a fierce recrimination on a nameless assailant, whom he calls the "motley doctor." The first and the more full is calm, cautious, guarded; yet on some of the more momentous questions significant enough. To the first five charges, which turn on subtle and scholastic points (Wycliffe was no contemptible Schoolman), he is subtle and scholastic. In the later articles two great principles transpire without disguise: 1, That the property of the Church is not

---

¹ There is a singular instance of the progress of Wycliffe's opinions. The Mayor of London, John of Northampton, like his puritanical successors in later days, to the great disparagement of the clergy, took the morals of the City under his own care. He arrested a number of loose women, cut off their hair, and exposed them to public derision, openly asserting that he was compelled to this act of authority by the remissness of the clergy, who for money would connive at any debauchery, and even sell licences for incestuous marriages.—Fox, ut supra.

² Walsingham.

inalienable, indefeasible, but may be forfeited if it be not applied to its proper use, and that it is for the temporal power to enforce that forfeiture; 2, That spiritual powers of censure, excommunication, absolution, are not absolute and unconditional, but depend for their validity, and will be ratified by God, only if uttered or promulgated in strict conformity with the law of God. Wycliffe declares his resolution by God's grace to be a sincere churchman, he by no means declines the jurisdiction of the Church; he is prepared to deliver his opinions in writing, he is ready to defend them to death. They are formed from the Sacred Scriptures and from holy doctors; if they are proved adverse to the faith he is ready and willing to retract them.* Nothing further was done, beyond an injunction to Wycliffe to keep silence, lest he should mislead the ignorant.

The death of Pope Gregory XI., as it annulled the authority held by the Prelates, stopped all further proceedings. The Schism which followed was not likely to re-establish the awe of the Pope in minds which had either shaken it off, or were ready to shake it off. Wycliffe sent out a tract on the Schism of the Church.

Wycliffe is now the head of a sect; he becomes more and more the antagonist of the hierarchy; as yet only of the higher and wealthier dignitaries, more immediately threatened by his democratic views as to their temporalities; and of the more saga-

Wycliffe teaches.

---

* Dr. Lingard and Dr. Vaughan differ as to the time of publication of these writings. It appears to me that there is no certain evidence on the point; nor is it material. The more violent was a polemic and personal tract; the other a calm and deliberate reply before a public judicature. I see no evasion or timidity, nothing beyond ordinary discretion, in Wycliffe's conduct.

cious divines, who might discern how rapidly and how far such a mind, once released from the yoke of the ancient theology, would break loose from the established opinions. He appears not as yet to be an object of alarm or unpopularity with the lower clergy; Oxford has not repudiated him. But he is now organising a kind of Order of his own, who travel through the land, preaching, where favoured by the clergy, in the churches, elsewhere in the highways and market-places. These itinerant teachers vied with and supplanted the Mendicant Orders in popularity. How they were maintained appears not; probably they were content with hospitable entertainment, with food and lodging. Such was the distinction drawn by Wycliffe between our Lord and his Apostles and the sturdy beggars whom he anathematised, and whose mode of exaction is so humorously described by Chaucer. There is always a depth of latent religiousness in the heart of the common people, and these men spoke with simplicity and earnestness the plainer truths of the Gospel in the vernacular tongue. The novelty, and no doubt, the bold attacks on the clergy, as well as the awfulness of the truths now first presented in their naked form of words, shook, thrilled, enthralled the souls of men, most of whom were entirely without instruction, the best content with the symbolic teaching of the ritual.

Wycliffe has now at least begun his great work, the Complete English Version of the Scriptures, *Translation of Scripture.* and as this work proceeds, it more entirely engrosses his mind, and assumes its place as the sole authority for religious belief. It must have been sent out and widely promulgated in different portions, or it could not, before the days of printing, have become so familiar to the popular mind as to give ground to the bitter complaint of one of Wycliffe's adversaries, that laymen and women who could read were better acquainted with the Scripture than the most lettered and intelligent of the Clergy.[1]

But as Wycliffe advanced in more exclusive devotion to the Sacred Writings; as by his own work of translation, and the translations of his coadjutors, he became more fully acquainted with the Bible,—he began to question not only the power of the Pope and of the Hierarchy, but some of the doctrines of the Church. He is now examining and rejecting with deliberate determination the materialism of the vulgar Transubstantiation. He is become not merely a dreaded and dangerous Reformer, but, according to the dominant creed, a daring and detested heresiarch. It might almost seem that Rome was in the conspiracy against her own power and sacred authority. "This very year," writes Walsingham (a high Papalist, who not the less dwells with honest energy on the venality of the Court of Rome), "came the Cardinal di S. Prassede into England, to treat of the marriage of the Emperor's sister with the King, and to drain the realm of its wealth. The whole kingdom poured out to him, for there was no grace which he would not sell, none which he would grant without money: he sold indulgences, formerly reserved by the Pope to himself, for two years, for three years, excommunications, absolutions, commutations for pilgrimages. At length, his men grew wanton in their avarice; they disdained silver, would take nothing but gold: he carried off in his bags more than a year's taxes of the realm."[2]

---

[1] "Unde per ipsam fit vulgare et magis apertum laicis et mulieribus legere scientibus, quam solet esse clericis admodum literatis et bene intelligentibus."—Knighton, p. 2644.
[2] Walsingham, p. 246. In the

At this time also broke out the insurrection of the Commons: six counties at least—Kent, Essex, Hertford, Norfolk, Suffolk, Cambridge—were in furious revolt. Wat Tyler and his rude Kentish peasantry were in possession of London. Among other noble victims, the Archbishop of Canterbury had been cruelly put to death on Tower Hill.* The resolution of the young King, the boldness of Walworth the Mayor of London, seem to have saved the whole realm from anarchy, the upper orders from massacre and ruin. This outburst had no connexion with religion. It was a political and social insurrection; it had its immediate origin in a heavy all-burthening tax, levied in a manner to awaken all the most ardent and generous feelings of the people. Men have borne every oppression, but have been maddened beyond control by insults to their wives and daughters. The popular fury was not against the sacerdotal order: it was against the judges, the lawyers, the jurymen. They did not doom to ruin the churches

---

13th Richard II. there is a protest of the Archbishops of York and Canterbury, both Papal Legates, in the name of their Suffragans and the Clergy, against any Statutes made in Parliament, so far as tending to restriction of apostolic power, or derogative of ecclesiastical liberty. This probably referred to the petitions of the Commons for the observance of the Statute of Provisors, and against the impositions of the Pope. To these the King had given a favourable answer. Writs were issued to the two Archbishops, other dignitaries, and the Pope's Nuncio, declaring that no impositions of any kind could be levied without the common counsel and assent of the kingdom. The par-

tions employed were prohibited from levying such impositions. — Lords' Report on the Dignity of a Peer, p. 344.

* The Monk of St. Denys was in London at this time. "Michi causam Ecclesiae nostrae in hoc regno promoventi (had S. Denys still property in England?) cum indignanter audirem ipsa die per villa biria illius Archiepiscopi caput sacratum plebem pedibus huc illucque projecisse, unusque assistentium diceret, Scias in regno Franciae abhominabiliora futura et in brevi, hoc scitum subjunxit, absit ut Galliae continuata fidelitas tanto monstro deformetur." This is a singular illustration of the public feeling. —P. 134.

or the monasteries, but the courts of law; they would destroy all the archives of the realm, probably esteeming them mere rolls and records of taxation. The Duke of Lancaster was the special object of hatred—Lancaster the patron of Wycliffe. They burned his splendid palace in the Savoy. It was not as Archbishop, but as Chancellor, that they murdered Simon of Sudbury, as one who had called them "shoeless ribalds," and urged no concession. They beheaded him as a false traitor to the Commons and to the realm.[a] At St. Alban's, at Edmondsbury, at Walsingham, it was the villeins demanding manumission from their lords, not Wycliffe's disciples despoiling possessioners. Not indeed that such insurrectionists were likely to look with much respect on the exorbitant wealth of the clergy. Some proclaimed that no taxes were to be paid till the whole Church property was confiscated and expended.[b]

No popular insurrection, in truth, can take place without stirring up all the dregs of society; all the turbulent, the designing, the political and religious fanatics, are then in their element. Among the first acts of the rebels was to break open the gaols. From the prison of the Archbishop of Canterbury came forth John Ball, who, years before Wycliffe had been heard of, had promulgated among the humblest classes the wildest levelling doctrines. He was a religious demagogue of the lowest order; his tenets are contained in the old popular rhyme, "When Adam delved and Eve span, Where was then the gentleman?" He had been seized and imprisoned; imprisonment was not likely to

---

[a] Knighton. Read the account of Sudbury's death in Godwin. He was a man of great eloquence, and died, it is said, imploring pardon on his enemies.

[b] Walsingham. He was a monk of St. Alban's. His account of the revolt against the abbot is prolix and curious.

soften his fierce temper. His release by a violent and victorious mob of peasants would offer too tempting opportunities for vengeance on his persecutors,[c] and stimulate and seem to justify the propagation of his tenets to the utmost.[d] Nor was John Ball alone; there were others who mingled up doctrines of social and religious anarchy. The confession of Jack Straw is that of one of the Fraticelli. He looked forward to the glorious time when the Mendicants should possess the whole earth.[e] Walsingham accuses the Mendicants as one of the great causes of the insurrection. Jack Straw's confession was obtained by the Lord Mayor of London, who promised not pardon, but to pay for masses for his soul: he was joined in this posthumous benevolence by other charitable citizens.

This insurrection, nevertheless, had two fatal consequences to Wycliffe and to his tenets. All reformers, even the wisest and most moderate, must make up their minds to bear the odium of the exaggeration of their own opinions. No religious or social innovation can be without its danger. It is the one profound and difficult question whether mankind is to linger on in any depth of darkness, ignorance, oppression, rather than undergo that danger. Wycliffe's enemies of course denounced John Ball as his par-

Effects on Wycliffe.

---

[c] Knighton says that some proposed to make John Ball their Archbishop of Canterbury. Was John Ball present at the beheading of Sudbury, and so wreaking vengeance for his imprisonment? Compare the account of John Ball in Lewis, p. 223, &c. A confession was extorted from John Ball that he had been two years a disciple of Wycliffe.—Fasciculi Zizaniorum, p. 273.

[d] There is an inhibition by Archbishop Islip against the Mendicants, issued at the same time with that against John Ball.—Wilkins, iii. 64, 5, A.D. 1366. There is another denunciation of John Ball by Archbishop Sudbury, April 21, 1381.

[e] "Soli Mendicantes virilement in terrâ." See Petition of the Four Orders to John of Gaunt, F. Z. L., p. 292.

tisan.' Between the two men there was no connexion, less sympathy. With Wycliffe religion was the sole, exclusive, ultimate aim; with the wilder insurgent teachers the religious was but one part of a wide, universal, social, political revolution. But those to whom all innovation is dangerous, naturally and without dishonesty refuse to discriminate between the darker and lighter shades, the anarchic and the Christian points, in the destructive doctrines which threaten their power, influence, interest, rank, authority. To them every opponent in religious matters is a blasphemer, a heretic; in civil, a demagogue and an anarchist.

But it was not this general suspicion and jealousy alone which darkened the minds of the clergy, and wrought them up to keener vigilance against the doctrines of Wycliffe. To the murdered Simon Sudbury, who seems to have been more gentle and moderate in his ecclesiastic rule,² succeeded the high-born and High-Church Prelate, William Courtenay, before whom Wycliffe had already twice appeared, and twice defied or escaped prosecution. Courtenay, with the indignation and terror excited by the terrible sight of his predecessor's headless trunk, was least likely to draw these just, no doubt, but not clearly discernible, distinctions between the opponents of authority. With his birth, education, position, haughty temper, all resistance to ecclesiastical superiority was rebellion, sacrilege, impiety. The first act of Courtenay was to summon a Synod to deliberate and determine on the measures to

Courtenay Archbishop.

---

¹ Compare Lewis, p. 221. The good sense of his observations is marred by his coarse language.

² Sudbury appears to have been tardy and irresolute, if not unwilling, in his prosecution of Wycliffe and his doctrines. His death was by some attributed to his guilty laxity in this prosecution.

be taken concerning certain strange and dangerous opinions widely prevalent, as well among the Nobility as among the Commons of the realm.[h] The Synod met (a dire and significant omen), not at St. Paul's or Lambeth, but at the Grey Friars (Mendicants) in London. There assembled eight Bishops, fourteen Doctors of Civil and Canon Law, six Bachelors of Divinity, four Monks, fifteen Mendicants (three of these Dominicans, four Minorites, four Augustinians, four Carmelites).[i] Hardly had the Synod taken its seat, when an earthquake shook the Metropolis.[k] The affrighted Synod trembled at this protest of Heaven at their proceedings. Courtenay, with no less promptitude than courage, turned it to a favourable prognostic. "The earth was throwing off its noxious vapours, that the Church might appear in her perfect purity." Twenty-four articles were gathered out of the writings of Wycliffe, ten condemned after three days' debate as heretical, the rest as erroneous. Among the heretical tenets were the denial of Transubstantiation; the assertion that the Sacraments administered by a priest in mortal sin were null; rejection of all confession but to God; a reprobate Pope had no spiritual power, only that conferred by Cæsar; there was no lawful Pope after Urban VI.; all Churches were to live like the Greeks, under their own laws; ecclesiastics were not to hold temporal possessions. One tenet ascribed to Wycliffe was that God ought to obey the devil! The

---

[h] Wycliffe asserts that the Bishops of old took part against the mendicants, now "Herod and Pilate have come together."—Fascic. Zizan. p. 284.

See the names in Fox, p. 568. The names in Fox and the Fasciculi are somewhat different. See also the curious Ballad on the Council of London. Wright, Political Songs, pp. 253, 263. There are other remarkable poems for and against the Lollards.

[k] Wycliffe himself compared this earthquake to that at the time of the Crucifixion. Confessio, apud Vaughan, ii. vii. Appendix.

erroneous doctrines from which, with some specious loyalty, it was dexterously endeavoured to show Wycliffe an enemy to temporal as to ecclesiastical authority, were: that a Prelate who excommunicated a person whom he did not know to be really excommunicate, was himself excommunicate; that it is treason to God and the King to excommunicate a person who has appealed to the King; that those who cease to preach, because excommunicated by priests, are excommunicate, and liable to answer in the Day of Judgement; that a Lord is no Lord, a Prelate no Prelate, while in mortal sin; that temporal Lords might take away temporal goods from delinquent ecclesiastics, and the people might aid in this; that tithes are alms to be granted to whom we will. The last article condemns altogether the religious Orders, especially the Mendicants: " He who gives alms to a Mendicant is excommunicate."

Archbishop Courtenay determined to give these decrees the most imposing solemnity. A great procession of clergy and laity walked barefoot to St. Paul's to hear a sermon by a Carmelite Friar. Strong measures were taken to suppress the Preachers. An act was passed by the Lords, and promulgated by the King (the first statute of heresy passed in the realm), commanding the apprehension of all the Preachers, with their maintainers and abettors, and their committal to prison, that they might answer in the Bishops' Courts. But Oxford was still the centre of Wycliffe's influence. A Carmelite, Peter Stokes, no doubt esteemed the most eloquent preacher, was sent down to confute the new opinions.[m] Peter Stokes preached in an empty church, while the

---

[m] Article VII. Lewis, ch. vi. p. 107, 9. Wilkins, Concilia, iii. p. 157. Compare on this Mr. Shirley, p. 13; Fasciculi Zizaniorum, p. 275. See Courtenay's Letter to Stokes, and Stokes's Letter, p. 300.

scholars crowded around the University pulpit, where Nicolas Hereford the Vice-Chancellor, and Philip Rypington, openly maintained the doctrines of Wycliffe. The Chancellor, Peter Rigge, notoriously, if not openly, favoured his cause. He answered the Archbishop's mandate to search the Colleges and Halls, and to force all who held such opinions to retract, that it was as much as his life was worth. "Is then the University," answered Courtenay, "such a fautor of heresy that Catholic truths cannot be asserted in her walls?"[o] Courtenay assumed the office and title of Grand Inquisitor. The Synod met again. The Chancellor, Peter Rigge, and Brightwell, a Doctor of Divinity, appeared.[o] Nicolas Hereford and Philip Rypington were compelled or permitted to recant,[p] but their recantation was held evasive and unsatisfactory. They were publicly excommunicated at St. Paul's. They fled to implore the protection of the Duke of Lancaster. John of Gaunt coldly recommended them to submit to their superiors. Rypington afterwards absolutely disowned Wycliffe and his tenets. His apostasy was rewarded by the Bishopric of Lincoln. He became, like most apostates, a violent persecutor of his old opinions. He died a Cardinal. Nicolas Hereford is said boldly to have gone to Rome to defend the opinions of Wycliffe; there he was imprisoned, and died a monk.[q] Wycliffe himself appears

---

[o] Lewis, p. 115. Documents, No. 34. Compare V. Z., p. 304. One of the charges against the Chancellor was his naming Hereford to preach the *English* Sermon before the University on Ascension Day.

[o] Rigge and Brightwell before the synod at Lambeth, June 12.

[p] Another Synod, June 18. Here Hereford and Rypington demand, Ashton refuses, delay. They sent in their answers June 20. These were declared insufficient, heretical, deceptive. They were excommunicated July 13. Same day was issued the King's Edict to Oxford.

[q] Yet he appears, if there is not some mistake or confusion, to have

neither at Oxford nor at Lambeth. He is cited, but no notice is taken of his contumacy. Perhaps he was suffering under his first attack of palsy, expected to be mortal: he was believed indeed to be at the point of death. "I shall not die," he said, "but live and declare the works of the Friars."

In a few months he is not only denouncing the Council of the Grey Friars in London, and haughtily casting back the calumny that he taught "God should obey the devil;" he proceeds to a bolder measure. He presents a petition to the King and Parliament that he may assert and maintain the articles contained in his writings, and proved by authority and reason to be the Christian faith; that all persons, now bound by vows of religion, may follow, instead thereof, the more perfect law of Christ; that tithes be bestowed, according to their proper use, for the maintenance of the poor; that Christ's own doctrine of the Eucharist be publicly taught; that neither King nor kingdom obey any See or Prelate further than their obedience be grounded on Scripture; that no money be sent out of the realm to the Court of Rome or of Avignon, unless proved by Scripture to be due; that no Cardinal or foreigner hold preferment in England; that if a Bishop or Curate be notoriously guilty of contempt of God, the King should confiscate his temporalities; that no Bishop or Curate should be enslaved to secular office; that no one should be imprisoned on account of excommunication.*

Danger seemed to be gathering around Wycliffe, but Wycliffe shrunk not from danger. The Parliament was

---

assented at Hereford to the persecution of Walter Brute. Compare the whole article on Hereford, as well as on Rypington and Ashton.—Lewis, p.

267, &c.

* The petition may be read in its main articles in Vaughan, ii. 97. It was printed by Dr. James, 1608.

summoned to Oxford; the Convocation, as of course, accompanied the Session of Parliament; a collision of mortal strife seemed inevitable. The Duke of Lancaster, though Wycliffite in all that concerned the limitation of the power and wealth of the hierarchy, urged the Reformer to submit to his spiritual superiors in matters purely spiritual. Convocation was afraid to stir those questions which concerned the wealth of the hierarchy, the Papal taxation, and other Papal privileges. Parliament respected the exclusive right of Convocation to judge on points of doctrine. Wycliffe was called to answer, but, as it were by common consent, on one doctrine alone—that of the Eucharist.

Nov. 19, 1382.

Wycliffe, at Lutterworth and in the villages around, before the people, was the plain, bold, vernacular preacher; at Oxford, before the Convocation, he was a school divine of acuteness, subtlety, and logical versatility, in which he was perhaps the greatest and most experienced master in the University. We may imagine that among the Prelates (the high-born Primate the Bishops of London, Norwich, Worcester, Lincoln, Sarum, Hereford, the Chancellor of the University, a host of Doctors), though some may have been, few were men of profound learning. The greater number must have found themselves fairly caught in the meshes of Wycliffe's metaphysic web; at one moment hearing words which sounded like the most rigid orthodoxy, at another trembling at nice distinctions which seemed to threaten the most fatal consequences. So completely does Wycliffe seem to have perplexed and bewildered his auditory, that of the monastic historians one boasts of his speech as a humble recantation; one as a bold confutation of the Doctors of the Second Millenary period of the Church, of all who had taught, after Transubstantiation, in its most materialistic form, had become a doctrine of the Church; as an assertion of the tenets of Berengar of Tours.* Nor can Wycliffe himself be fairly charged with insincerity, disingenuousness, or even politic art. His view of the Eucharist is singularly consistent, as much so as may be on so abstruse a subject. He is throughout labouring to reconcile a Real Presence with the rejection of the grosser Transubstantiation. The Eucharist is Christ's Body and Blood spiritually, sacramentally; but the bread and wine are not annihilated by transmutation. They co-exist, though to the mind of the believer the elements are virtually the veritable Body and Blood of the Redeemer.¹

That he was condemned by such a Court was matter of course. The condemnation was publicly promulgated in the school of the Augustinian Monks. Wycliffe was sitting in his chair as Professor, and holding, in academic phrase, his Determinations" on the other side. He is said to have been confounded by his condemnation. He might well be somewhat appalled: all his followers —even Ashton, who till now had adhered to him—had been reconciled or consented to reconciliation.* Lancaster advised submission. But he soon resumed his intrepidity; he appealed, to their indignation, not to the spiritual but to the temporal authority; not to the Pope

---

* Knighton. Walsingham, p. 283.
¹ Apud Vaughan, Appendix, vols. II. vi. and vii. Wycliffe asserts that a third part of the Clergy believed with him, and would die for their belief.
" "Tota prædicta condemnatio promulgata est publicè in scholis Augustinensium, ipso sedente in cathedrâ, et determinante contrarium. Sed confusus

"est auditâ condemnatione." From the official report, Wilkins, iii. 176. See the condemnation by the Chancellor of the University, William Berton. Spelman, Concilia, ii. 627. Fasciculi Zizaniorum, p. 100.

* Rypington was reconciled Oct. 30; Ashton, Dec. 27; Laurence Bedeman, earlier.

but to the King.* Lancaster in vain urged him to yield; he refused with calm pertinacity: "On this point all have erred but Berengarius."

Wycliffe retired unmolested to Lutterworth: no one can doubt that he would have shown the dauntlessness of a martyr. But there was as yet no statute in England for the burning of heretics: no officer, without legal warrant, would have obeyed, as in other countries, the mandate of the Church. His adversaries were too wise or too timid to urge extreme measures, such as imprisonment. It is extremely doubtful whether Lancaster and the Parliament would have consented to any act of rigour, and the Primate would not unnecessarily submit to the refusal of the secular power to execute his warrant: his own person had not been safe. Perhaps there was a tacit understanding that Wycliffe should leave Oxford, the most dangerous field of his influence.

In the two years' interval between the appearance of Wycliffe before the Convocation in Oxford and his death, an event occurred not likely with the thoughtful, or with those whose reverence for the Pope and the hierarchy was already shaken, to impair the cause of the Reformers. If the followers of Wycliffe gradually surrendered themselves to a fanatic madness, and became more and more daringly and insultingly hostile to the Clergy, the Clergy might seem under a judicial determination to justify those worst extravagances of hatred.

---

* "Volens per hoc se protegere regali potestate quod non premeretur vel ecclesiasticâ potestate."—In the report of the twelve judges appointed to examine into his opinions, he is said to have appealed "ad seculare brachium." They compare him to Arius. Peter Stokes, the Carmelite, had now become involved in heresy.

Just at the time when the Schism had shaken the Papacy to its base, and Wycliffe had denounced both Popes alike as Antichrist,[y] and had found strong sympathy in the hearts and minds of men; when the malappropriation of the vast revenues of the Church, which were asserted to be the patrimony of the poor, had been declared in many quarters to demand their confiscation for the public good; when the people had been abused by the fond but captivating notion that by such measures they might be relieved for ever from the burthen of taxation; when motions were entertained in the English Parliament to expel churchmen even from the more peaceful functions in the state; and, indeed, in some quarters notions of the unlawfulness of war were beginning to dawn: for the first time a holy civil war is proclaimed in Christendom, especially in England, the seat of these new opinions; a war of Pope against Pope. The Pontiff of Rome promulgates a crusade against the Pontiff of Avignon. A Bishop (Norwich) is at the head of the English host. Public prayers are put up, by order of the Primate, in every church of the realm, for the success of the expedition into Flanders. The Bishops and the Clergy are called on by the Archbishop to enforce upon their flocks the duty of contribution to this sacred purpose. Money, jewels, property of all kinds, are lavishly brought in, or rigidly extorted; it is declared meritorious to fight for the faith, glorious to combat for the Lord. The same indulgences are granted as to Crusaders to the Holy Land.[z]

---

[y] Wycliffe was more inclined to Urban VI.—See Lewis, p. 120, note.

[z] The preamble to the Archbishop's mandate for public prayers throughout the realm begins with "Rex pacificus, Jesus Christus." It enlarges on the blessings of peace, and goes on: "Quam meritorium sit pugnare pro fide; quamque decorum pugnare pro Domino." Courtenay's own words!

Spencer, the young and martial Bishop of Norwich, had distinguished himself during the peasant insurrection in Norfolk.[a] At the head of eight lances and a few archers, he had boldly arrested one of the ringleaders. A few knights gathered round him. Armed from head to foot, with a huge two-handed sword, he attacked an immense rabble, hewed them down, put the rest to flight, seized the captain, a dyer of Norwich, and reduced his diocese to peace by these victories, and by remorseless executions. This same Bishop set himself at the head of the crusade. The powers entrusted to him by the Pope were enormous: he had full Papal authority. He addressed all the parish priests in the province of York, urging them to compel contributions by every means, by confessions, by indulgences. Parliament murmured that such a vast array of the king's forces should be sent out of the realm under so inexperienced a general: but Hugh Calverly, and some of the old soldiers of the French wars, scrupled not to serve under the mitred captain.[b]

But after all, the issue of the expedition, at first successful, was in the end as shameful and disastrous as it was insulting to all sound religious feeling. The crusaders took Gravelines, they took Dunkirk; and this army of the Pope, headed by a Christian Bishop, in a war so-called religious, surpassed the ordinary inhumanity of the times. Men, women, and children, were

---

[a] Spencer figures among the distinguished Henrys in Capgrave's Liber de Henricis. There are some curious incidents about his suppression of the rebellion in Norfolk. But even Capgrave, the ardent admirer of Spencer, is obliged to enter into an apologetic discussion about Bishops bearing arms. The Flemings are wretched schismatics. This passage had been printed in Wharton's Anglia Sacra.

[b] See in the Close Rolls (edited by Mr. Devon) the issue of money for Spencer's crusade by the hands of John Philpot, for wages in the war, and reward for 2500 men-at-arms and 2500 archers, 6266l. 13s. 4d.—9th year of Richard II., 1385.

hewn to pieces in one vast massacre. After these first
successes the London apprentices, and the villeins
throughout the kingdom, were seized with a crusading
ardour. They mounted white cloaks, with red crosses
on their shoulders, red scabbards to their swords, and
marched off defying their masters.* Many religious,
monks and friars, followed their example.ᵈ The crusaders had neither the pride nor consolation of permanent success. The army of Spencer returned as
ingloriously as it had conducted itself atrociously. He
had 60,000 men, besides auxiliaries from Ghent. Before
Ypres he failed shamefully. At the first approach of
the French army he withdrew to Gravelines, and was
glad to buy a safe retreat by the surrender of the
town.*

On Innocents' Day, two years after the condemnation
at Oxford, during the celebration of the Mass in the
church of Lutterworth, Wycliffe was struck again with
paralysis. He died on the last day of the year. In
the suddenness of his death, in the day of his death, in
the fearful distortions which usually accompany that
kind of death, nothing was lost upon his adversaries,
who of course held him to be a victim of Divine wrath.
He died, it was said, on the day of St. Silvester: to the
memory of that Saint, as the fatal receiver of the dona-

---

* John Philpot, the magnificent Mayor of London, had raised 1000 men-at-arms at his own expense. He took great interest in the Bishop's expedition, and kept ships to give these volunteers free passage.

ᵈ Of these religious, says Walsingham, it was "in magnum personarum suarum dedecus et detrimentum, quia non propter Jesum Christum peregrinare decreverant sed ut patriam mundumque viderent."—P. 301.

* At a later period, when the Lollards, by preaching against pilgrimages, endangered the interests of our Lady of Walsingham, Bishop Spencer swore that if any of Wycliffe's preachers came into his diocese, he would burn or behead him. " Faith and religion remained inviolate in the diocese of Norwich."—Walsingham, 341.

tion of Constantine, he had ever been implacably hostile. By another account he died on the day of St. Thomas of Canterbury: he was struck while impiously inveighing against that Martyr of the Church.[f]

Yet Wycliffe, though the object of the bitterest hatred, even in his own day awed his most violent antagonists into something approaching to admiration. His austere exemplary life has defied even calumny: his vigorous incessant efforts to reduce the whole clergy to primitive poverty, have provoked no retort as to his own pride, self-interest, or indulgence, inconsistent with his earnest severity. His industry, even in those laborious days, was astonishing. The number of his books, mostly indeed brief tracts, baffles calculation. Two hundred are said to have been burned in Bohemia. How much of the translation of the Scripture he executed himself, is not precisely known; but even if in parts only superintended, it was a prodigious achievement for one man, so deeply involved as he was in polemic warfare with the hierarchy, the monks, and the Mendicant Orders.[g] He was acknowledged to be a consummate master in the dialectics of the Schools: he was the pride, as well as the terror of Oxford. "He was second to none," so writes a monk, "in philosophy; in the discipline of the Schools, incomparable."[h] In this, indeed, appear at once his strength, and the source of the apparent contradictions in the style and matter of his writings. Wycliffe was a subtle schoolman, and a popular religious pamphleteer. He addressed the students of the University

---

[f] Walsingham, p. 312. The historian consigns him to the companionship of Cain.

[g] The most curious charge against the translators of the Bible is that it was the Everlasting Gospel of Joachim and John Peter Oliva which they were publishing. Was this ignorance or malice?

[h] Knighton.

in the language and in the logic of their schools; he addressed the vulgar, which included no doubt the whole laity and a vast number of the parochial clergy, in the simplest and most homely vernacular phrase. Hence he is, as it were, two writers: his Latin is dry, argumentative, syllogistic, abstruse, obscure: his English rude, coarse, but clear, emphatic, brief, vehement; with short stinging sentences, and perpetual hard antithesis.[1]

His life shows that his religious views were progressive. His ideal was the restoration of the pure moral and religious supremacy to religion. This was the secret, the vital principle of his anti-sacerdotalism, of his pertinacious enmity to the whole hierarchical system of his day. That the caste of the Clergy was then discharging its lofty moral and religious mission, was denied by every pure and holy mind of the time; the charge was admitted by all the wise, even by Councils. The cause of all this evil, Wycliffe, like many others, saw in their exorbitant wealth. He could not but contrast with the primitive poverty of Christ and his Apostles, that wealth, whether in estates held by those whom he called "possessioners," the tithes exacted from the whole realm, and all which was extorted, chiefly in kind, by the sturdy beggars among the Mendicants. The Clergy had a right to a frugal, hospitable maintenance, but no more. This wealth was at once held by a false tenure, being the patrimony of the poor, and was forfeited by misuse, and by the neglect and non-performance of the conditions on which it was held. It was therefore not merely lawful, it was the bounden duty of the State, of the King, or the Emperor, to confiscate the whole of these escheated

---

[1] See, for instance, the long passage in the tract "Antichrist and his Meynie," published by Dr. Todd of Dublin.

riches; it was the duty of every one to refuse tithe to a priest, who, according to his notions, did not discharge his duty (Wycliffe could not or would not see the wide field he opened, by investing fallible and interested men with this judgement, to avarice, and bad passions). It was a sin, a sin deserving excommunication, to contribute to the rapacious quests of the Mendicants.

Wycliffe is charged with holding and urging in the broadest and most comprehensive form, what is called the doctrine of dominion founded in grace; that is, that the possession of anything whatever, even of a wife, depended on the state of grace in which a man might be. Wycliffe no doubt maintained in theory, that all the gifts of God (God, as it were, the One great feudal Suzerain), and of Christ, on account of his original righteousness,[k] were held on the condition of holiness.[m] But I have never read, nor seen adduced, any sentence of his writings, in which he urges the application or enforcement of this principle. He recognises civil possession as something totally distinct, as a full and legal right. This notion of dominion is diametrically opposed to all his arguments for the right to the resumption of ecclesiastical property by the State. But the ecclesiastics, to whose possessions, as held by sinful and unworthy men, Wycliffe remorselessly applies this rule,[n]

---

[k] "Titulo autem originalis justitiæ habuit Christus omnia bona mundi, ut sæpe declarat Augustinus, illo titulo, vel titulo gratiæ justorum sunt omnia, sed longe ab illo titulo civilis possessio. Unde Christus et sui Apostoli spretâ dominatione civili, fuerunt de habitatione pura, secundum illum titulum contentati," &c. &c. See the whole curious passage (strangely misprinted) in Vaughan, II. 235. Compare too Mr. Shirley (p. lxvii.) who has arrived at the same conclusion.

[m] So he seems to interpret the "saints shall inherit the earth."

[n] "Si Deus est, domini temporales possunt legitimè ac meritoriè auferre bona fortunæ ab ecclesiâ delinquente."— Fasciculi Zizaniorum, p. 249. Compare 251-2, where "excommunicatio propter

had the sagacity to see that this was a logical inference, an inference which Wycliffe himself may, in his incautious intrepidity, not always have avoided. They argued upon, refuted, condemned it, as if it were in truth, his favourite, fundamental maxim. A demagogue so dangerous to their order must be made out a demagogue dangerous to all orders. The religious reformer must be convicted on his own principles, as a political and social anarchist. Nor in their view was this difficult, hardly dishonest. Their property, they averred, was that of God, or at least of his Saints; it boasted a far higher, and a more sacred title than civil possessions: to despoil them was sacrilege, impiety, the spoliation of others only the less heinous crime of robbery: one was an outrage on the divine, the other but a breach of human law.*

Wycliffe, after all, was not merely premature as a Reformer of Christianity, he was incomplete and insufficient. He was destructive of the existing system, not reconstructive of a new one. In the translation of the Latin Scripture, and the assertion of the sole authority of Scripture, he had laid the foundation, but he had built on it no new edifice. He had swept away one by one almost all the peculiar tenets of mediæval Latin Christianity, pardons, indulgences, excommunications, absolutions, pilgrimages; he had condemned images, at least of the Persons of the Trinity; he had rejected Transubstantiation. But Teutonic Christianity had to await more than two centuries and a half before it

negationem temporalium," is no excommunication, and 254-5. Ecclesiastics subject to lay tribunals.

* This is among the singular facts, which appear from the refutation by Woodford (apud Brown, Fasciculus), one of the most instructive documents concerning Wycliffism. This was the doctrine also of Armachanus, Fitz Ralph, Archbishop of Armagh.

offered a new system of doctrine to the religious necessities of man. Lutheranism, Anglicanism, Calvinism, are forms of faith; from Wycliffism it would be difficult, perhaps impossible, to frame a creed like that of Augsburg, Articles like those of the Church of England, or even those of Westminster.

CHAPTER VII.

The Lollards.

<small>The Lollards.</small> WYCLIFFE left no heir to his authority or his influence; he had organised no sect. But his opinions, or some of his opinions, had sunk into the hearts of multitudes. Knighton (but Knighton wrote at Leicester in the immediate neighbourhood of Wycliffe) declares, in his bitterness, that every second man you met was a Wycliffite. Under the vague name of Lollards, they were everywhere; bound together by no public, as far as is known, by no secret association; only by common sympathies and common jealousy of the clergy. Many of them no doubt were more, many less, than Wycliffites. They were of all orders, ranks, classes; they were near, and even on, the throne; they were in the baronial castle, in the city among the substantial burghers, in the peasant's hut, even in the monastery. Wycliffe's own personal influence had cast a spell over some of the highest personages in the realm. His doctrines were looked on with favour by the widow of the Black Prince, by John of Gaunt, above all by the Queen of Richard II., Anne of Bohemia. The Good Queen Anne,* as she was popularly called, if not in doctrine,

---

* It is an observable indication of popular feeling that "good" seems to be the especial appellative of those most hostile to the Clergy. The "good" Queen Anne; the "good" Parliament, though its popularity was no doubt much out of its attachment to the Black Prince; the "good" Duke Humphrey, the adversary of Cardinal Beaufort, who had been the

in the foundation of her doctrine, reverence for the Scripture, was a Wycliffite. She had the Gospels at least in Bohemian, in English, and in Latin.[b] It was through her attendants that grew up not only the political, but the close and intimate religious connexion between Bohemia and England. Through them these doctrines passed to John Huss and Jerome of Prague. Not only does the Council of Constance denounce these teachers as disciples of Wycliffe; in repelling and anathematising Wycliffe, it assumes that it is repelling and anathematising the Bohemian Reformers. An Englishman, Peter Payne,[c] throughout the Hussite War, is one of the leaders of religion, one of the great authorities of the Bohemian faith. Among the Wycliffite noblemen the Earl of Salisbury is claimed by Fox, and branded by Walsingham as an obstinate and shameless Lollard, a despiser of images, a scoffer at the Sacraments.[d] His fate will ere long appear. A list of ten or twelve knights of property and influence has been preserved, who openly avowed the Wycliffite opinions: among these was the hero and martyr of Lollardism, Sir John Oldcastle, Lord Cobham.[e] London was their stronghold. The

Anne Queen of Bohemia.

---

most distinguished general in the Anti-Hussite wars. I suspect, too, some latent connexion between the Lollard party and Duke Humphrey.

[b] "Nobilis regina Angliæ, soror Cæsaris, habet Evangelium, in linguâ triplici, exaratum, scilicet in linguâ Bohemicâ, Teutonicâ, et Latinâ." I translate "Teutonicâ" English.— Wycliffe, apud Lewis. Anne of Bohemia died 1392.

[c] On Peter Payne, Lewis, p. 229. Compare Palacky, Geschichte von Böhmen, especially ill. 2, p. 485.

[d] "Lolardorum fautor in totâ vitâ, et imaginum vilipensor, contemptor canonum, sacramentorumque derisor."

[e] See ch. x., Lewis's Life of Wycliffe. Sir Thomas Latymer, Sir Lewis Clifforde, Sir John Peeche, Sir Richard Story, Sir Reginald de Hylton, Sir John Trussel, with Dukes and Earls. Lewis is quoting Knighton. Lewis gives an account of these men. To these he adds (p. 242) Sir William Nevyll, Sir John Clanbourn, Sir John

sober and wealthy citizens were advancing in intelligence and freedom, jealous no doubt of the riches of the clergy gained without risk or labour, and spent with splendour and ostentation which shamed their more homely and frugal living.ᶠ Nor were they without active proselytes in the lower and more unruly classes. Peter Patishull, an Augustinian Monk, though appointed one of the Pope's chaplains (a lucrative and honourable office, which conferred great privileges, and was commonly bought at a great price), embraced Wycliffism. He preached publicly on the vices of the clergy, at St. Christopher's in London. The Augustinians burst into the church, and served an interdict on the unsilenced teacher. The Lollards drove them out. Patishull affixed a writing on the doors of St. Paul's, "that he had escaped from the companionship of the worst of men to the most perfect and holy life of the Lollards."ᵍ The midland towns, rising into opulence, were full of Wycliffism, especially Leicester. There the Primate Courtenay took his seat in full Pontificals on the trial of certain heretics, who seem to have been of note; their accusers were the clergy of the town. They were anathematised with bell, book, and candle, and read their recantation.ʰ But the strength of the party was in the lower orders of society. Among them the name of Lollard, of uncertain origin (it is doubtful whether it was a name adopted by themselves or affixed as odious and derisive by their enemiesⁱ),

A.D. 1387.

Montague (p. 243), and Sir Laurence de St. Martin (p. 244).

ᶠ Among Walsingham's reproachful appellations bestowed on the Londoners is " Lolardorum sustentatores." Compare Lewis's account of the reforming Mayor, John of Northampton, p. 255.

He was connected with Chaucer.— *Life of Chaucer,* and Note forward.

ᵍ Fox, i. p. 681, from Chronicle of St. Alban's.

ʰ Wilkins, iii. 208.

ⁱ I cannot satisfy myself on this point.

comprehended no doubt, besides the religious, a vast mass of the discontented and revolutionary. In the latter years of his reign the King, Richard II., was hastily summoned from Ireland by the urgent solicitations of the Archbishop of York and the Bishop of London. An outbreak of the Lollards was said to threaten the peace of the realm. London was placarded with menacing sentences; they were affixed on the doors of St. Paul's and of St. Peter in Westminster. A remonstrance was addressed to the Houses of Parliament. This expostulatory petition showed that the grave and more prudent influence of the master was withdrawn; that his opinions had worked deeply down into a lower region. It does not appear that the more noble or distinguished followers of Wycliffe were concerned in the movement, which was an outburst of popular fanaticism. It was vehemently, in every point, anti-papal, anti-Roman. It was Wycliffite, but beyond Wycliffism. "Since the Church of England, fatally following that of Rome, has been endowed with temporalities, faith, hope, and charity have deserted her communion. Their Priesthood is no Priesthood; men in mortal sin cannot convey the Holy Ghost. The Clergy profess celibacy, but from their pampered living are unable to practise it. The pretended miracle of Transubstantiation leads to idolatry. Exorcisms or Benedictions are vain, delusive, and diabolical. The realm cannot prosper so long as spiritual persons hold secular offices. One who unites the two is an hermaphrodite. All chantries of prayer for the dead should be suppressed: 100 religious houses would be enough for the spiritual wants of the realm. Pilgrimages, the worshipping images or the Cross, or reliques, are idolatry. Auricular confession, indulgences, are mischievous or a

Petition of Lollards.

mockery. Capital punishments are to be abolished as contrary to the New Testament. Convents of females are defiled by licentiousness and the worst crimes. All trades which minister to pride or luxury, especially goldsmiths and sword-cutlers, are unlawful."[k]

These murmurs of a burthened and discontented populace were lost in the stir of great political events, the dethronement of the King, his death, and the accession of the Lancastrian dynasty.

The son and successors of John of Gaunt inherited neither the policy nor the religion, if it was the religion, of their ancestor. Henry IV. to strengthen himself on his usurped throne, Henry V. to obtain more lavish subsidies for his French wars, Henry VI. from his meek and pious character, entered into close and intimate alliance with the Church. Religious differences are but faintly traced in the Wars of the Roses.

Accession of Henry IV.

The high-born Arundel had succeeded the high-born Courtenay in the See of Canterbury. It is remarkable to see the two Primates, Canterbury and York, on adverse sides in the revolution which dispossessed Richard II. of his throne. Arundel was already before the landing of Henry at Ravenspurg, deep in conspiracy against King Richard. His brother, the Earl of Arundel, had been executed before his face; himself had fled, or had been banished to France. Neville of York had once adhered to Richard's fortunes, and suffered degradation, or a kind of ignominious translation to St. Andrew's in Scotland.[m] The name, rank,

Arundel Archbishop, 1897.

---

[k] See the Petition in F. Z. p. 300.
[m] The northern prelates seem to have adhered to Richard II. Marks, Bishop of Carlisle, in a speech of singular boldness and force, defended the deposed monarch.—See Collier, l. p. 616. See above reference to Papal Letter, p. 197.

influence, bold character of Arundel contributed more than all other adherents to the usurpation of Henry Bolingbroke. The Archbishop of Canterbury received the abdication of Richard. Scrope, who succeeded Arundel after Neville as Archbishop of York, was one of the King's Proctors on his renunciation of the crown. Arundel presented Henry to the people as their king. Arundel set the crown on his brow. When the heads of the Earls of Kent and Salisbury (the famous Lollard) and of six knights after their vain insurrection and their defeat near Cirencester, were sent to London to be exposed on the bridge, they were received and accompanied by the Bishops and Clergy in solemn procession, in full pontificals, chanting Te Deum.ⁿ Arundel might seem to have forgotten, in his loyal zeal, that he was the successor of Becket. In that insurrection two clergymen were hanged, drawn, and quartered without remonstrance from the Primate.° When Archbishop Scrope, after the revolt of the Percies, is beheaded as a traitor, Arundel keeps silence.

Archbishop Arundel was to be propitiated or rewarded by all concessions which could be demanded by a partisan so unscrupulous and of so much influence. Almost the first act of Henry IV., notwithstanding these

---

ⁿ So writes the Monk of St. Denys, as if present. "Aderant et præcedentes, qui capita comitum Cantiæ et de Salisberry, sex queque allorum militum, longis lanceis affixa defferebant cum lituis et instrumentis musicis, ut sic cives ad horrendum spectaculum convenirent. Cumque Pontificum cum Clero sacris vestibus induti processionabantur, Te Deum laudamus altis vocibus cantando obviam sceleri (o?) muneri processisent, taodem ad introl- tum pontis suspensa sunt capita, membra quoque per campestria sparsa sunt, feris et avibus devoranda."—L. xx. c. 16, p. 738. When the quarters of these unhappy men were brought to London, no less than 18 bishops and 52 mitred abbots joined the populace, and met them with the most indecent marks of joy and exultation. See, too, the conduct of the Earl of Rutland.—Hume, Henry IV.

° Walsingham, p. 363.

bold infringements on the personal sanctity of consecrated persons, was to declare himself the champion of the hierarchy against her dangerous enemies. In the first Convocation a welcome message was delivered, that the new King would be the Protector of the Church. The Prelates were urged to take measures for the suppression of itinerant preachers; the Crown promised its aid and support. The King, in his first speech in Parliament, announced the same deliberate determination to maintain the Catholic faith. The Commons returned their humble thanks for his Majesty's zeal in the assertion of the Catholic faith and the liberties of the Church.

<small>A.D. 1399.</small>

In England alone a Statute was necessary to legalise the burning of heretics.[p] In all other parts of Christendom the magistrate had obeyed the summons of the clergy. The Sovereign, either of his own supreme authority, or under the old Roman Imperial Law, had obsequiously executed the mandates of the Bishop. The secular arm received the delinquent against the law of the Church. The judgement was passed in the Ecclesiastical Court or that of the Inquisition; but the Church, with a kind of evasion which it is difficult to clear from hypocrisy, would not be stained with blood. The Clergy commanded, and that under the most awful threats, the fire to be lighted and the victim tied to the stake by others, and acquitted themselves of the cruelty of burning their fellow-creatures.

<small>Statute de Hæretico Comburendo.</small>

King Henry IV. and the Parliament (even the

---

[p] Blackstone indeed says (B. iv. c. 4) of the writ de hæretico comburendo that "it is thought by some to be as ancient as the common law itself." Compare Hales' Pleas of the Crown. The king might issue such a writ. But is there any instance of such writ actually issued in England?"

Commons, now affrighted no doubt by the wild and revolutionary tenets ascribed to all the Lollards, and avowed by some) enacted the Statute which bears the ill-omened appellation, "for the burning of heretics." The preamble was directed in the most comprehensive terms against the new preachers.[1] It was averred that in their public preachings, in their schools, through their books, they stirred up and inflamed the people to sedition, insurrection, and other enormities too horrible to be heard, in subversion of the Catholic Faith and the doctrine of Holy Church, in diminution of God's honour, and also in destruction of the estate, rights, and liberties of the Church of England. These preachings, schools, books were strictly inhibited. The Bishop of the diocese was empowered to arrest all persons accused or suspected of these acts, to imprison them, to bring them to trial in his court. "If he shall refuse to abjure such doctrines, or, having abjured, relapse, sentence is to be recorded: a writ issued to the sheriff of the county, the mayor or bailiff of the nearest borough, who is to take order that on a high place in public, before the face of the people he be burned."

A.D. 1400.

Nor was this Statute an idle menace; the Primate and the Bishops hastened to make examples under its terrible provisions.

William Sautree is the protomartyr of Wycliffism. But the first victim, while he displays most fully the barbarity of the persecutors, does not lead the holy army with much dignity. His sufferings alone entitle him to profound commiseration. He was chosen perhaps as an example to overawe London, and as one whose fate would not provoke dangerous sympathy.

William Sautre.

---

[1] But see Hallam, Middle Ages, ii. p. 221.

William Sautree had been Priest of St. Margaret's in King's Lynn: he was now a preacher at St. Osyth in the City. He had been already arraigned and convicted before that model of a Christian Prelate, the warlike Bishop of Norwich. On his trial in London, he not only recanted and withdrew his recantation (a more pardonable weakness), he daringly denied that he had ever been on trial before. The record of the Court of Norwich was produced before him. He had already been condemned as a heretic for the denial of Transubstantiation. He was now doomed to the flames, as a relapsed heretic. The ceremony of his degradation took place at St. Paul's, with all its minute, harassing, impressive formalities. He was then delivered over, and for the first time the air of London was darkened by the smoke of this kind of human sacrifice. The writ for the execution of Sautree distinctly stated that the burning of heretics is enjoined by the law of God as well as of man, and by the canons of the Church. The act was that of the King, by the advice of the Lords and Commons. The burning was in abhorrence of the crime, and as an example to all other Christians.[r]

Yet if the Commons had assented (if they did formally assent to the persecuting Statute), if they had petitioned for its rigid enforcement against the Lollards, and those who rejected the Catholic doctrines, there was still great jealousy of the more unpopular abuses in the Church. In the fourth year of Henry petitions were presented,[s] that all Monks of French birth should be expelled from the country, all priories held by foreigners seized, every benefice have its vicar bound to reside,

---

[r] The account is in Fox. Compare House of Lancaster, p. 85.
[s] Rot. Parliament. iii. 459.

and to exercise hospitality; that no one should be allowed to enter into any of the four Mendicant Orders under the age of 24. The King assented to limit the age to 18.¹ The next session the King, by his Chancellor, as though to awe the boldness of Parliament, again declared it to be his royal will to maintain the Church, as his ancestors had maintained it, in all its liberties and franchises. He compared the realm and its three estates to the human body. The Church was the right side, the King the left, the Commonalty the other members. The answer of the Commons was an address to the King to dismiss his Confessor and two others of his household. Henry not merely submitted, but declared that he would retain no one about his person who had incurred the hatred of his people. Nothing could equal the apparent harmony of the King and his Parliament. He entreated them not to be abashed or to refrain from giving their good counsel. They desired that he would notify to them the honourable and virtuous persons whom he named for his household, and that he would appoint no foreigners. The King again graciously assented: he even promised to live upon his own. "The King is willing so to do, as soon as he well may." But the Commons were well aware of the weakness of Henry's title. So far as that the Commonalty might relieve themselves from taxation by throwing the burthen on the wealth of the Church, they were all Lollards. They represented that while the knights were worn out in service against the King's

---

¹ Walsingham gives a whimsical illustration of the feeling about the Mendicants. He says that Owen Glendower's dealings with devils were instigated and aided by the Friar Minors. But he is shocked at his own words. "Absit ab hominibus tam sanctam professae regulam ut cum dæmonibus tantam contraherent familiaritatem."—P. 366.

enemies, the clergy sat idle at home. Primate Arundel answered that their vassals followed the King to his wars; that they paid their tenths more promptly than the laity their fifteenths, besides the potent aid of their prayers. The Speaker (he was a knight, John Cheyne,* who had been in deacon's orders, and thrown them off without licence) betrayed in his voice and look something of heretical or knightly disparagement of the value of their prayers. Arundel broke out, "No kingdom ever prospered without devotion; nor think thou to plunder the Church; so long as there is an Archbishop of Canterbury, thou wilt do it at thy peril." The Primate fell on his knees before the wavering King, imploring him to respect his oaths, and to protect the rights of the Church. The obstinate Commons persisted in their unwelcome representations. They urged from a schedule, with tempting and nicely-calculated particulars, that the temporal possessions of the Bishops, Abbots, Priors, now idly wasted, would furnish to the realm 15 Earls, 1500 Knights, 6200 Squires. The King forbade them to discuss such high matters. They began still more to show their anti-hierarchical spirit. They demanded a mitigation of the statute against the Lollards. The King answered that it ought to be made more severe. But for some unexplained reason a subsequent answer to the same petition was in milder terms, yet, "this relaxation was not to be alleged as an example."

In the midst of these significant struggles between the King and the Commons—the King pledged by gratitude and by his interests to maintain the hierarchy to the utmost; the Commons, if not in open assertion

---

* Walsingham, p. 572.

of religious liberty, looking with greedy and jealous eyes on the estates of the clergy: the second victim on record of the sanguinary law was sent to public execution. He was but a humble tailor of the diocese of Worcester. Why, among all the Lollards, who boasted that they were 100,000, this poor man was chosen for this melancholy distinction does not appear. John Badbee had already been tried and condemned in the Court of the Bishop of Worcester. His crime was the ordinary one, the denial of Transubstantiation; and this, excepting that in one respect it was coarsely expressed,* from the usual objections which formed part of the Wycliffite creed. He was summoned to London before a more dignified and solemn tribunal. The Primate sat with the Archbishop of York, the Bishops of London, Winchester, Norwich, Salisbury, Bath, Bangor, St. David's. Edmund Duke of York, the Chancellor, and the Master of the Rolls. The poor man's answers were given with courage and firmness in words of simplicity and plain sense. He said that he would believe "the Omnipotent God in Trinitie," and said, moreover, "if every Host being consecrated at the altar were the Lord's body, that then there be 20,000 Gods in England. But he believed in one God Omnipotent." Every effort was made to incline him to retract. Arundel the Primate condescended to urge him in the strongest terms to submission. He was condemned in a second great Court, held in St. Paul's. He was led forth to be burned in Smithfield. The Prior of St. Bartholomew's, as if to overawe him, brought out the Sacrament. The

March 1, 1409.

Badbee burned.

---

* He said that John Bates of Bristol had as much power and authority to make the like body of Christ as any priest had.—Fox, I. 679.

Prince of Wales, Henry, chanced to be present. At the first sensation of the fire, the poor man cried out "Mercy!" The Prince ordered the fire to be removed. But it was to the mercy of God, not of man, that Badbee appealed. Neither persuasions nor the promises of a yearly maintenance could subdue his quiet but inflexible courage; he was thrust back into the blazing cask, and perished in the flames. Did Prince Henry turn away his eyes?[r]

William Thorpe, arraigned before this time, was a man of higher station and character. He was tried before Arundel; his trial lasted a considerable time; it almost appears that it was protracted for more than a year. But it is most remarkable that, after all, it is not known what was his fate. He lived to write an account of his trial; it is probable that he was kept in prison.[s]

On the accession of Henry V., the religious conduct of the gay and dissolute Prince might have been an object of apprehension; the Lollards might hope that at least, notwithstanding his doubtful conduct at the execution of Badbee, he would not be the slave of the hierarchy. These apprehensions and these hopes were speedily dissipated (whether by any acts or words of Henry) by the early betrayal of his ambitious designs, into which the sagacious Church afterwards threw itself with the most loyal ardour; or from the no less sagacious prescience of his character among the Lollards. The Lollards might well mistrust the son of Henry IV.; and such men, among many of whom fanaticism was the height of virtue, were not

Accession of Henry V.

---

[r] Walsingham as well as Fox relates his death.—P. 379.

[s] This is the conjecture of Fox. The trial is curious. The trial or arraignment began in 1407.

likely to disguise their mistrust, or to refrain from taking measures perhaps for their safety, perhaps for more than safety. Whatever the causes of this mutual jealousy, the Lollards seem to have begun the strife. On the doors of the churches in London appeared menacing notices, that to the number of 100,000 men, they were prepared to maintain their opinions by force of arms.

The head of the Lollards was Sir John Oldcastle, Lord Cobham, a man of the highest military reputation, who had served with great distinction in the French wars. His whole soul was now devoted to his religion. Through his influence unlicensed preachers swarmed through the country, especially in the dioceses of London, Rochester, and Hereford. The Primate Arundel was not a man to shrink from bold and decisive measures in his own diocese, or not to force to issue the King's yet undeclared opinions on this momentous question. He summoned the Convocation of the Clergy. Lord Cobham was accused as having spoken contemptuously of the power and authority of the Archbishop of Canterbury, of holding heretical opinions on the Eucharist, on Penance, Pilgrimages, the Power of the Keys. On these crimes he was denounced to the King. Henry honoured the valiant knight, the skilful general, who had already distinguished himself in the wars of France, who might hereafter (for Henry's ambitious schemes were assuredly within his heart) be of signal service in the same fields. He had no doubt that his own arguments would convince so noble a subject, so brave a soldier, so aspiring a knight. But Henry was just emerged from his merry life; at least, with all mistrust of the potent enchantments of Shakspeare, Henry's

Oldcastle, Lord Cobham.

youth can have been no school for serious theology. He knew not much of the depth of religious feeling which possessed the disciples of Wycliffe. He resented the more the unexpected resistance of Cobham; his disobedience was almost treason. Cobham, as it is related, protested the most submissive loyalty. "You I am most prompt and willing to obey: you are a Christian King, the Minister of God, that bears not the sword in vain for the punishment of wicked doers and the reward of the virtuous. To you, under God, I owe my whole obedience. Whatsoever you command me in the name of the Lord, that am I ready to fulfil. To the Pope I owe neither suit nor service: he is the great Antichrist, the son of perdition, the abomination of desolation in the holy place."

Lord Cobham* retired to his strong castle of Cowling, near Rochester. He treated the citations, the excommunications of the Archbishop with utter contempt, and seemed determined to assert the independence of a bold baron, and to defend his house against all aggressors. The summoners, one after another, were repelled: letters citatory affixed on the doors of Rochester Cathedral, three miles off, were torn down and burned. The Summoner at length found his way into the castle accompanied by a King's officer. To the royal officer Cobham was too prudent or too loyal to offer resistance. He was committed to the Tower. There (perhaps

---

* He was Lord Cobham by right.

* Hit is uckindly for a knight, that should
  a kynges castel kepe,
  To bable the bible day and night in
  restlng time when he sholde slepe;
  And carefully away to crepe for all the
  chief of chivalrie,
  Well ought him to walle and weepe that
  swych lest hath in lolardie.

An old castel and not repaired, with wast walls and wowes wide,
The wages ben full yoel with such a capitayn to abide;
That reveth not to ride agayns the kyng and his clergie,
With privye jents and pore pride, there is a pound of lollardie."
—Quoted from a satirical song, MS. Cotton, by Pauli, Geschichte Englands, v. p. 297.

shortly before) he published a full confession of his belief. Its language was calm, guarded, conciliatory. If the Clergy had chosen to be satisfied, they might have been satisfied. Cobham was again admitted to the King's presence. He offered one hundred knights as his compurgators. He offered wager of battle; he would fight for life or death with Christian or heathen, on the quarrel of his faith, saving the King and his Counsellors.[b]

But Arundel was determined to crush his antagonist. He admitted that Cobham's confession contained much which was good. Articles were framed declaring Transubstantiation in its grossest form, the absolute annihilation of the material bread and wine; Confession in the most rigid terms, obedience to the hierarchy, the worship of images, and pilgrimages. Cobham was arraigned before the Primate, the Bishops of London and Winchester (the Bishop of Bangor joined the tribunal), with a number of Doctors of the Canon and Civil Law.[c] The Archbishop's language was mild, his purpose stern and inflexible. Cobham knelt down and spake: "Many have been my crimes against man; for the breaking of God's commandments they never cursed me, for breaking their laws and traditions I and others are thus cruelly entreated." He was committed, and appeared a second time in the Dominican convent. He was submitted to a long, weary, intricate, scholastic

---

[b] It is said, but most improbably, that he appealed from the Archbishop to the Pope.

[c] During the search for Wycliffe's writings, which were publicly burned at Paul's Cross, a book was found at a limner's, where it had been left to be illuminated, belonging to Oldcastle. The King read a few pages, and declared that he had never read such dangerous doctrines. Oldcastle owned the book to be his property, but asserted that he had read only two or three pages of it, and could not be answerable for its contents.

cross-examination. He gradually lost his calm self-command. The suppressed enthusiasm burst out into a wild prophetic denunciation of the Pope and the Prelates. He denounced the wealth of the Church as the venom of the Church. "What meanest thou," said Arundel, "by venom?" "Your possessions and your lordships. Then cried an angel in the air, as your own chronicles witness: 'Woe, woe, woe! this day is venom poured into the Church of God.' Since that day Pope hath put down Pope; one has poisoned, one has cursed, one has slain another. Consider ye this, all men. Christ was meek and merciful; the Pope haughty and a tyrant. Christ was poor and forgave; the Pope is rich and a homicide. Rome is the nest of Antichrist: out of that nest come his disciples. The Prelates, the Priests, the Monks are the body; these shaven Friars the tail." "That is uncharitably spoken," said the Prior of the Augustines. The blood of Cobham was on fire; he went on in his fierce declamation. He soon resumed his calm courage, and argued with close precision. After his sentence, he said: "Though ye judge my body, ye have no power over my soul." He knelt and prayed for his enemies. He was condemned, adjudged a heretic, and committed to the Tower.[d]

He made his escape from the Tower, and from that time became an object of terror to the government, who dreaded a general rising of the Lollards under a man of such known intrepidity, valour, and military science. Rumours of conspiracies, of insurrections, of designs on the person of the King, spread abroad. A royal proclamation, subsequently issued, accused the Lollards of a deliberate, wide-spread plot to destroy

---

[d] Fox. The sentence passed by Arundel may be read.

the hierarchy, to suppress all monasteries, to confiscate the estates of the Church, to proclaim Cobham Protector of the realm. Cobham is said to have instigated a Scottish invasion.*

It must be remembered that the title of Henry V. was at this time by no means generally acknowledged; his throne not secure. Reports that Richard II. was still alive in Scotland were credited by many; the elder line of Lionel Duke of Clarence (as appears by the conspiracy of the Earl of Cambridge, Scrope, and Grey of Heton, during the next year) had its partisans. Henry was known, till the battle of Agincourt, only as a wild and dissolute, if gallant, generous, and active youth, accused of having designed to seize his father's crown in his lifetime. The lower orders, till they were intoxicated into loyalty by the French conquests, cherished the memory of Richard II., hated the usurper, loved not his main support, the Church. The levelling doctrines of the peasant insurgents under Richard cannot have been entirely crushed. Of the more fanatic Lollards some may have embraced those tenets. The whole sect may have begun to madden into despair at this close and manifest alliance between the Lancastrian Kings and the hierarchy. It is not improbable that wild schemes may have been formed, it is certain that they were dreaded and suspected.

The King, with his bold military decision, suddenly moved from his palace at Eltham, in which it had been rumoured that the conspirators were preparing to surprise him and put him to death. He appeared in Westminster. Immediately, St. Giles's Fields, the place of assembly, as it was bruited abroad, for the

---

* Walsingham.

whole host of the Lollards, was on a sudden surrounded by the royal troops. It was given out, that in the dusk of that very evening, or in the night, countless armed men were seen creeping along the lanes and under the hedges to the place of rendezvous. A few persons were seized, Sir Roger Acton, Sir John Browne, and J. Burnley, a rector. Their excuse was that they came to hear Burnley preach. From others was extorted a confession that they expected the Lord Cobham. The King had ordered the City gates to be closed, for it was further rumoured that 50,000 servants and apprentices were prepared to sally forth.

No outbreak took place; there was not the least commotion or resistance. Nine and thirty persons were instantly put on trial and executed.[f] Confessions, whether voluntary or extorted, true or false, were announced, of the vast and formidable conspiracy. After the execution, a new and violent Statute was passed for the suppression of Lollards.

The royal proclamation and the indictment of Oldcastle Lord Cobham, Sir Roger Acton, and others, announced to the nation, which had hardly time for amazement and terror from the rapidity of the King's movements, the menaced insurrection, the secret conspiracy, the gathering together of the conspirators, the 20,000 men said to be ready in arms. It declared their object to have been the utter abolition of the State, the abrogation of the office of Prelate, the sup-

---

[f] The meeting was on the night of the 7th Jan. (Sunday). Was a preaching to take place? was it to cover the movements of the conspirators? or was it a pretext seized by the government? On Monday (8th) the prisoners had been taken and sent to gaol. The bill was preferred against the 27 (or 39) prisoners on the 9th. On that day and the 10th, all, including three peers, were tried and condemned for treason and heresy. On the 12th they were executed. Compare House of Lancaster, note xxviii.

pression of all religious orders, the slaying of our Lord the King, his brothers, the Prelates, and other nobles of the realm; the proscription of all monks and friars, the despoiling and destruction of all Cathedral churches, of many other churches and holy monasteries; they designed to raise Sir John Oldcastle, Lord Cobham, to be Regent of the realm.[a]

How far were the fears of the government real? On what were they grounded? How far was the proclamation intended to strike terror into the Lollards and their abettors, to arouse the hatred of all loyal subjects and lovers of order against them? The whole was an affair of four days: the pretended insurrection, its suppression, the trial, the execution of at least between twenty and thirty men, some of high rank.[b] And where all this time was the terrible and mysterious Cobham? Of his agency, still less of his presence, there is neither proof nor vestige. It is only known that he was proscribed; that for three years he lay concealed from all the keen bloodhounds who were induced to trace him by honest hatred of his treasons, or by the baser hope of favour or reward.

At the end of this period (yet this is but a doubtful rumour) he suddenly appeared near St. Alban's. If

---

[a] The Indictment is in Fox. "Et dictum Johannem Oldcastle regentem ejusdem regni constituere, et quamplurima regimina secundum eorum voluntatem intra regnum prædictum quasi gens sine capite in finalem destructionem tam fidei Catholicæ et cleri, quam status et majestatis dignitatis regal. infra idem regnum ordinare."

[b] In the Close Rolls at this time appears an entry: "To John Mathewe and others, his companion jurors upon an inquest held for the King at Westminster upon certain traitors and rebels against the King's person, the money paid by the hands of the said John in discharge of 6l., which the Lord the King ordered them of his gift, by writ 6l.: also for a breakfast to others, including the Lord Mayor, 2l. 16s. 8d." There is another to Thomas Burton (the King's spy), for watching the Lollards, 100 shillings.

accidental, this apparition was singularly ill-timed. It was during an invasion of the Scots, with whom he had before been charged as being in secret correspondence. Again he was lost to the keen sight alike of his admirers and his enemies. At length he was taken, after a vigorous resistance, by Sir Edward Charlton, Lord of Powis. Such importance was attached to his arrest, that Charlton received 1000 marks as reward.

Cobham suffered at once the punishment of a traitor and a heretic. This punishment was inflicted in St. Giles's Fields, with all the blended barbarity of both modes of execution. He was hung on a gallows, with a fire at his feet, and slowly consumed. He was said to have declared himself a faithful subject of his liege Lord, Richard II., thus avouching, as though in secret intelligence with the Scots, the wild tale, unquestionably current, that Richard was still living in that kingdom. These and other strange rumours rest on slight authority. His conduct was throughout (this we would believe more fully) that of a noble religious man. Before his execution he fell on his knees, and implored forgiveness on his enemies. He addressed the multitude in a few words, urging them to obey the law of God in the Scripture, to reject all evil in their lives. He refused the aid of a priest: "to God only, now as ever present, he would confess, and of him entreat pardon." His last words, drowned by the crackling flames, were praise of God. The people wept and prayed with him; they heard in contemptuous silence the declarations of the priests, that Cobham died an enemy o God, an heretic to the Church.[1]

_{Death of Cobham, 1411.}

---

[1] Though rapid in my relation, I have been slow, if I may say so, faltering, in all this history of Cobham. All is obscure and contradictory, especially the St. Giles's Fields insurrection. To all Roman Catholic writers

We have followed English Wycliffism to the martyrdom of Lord Cobham. It is singular that it was not in a Teutonic but a Sclavonian kingdom, not in a language kindred to the English, but in one of a totally different stock, dissonant in most of its words and ideas, that the opinions of Wycliffe were to be received with eager zeal, and propagated with cordial acceptance. In Bohemia, the Reformer's works—jealously watched, trampled under foot, burned by the hierarchy—were received, multiplied, translated, honoured as the exposition of the true and genuine Gospel. The apostles, the heirs, of Wycliffism, were John Huss and Jerome of Prague; we must return to Constance to witness their influence, their death-defying strength, their unextinguishable vitality: the death of Huss preceded that of Cobham two years.

Oldcastle is a turbulent, dangerous rebel, as well as a heretic; to Protestants, a loyal subject, as well as a martyr. The authorities are heaped together, but require most diligent and suspicious sifting, in Fox. The abjuration which he is said to have made (Fox, Z. 414), and to which Mr. Shirley seems to give some credit, may possibly have been the form offered to him; but if he had abjured before, he would have been executed at once as a relapsed heretic; if just before his death, why was he burned as a heretic? I believe it to be a forgery.

CHAPTER VIII

Council of Constance.

THROUGHOUT Christendom all eyes, all minds were centered on the German city of Constance. There for the first time was to meet the great Universal Council, the representative assembly of Latin Christianity. The older Œcumenic Councils had been Eastern and Greek, with a few, a very few, delegates from the West. The more famous Latin Councils, as those of the Lateran, of Vienne, of Lyons, were assemblages of prelates, whom the Pope condescended to summon, in order to take counsel with him, and under him, on the affairs of the Church. The Council of Pisa had been hardly more than a college of Cardinals, with the advice and support of certain prelates and ambassadors of sovereign princes. The Council of Constance assumed more than the power of judging on the claims of rival Pontiffs; the supremacy of the Pope over a General Council, of a General Council over the Pope, was now an inevitable question. The Council placed itself at once above the three contesting Popes, each with a doubtful and disputed title; each with some part, though but a small part, of Christendom adhering to his obedience. If such a Council, sweeping away these ignoble rivals, might create a new successor of St. Peter, they might impose conditions and limit his autocracy. Who could foresee the power which they would assume, the power which they would have the ambition, the strength to exercise? Nor was

the one absorbing paramount question the election of
the Pope: it was not only from its anarchy but its
sunken state that the Church must be vindicated and
re-established. The reformation of the Church in its
head and in all its members, was among the avowed
objects, it was the special function, of the Council; the
maintenance of the unity of the Church against formidable heresiarchs; the suppression of heresies, which had
ceased to be those of rebellious sects, had become those
of rebellious nations. In Constance would be seen of
the monarchs of Christendom perhaps one only, but he
the greatest, the Emperor, who stood higher than any
successor of Charlemagne since the Othos, the Fredericks,
or Rodolph of Hapsburg. But there might be three
Pontiffs, each of whom had worn, each boasted himself
the rightful wearer of the Papal tiara. There would
certainly be the whole College of Cardinals; the most
famous and learned churchmen from every kingdom of
the West; even those dreaded heresiarchs, the heirs
and successors of the English Wycliffe, who had nearly
severed the kingdom of Bohemia from Latin Christendom.

In June the quiet streets of ancient Constance were
disturbed by the first preparations for the
great drama which was to be performed within A.D. 1414.
her walls. The Bishop elect of Augsburg and Count
Eberhard of Nellenberg entered the city to choose
quarters for the Emperor. Hopes began to spread, to
strengthen, that the high contracting parties were in
earnest; that the Universal Council, so often announced,
so often eluded, would at length take place. In August
came the Cardinal of Viviers, the Bishop of Ostia, with
a distinguished suite, to take order for the accommodation of the Pope John XXIII. and of his Cardinals.

From that period to the Feast of All Saints, the day named for the opening of the Council, and for several months after, the converging roads which led to this central city were crowded with all ranks and orders, ecclesiastics and laymen, Sovereign Princes, and Ambassadors of Sovereigns, Archbishops and Bishops, the heads or representatives of the great Monastic Orders, theologians, doctors of Canon or of Civil Law, delegates from renowned Universities, some with splendid and numerous retainers, some like trains of pilgrims, some singly and on foot. With these, merchants, traders of every kind and degree, and every sort of wild and strange vehicle. It was not only, it might seem, to be a solemn Christian Council, but an European congress, a vast central fair, where every kind of commerce was to be conducted on the boldest scale, and where chivalrous or histrionic or other common amusements were provided for idle hours and for idle people. It might seem a final and concentrated burst and manifestation of mediæval devotion, mediæval splendour, mediæval diversions: all ranks, all orders, all pursuits, all professions, all trades, all artisans, with their various attire, habits, manners, language, crowded to one single city.

On the steep slope of the Alps were seen winding down, now emerging from the autumn-tinted chestnut groves, now lost again, the rich cavalcades of the Cardinals, the Prelates, the Princes of Italy, each with their martial guard or their ecclesiastical pomp. The blue spacious lake was studded with boats and barks, conveying the Bishops and Abbots, the knights and grave burghers, of the Tyrol, of Eastern and Northern Germany, Hungary, and from the Black Forest and Thuringia. Along the whole course of the Rhine, from Cologne, even from Brabant, Flanders, or the farthest

North, from England and from France, marched Prelates, Abbots, Doctors of Law, celebrated Schoolmen, following the upward course of the stream, and gathering as they advanced new hosts from the provinces and cities to the east or west. Day after day the air was alive with the standards of Princes, and the banners emblazoned with the armorial bearings of Sovereigns, of Nobles, of Knights, of Imperial Cities; or glittered with the silver crosier, borne before some magnificent Bishop or mitred Abbot. Night after night the silence was broken by the pursuivants and trumpeters announcing the arrival of some high and mighty Count or Duke, or the tinkling mule-bells of some lowlier caravan. The streets were crowded with curious spectators, eager to behold some splendid prince or ambassador, some churchman famous in the pulpit, in the school, in the council, it might be in the battle-field, or even some renowned minnesinger, or popular jongleur. The city almost appeared to enlarge itself to welcome week after week the gathering strangers. The magistrates had taken admirable measures to maintain order. Every one seemed to glide into and settle down in his proper place. Everywhere were gathering crowds, yet no tumult: among these crowds now a low deep murmur, now a hush of expectation, no clamour, no confusion, no quarrel, no riot. Constance might seem determined to support her dignity, as chosen for a kind of temporary capital of Christendom. The awfulness of the great subjects which were to be discussed had, as it were, enthralled the mind of man to a calm seriousness; even amusements and diversions were under sober discipline. Whatever there was, and doubtless there was much, of gross and licentious, was kept out of sight.

Of all those vast multitudes there was no one whose

fate might seem so to tremble on the balance; who could look on this wonderful scene with such profound emotions of hope and fear; to whom the Council was at once so full of awe, yet at the same time, to his yet unextinguished ambition, might eventually prove such a scene of pride, of triumph, as John XXIII. The Pope had every imaginable guarantee, notwithstanding some dubious words,[a] not only for his person, but for his dignity. His right, in concurrence with the Emperor, to summon the Council had been admitted by Sigismund. The Imperial Edict asserted his plenary jurisdiction; the magistrates of Constance had taken a solemn oath on the direct demand of the Emperor, to receive him with all befitting honours as the one true Pope, to protect him to the utmost, to give him free liberty to enter, to remain, or to depart from their city.[b] He was to have entire independent authority over his own court: his safe-conduct was to be respected by all the officers of the city.

Yet had the Pope, notwithstanding all these solemn guarantees, notwithstanding his wealth, and the array of Cardinals attached, as he hoped, to his interests, with the Italian Bishops, almost in number enough to overrule the Council,[c] strong and sad misgivings. He sought to make friends in every quarter in his hour of need. Frederick, Duke of Austria, was the hereditary enemy of the House of Luxemburg. His territories almost

---

[a] "Ne exinde occasionem non veniendi habeat." Such is the suspicious language of Sigismund.

[b] "Ita quod semper et omni tempore, liceblt el stare in dictâ civitate et ab eâ recedere, non obstante quocunque impedimento." See the oath in Von der Hardt, l. v. p. 5. The Emperor's stipulations to the Pope were not of much more value than those to John Huss.

[c] "Johannes venit Constantiam, cum multis Prælatis Italiæ, ut per votorum pluralitatem se conservaret in Papatu."—Ebendorfer in Pez Script. Austria, ii. 825.

surrounded the city of Constance; his strong castles crowned many of the hills around, which might be seen from the borders of the lake; the Tyrol and the Black Forest were among his possessions. Frederick, as if to show the utmost respect to the Pope, met him at Trent. The Pope was lavish of honours, gifts, and promises. At Meran he named the Austrian Gonfalonier of the Church, and of his privy council. He assigned him as stipend for these functions 6000 florins a year. Frederick, besides these advantages, looked to the support of the Pope in certain feuds with the Bishops of Trent, Coire, and Brixen. He swore fealty to the Pope; he promised all aid and protection on the road, and in the city of Constance, and to secure his free retreat from that city.[d] Frederick of Austria was closely allied with the Duke of Burgundy; the Duke's sister was the widow of Frederick's brother, Leopold of Austria; she resided on her dowry lands in the Austrian States. The Duke of Burgundy had strong reasons for courting the favour of the Pope. Among the causes to be judged by the Council of Constance was that of Jean Petit, whose atrocious defence of the atrocious murder of the Duke of Orleans by Burgundy or his partisans, was to be arraigned in the face of Christendom. An alliance with Austria was almost an alliance with Burgundy, now, whether on the French or English side, almost commanding France. The Marquis of Baden, too, and the Count of Nassau received significant presents from John XXIII.; and if the Emperor should show hostility to the Pope, the Pope seemed sure of a partisan in

---

[d] Gerhard de Rio asserts, from Austrian documents, that the Pope communicated this treaty to Sigismund: probably the articles which could not be concealed; the honours and dignities conferred on the Austrian, not the secret stipulations for protection.

the mightiest Prelate of the empire, the Archbishop of Mentz. As John descended towards Constance he invested the Abbot of S. Ulric at Kreuzlingen with the mitre, the usual privilege of Bishops alone. Thus, even at the gates of Constance, he would secure a powerful friend.

Yet, despite of all these precautions, there were dismal moments of despondency. As he came down the steep Arlberg his sledge was overset; his attendants crowded round to know if he was hurt. "In the devil's name what do I lying here?" As he wound round the last declivity, and Constance lay below in her deep valley, washed by the lake, the Pope looked down and exclaimed, "A trap for foxes!"

<small>Oct. 26.</small>

Constance received the Pope with every sign of respect and spiritual loyalty. The magistrates and the clergy attended him through the streets, and to the venerable Minster. Nine Cardinals, about six hundred followers, formed the pompous retinue of his Holiness. The great Festival of All Saints had been named as peculiarly appropriate for the opening of the saintly Council; but from various causes, of the Prelates, except those of Italy, few had arrived. Though the Council was opened by the Pope in person on the 5th November, the first public session was adjourned to November 16. In the mean time certain preliminaries were arranged. Twelve auditors of the Rota were named to judge ecclesiastical causes. Congregations were held to regulate the order of the sittings and to appoint officers. At one of these congregations the Pope issued his inhibition to all members of the Council that no one might depart without permission. On the 2nd December six more Cardinals had arrived; these with the nine present formed a fair College. But on

<small>Oct. 28.</small>

the 3rd another arrival caused still greater excitement. There entered the city a pale thin man, in mean attire, yet escorted by three nobles of his country, with a great troop of other followers from attachment or curiosity; he came under a special safe-conduct from the Emperor, which guaranteed in the strictest and amplest terms his safe entrance and safe departure from the Imperial City. This was the famous heresiarch of Bohemia, John Huss. Nothing could be more opportune than his early arrival for the Papal policy.

John Huss.

The Council had been summoned for three principal objects. I. The union of the Church under one acknowledged Pope. II. The reformation of the Clergy in its head and in its members. III. The extirpation of erroneous and heretical doctrines. Other subordinate questions were to be submitted to the supreme tribunal of Christendom: the examination of Jean Petit's defence of the assassination of the Duke of Orleans, the proceedings of the Flagellants, and some less important matters. On the order in which the Council should proceed as to the three great leading topics depended the influence, the title, perhaps the fate of the Pope. The vital question of all, not deliberately proposed, but at the root of all the other questions—the superiority of the Council to the Pope, of the Pope to the Council—might be postponed; if postponed, eluded. This would be the case if the Council could be occupied by matter on which Pope and Council might agree, which might inflame the common passions, and direct their almost maddening zeal against one common foe, one common victim. Let, then, the suppression of heresy be the first paramount absorbing subject of debate. All precedent was in the Pope's favour; it had ever been the first act of Œcumenic Councils, from that of Nicæa, to guard the faith and to condemn heresy. So, too, the Council of Constance, commencing at this point, might be held a continuation, hardly more than a prorogation, of the Council of Pisa. And this to the Pope was life or death. For if the Council of Pisa was thus even tacitly recognised, his title among the three claimants to the Papacy, his absolute title, resting on the solemn decree of that Council, was irrefragable. Could he not, begirt with his Cardinals (their common interest might guarantee their fidelity), and with the overpowering suffrages of the Italian Prelates, centre the whole attention of the Council on this one subject? Could he not set the whole host in full cry on the track of this quarry? At least during this discussion he and his Italians would have been gaining a preponderating influence; he, for months, would have been permitted to guide and rule the Council. What if he should render the signal service of condemning, still better of inducing these dreaded heresiarchs to recant, could the ungrateful Church then cast him off? Then he would return to Italy the recognised Pope of the Council of Constance. If not, some time having been thus occupied, a thousand accidents, dissensions, plague, famine, the opportune death of some important personage, might dissipate the Council before they could enter on more dangerous ground.

Nor was this an unwarranted, ungrounded hope; the policy had every promise of success. The doctrines of Wycliffe, which Huss and his followers were accused of propagating in the villages and cities of Bohemia, even in the University of Prague, were generally odious. Those who knew least of them, looked on them with the terror of ignorance; those who knew them best saw that they struck at the root of the whole hierarchical system, in the common view the whole religion of Christ. The foremost Reformers, D'Ailly, Gerson, Zabarella, and the few Cardinals in that party, would behold perhaps with greater horror, as crossing their more moderate and sober designs, those innovators who laid their hands not on the corruptions of the Clergy only, but on their possessions, their rights, their immunities, their privileges, their spiritual powers, and even on the accredited orthodox doctrines of the faith. They, too, might be tempted to assert this suppression of heresy, which they dreaded with such profound dread, hated with such unmitigated hatred, to be the first, preliminary, inevitable duty of the great Council.

This insurrection, moreover, against the sublime autocracy of the Latin hierarchy; this appeal from the traditional Christianity of the West, the growth of ages, with all its mythology, legendary history, law, philosophy, ritual, venerable usages, and with all its vast system of rights and obligations and its tenure of property, to the primal and simpler Christianity of the Lord and his Apostles; this first attempt to substitute for an obedience to an outward law, and to an all-embracing discipline enforced by ecclesiastical penal statute, the religion of the inward conscience, self-dependent rather than dependent on the ghostly adviser: this assertion of the freedom of thought, limited only by the boundaries of the human faculties and the plain written word of God; this dawning moral and religious revolution, though it had begun in Teutonic England, and had been first embodied in the vernacular Anglo-Saxon of Wycliffe's Bible and Tracts, and in the poetry of Langland and of Chaucer, was not yet taken up by the Teutonic mind. It was propagated only under most

unfavourable auspices, in a remote corner of Christendom,
among a nation which spoke an unformed language, intelligible to themselves alone, and
not more akin to German than to Latin; a nation, as it
were, intruded into the Teutonic Empire, thought barbarian, and from late circumstances held in hostile
jealousy by the Teutonic commonwealth.

<small>Reformation not yet Teutonic.</small>

Bohemia was thus an insulated stranger among the
German principalities, a stranger with a right
of suffrage for the Imperial crown, but striving
to preserve her Sclavonic nationality against the Teutonic element which, from her connexion with the
Empire, was forcing itself into her territory, her usages,
and even pressing on her language. Bohemia, too,
laboured under the unpopularity of having given to
the Imperial throne a Sovereign, Charles IV., of whom
the German annals speak with bitter hatred and contempt, but who had been beloved, and deservedly
beloved, for his wise laws, admirable institutions, and
for his national policy in his native kingdom. His
father, John of Bohemia, that restless chivalrous adventurer who fell at Crecy, was a German in manners
and in heart; Charles a Bohemian who might seem to
sacrifice the ungrateful and intractable Empire to his
hereditary Kingdom. As King of Bohemia, Charles
was the creator of the realm; to him she owed equal
laws, sound institutions, magnificent cities, at least
Prague, which Charles adorned with splendid churches,
noble palaces, stately bridges, her famous University.*

<small>Bohemia.</small>

Charles IV. had at least not discouraged the first Reformers, who before the time of Huss protested in the

---

* Read the glowing description of the reign of Charles IV., in Palacky, Geschichte von Böhmen, II. p. 2, p. 328 et seqq.

strongest terms against the vices of the clergy, and the abuses of the Roman Court. The Prelate Conrad Stricknn, during his reign, had denounced the progress of these opinions. The Reformer, Milecz von Kremsar, was the King's Court Preacher.

The deposition of King Wenzel, the son of Charles, from the Empire by the Electors on the Rhine, was at once a sign and an aggravation of the jealousy of Teutonism against Bohemia. During the reign of Wenzel, a still more stirring teacher, Matthias von Zanow, had advanced the bolder axiom that it was gross superstition to reverence the edicts of the Pope on articles of faith, equally with the words of Christ and his Apostles. The Church, to resume her dignity, must be entirely renewed in the spirit of the Gospel.[f] The marriage of King Wenzel's sister, Anne of Bohemia, to Richard II. of England, had brought the two realms into close connexion, exactly at the time when the doctrines of Wycliffe were making their most rapid progress. The Queen herself, as has been said, was strongly impressed with the new doctrines. Bohemian scholars sat at the feet of the bold professor of theology at Oxford; English students were found at Prague. The writings of Wycliffe were brought in great numbers, some in Latin, some translated into Bohemian, and disseminated by admiring partisans.

John of Hussinetz, a Bohemian village, was a man of eloquence and an accomplished scholar, of severe morals, but gentle, friendly, accessible to all. He became Preacher in the University chapel called Bethlehem, and Confessor to the Queen Sophia. So long as his fervid sermons denounced the vices of

---

[f] Weissenburg, II. p. 121.

the world, the Clergy, the Monks and the Friars were among his most admiring hearers; but as he began to condemn the luxury, the pride, the licentiousness of the Clergy and the abuses of the Church, their admiration turned to animosity. He would have been persecuted, if he had not been protected by the Court; for such doctrines were not the less heard with favour by the Court because they were repulsive to the Clergy. The Schism in the Papacy had shaken the awe of the hierarchy to its base, and King Wenzel had strong grounds for personal hostility against that hierarchy. The Archbishop-Electors had been the leaders in the defection, the prime movers in his deposal from the Empire. The Pope, Boniface IX., had sanctioned their haughty proceedings. For many years, too, the sale of benefices had been so notorious by both Popes, that Wenzel in Bohemia, Sigismund in Hungary,[a] had not only prohibited the exportation of money to Rome, but had broken off all intercourse with the Papal Court.

Just at this time a scholar of John Huss[b] returned from his studies in Paris and Oxford: he brought many writings of Wycliffe. These writings not merely inveighed against the idleness and corruptions of the Clergy and of the Monks, but broke in at once on more perilous ground. Wycliffe had been already condemned by the Church as an heresiarch. Huss shrunk at first from the infection: he read the books with suspicion and dislike, so much so that he had nearly committed the godless volumes to the flames. He found, on more careful study, deeper and neglected truths. Still, however, much of Wycliffe's doctrine could not command

---

[a] Aschbach, Kaiser Sigmund, II. 24.
[b] He had the ill-sounding name of Faulfisch.

his assent, but much worked by slow degrees into his mind and into his teaching.

The Archbishop Sbinko of Prague had looked on Huss with favour; he could neither be ignorant of the change in the Preacher's views, nor of the cause of that change. He issued his sentence of condemnation; he threatened all who should promulgate the tenets of Wycliffe with the heretics' death, the stake. Huss was at first appalled; he was quiet for a time; but the Confessor of the Queen, and the idol of one-half the University of Prague, could not long hold his peace, for he was not the champion of Wycliffe's free opinions alone, now forcing themselves into a slow popularity, but of the Bohemian against the German students; and, extraordinary as it may seem, on a subject which stirred the hearts of the scholars to as great a depth, of the Realist against the Nominalist philosophy. This strife hurried on the conflicting parties to the inevitable schism. The deposition of their King Wenzel from the Empire had wounded the Bohemian pride: they held the Germans as strangers and aliens in their national University. The German Professors had taken part with the Archbishop in the implied censure of Huss. By a singular revolution, the Realistic philosophy, which had been the sworn ally of orthodoxy, the philosophy of Lanfranc and Anselm against Abélard, of Aquinas against Ockham, had changed sides. The great French divines, Gerson, D'Ailly (perhaps partly from their French perspicacity), the Germans in general, from the more exclusive study of the Aristotelian Scholasticism, had warped round to the more rationalistic Nominalism. The University of Prague was rent with feuds; students met students, not in the schools of disputation, but in the streets and on the bridges, and fought out the battles of Churchmen and

Wycliffites, of Germans and Bohemians, of Nominalists and Realists. At length the Bohemian faction, with Huss at their head, obtained from the King the abrogation of the privileges of the Germans in the votes for academic offices. The sullen Germans, and with them the Poles, abandoned the city. Of thirty thousand, a great part wandered to Leipsic, and founded a rival University. Huss became Rector of the University of Prague. His popularity triumphed even over the interests of the citizens, which suffered severely from the departure of the German students.

A.D. 1409.

Huss now preached boldly and without reserve the Wycliffite doctrines, at least as far as denunciations, not only against the corruptions, but against the wealth of the Clergy. The King heard with satisfaction the grateful maxim that the royal power was far above that of the hierarchy; the Archbishop and the Clergy were constrained to murmuring silence, while all Bohemia seemed falling off to these fearful opinions.

The Council of Pisa had uttered its sentence of deposition against Benedict XIII. and Gregory XII. The Archbishop of Prague adhered to Gregory; the King, Huss, and the Bohemians to the Council. Huss was emboldened to assail the Papal power itself. The King answered to the complaints of the Archbishop, "So long as Master Huss preached against us of the world, you rejoiced, and declared that the Spirit of God spoke in him. It is now your turn." But the accession of Alexander V., whom Bohemia, having acknowledged the Council of Pisa, could not refuse to accept, gave the Archbishop courage. He obtained a Bull from the Pope for the suppression of the Wycliffite doctrines. He threatened the refractory teachers. He collected no less than two hundred writings of the odious English

heresiarch, and committed them publicly to the flames;
but the King compelled him to pay the value of the
books to those from whom he had seized them by his
arbitrary ecclesiastical power. Huss continued to
preach. He appealed from the Pope to Christ himself,
the one final unerring Judge: "I, John Huss, offer this
appeal to Jesus Christ, my Master and my just Judge,
who knows, defends, and judges the just cause."[1]

The pious Alexander was succeeded by Balthasar
Cossa, John XXIII. Among the first acts of Pope John
was a citation to John Huss, the man of irreproachable
morals, to appear before the tribunal of a Pope charged
at least with every imaginable crime. The Bohemian
King and the nation would not permit Huss to cross
the Alps; they alleged fear of his German enemies;
a pompous embassy of three theologians appeared in
his stead. The Archbishop, from prudence or more
generous feeling, received from Huss a confession of
faith, with which he declared himself satisfied. He announced to the Roman Court that heresy no longer con-
taminated his diocese.

No answer came from Rome, but there came the
vendors of indulgences for the war of the Pope against
King Ladislaus of Naples. The vendors abstained from
none of those insolent exaggerations of the value of
their wares which were so obnoxious to sounder piety.
Huss broke out in a torrent of eloquent indignation. His
scholar, Jerome Faulfisch, burned the Bull of Indulgences under the gallows. The preachers of the Indulgences were exposed to insult, outrage, persecution.
The magistrates interfered; some rioters were seized
and executed; the people rose; the town-house was

---

[1] Opera, John Huss, I. 17. L'Enfant, Concile de Constance, I. p. 83.

stormed; the remains of the rioters taken up and venerated as reliques. News arrived that the ambassadors of Huss, of the University, and of the King, had been thrown into prison at Rome; that Huss was under the ban of excommunication, Prague under interdict. The timid King shrunk from the contest. Huss withdrew for a time from the city, but only by his eloquent preachings all over the country to influence now not Prague alone, but all Bohemia, with indignation against the abuses of the hierarchy. His writings, some in Latin, some in his native dialect, spread with rapidity. If in these he maintained some prudent or perhaps indeterminate ambiguity on the established doctrines, he struck boldly at all the bearings of those doctrines on Papal and on priestly authority.

John Huss then was no isolated teacher, no follower of a condemned English heretic: he was more even than head of a sect; he almost represented a kingdom, no doubt much more than half of Bohemia. King Wenzel and his Queen were on his side, at least as against the Clergy.

The Emperor Sigismund aspired to restore peace to the Church. The Council of Constance had been summoned to reform the Church in its head and in its members; its proclaimed object was the extirpation of all abuses throughout Christendom. It was not for Huss to stand aloof in fear or suspicion. He had appealed to a Council. If his opinions were just and true, he could not shrink from bringing their justice and truth before a Council which comprehended not the high dignitaries alone, but also the most consummate theologians of Christendom. As yet, however some of his opinions might seem to lean to speculative Wycliffitism, he was, like others of great name, avowedly no more

Why Huss appeared at Constance.

than an ardent reformer of abuses. He obtained from the University of Prague, from the Estates of Bohemia, from Conrad Archbishop of Prague, and even from Nicolas Bishop of Nazareth, the Grand Inquisitor, testimonials to his orthodoxy and irreproachable life. Yet he was not, he could not be, without dark misgivings. He left a letter only to be opened in case of his death at Constance: it contained his last will and his confession.[k] His valedictory address to his followers enjoined them to maintain their faith, to pray earnestly for his safe return. "He expected to meet as many enemies at Constance as our Lord at Jerusalem—the wicked Clergy, and even some secular Princes, and those Pharisees the Monks."

The fame of Huss travelled before him: curiosity or interest in his doctrines triumphed over the German aversion to the Bohemian. In many towns he held conferences even with the clergy, and parted from them on amicable terms. At Nuremburg he was met by three Bohemian nobles, who bore from Spires the Imperial safe-conduct, couched in the strictest and fullest terms, guaranteeing his safe entrance and his safe return from Constance.[m] John of Chlum, Wenzel of Duba, Henry of Lazenbach, were charged to watch and keep guard over their countryman, who travelled under the special protection of the Emperor.

Huss sets out for Constance. Oct. 21.

Not many days after the arrival of the Pope, John Huss, as has been said, entered Constance. He was graciously received by the Pope himself. Nothing was

---

[k] Among the sins that burthened his conscience was playing at chess and losing his temper when beaten.

[m] The safe-conduct may be seen in many publications, L'Enfant, Von der Hardt; the latest and perhaps most accurate version in Aschbach, Kaiser Sigmund, ii. 29.

said of the ban of excommunication which still hung over him: it is doubtful whether it was not legally annulled by his reception before the Pope. Strong expressions are attributed to the Pope: "If he had slain my brother, I would not permit, as far as is in my power, any harm to be done to him in Constance."* The Pope, on whom religion hung so loosely, may not have had that deep aversion for, he may not fully have comprehended, the bearing of the Wycliffite tenets; still less could he comprehend the stern, stubborn conscientiousness which would not swerve from, and which would boldly assert such opinions in the face of danger or death. Noble religious fanaticism has constantly baffled the reckoning of the most profound worldly sagacity. He might fondly suppose the possibility of the Bohemian's submission to Papal arguments, impressed by Papal majesty; and the submission of so famous a heretic to his milder admonitions would give him overweening weight in the Council. But with the more keen-eyed and inflexible Italian Cardinals, Huss was only a barbarian and a heretic. They could not but discern (for they had nothing to blind their instinct) the vital oppugnancy of his views to the hierarchical system. Huss himself could not remain in modest and inoffensive privacy. Partisans, admirers, would crowd around him; his zeal would not permit him in base timidity to shrink from the avowal of his creed, whether by preaching in his house or among his followers. The Bishop of Constance admonished him, but in vain, and forbade his celebrating Mass while yet unabsolved.

---

* "Etiamsi Johannes Hus fratrem sibi germanum occidisset, se tamen nullo modo commissurum, quantum in ipso sitem est, ut aliqua ei fiat injuria, quamdiu Constantiæ esset."— Von der Hardt, iv. p. 11.

The arrival of Stephen Palecz and Michael de Causis, the bitter and implacable adversaries of Huss, with whom he had been involved in fierce controversy, changed the suspended state of affairs. These men stood forward openly as his accusers: they swept away all the fairer, milder, or more subtile interpretations by which Huss reconciled his own doctrines with the orthodox creed, especially as regarded the clergy. Huss had declared wicked Popes, wicked Cardinals, wicked Prelates, to be utterly without authority, their excommunications void, their administration of the Sacraments as only to be valid by some nice distinction. Palecz and De Causis cast all these maxims in their naked, unmitigated offensiveness before the indignant hierarchy. Huss was summoned, yet by a deputation which still showed respect, the Bishops of Augsburg and Trent, to appear before the Consistory of the Pope and Cardinals. He obeyed, protesting, nevertheless, that he came to render account to the Council, not to the Consistory. The charges of heresy were read. Huss quietly declared that he had rather die than be justly condemned as a heretic. "If convinced of error, he would make full recantation." He retired, but his lodging was encircled from that time by watchful sentinels.[*] A monk was let loose upon him, to ensnare him with dangerous questions. Huss had the shrewdness to detect in the monk, who affected the utmost simplicity, one of the subtlest theologians of the day.

Four weeks after his arrival at Constance, notwith-

---

[*] Aschbach (p. 30) here inserts the attempt of Huss at flight, which the two authors (perhaps they are but one authority), Reichenthal and the author in D'Achery, assign to a much later period. To my judgement, Aschbach's view is utterly improbable; and on such points Reichenthal, who does not care much for religious questions, is worthy of full confidence.

standing his appeal to the Imperial safe-conduct, notwithstanding the protest of his noble Bohemian protector, John de Chlum, Huss was committed to prison in the Bishop's palace. To De Chlum the Pope protested that it was done without his authority. The Pope might find it expedient to disclaim such an act. A congregation was summoned to hear eight articles promoted by the Bohemian, Michael de Causis, against John Huss. Three Commissioners had been named by the Pope. A more numerous Commission of Cardinals, Bishops, and Doctors was appointed to conduct the inquiry. From his first prison he was conducted to a closer and more safe one in the Dominican Convent.[p] There he fell ill, and was attended by the Pope's physicians. He recovered, and in his prison wrote several works, which were eagerly dispersed among his brethren.

John de Chlum took bold and active measures for the release of Huss. He communicated this insolent violation of the Imperial safe-conduct to Sigismund, who was on his way from his coronation at Aix-la-Chapelle. The Emperor broke into wrath: he gave orders, that if the Pope and Cardinals did not obey his mandate, the doors of the prison should be opened by force. But no one ventured to invade the Dominican cloister, and the Council yet respected the ordinances of the Pope and Cardinals. De Chlum affixed writings on all the church-doors in Constance, declaring, in strong language, the imprisonment of Huss to be an outrage against the Emperor; that all who had presumed to violate the Imperial safe-conduct, and still presumed to resist the demands of the Imperial Ambassador for his release, would be called to account.

[p] L'Enfant, I. p. 64.

So far, even up to the arrival of the Emperor, Pope John had maintained uncontested supremacy in the Council. His Bull had been read at the first Session, as the authority for its proceedings. Zabarella, the all-honoured Cardinal of Florence, in his opening speech, assumed throughout the presidency of the Pope. The Pope named all the officers, and distributed the functions which were submitted to and accepted by the Council. One incident alone threatened his sole dignity. The Archbishop of Ragusa, and other legates of Gregory XII., had made their entrance. On the same night the Archbishop affixed over the gates of his lodging the Papal arms of Gregory XII, with the keys and the triple crown. John resisted this daring invasion in the name of a Pope deposed by the Council of Pisa. The Council, after some stormy debate, pronounced in favour of the Pope, thus again recognising the acts of the Council at Pisa. The obnoxious arms disappeared.

On Christmas Eve tidings arrived that Sigismund, now having received the Imperial crown at Aix-la-Chapelle, had reached Oberlingen, on the northern shore of the lake. Before morning-dawn he entered Constance. Among his first acts was attendance at the Mass. The Emperor, according to usage, in the dalmatic of a deacon, read the Gospel—the Gospel which sounded ominous in the ears of the Pope: "There went out a decree from Cæsar Augustus." The sermon preached three days after by Peter d'Ailly, Cardinal of Cambray, must at times have sent a cold shudder of dismay to the heart of John. The text was, "There shall be signs in the Sun, and in the Moon, and in the Stars:" a text literally applicable to the last advent of Christ, spiritually to his advent in an Œcumenic Council. The Sun was the spiritual power, the Pope ; the Moon the temporal, the Emperor; the Stars, the Cardinals, Prelates, and Doctors in the firmament of the Council. But the Sun, for the plenitude of his power, must fulfil certain conditions. If the supreme Pastor shall have risen by bad means, by unjust and reprobate ambition; if he shall have led a scandalous and dishonest life; if he shall have ruled negligently or tyrannically, he is but the phantom of a sun. "Oh! that the Omnipotent Trinity would dash down these three statues in the Sun's house, the Church of Rome. .... The Holy Trinity of the Divine Persons is not more adorable than a trinity of Popes abominable." But the lofty churchman kept the Moon, the temporal power, in its due subordination. To the Emperor himself he uttered no words but those of high honour; "yet the Imperial power must not think to preside in the Council, but to execute her decrees." The Council, he distinctly avers, derived its legitimate authority from being summoned by the Pope; but once met, its power was above the Pope. St. James, in the first Great Council in the Acts, did not publish its decrees in the name of St. Peter, but in that of the Council. "It seemed good to the Holy Ghost and to us."[q]

There was no outward disturbance in the seeming amity between the Emperor and the Pope; they appeared together in public; all was mutual deference and respect. The Pope knew the necessities of the Emperor. The great weakness of the Empire was the utter inadequacy of the Imperial revenues to the dignity of the station. The more magnificent or ambitious the Emperor, the more difficult, often degrading,

[q] "Ubi non ait, placuit Petro, sed placuit nobis collectis in unum; et sequitur, 'Visum est Spiritui Sancto et nobis.'"—Read the sermon, in Von der Hardt, l. 438, 450.

CHAP. VIII.   THE COUNCIL.   249

was the struggle with his narrow finances. Sigismund aspired to be amongst the most splendid of sovereigns; his enemies scoffed at the mean artifices to which he was reduced to maintain that splendour. The Pope made a skilful attempt to avail himself of his weakness; he offered him a grant, or donative, or subsidy of 200,000 florins. But Sigismund was too deeply pledged, too resolutely determined; he had set his fame on the union and reform of the Church. He could not but refuse the tempting lure.[r] From the lordly prelates of Germany he might easily raise such a sum.

The Council at first had been hardly more than an assemblage of Italian Cardinals and Prelates; it had filled gradually, but rapidly, from all parts of Europe. The first to appear before the arrival of the Emperor had been the Cardinal of Cambray, Peter d'Ailly, accompanied by many French prelates; others came soon after. The Cardinal of Cambray took the lead of all the Transalpine prelates, as Zabarella, Cardinal of Florence, of the Italian. All the rest did homage to their superior learning, abilities, and virtues. It was not till three months afterwards that the more learned and not less pious Chancellor Gerson appeared at the head of the deputies from the University of Paris. The French prelates and divines formed, in modern phrase, the constitutional party: they adhered with the severest orthodoxy to the Catholic doctrines; they admitted the supremacy of the Pope, but not an absolute autocracy.

---

[r] Sigismund came "mit Warnung, er soll, von Johann die 200,000 Gulden ja nicht nehmen: diese Summa könne man von den reichen Bischofen Teutschlands leicht bekommen."— J. Müller, Geschichte von Schweitz, aus Handschriften der Bibliothek von Wien. John de Monterolls, a bitter enemy of Sigismund, ascribes his hostility to John to the Pope's refusal of this sum. John was not likely to refuse it.—Apud Martene et Durand, t. II. p. 1444.

That supremacy was limited, not only by the College of Cardinals, but by the universal voice of the Church. A General Council was above the Pope. Beyond this the Church of France stood on some of her peculiar rights and privileges, which the Pope could not infringe or abrogate. There was a law and prerogative superior to the Pope. The Gallican Church is already asserting her liberties; her antagonism is hardly yet on distinct or defined grounds, but still it is antagonism. And all this bold assertion of superiority or independence was while a lunatic was on the throne of France; while Henry of England was in the heart of the land, one year before the battle of Agincourt.

The English, at least Robert Hallam, Bishop of Salisbury, the representative of their Church and of the insular character, were likewise as yet rigidly attached to the old traditional faith. With him the Teutonic independence of thought had not advanced farther than the strong impatience, which had long brooded in England, of the Papal tyranny, and its encroachment on the power of the State and of the nation. Throughout Hallam was the right hand of the Emperor, as asserting the civil supremacy. He alone took a high moral tone: to him a wicked Pope was but a wicked man. There was an unconscious Wycliffism in the Bishop, who would perhaps hardly have hesitated to have burned Wycliffe himself.

The powerful hierarchy of Germany did not hold its proper rank in the Council of Constance. Of the three great electoral prelacies, Cologne was vacant and contested. Treves was still in the obedience of Gregory XII.* Mentz appeared, but

---

* Cologne and Treves were, it seems, present by deputy.

Archbishop John of Nassau was more fitted to shine in a camp than in a Council. He entered Constance at the head of a splendid and numerous retinue, in military attire, with helmet, cuirass, and boots of iron. His jealousy of the Emperor attached him recklessly to the cause of Pope John. The more remote kingdoms, Prussia, Poland, Hungary, sent their Archbishops, Posen, Riga, Gnesen, Colocz, and Canitz. There were two Danish Bishops, Kypen and Schleswig.

The total number of Clergy, not perhaps all present at one time,[1] was four Patriarchs, Constantinople, Grado, Antioch, Aquileia; twenty-nine Cardinals, Italians by birth, excepting five Frenchmen, chiefly of the creation of Benedict XIII., and one Portuguese; thirty-three Archbishops; about one hundred and fifty Bishops,[2] including thirty-two titulars; one hundred and thirty-four Abbots; two hundred and fifty Doctors; one hundred and twenty-five Provosts, and other superiors. With their whole attendance the Clergy amounted to eighteen thousand.

If the German hierarchy were less fully or rather less effectively represented, Germany alone sent her Princes to this Diet-Council, the Prince Palatine, Louis of Heidelberg, the Dukes Louis and Henry of Bavaria. The Palatine headed the embassy of France. The Burgraves John and Frederick of Nuremburg, the latter Margrave of Brandenburg; Rodolf, Elector of Saxony, the Margrave of Baden.

All the great Free Cities sent their deputies. Over their doors the arms of their cities were ostentatiously displayed, as taking rank among sovereigns.[3]

---

[1] The numbers vary, perhaps on that account.
[2] The English Bishops were Bath, Hereford, Salisbury, Bangor; later, Winchester, London, Lichfield, Norwich.
[3] See Reichenthal (Augsburg, 1483)

Ordinarily 50,000, at certain periods at least 100,000 persons and 30,000 horses were kept in ease and plenty; 30,000 beds were provided by the city. Four Imperial Commissioners regulated the price of provisions, which throughout were abundant, and at moderate cost. The police regulations were excellent; the garrison was but of 2000 men; to the last, as at first, no disturbance, no riot took place during the Council. This is the universal testimony.

---

reprinted in latter collections, a kind of King-at-Arms. He has left a chronicle of what may be called the State proceedings. See on Reichenthal, L'Enfant, Preface, p. xxxii.

CHAPTER IX.

Council of Constance. John XXIII. John Huss.

POPE JOHN opened the year with a magnificent religious ceremony; he appeared amid the assembled myriads in the most solemn function of the Church as the acknowledged head of Christendom, almost for the last time! The sermon of the Cardinal of Cambray had not been the only sign of the danger that was looming over him. In the first General Congregation the Emperor had solemnly sworn to take the Pope under his sovereign protection.[a] So far the Pope and the Cardinals had heard with satisfaction; but he also avowed his expectation that the Legates of the two rival Pontiffs would be admitted to the Council. This was to sever the link which bound the Council of Constance to the Council of Pisa; it disclaimed the authority of Pisa, if it recognised as Popes those who had been there deposed. A Parisian divine, Matthew Roder, had delivered a sermon in which he suggested the election of a new Pontiff.[b]

A.D. 1415.

Threatening signs against Pope John, Dec. 29.

But that act of the Emperor, which might seem least connected with the fate of Pope John, was in fact, no doubt to his own sagacity, at once the direst omen and the immediate cause of his fall. The Emperor consented to violate his own safe-conduct, to abandon John Huss. The Bohemian was, with the

The Emperor abandons John Huss.

---

[a] Von der Hardt, iv. p. 31.   [b] L'Enfant, L p. 79.

consent of Sigismund, committed to closer custody. It was understood that he was to be tried by the Council, doomed by the Council, and that whatever might be the sentence of the Council, it would be carried into execution by the secular arm. The Council was thus relieved from all further debate on that question: it was out of the way of their ulterior proceedings; the rock on which they might have split was avoided; their onward course was straight, clear, open.

Breach of faith admits no excuse; perfidy is twice perfidious in an Emperor. Yet it is but justice to Sigismund fairly to state the inextricable difficulty of his position. He had to choose between the violation of faith to one whom he himself no doubt esteemed a dangerous and turbulent heretic, and, it might be, the dissolution of the Council. With the Council he abandoned all the hopes on which he had rested his fame, his influence, his authority, the restoration of peace to the Church, the reformation of the Church. Huss was already arraigned as a heretic; the Pope, the Cardinals, the Council, had committed themselves to that arraignment. According to the view of almost the whole hierarchy, and the prelates of every nation, the suppression of heresy was their first imperious duty: it was the deepest and most passionate vow of every high-churchman; and which of them on such a point was not a high-churchman? Arguments were ready, which, on the principles dominant and long admitted in those days, it was not easy to parry or confute. The Emperor had no right to protect heretics, over whom throughout the world, and in every part of it, the hierarchy, especially such a council of the hierarchy, had indefeasible cognisance, could proceed, and were bound to proceed, according to the canons of the Church. And the fatal doctrine, confirmed by long usage, by the decrees of Pontiffs, by the assent of all ecclesiastics, and the acquiescence of the Christian world, that no promise, no oath, was binding to a heretic, had hardly been questioned, never repudiated.

Had Sigismund with a high hand released the prisoner; had he in the slightest degree infringed on the recognised province of the hierarchy, their sole adjudication in causes of heresy, Pope John might either have lengthened out an interminable discussion, or, if he had broken up the Council, or left it himself, he would have carried with him probably all the Italian Cardinals, and thrown an irreconcileable schism among the rest of the prelates. He would have become the champion of a great cause, a cause popular with the whole hierarchy, and with all under the immediate influence of the hierarchy.

Sigismund yielded, perhaps not without self-reproach, certainly not without remonstrance which must have galled a man of his high feeling to the quick. The Bohemian lords, the Burgrave of Prague and others, had already written a strong demand, which arrived about this time, for the liberty of John Huss. He had been proclaimed, as they averred, by Conrad Archbishop of Prague, under his seal, guiltless of the slightest word of heresy. A second still more vigorous protest had followed, on his removal from the Dominican Convent, against this flagrant violation of public faith. "They would deeply grieve if they should hear that his august Majesty was polluted by such an enormous iniquity. Every one hereafter would spurn and despise an Imperial s.fe-conduct." *

---

* Von der Hardt, iv. p. 33.

The sacrifice of Huss (and now that perfidious sacrifice was resolved) established perfect harmony between the Emperor and the whole reforming part of the Council. Notwithstanding all the remonstrances of the Pope and his partisans, it was immediately determined to receive the ambassadors of the Antipopes, if armed with full powers, and to admit them with full recognition of their dignity into the Council. Those of Benedict presented themselves first, but not being provided with full powers, they were contemptuously rejected by the Emperor.⁴ Their proposal, however, that Benedict XIII. and the King of Arragon should hold a conference with the Emperor at Nice, was not absolutely discarded. A few days after presented themselves the Archbishop of Ragusa and the other Legates of Gregory XII. They had been preceded by Louis Count Palatine, the delegates of the Archbishop of Treves, and the Bishops of Worms, Spires, and Verden, who still adhered to his obedience. The ambassadors, under this powerful support, were received with courteous honour; they declared their master, Gregory XII., prepared at once to resign the Papacy on condition that Benedict and John did the same; that no one of the three should preside in the Council.*

John's cession demanded. The demand for the cession of John, which had been at first a low and timid murmur, became the general clamour. Notwithstanding intrigues, bribes, promises, menaces, his partisans fell off daily.⁶ Some appealed to his higher feelings; some uttered more or less disguised threats. The ambassador of Poland, Andrew Lascaris, Archbishop elect of Posen,

---

⁴ " Da ward der König zornig, und sprach zu ihnen, den Boten des Peter Luna, nesclo vos."—Justinger, Bern. Chronik, 291, cited by Aschbach. p. 46.
* Aschbach, p. 47.
ᶠ Von der Hardt, ii. 478, 479.

urged his free abdication as a generous sacrifice for the peace of the Church. The Cardinal of St. Mark, in a writing communicated to the Council, the Emperor, and the Pope, urged upon John XXIII., that the stronger his grounds to be recognised as lawful Pope, the greater was his obligation to make this noble oblation for the good of the Church.[f] He more than hinted the power of the Council to enforce abdication.[h] John's Italian Cardinals raised a loud cry, that it was almost, if not absolute, heresy to put the Pope on the same footing with those deposed at Pisa.[i] The Cardinal d'Ailly at length summed up the whole in the fatal sentence, "The Universal Church, represented by a General Council, has full power to depose even a lawful Pontiff of blameless character, if it be necessary for the welfare of the Church."[k]

But these two Cardinals, Cambray and St. Mark, were preparing a measure still more disastrous to the Pope. The right of suffrage in an Œcumenic Council was by no means fixed and certain. In most of the later Councils the aristocratic principle had prevailed. No one below the Bishop or the Abbot had presumed to the right of voting on such high and mysterious matters. The Council of Pisa had admitted the right of professors and doctors of theology. The Pope, who knew his own strength, in the first session of the Council of Constance had rejected this claim. The Cardinal d'Ailly, in a memorial to the Council, not only asserted the right of these learned men to free suffrage, but demanded it for princes and ambassadors in all matters not directly concerning the faith. The Cardinal of St. Mark went still

---

[f] Von der Hardt, II. 178 et seqq.
[g] Ibid. ii. 209.
[i] Ibid. II. 213.
[k] L'Enfant, I. p. 105.

further; he asserted the right of the lower clergy.
"Was the Council not to profit by the profound learning of doctors in civil or canon law, and the wisest of the clergy?" "An ignorant prince or prelate," he said in coarse phrase, "is but a crowned ass. Is one entrusted with the cure of souls in a large parish less able to judge than the abbot who rules a few monks?"

The first proposition wrested the superiority in the Council from the hands of the Pope. The Italian Bishops were numerous and poor. Fear, interest, nationality, contempt of Transalpine barbarians, bound them to the service of the Pope. But this was not the worst or most menacing proposal. Already, according to the usage of most Universities, the Congregations, which prepared the business for the general Sessions of the Council, had met in Nations. The prelates, doctors, and ambassadors of the four great powers assembled each in a separate chamber, with a President changing every month, a secretary, notaries, and other officers. The Nations were; I. The Italians; II. The Germans, comprehending the Poles, Hungarians, Danes, and Scandinavians; III. The French; IV. The English. At a later period the Spaniards, who had not yet joined the Council, formed a fifth Nation. It was proposed to vote by Nations; and this decree, which reduced the Italians to a single suffrage, notwithstanding the Pope's remonstrance, passed with irresistible acclamation.

Feb. 7.

Pope John was in the toils; his most obstinate struggles only drew around him more closely the galling meshes. The subtle Italians found themselves circumvented by the steady aggression of the Tramontanes. Now came a more tremendous blow. A memoir was secretly presented to the Council, it was

Charges against the Pope.

presumed by an Italian, with a full and darkly-coloured statement of the detestable wickedness, the vices and crimes of the Pope's whole life.! The more noble-minded of the Germans and the Poles recoiled from the scandalous exposure. They refused the public inquisition into these articles, as degrading to the Roman See, as throwing a fatal slur on all the Prelates and dignitaries promoted by the Pope. They generously insisted on its suppression. But these sinister tidings did not escape the Pope, who had his secret intelligence of the most trivial proceedings in the Council. He was struck with utter consternation.⁕ He summoned the Cardinals: he denied much, but he admitted some of the charges. He heaped upon them gifts and promises: he proposed desperately to confront the Council; to make ample confession and to stand on the great principle, that a Pope could not be deposed but for heresy. The Cardinals coldly advised him not to be precipitate, but to take some days to mature his determination.

His adversaries pursued their advantage. While the Pope was quailing under this peril, deputies appeared before him to persuade him to the cession of the Papacy. To their surprise and joy, the Pope consented; he drew up himself a form which was submitted to the Nations. But every word of the

The Pope determines to abdicate. Feb. 14.

---

[1] "Quidam, ut præsumitur, Italicus, multos articulos valde famosos, et omnia parenta mortalia, nec non impacta quodammodo abominabilia continentes, contra eundem Balthasarem, in eodem Concilio exhibuit in scriptis tamen secreto, quod super illis contra eundem Balthasarem fieret Inquisitio, et provideretur instanter per Concilium memoratum."—A Niem, p. 25.

⁕ "Quibus etiam interim clanculo et proditorie ad notitiam dicti Balthasaris deductis, illico mente consternatus est, et cœpit valde tremere et timere ac etiam quosdam sibi secreto Cardinales, et de quibus fiduciam habuit donis ac promissis allicere et consulere quid esset in eâ parte pro ejus honoris conservatione facturus, asserens, quod quædam in ipsis articulis descripta, tanquam homo, peccando commisisset, et aliqua non."—Ibid.

Papal form was scrutinised with the most suspicious jealousy. It was thought vague and ambiguous; doubtful pretensions, doubtful meanings lurked under its artful phrases. There was a long discussion. The Pope presented a second form; it was rejected. A third, proposed by the Emperor, was repudiated by the Pope. At that instant arrived the Delegates from the University of Paris, with the famous Gerson at their head. All did homage to the high authority of this learned body, and their world-renowned Chancellor. A new form was prepared, it was supposed under the direction of Gerson, and presented by the Emperor with more peremptory demand of acceptance. The Pope stifled his grief, tried every subterfuge, raised every subtle objection; but the three Nations, the Germans, the French, and the English, held resolutely together; the Italians supported him with but feeble fidelity. The one alteration admitted only made the words more stringent, severe, not to be eluded. In his despair he assumed a kind of sullen magnanimity. A general Congregation was summoned: the Emperor and the Deputies of all the Nations were present. The form was offered to the Pope by the Patriarch of Antioch. He read it to himself, and seemed to ponder over it. None of the bitterness of his heart betrayed itself in his countenance. With a calm clear voice he read publicly the irrevocable words: "I, Pope John XXIII., for the repose of the whole Christian people, profess, engage, promise, swear, and vow to God, the Church, and this holy Council, willingly and freely to give peace to the Church, by the way of my simple cession of the Papacy; to do and to fulfil this effectually, according to the determination of this present Council, when and so soon as Peter di Luna and Angelo Corario, called in their respective obediences Benedict XIII. and Gregory XII., shall in like manner cede the Papacy, to which they pretend, by themselves or by their lawful Proctors: and even in any case of vacancy by decease or otherwise, in which by my cession unity can be restored to the Church of God through the extirpation of the present Schism."

Ere he closed, the whole Assembly broke out into a paroxysm of rapture. The Emperor, the Cardinals, the Deputies of the Nations and of the University of Paris crowded round the throne, all rendering thanks. Te Deum was sung; the chant was interrupted by tears of joy; more wept than sang.[a]

The next day was the second public Session. The Pope himself celebrated Mass. At its close he took his seat before the altar, with his face to the Council, and read the same form handed to him by the Patriarch of Antioch. At the words, "I swear and vow," he knelt before the altar, clasped his hands together, and uttered the words "Thus I promise," with profound solemnity. He returned to his chair, and concluded the service. The Emperor advanced, took off his crown, threw himself at the feet of the Pope, and kissed them, expressing his fervent gratitude. So did the Patriarch of Antioch in the name of the Council.

March 2.

Two days had hardly passed, when dark mutual suspicions began to transpire. Each party had ulterior views. Pope John had manifestly the hope that by his frank and full confession he might propitiate the Council; perhaps be able to throw on his competitors the odium of refusing these equal terms; or he might delude

---

[a] Von der Hardt and L'Enfant throughout.

himself with fonder expectations. The Council felt that he was at their mercy, and were disposed to clench rather than relax their iron grasp. They had determined to press the conditional into an absolute abdication. This dire reality broke gradually but rapidly upon the Pope. First they demanded a Bull, declaring his abdication according to the customary form. The Pope treated this proposition as an insult, and haughtily repelled the Prelates from his presence: they dared not venture again on this perilous subject. But to the Emperor he was less intractable. Sigismund extorted from him a Bull, still, indeed, guarded in its language.

March 4. John renewed his sacred promise; but his abdication yet depended on the simultaneous abdication of his rivals. The next demand was more insidious, more imperious, more embarrassing. Of the two rival Popes, most respect was paid to Benedict XIII. He had still a King, the King of Arragon, for his partisan. It had been proposed that the Emperor and the King of Arragon, accompanied by Benedict, should meet at Nice. John was required to invest ambassadors with full powers to execute his abdication at the same instant with that of Benedict. Of these ambassadors the Emperor was to be one. With such irrevocable powers Pope John would have delivered himself bound hand and foot into the hands of Sigismund.

This proposal was made in a full Congregation by the Germans, French, and English, it was indignantly rejected by the Pope, supported by the Italian Prelates. The Italians threatened to leave the Council if such rigorous demands were urged further.

March 8.

Yet there was still the most bland and respectful outward amity. The next day the Pope presented to the Emperor the Golden Rose. That mysterious gift, according to Pope Innocent III,* represented by its gold, its odour and its balm, the Godhead, the Body and Soul of the Redeemer. It was only bestowed by Popes on Sovereigns the most loyal servants of the Church. The Emperor received it with words of the most devout gratefulness. They dined together. The Emperor offered the consecrated Rose in the Church of the Virgin Mary.

The very next day, whether there was a deep latent hypocrisy under this seeming amity; whether the Emperor had discovered treachery in the Pope, and that he already meditated flight; or that he thought it no longer worth while to dissemble his uncompromising hostility, the proposal was openly made to elect a new Pope. This proposal in itself proclaimed John XXIII. no longer Pope; it assumed the power in the Council of deposing him, and of proceeding to another choice. Among the vague, fond hopes of John had been that he himself might be re-elected to the Pontificate. Such had been the design of his more steadfast partisans. The warlike Archbishop of Mentz declared that he would never render allegiance but to John. Words ran high; the suppressed charges against the abominable life of the Pope were revived in their unmitigated blackness. Robert Hallam, Bishop of Salisbury, at the head of the English, had already espoused the Emperor's cause, and had urged unswervingly the searching reformation of all orders in the Church. The honest islander broke out in righteous indignation, "that the Pope deserved to be burned at the stake."

March 18.

Proposal for a new Pope.

---

* Innocent III., Prædicatio, see Hurter. Compare also Durand, Rationale, vi. 121.

All confidence was now at an end. It was notorious that Pope John meditated escape: and should he escape would boldly appeal to Christendom against the decrees of a headless Council. The Council was determined that he should not leave the city. An attempt was made by the Cardinal St. Angelo to pass the gates; he was rudely arrested by the burgher guard. The Pope loudly complained of the violation of the Imperial safe-conduct, that safe-conduct which in the case of John Huss he had trampled under foot. The Magistrates of Constance threw the blame on the orders of the Emperor. Frederick of Austria alone declared that he at least would respect the person and liberty of the Pope.[p]

Another Congregation of the Nations was held; the Italians stood aloof. It was resolved to urge the Pope at once to appoint plenipotentiaries to execute his abdication, and that the Emperor should be one of these plenipotentiaries. They further required the Pope to give security that he would neither leave the Council, nor adjourn it to any other place. The Emperor excused the rigid watch, now avowedly maintained at the gates of the city, by declaring that it was on account of the notorious design of many Cardinals clandestinely to leave Constance. It was his duty to prevent this unauthorised dissolution of the Council.

March 15.

The Pope yielded to this last demand, the promise not to dissolve or adjourn the Council till the end of the Schism, and to do everything he could to promote the restoration of unity. This was a promise which, were it in his power, he could without difficulty violate or elude. But the immediate fatal step of authorising

---

[p] Cerretanus, apud Von der Hardt, iv. 55.

others to execute his abdication, he refused with stubborn obstinacy. "He had no proof that Angelo Corario had resigned; he had only heard that Peter di Luna would resign."

The gloom which was gathering round John was broken by a faint but transient gleam of hope. The French Cardinals began to relent, to murmur at his harsh usage. The Italians seized the opportunity, and endeavoured to detach them from the hostile league. They began to revive the question of voting by voices, not by Nations. The Germans and the English adhered to each other in resolute hostility to the Pope. In the French, the hatred and jealousy of the English, fostered by their long, cruel, and humiliating wars, struggled with their zeal for the unity and for the reform of the Church. The Cardinals, as Italian Prelates, sat with the Italian nation. The Five, the Cardinal of Cambray at their head, were deputed to persuade the French nation to milder measures. The Germans and English held only the more closely together, and were more inflexibly resolved by this opposition. The Bishop of Salisbury boldly proposed that if the Pope refused to appoint his Procurators, he should be put under arrest. The Emperor and his supporters of the other two nations presented themselves in the French Congregation, and laid before them the result of their deliberations. The French insisted that they should withdraw. Sigismund broke out in a wrathful menace: "Now will be shown who are for the unity of the Church and for the Empire." The Cardinal of Cambray indignantly retired: the other four Cardinals protested against the violation of the liberty of debate. The Emperor answered that the word had escaped him in passion, that the

Quarrel in the Council.

March 19.

French had perfect liberty, but the Cardinals were Italians, not French; if they withdrew not to their own chamber, he threatened them with imprisonment.

The quarrel, the Pope's last desperate hope, was appeased by the skilful influence of the ambassadors of France, especially by Duke Louis of Bavaria.

Late the following evening, after vespers, Sigismund visited the Pope; he found him reclining on his bed, somewhat indisposed. John complained of the oppressive air of Constance, he required change.[a] The Emperor earnestly dissuaded him from leaving Constance before the close of the Council, above all not clandestinely. "This would be to his eternal dishonour." He declared himself prepared to maintain his safe-conduct inviolable, but he had not power to permit him to depart from the city. The Pope answered in ambiguous phrase, that he would not quit Constance till the dissolution of the Council.[r] Many other rumours spread abroad of what took place at this memorable interview. The Emperor had demanded, or the Pope had offered, large sums for his liberty, under pretence of the great expense of maintaining the Council. The Pope, by one account, refused to buy the Emperor or to sell the Council. The Bishop of Salisbury, said to have been present, asserted to the face of the Pope the superiority of the Council over the Pope. The Pope kept no reserve. As soon as the Emperor had departed, to his attendants he taunted Sigismund as a drunkard, a fool, a madman, and a beggar.[s]

Interview of the Emperor and the Pope. March 19.

All this time the plot for his escape had been laid

---

[a] Theodoric à Niem here breaks out into praise of the salubrity of Constance.

[r] "Credens forte, quod eo recordente, abbine illud dissolveretur omnino."—A Niem, 27.

[s] A Niem, ibid.

and fully matured. Frederick, Duke of Austria, had been a month in Constance, a month of humiliation and aggravation of his hatred towards the Emperor. He had been compelled to do homage for all his fiefs. He had attempted to delude the Emperor into favouring a breach of the peace which he had sworn to the Swiss Cantons. The Emperor, more crafty than himself, had betrayed him to the Swiss. Delegates from the cantons and cities had exposed the Duke's perfidy before the Emperor. That Frederick of Austria was in secret communication with the Pope, all suspected. The Emperor admonished the Duke concerning the peril of these intrigues. Frederick solemnly protested his innocence.

Frederick of Austria.

The afternoon of the very day after the interview with the Pope, the Duke of Austria had proclaimed a splendid tournament without the gates of the city. Himself was to joust with the young Count of Cilly, brother of the Empress. All Constance thronged forth to the spectacle; the streets were a desert. Pope John, in the dress of a groom, with a grey cloak, and a kerchief wrapt close over his face, mounted a wretched ill-accoutred horse, with a cross-bow on the pommel of his saddle. He passed the gates unperceived, unchallenged, and rode about two hours to Ermatingen, at the efflux of the Rhine from the Lake of Constance. A boat was ready, he glided down the rapid stream to Schaffhausen, the castle of which was a stronghold of the Duke of Austria. Tidings were whispered in the ear of the Duke in the very act of his tourney. He continued the contest a short time, then courteously ceded the prize to his adversary De Cilly; in the evening he rode with a few attendants to Schaffhausen.

March 20. Flight of the Pope.

The news of the Pope's flight spread like wildfire.[1] The streets of Constance were thronged with prelates, priests, and populace, some in dismay, some in undisguised joy. A few Italians and Austrians stole out of the gates, and took to flight. The rabble broke into the palace from which the Pope had fled, to assert their privilege of plunder. The goldsmiths, money-changers, traders shut their shops.[2] The Burgomaster called the inhabitants to arms; the imperial soldiery occupied the principal streets and squares. The adversaries of the Pope were appalled. Some declared the Council actually dissolved by the departure of the Pope. The superstitious shuddered at the ban which no doubt the Pope would hurl at the devoted city and the contumacious Council. Five Cardinals in the confusion stole away to the Pope.

In the morning the Emperor rode through the streets with the Count Palatine, Louis of Bavaria, and a long retinue of princes and nobles. He allayed the tumult among the people by the assurance of his protection to their liberties and properties. He summoned the Princes, Cardinals, Prelates, Ambassadors; he declared his resolute determination, with all his power, and at the hazard of his life, to maintain the authority of the assembly. He exhorted them not to disquiet themselves on account of the Pope's flight. The fathers of the Council resolved to send ambassadors to summon the Pope to return, and to commission plenipotentiaries for his absolute cession. These ambassadors were the Cardinals Orsini, St. Mark, Saluces, with the Archbishop of Rheims.

---

[1] Von der Hardt. Almost all the authorities are collected, and references made to the rest.—Vol. iv. pp. 59, 66.

[2] This can hardly be called a riot, or a breach of the boasted peace in Constance.

Pope John, almost immediately on his arrival at Schaffhausen had written letters to the Council. "By the grace of God Almighty I have arrived at Schaffhausen, where I enjoy liberty and breathe air suited to the state of my health. I have come hither without the knowledge of my son, the Duke of Austria,[a] not to dispense myself from the promise of abdicating the Papacy in favour of the Church of God, but to execute it with greater freedom, as well as for the recovery of my health."

The Pope's Letter.

The letter of the Pope was treated as an audacious falsehood. On the walls of the palace at Constance was affixed a terrible writing, proclaiming the Pope Antichrist, denouncing his base and perfidious arts and cajoleries, and those of the Cardinals, in order to dissolve the Council, recounting all his crimes, tyrannies, murders, simonies, sordid merchandise of the Church; calling on the Council to proceed against him, and to depose him at once from his throne. The Emperor in a full assembly arraigned the Duke of Austria as a perfidious traitor to the Church, the Council, and the Empire. Not a voice was raised in his defence.

The Council was now to proclaim itself the supreme, indefeasible, independent authority of Christendom. In the assertion of these new principles, which changed the Church from an autocracy to an aristocracy, the lead was taken by the French Nation, by the Chancellor Gerson, the voice of that Nation; but with the full concurrence of the Germans, the English, even of the Italians except the Cardinals. The Cardinals, as the Privy Council of the Pope, refused to

The Council supreme.

---

[a] "Inscio filio meo Duce Austriæ." Schaffhausen, March 21.

be present, and to sanction doctrines limitary if not subversive of the Papal power.

Gerson laid down twelve great revolutionary maxims. Among them that Jesus Christ himself was the one primal and perfect Head of the Church, the Pope so only in a secondary sense; the union of Christ as the Spouse with his Church was alone indissoluble, that of the Pope might be dissolved; a Pope is necessary to complete the Church, but any particular Pope may be removed; the Church, or an Œcumenic Council representing the Church is under the direction of the Holy Ghost, it may enact canons which the Pope is bound to obey, and cannot annul; a Council can be assembled in some cases without the authority even of a legitimate Pope; the Council can command the cession of a Pope for the welfare of the Church, or the termination of a schism; the reformation of the Church both in faith and discipline rests ultimately with the Council; Councils ought to be held from time to time, as the one supreme, irrefragable representative of the Church.[r]

[r] Gerson had already promulgated these doctrines in a more contemptuous and offensive form. He had raised the Imperial power high above the Papal. "If an hereditary monarch may be deposed, how much more an elective! If an Emperor descended from a long unbroken royal lineage, how much more the son of a Venetian fisherman, whose father and grandfather had not beans enough to fill their stomachs! The Pope ought to be more easily deposed than another prelate. If the Pope sins, all partake of his sin; not so if a bishop. The canons on which rests the Papal authority were framed by fraud and craft." Gerson throws disdainfully aside the 6th book of Decretals and the Clementines. "What is a Pope? A man! the son of a man! clay of clay! a sinner, liable to sin! Two days before the son of a poor peasant, he is raised to be Pope. Is he then above repentance, confession, contrition? a sinless angel? a saint?" Wycliffe himself gives not a more awful catalogue of Papal crimes than this doughty churchman. "He is not above the Gospel."—Apud Von der Hardt, i. p. 76 et seqq.; et Oper. vol. ii. p. 162 et seqq. Tractatus pertinentes ad Concilium Constantiense.

CHAP. IX.   THE POPE AT SCHAFFHAUSEN.   271

The Pope was not idle at Schaffhausen ; he summoned all his officers and the whole Papal Court to attend upon him.[1] He published an appeal addressed to the French; he hoped to touch their pride and their jealousy of the Germans and English. Among his first and bitterest charges was their refusal to proceed at once to the extirpation of heresy in the person of John Huss. He complained of the division of the Council into four Nations, by which the French and Italians—by far the most numerous and learned—were reduced to the level of the English and the Germans; of the extension of the suffrage, which had ever been confined to Cardinals, Prelates, and the Hierarchy; of its usurpation by laymen as by priests, married and unmarried, ignorant and erudite. This turbulent rabble had hissed down grave Cardinals. His undoubted presidency of the Council had been usurped by the Emperor. He complained of the tyranny and force exercised by the Emperor; the insults to his person— jousts had been celebrated under his windows, with intolerable clang of trumpets. He complained of the insolence of the English, who had threatened him with arrest, especially Robert Hallam of Salisbury. The most extraordinary paragraph was that in which he gave himself the lie, and now asserted that his flight was with the aid of the Duke of Austria.[a] He wrote to the King of France and to the Duke of Orleans in the same strain ; it was his hope to enlist them in his cause against the Emperor, whom he represented as exercising a cruel tyranny over the Council.

The Pope at Schaffhausen was almost as much at the mercy of his enemies as at Constance. Could he have

The Pope at Schaff- hausen.

---

[1] Von der Hardt, ii. 153.   [a] Apud Von der Hardt, ii. 257.

crossed the Alps, followed as he would have been by some of the Cardinals, and appealed to the loyalty and anti-Ghibellinism of some of the Guelfic cities, he might possibly have maintained the contest. But he had neither strength nor courage. A Gregory VII. or a Gregory IX. would instantly have issued his ban against the perfidious Emperor, who had violated his own safe-conduct, and the contumacious Council. He would have declared the assumption of supreme power by the Council an impious affront to St. Peter, a denial of Christ in his Vicar: he would have laid half Christendom under an Interdict, and placed before the hierarchy the alternative of forfeiting or endangering their own authority, or asserting that of the Pope. But John XXIII.

<small>John's conduct.</small> wanted faith in himself and in his office. The truth, no doubt, of some of the damning charges against his life weighed heavily on his spirit, and no one could discern with more sagacity how much in the course of things, and through the long Schism, the old awe had fallen away from the name of the Pope. He was embarrassed, too, by the services of his now avowed ally, the Duke of Austria. The Emperor eagerly seized the opportunity of crushing his refractory and hated vassal. The Pope could not abandon Frederick to his wrath, his only refuge was an Austrian castle. His other great partisan, the Archbishop of Mentz, had not dared to own his complicity in the flight; he had retired to his own city, and Mentz was too far from Italy, too deep in Germany to offer an asylum. The whole conduct, therefore, of John was that of timidity, vacillation, tergiversation. His object was to detach the Cardinals from the Council, to gather them round himself, and to obtain for the Pope and the Sacred College that respect which the Pope alone had irre-

coverably lost. The Archbishop of Rheims returned before the other ambassadors of the Council, with a proposition to appoint the Cardinals collectively, with four Bishops, one of each Nation, Bath, Lebus (in Poland), Narbonne (the Italian was not named), the Procurators for his absolute cession.

The proceedings of the Council, on the other hand, were resolute, aggressive, imperious. Congregation after Congregation, and two Sessions of the whole Council, were held between the Pope's flight and the end of the month. At every meeting there was the same scornful rejection of all the Pope's advances, the same inflexible determination to vindicate their own superior authority. The Cardinals were divided, perplexed; they could not support, they would not abandon the Pope; with his integral authority fell theirs; they could not acknowledge, they dared not defy the Council. Hence at the First General Session after the flight two only were present, one French, the Cardinal of Cambray, one Venetian, St. Mark. *March 26.*

Proceedings of the Council.

Yet the Council without the Cardinals appeared wanting in dignity. After much stormy discussion in the Congregations, the memorable Fourth Session of the Council was summoned for the 31st March. The President (the Cardinal of Naples, an Orsini) took his seat: on one side was Sigismund the Emperor, and the hierarchy in their ranks; on the other the great laymen, Ambassadors, Princes, Dukes, and Counts. The resolutions, the final fatal resolutions, agreed upon the day before, or averred by one party to have been agreed upon at a full Congregation of the Nations, were placed in the hands of Zabarella, the Cardinal of Florence. He read in calm tone the Preface and the Decree:—

"The said Council of Constance, lawfully assembled in the name of the Holy Ghost, an Œcumenic Council, which represents the Catholic Church Militant, has received immediately from Jesus Christ power which every one of every estate and dignity, even Papal, is obliged to obey in all which regards the faith and the extirpation of the present Schism." Here the voice of the Cardinal faltered at the unexpected or unwelcome words. He either refused to read on or read imperfectly, with faint and trembling accents, "and the reformation of the Church in its head and in its members." In the tumult which rose the two other resolutions were hardly heard. These declared that the Pope should not adjourn the Council from Constance to any other place, nor summon his Court to attend him elsewhere; that all promotions made by him from that time were null and void.

The Council would not permit the Cardinals to elude their stern determination. At a Fifth General Session, notwithstanding much altercation and strife with the Cardinals, the three Decrees were read fully, distinctly, dictatorially, by the Archbishop of Posen.[b] The Pope had not awaited this act: he had dropped down the Rhine to another strong fortress, Laufenburg. But his Cardinals and most of his Court refused to follow him; they returned in shame and contempt to Constance.

April 10.

Further Flight of the Pope.

The rapid, total, and unpitied humiliation of the Duke of Austria left the Pope a miserable defenceless fugitive. On April 7th the ban of the Empire, the excommunication of the Council, were promulgated against this capital traitor. All his vassals

Humiliation of the Duke of Austria.

---

[b] Von der Hardt iv. 105.

were released from their sworn fealty; all treaties, contracts, oaths, vows, concerning the man excommunicated alike by the Church and by the Empire, were declared null and void. Whoever could conquer might possess the territory, the towns, the castles of the outlaw. The Swabian Princes fell on his possessions in Alsace; the Swiss Cantons (they only with some reluctance to violate solemn treaties) seized his hereditary dominions, even Hapsburg itself. The Duke of Upper Bavaria, the Bishops of Augsburg and Coire, the Patriarch of Aquileia, the Archbishop of Saltzburg, Albert of Austria, the Count of Cilly, overran the Tyrol. Before the month had expired, this powerful Duke was hardly permitted to humble himself *April 30.* in person before the Emperor, whose insatiate revenge spared nothing that could abase his ancient foe. It was a suppliant entreating pardon in the most abject terms, a Sovereign granting it with the most hard and haughty condescension. Frederick surrendered all his lands and possessions to be held at the will of the Emperor, until he should deign to reinvest the Duke with them under the most degrading tenure of allegiance and fealty.

The Pope in the mean time had fled again in mean disguise to Fribourg in the Brisgau, a pleasant *The Pope at* city, which still owned the dominion of the *Fribourg.* Duke of Austria. He had sent certain articles to the Council from Laufenburg; he sent others more ambiguous and unsatisfactory from Fribourg. The Council, while the Pope was thus sinking into despicable insignificance, was still rising in pretensions and power. An address to all Christendom vindicated their proceedings towards the Pope. "The King of the Romans (the Emperor), only at their request, had closed the gates to prevent some faithless Prelates from leaving the Council." "The Pope had deserted the Council after having deliberately sworn to maintain it. He had summoned his Cardinals and his Court to follow him in his ignominious flight, in order to dissolve the Council." As yet, however, there was no acrimonious persecution of the Pope. A mandate was issued by the Council prohibiting scurrilous and abusive libels against the Pontiff and the Court of Rome. A motion to refuse the Cardinals admission and the right of suffrage was rejected.

The Pope had one wild hope: he had looked to France, to the King; he now looked to the Duke of Burgundy. Under his protection he meditated an escape to Avignon; to be nearer the Rhine he removed to Brisach; but the Duke of Burgundy had his reasons for declining to offend the Council. His own cause, Jean Petit's defence of his assassination of the Duke of Orleans, rested on their decision. Even Frederick of Austria was compelled to the hard terms of surrendering the Pope to the Council. At the Sixth Session instructions were given to deputies from the Council to compel the surrender of the Pope. They found him not at Fribourg; they followed him to Brisach. He promised an answer the next day; the next day he had disappeared.

April 17.

April 18.
April 22.

The ensuing Session determined to cite the Pope, and proceed to the utmost extremity. The citation was fixed on the gates of the city, on the doors of all the churches. It summoned Pope John XXIII. to answer for the maintenance of the Schism, for heresy, simony, maladministration and notorious dilapidation of the estates and possessions of the Papacy; for the scandals and notorious criminalities

May 2.

of his life and conversation. A body of three hundred
armed men, under Frederick of Nuremburg,
were sent to seize the fugitive. In vain the *May 13.*
Pope sent full powers to the Cardinals of Cambray, St.
Mark, and Florence, to act in his behalf; the Cardinals
refused to undertake the trust. The next day,
the time assigned to the Pope for his appear- *May 14.*
ance having expired, the Council proceeded in its course.
Seventy articles were exhibited: never probably were
seventy more awful accusations brought against man
than against the Vicar of Christ. The Cardinal of St.
Mark made a feeble attempt to repel the charge of
heresy; against the darker charges no one spoke a
word. Before the final decree, sixteen of those of the
most indescribable depravity were dropped, out of
respect not to the Pope, but to public decency *Eleventh*
and the dignity of the office. On the remain- *Session. May 25.*
ing undefended fifty-four the Council gravely, deliberately, pronounced the sentence of deposition against
the Pope.*

Weary, deserted by all, conscience-stricken, betrayed
perforce by the Duke of Austria, pursued by *Surrender*
the Imperial soldiers, John in his fall was with- *and impri- sonment of*
out courage as without dignity. He had already *the Pope. May 27.*
been brought to Rodolfzell, and imprisoned in the castle
under an Hungarian guard. On the first demand he
yielded up the insignia of universal spiritual power, the

---

* Among the sentences was "suis ipse graviter fuit infamatus, quod
detestabilibus inhonestisque vitâ et cum uxore fratris sui concubuerit;
moribus ecclesiam Dei et populum cum sanctimonialibus incestum, cum
Christianum scandalizantem, ante ejus virginibus stuprum, et cum conjugatis
assumptionem ad Papatum et post adulterium perpetraverit, nec non alia
usque ad ista tempora."—Apud Von flagitia, propter qualia ira Dei descendit
der Hardt. I give one class of charges in filios diffidentiæ."—P. 341. See
in the words of Gobelinus: "Item the 6th article.

Papal Seal, the Fisherman's Ring, the Book of Petitions.[d] His sentence was read to him by two Cardinals. He acknowledged its justice, protested that he surrendered of his free will the Papal dignity, and would never attempt to resume it. This one vow John XXIII. religiously observed: he had neither opportunity nor temptation to break it. He was brought to the strong Castle of Gotleben, without the walls of Constance. To his sentence of deposition had been subjoined a sentence of imprisonment, at least for safe custody. He was afterwards committed to the charge of the Elector Palatine. The Castle of Heidelberg was assigned as his residence and his prison.

There was another prisoner in Gotleben, a man against whose life his worst enemies brought no word of reproach. John Huss had been for some months in irons pining in a dungeon of this fortress, under custody of the Bishop of Constance. To Huss the fall of the Pope, though it might seem to deliver him from his most implacable enemy, was fatal. His friends had fondly supposed that he would meet with more calm and equable justice, if not with favour, before a Council of which all the leading members had concurred in denouncing ecclesiastical abuses, the vices and ignorance of the clergy in terms as strong and uncompromising as the Reformers of Bohemia, as Wycliffe himself: a Council which had ventured on so bold an innovation, a heresy so manifest according to the principles long dominant in Christendom, as to set itself above the Pope, to assume the power of deposing a Pope. Now too would appear in his proper character an Emperor whose noble ambition seemed to be the

John Huss.

---

[d] Liber Supplicationum.

restoration of the Church to purity as well as to unity, under whose safe-conduct he had to come to Constance. Sigismund had reluctantly yielded to the violation of that safe-conduct, and might now redeem his pledge, which the Pope had almost compelled him to forfeit.

So entirely were the friends of Huss under this delusion, that Jerome of Prague, the second in influence and character among the Bohemian Reformers, had thought it a favourable opportunity to join his friend. Jerome, notwithstanding the remonstrances of Huss, had set out from Prague to share the dangers and to support the cause of his brother teacher of the truth. He entered Constance secretly, without a safe-conduct. The Council issued a summons to him to appear within fourteen days. They offered full freedom of entrance into Constance; his departure must depend on their judgement in his cause. Jerome turned his face back towards Prague; but at Hirschau, in the Upper Palatinate, he rashly broke out, in the presence of many clergy, into denunciations against the Council. He was seized and sent prisoner to Constance.

Huss and his followers, in their infatuated expectations of leniency, or of respect for the freedom of such opinions as theirs, showed their ignorance of mankind, of the hierarchy, as well as of the bounds beyond which it was premature to attempt the emancipation of the religious mind of Europe. The leaders in the Council of Constance, the Cardinal d'Ailly, Gerson, still more the better Italian Cardinals, St. Mark and Zabarella of Florence, had no conception beyond a purely aristocratic and hierarchical reformation, which should restore its strength to the ecclesiastical system by raising the morals of the corrupt clergy and the ignorant monks and friars. But they would have shuddered with horror and indignation at the examination of any established doctrine, or even of any ancient ritual observance. They had not only the pride of ecclesiastical rank, but the pride of that learning which consisted in a laborious and masterly command of the vast and voluminous theology, and of the Canon Law, the established code of Christendom. They were conscientiously convinced that there was no knowledge, at least of religious things, beyond this circle. The most far-sighted might not perceive the full bearings, but they had an instinctive sagacity which shrunk from the democratic doctrines which had been preached by Wycliffe, and were partially, at least, embraced by the Bohemian Reformers: their mistrust was more likely to exaggerate than diminish the danger. These doctrines without doubt called in question, and submitted to bold inquiry, some which were thought the fundamental articles of the dominant creed, withdrew in fact the ritual and the instruction of the Church from the sacred Latin, and vulgarised it into the national language. They already spoke of an authority to which all the theology of the Church, which had been accumulating for centuries, and all the law of the Church (their proud possession), must submit, that of the Bible—the Bible translated and popularised for general use. Above all, they owned the great vital principle of Wycliffism, that the wicked or unworthy priest was no priest. Be he Pope, Cardinal, Bishop, Curate, or Friar, his vices absolutely annulled all his privileges, his immunities, his rights to his estates, his claim to tithes or church-dues. The efficacy of the Sacraments which he administered, perplexed or divided the teachers of this bewildering doctrine.

It was in truth, in its broad enunciation, a specious and noble theory; but to the calmest, still more to the interested, the objections raised against Wycliffe could not but occur in appalling force. Without an infallible tribunal, without an omniscient Judge to pronounce sentence against the whole hierarchy or any individual priest, how impracticable, how iniquitous! Was this sentence to be intrusted for its award and execution to Kings coveting the wealth of the Church; to an ignorant populace, who knew not the difference between unchristian arrogance or the calm and holy severity of good Churchmen; or even to the honest but fanatic teachers of purer doctrines, usually as intolerant as those against whose intolerance they have risen up? In such a strife must fall law, order, property, government, the salutary restraints of religion.

John Huss and Jerome of Prague, as among the first distinguished martyrs for Christian liberty, and as condemned by a Council in the face of Christendom, have obtained perhaps importance, not fully recognised in their own day, assuredly not till after the Bohemian war. It could not be supposed that a great hierarchical Senate from the four most powerful kingdoms, indeed from all Europe, with the Emperor, who took a pride in exalting its authority, at its head, a Council which had deposed Popes, would be bearded and defied by two or three contumacious priests from a remote, obscure, and half-barbarous land. The burning of heretics was now so completely part of the established usage of the Church, as to cause, if compassion, none of that revulsion of feeling which has happily grown into our Christianity. And it is but justice to the "Fathers of Constance," as they are called, to admit that they tried all milder means of persuasion. Even the bitterest opponents of Huss, Michael de Causis and Stephen Palecz, earnestly besought him to make disavowal of his errors. The course of the Churchman seemed to him

clear and determinate, and unavoidable. In the Emperor
his pride and his honour, and even his interest,
came into perilous collision with these opponents.
Was he to recede before a simple Bohemian?—
and Sigismund had an old hereditary grudge, as well as
a German aversion, to Bohemia. He was beset on all
sides. The Churchmen pressed him with the argument
that he had gone beyond his powers in granting security
to a heretic over whom the Church alone has jurisdiction.
"He that is false to God, has no right to appeal to
truth or faith."* The King of Arragon addressed a
letter to Sigismund, taunting him with his manifest
favour to a notorious heretic, and avowing astonishment
that he had not long before done justice upon Huss.
Yet, on the other hand, there still was his safe-conduct,
full, distinct, not to be disavowed. He looked too,
hereafter, to the succession to the throne of Bohemia.
That kingdom had already sent another petition, almost
imperious, expressing the sentiments of the magnates
of the realm, and demanding the release of John
Huss.

The affair of Huss had been revived almost simultaneously
with that of the deposition of Pope John. The
Council seemed resolved, while it proceeded to extremities
in one direction, to show to Christendom that it had
no disposition to dangerous latitude on the other. Early
in May, in a numerous Session of the Council (the
Eighth), came forth a full condemnation of Wycliffe
and his doctrines. During the imprisonment of Huss
the controversy concerning the administration of the
Cup to the laity had been renewed in Prague. The

---

* See Andrew Ratisbon Chronic. Eccard, i. p. 2146; and Pez, Thes.
Anecdot. Novissim. II. 8, 626.

Curate of St. Michael in that city, James von Mies, commonly called Jacobel, had embarked in violent warfare with the opponents of this innovation. The Bishop of Lieutomyssel had denounced the proceedings of Jacobel at Constance; and this denunciation could not but exasperate the general animosity against Huss.

On the last day of May the Bohemians presented a memorial to the Council. They expostulated on the neglect of their former petition: they recited the declaration of faith which had been disseminated throughout Bohemia by the friends of Huss, asserting his full belief in all the articles of the Creed, his determination to defend them to death, and the testimonial of the Grand Inquisitor, the Bishop of Nazareth, acquitting him of all heterodox opinions. They demanded his release from his noisome prison, by which his health was affected, and that he should be heard before the Council against his calumnious enemies. The Patriarch of Antioch answered coldly in the name of the Council, that the testimonials were of no avail, till they should have undergone close examination before themselves; they had no faith in his statements. Yet they would condescend, as an act of grace, to grant him a public hearing; for this end he would be removed from his present confinement. Sigismund so expressed his approbation of that resolution to grant a hearing, that the partisans of Huss weakly concluded that the royal favour would protect their teacher.

Bohemian memorial.

The Council would willingly have avoided the notoriety of a public examination. Huss was visited in his cell at Gotleben by the Patriarch of Antioch, by Michael de Causis, and Stephen Palecz. He was urged to retract. They now, however, interrogated him, as he complains, with the captious and en-

June 1.

snaring severity of Inquisitors, adducing against him words culled out of all his letters and discourses; Palecz adduced phrases uttered in frank and careless conversation.* The Patriarch reproached him with the wealth he had obtained: "Have you not seventy thousand florins?" His answers were brief and cautious: "I will retract when convinced of my error."

He was removed to the Franciscan cloister. In the mean time, the utmost industry had been employed in collecting obnoxious passages from all his writings, and from adverse witnesses. The Cardinals sat in Council on these in order to frame articles of accusation. Sigismund required that these articles should be communicated to Huss. The Cardinals deigned to accede, not as of right, but as of favour. The partisans of Huss were prepared, on the other hand, with authenticated copies of all his writings to confront false citations, or contest unjust inferences.

On the 5th of June John Huss was brought in chains into the Council. His works were presented to him; he acknowledged them for his own. The articles were read; but either the indignation of his adversaries, or the zeal of his partisans, or both, raised such an uproar, that silence could hardly be enforced. Huss calmly declared himself ready to maintain his opinions by Scripture and the Fathers. Another outburst of abuse and mockery compelled the Council to adjourn its proceedings.

On the morning of the 7th of June, Constance was darkened by an eclipse of the sun. At Prague the eclipse was total, a sinister omen to the followers of Huss. Two hours after the darkness had

---

* Compare L'Enfant, L. p. 306, with references to the letters of Huss.

passed away, John Huss stood again before the Council. All the more distinguished Fathers sat in their order. The Emperor was on his throne; a strong guard attended to keep order. Wenzel de Duba and John de Chlum, Nobles, and other Bohemians watched the course of things with grave solicitude. The accusers began on the perilous article of Transubstantiation. But the answer of Huss was clear, distinct, unimpeachable. The Cardinal of Cambray alone, as jealous for his nominalist philosophy as for his orthodox religion, endeavoured by a syllogism about universals, intelligible only according to the scholastic jargon,* to prove that Huss must assert that the material bread remained after consecration. Huss extricated himself with address and triumph. "His philosophic doctrine was that of S. Anselm." He averred Transubstantiation to be a perpetual miracle, and so exempt from all logical form. An English Bishop took up the Cardinal's cause. "A boy in the schools," said Huss, "might answer such puerility." To the other more general charges, that he had preached Wycliffite doctrines; that he officiated as priest when under excommunication by the Pope; that he had spoken with contempt of some of the most learned Prelates of the day, even the Chancellor Gerson; that he had excited tumults in Bohemia; he replied with admirable presence of mind and perfect self-command. Once, indeed, he admitted that he had said, "Wycliffe, I trust, will be saved; but could I think he would be damned, I would my soul were with his." A burst of contemptuous laughter followed this avowal, of which, however, it is not difficult to see the hidden meaning. After some hours of turbulent discussion, he was ordered to with-

---

* " Credimo universale a parte rei?"

draw, under custody of the Archbishop of Riga, Keeper of the Seals to the Council.

Before he was removed, the Cardinal of Cambray rose and demanded, whether he had not boasted that, if he had not come to the Council of his own free-will, neither King nor Emperor could have compelled his appearance. "There are many nobles in Bohemia," answered Huss, "who honour me with their protection. Had I not willed to come to the Council, they would have placed me in some stronghold beyond the power of King or Emperor." The Cardinal lifted up his hands in amazement at this insolence; a fierce murmur ran through the assembly. Thereat arose John de Chlum: "John Huss speaks truth; I am one of the least of the nobles of Bohemia; in my castle I would have defended him for a year against all the forces of Emperor or King. How much more, Lords mightier than I, with castles far more impregnable!" The Cardinal said in a lower tone, "Huss, I admonish you for your safety and your honour to submit to the Council, as you have promised in prison." All eyes were turned upon the Emperor. Sigismund rose; the purport of his speech was that he had issued the safe-conduct in order to give Huss an opportunity of rendering account of his faith before the Council. The Cardinals and Prelates (he thanked them for it) had granted him this favour; though many asserted that it was beyond his power to take a heretic under his protection. He counselled Huss to maintain nothing with obstinacy, but to submit to the Council on all articles charged and proved against him. So doing he might return in the good graces of the Council to his home, after some slight penance and moderate satisfaction. "If not, the Council will know how to deal with you. For myself, far from defending you in your errors and in your contumacy, I will be the first to light the fire with my own hands." Huss began to thank the Emperor for his clemency in granting him safe-conduct. The friendly interruption of John de Chlum reminded him that the Emperor had charged him with obstinacy. He protested in God's name that he had no such intention. "He had come of his own free will to Constance, determined, if better instructed, to surrender his opinions." He was conducted back to prison.

The next day Huss stood the third time before the Council. Thirty-nine articles were exhibited against him, twenty-six from his book on the Church, seven from a controversial Tract against Stephen Palecz, six from one against Stanislaus of Znaym. Huss, like most Reformers, held the high Augustinian notion of Predestination. "None were members of the true indefeasible Church, but those predestined to eternal life." On these points he appealed triumphantly to the all-honoured name of Augustine. None dared to answer. But when this theory was applied to Churchmen, to Prelates, to the Pope himself; and when their whole authority was set on their succession not to the titles, but to the virtues of the Apostles, the Council sat amazed and embarrassed. "The Pontiff, who lives not the life of Peter, is no Vicar of Christ, but the forerunner of Antichrist." A citation from S. Bernard seemed to confirm that dread sentence. "The slave of avarice is the successor not of Peter, but of Judas Iscariot." The Churchmen looked at each other and smiled, no doubt some a bitter smile. In an evil moment Huss pressed his fearless logic. "A King in mortal sin is no King before God." Sigismund was looking out of a window: "There never," he was saying, "lived a more pernicious heretic." The Cardinal of Cambray roused his attention to this last perilous conclusion. Huss repeated his words aloud. The Emperor only answered, "There is no man that sinneth not." "What!" burst out the Cardinal, "art thou not content with degrading the ecclesiastical power, wouldst thou thrust Kings from their thrones?" "A man," argued Palecz, "may be a true Pope, Prelate, or King, though not a true Christian." "Why, then, have you deposed John XXIII.?" The Emperor answered, "For his notorious misdeeds." Huss had been guilty of the rashness of discomfiting and perplexing his adversaries. The Cardinals were most indignant at what Cambray denounced as an unjust and overdrawn appeal to popular animosity against them. They constantly urged that the articles gave but a mild and mitigated notion of the language of Huss. Huss was arraigned for this assertion: "No heretic should suffer more than ecclesiastical punishment, none be delivered to the secular arm to be punished by death." Yet even Huss, and Huss at that moment, shrank from the full avowal of that simple Evangelic maxim. "The heretic was first to be instructed fairly, mildly, humbly, out of the Scriptures and by reason; if he refused to desist from his errors, to be punished according to St. Augustine, in the body."[b] He acknowledged a sentence in his works, which likened those who gave up a heretic to the secular arm unconvicted, to the Pharisees. "Whom," cried the Cardinals, "meanest thou by the Pharisees?" "Those who deliver an innocent man to the civil sword."[1]

At the close of the Session the Cardinal of Cambray urged Huss, who had heard the atrocious charges adduced

---

[a] "Corporaliter puniri debere."
[1] Von der Hardt, p. 319. The fullest report of the whole trial.

against him, to make unqualified submission to the Council, and to abjure all his errors: "if he persisted, the Council would know how to proceed." The Emperor condescended to argue with him in the same tone. His two accusers, Palecz and De Causis, appealed to Heaven, that they were actuated by no personal hostility towards Huss.

Huss replied with firm humility, that he sought instruction; he could not abjure errors of which he was not convinced. Many things charged against him were forged, many perverted from their true meaning; he could not abjure those, he could not sin against his conscience. He was remanded to prison; the faithful Bohemian Knight, John de Chlum, followed to console his weary friend.

The Emperor rose: "You have heard the charges against Huss proved by trustworthy witnesses, some confessed by himself. In my judgement, each of these crimes is deserving of death. If he does not forswear all his errors, he must be burned. If he submits, he must be stripped of his preacher's office, and banished from Bohemia: there he would only disseminate more dangerous errors..... The evil must be extirpated root and branch..... If any of his partisans are in Constance, they must be proceeded against with the utmost severity, especially his disciple, Jerome of Prague." Sigismund had wrought himself, no doubt as an excuse to his remonstrant conscience, to a fanaticism of obedience to the Church.

Huss heard in his prison the Emperor's declaration. "I was warned not to trust to his safe-conduct. I have been under a sad delusion; he has condemned me even before mine enemies."

The fatal hour had now come. The Council which

asserted itself to be under the actual inspiration of the Holy Ghost, could not recede without the impeachment of indifference to doctrines which itself had declared to be deadly heresy, or without disavowing the right established by the terrible usage of centuries, of awarding capital punishment for that which the Church had been so long teaching the world was a mortal crime; a crime which it was the most sacred duty to God and man in the Priest to avenge, in the temporal Sovereign, at the demand of the Priest, to punish by fire. Huss could not retract without perjury to his own conscience; without base treachery to his followers, whom he had instructed, whom he had kindled to a fanatic faith in that which himself had believed, which he still believed, to be the saving Gospel of Christ; and this from the fear of death, death which, as he himself was assured, as his partisans had no less confidence, would secure him the martyr's crown.

A form of recantation was drawn by Cardinal Zabarella, studiously mild in its terms, but of necessity an explicit renunciation of his errors, a humble submission to the determinations, to the definitions of the Holy Council. He was to abjure, retract, revoke all his errors, and undergo whatever penance the Council might decree for his soul's health.

The answer of Huss was a prayer to God Almighty for everlasting life, through Christ Jesus. He thanked the reverend Father, Zabarella of Florence, for his pious and paternal kindness. "But if Eleazar under the Old Law refused to eat forbidden food, lest he should sin against God, and leave a bad example to posterity, how can I, a Priest of the New Law, however unworthy, from fear of a punishment so brief and transitory, sin so heinously against the law of

God, first by departure from truth, secondly by perjury, thirdly by grievous scandal to my brethren? It is better for me to die, than by avoiding momentary punishment to fall into the hands of God, and perhaps into everlasting fire. I have appealed to Jesus Christ, the One All-powerful and All-just Judge; to Him I commit my cause, who will judge every man, not according to false witnesses and erring Councils, but according to truth and man's desert."[b]

Persons of the highest rank, Cardinals, Prelates, the Emperor, even his adversary, Stephen Palecz, again entreated him, and with tears, to depart from his stubborn resolution. *Attempt to persuade him to yield.* His answer was calm, unboastful, with nothing of the vehemence or contemptuousness of fanaticism; he acknowledged how hardly his soul was tried; at the same time, in his letters to Bohemia, some of which were publicly read in the Bethlehem Chapel at Prague, and in others addressed to the University of Prague, he declared that he could forswear no one of his doctrines. He had not been convinced out of the Scriptures, he awaited in tranquillity the judgement of the Lord.

The Council proceeded in full Session to condemn the doctrine of Jacob de Mies concerning the Cup: an omen and a warning! The writings of Huss were ordered to be publicly burned. The Council itself sent another deputation to urge submission. The Emperor had been a short time absent; the day before the final judgement, he sent four Bishops, Wenzel of Duba, and John de Chlum, with a still mitigated form of recantation. Huss was only to retract those tenets which he acknowledged to be his *July 1.*

---

[b] Von der Hardt, iv. 329.

own. Even John de Chlum endeavoured to move, or rather to strengthen him. "I am but an unlettered man, unfit to counsel one so learned. If you are conscious of error, be not ashamed to confess it to the Council. If not, I cannot advise you to act against your conscience. Bear any punishment rather than renounce the truth." Huss answered, that he would abandon any opinion on proofs adduced from the Holy Scriptures. A Bishop reproached him with arrogantly setting up his opinion against the whole Council. "Let the lowest in the Council convince me, I will humbly own my error." The night before his condemnation Huss made confession, and, it is asserted, received absolution from a monk.

The Council met in the Cathedral; the Cardinal Bishop of Ostia presided. Sigismund and the Princes of the Empire were present. While Mass was celebrated, Huss, as a heretic, stood in the porch. The Bishop of Lodi preached from the text, "That the body of sin might be destroyed."[*] It was a fierce declamation: it suggested that Huss was as "bad as Arius, worse than Sabellius." The preacher closed with adulatory praise of the Emperor. "It is thy glorious office to destroy heresies and schism, especially this obstinate heretic." He pointed to Huss, who was kneeling in an elevated place and in fervent prayer.

A Decree of the Council was read, inhibiting all present, without exception, Prelates, Princes, Kings, Emperors, under pain of excommunication and two months' imprisonment, to speak without permission, to reply, to interrupt the proceedings, to give any sign or murmur of applause or disapprobation either with the

---

[*] Rom. vi. 6. The sermon may be read in Van der Hardt, iii. 1.

hands or feet. Certain tenets of Wycliffe were here recited and condemned; afterwards thirty articles containing the doctrines of Huss.* Often, while these articles were read, Huss attempted to speak; as often he was put to silence. At length, while he was arraigned as believing that the material bread remained after the consecration, he broke out, "That I deny, so I have never believed or taught." He renounced with equal vehemence a charge that he had added a fourth person to the Trinity; he defied them to produce their nameless witness. His appeal to Christ was treated as an impious error. "Oh, blessed Jesus!" he uttered with a loud voice, "This thy Council condemns us, because in our afflictions we have sought refuge with Thee, the One just Judge." He added, "This I constantly affirm, that the surest and most safe appeal is to the Lord Jesus; Him none can pervert or bribe by gifts, none deceive by false witnesses, or beguile by craft. He will render unto every one his own." He justified himself for having continued to officiate as Priest after his excommunication by the Pope. "Freely came I hither under the safe-conduct of the Emperor." He turned and looked steadily at Sigismund. A deep blush passed over the face of the Emperor.

The Bishop of Concordia, an aged, bald Italian Prelate, rose to read the two sentences, one condemning the writings, the other the person of John Huss to the flames; his writings, as propagating the tenets of the heresiarch Wycliffe, and as containing many things erroneous, scandalous, offensive to pious ears, some notoriously heretical; all, both in Latin and Bohemian, were adjudged to be publicly and solemnly burned.

---

* Von der Hardt; more briefly in L'Enfant, p. 403.

Huss was commanded to kneel and hear his own sentence. The Council, having God before its eyes, declared Huss a real and manifest heresiarch, who had advanced doctrines offensive, rash, seditious, had trampled under foot the power of the Keys and the censures of the Church, had scandalised all true Christians, by his appeal to Jesus Christ. "This John Huss, being thus obstinate and incorrigible, who has refused to enter into the bosom of the Church, and abjure his errors." Huss broke in, "I have ever desired, and still desire, to be instructed out of the Holy Scriptures." The Bishop concluded with condemning him to be degraded and despoiled of his Orders. Huss rose from his knees; he uttered a fervent prayer to God to pardon his enemies. Some of the older Priests, even Bishops, looked sternly at him, and laughed his prayers to scorn. The Archbishop of Milan, the Bishops of Bangor, Feltre, Ast (in Hungary), Alexandria, and Lavaur were designated for the office of degradation. Huss was clad in all the attire of the Priesthood, and led with the cup in his hand to the high altar, as if about to celebrate Mass. As they put on the alb, he said, "They put a white robe on our Lord to mock him, when Herod sent him to Pilate." Once more the Bishops implored him to recant. He declined for the same reasons alleged before. "Behold," said the Bishops, "how obstinate he is in his malice." The cup was taken from his hand: "Accursed Judas, thou hast deserted the way of peace, thou hast entered into counsel with the Jews. We take away this cup in which the blood of Christ is offered for the redemption of souls." Huss said, "I trust that I shall drink it this day in the kingdom of heaven." He was stripped one by one of his robes, on each a curse was pronounced. "These mockeries I bear with equal mind for the name and the truth of Christ." The tonsure was now to be effaced. They disputed whether it was to be done with scissors or with a razor. "Lo! they cannot agree," said Huss, "how to put me to shame." It was done with scissors; the hair cut in the form of a cross; a high paper crown, daubed over with devils, was set on his head. "We devote thy soul to the devils in hell." "And I commend my soul to the most merciful Lord, Christ Jesus." So the Church made over the heresiarch to the secular arm. The Emperor delivered him to Louis, Elector Palatine, the Imperial Vicar; the Elector to the Magistrates of Constance, the Magistrates to the executioners.

Huss was led away with two of the headsman's servants before him, two behind. Eight hundred horse followed, and the whole multitude from the city. Over a narrow bridge they went in single file, lest it should break with their weight. They stopped before the Bishop's palace, that Huss might gaze on the pile on which his books lay burning. He only smiled at this ineffectual act of vengeance. As he went along he addressed the people in German, protesting against the injustice of his sentence, "His adversaries had been able to convince him of no error." The place of execution was a meadow without the walls. He knelt, recited several psalms, with the perpetual burthen, "Lord Jesus, have mercy upon me. Into thy hands I commend my spirit." "We know not," said the people, "what this man may have done, we only know that his prayers to God are excellent." They asked if he would have a confessor. A Priest on a stately horse, and richly attired, protested that no confessor should be granted to a heretic. But Reichenthal, as himself relates, called forth Ulric Schorand, a man of piety and wisdom. Ulric required that Huss should first retract the errors for which he was condemned. Huss declined to confess on such terms. "I have no need, I am guilty of no mortal sin." He endeavoured to address the people again in German. The Elector Palatine refused permission. Then Huss prayed aloud, "Lord Jesus, for thy sake I endure with patience this cruel death. I beseech thee to pardon mine enemies." As he spoke, the paper mitre fell from his head. The rude soldiers replaced it: "He shall be burned with all his devils." He spoke gently to his guards. "I trust that I shall reign with Christ, since I die for his Gospel."

He was then tied fast by an old rusty chain to the stake affixed on a platform. The Elector Palatine and the Marshal Oppenheim advanced, and again urged him to recant. Huss replied, that he willingly signed his testimony with his blood. All he had taught and written was to save men's souls from Satan, and from the dominion of sin. The fire blazed up; it is said that an old woman was busy in heaping the wood. "Oh, holy simplicity!" said Huss. With the last feeble sounds of his voice he was heard to chant verses of the Psalms, and to pray to the Redeemer. All the remains of the body were torn in pieces, even his clothes thrown into the fire; the ashes were gathered and thrown into the lake, lest his disciples should make reliques of them. But their faithful piety scraped together the earth around the pile, and carried it to Bohemia.*

* The whole description of the last hours of Huss is from Reichenthal and the two nameless biographers of Huss, who all were eye-witnesses. Compare L'Enfant, and Aschbach, Kaiser Sigmund.

So perished John Huss as an obstinate incorrigible heretic, but his heresy has never been clearly defined. It was not a denial of any of the great doctrinal truths of universal Christianity, nor any of those tenets of belief rejected afterwards by the German and English Reformers. On Transubstantiation (notwithstanding the subtleties of his adversaries), the Communion in one kind, worship of the Saints and of the Virgin Mary, Huss was scrupulously, unimpeachably orthodox. He was the martyr to the power of the hierarchy, not the power of the Pope, which the Council itself had renounced in its extreme theory; his testimony was against that supreme ecclesiastical dominion, which had so long ruled the mind of man.

Bohemia, at the news of the burning of Huss, seemed to rise with one impulse of sorrow and indignation. National and religious zeal animated all ranks, all orders. The King openly denounced the treachery of Sigismund and the barbarous injustice of the Council. The Bishop of Lieutomyssel had been commanded by the Council to communicate their act, and to exhort the Bohemians to extirpate the heresies which were teeming in the kingdom. The Magnates of Bohemia met in the Chapel of Bethlehem, whose walls might still seem to sound with the eloquent preachings of Huss. An address to the Council was framed and signed by sixty of the greatest names, nobles, barons, knights, gentlemen, denouncing the execution of Huss, as inflicting perpetual infamy and disgrace on the kingdom of Bohemia and the Marquisate of Moravia. They protested that Huss was a good Catholic Christian, of the holiest conversation and most Evangelic doctrine; a man who detested and never taught error or heresy, whose life was devoted to

Proceedings in Bohemia.

Sept. 2.

the edification of the people. They complained of the imprisonment, perhaps the death of the eloquent Jerome of Prague, that "illustrious philosopher," like Huss convicted of no crime, but accused, like Huss, by wicked and treacherous informers, the enemies of Bohemia. They declared that whoever averred heresies to prevail in the kingdom of Bohemia lied in his throat; they concluded with leaving the redress of their injuries to God, who will punish the proud, being determined when the Church should be united under one supreme and undisputed pastor, to prosecute to the utmost this violation of the rights and dignity, this execution of the innocent subjects, of their realm. Strong measures were taken in a subsequent meeting to protect the Hussite priests against their Bishops. The popular fury had broken out in acts of persecution against the old clergy, and against the monks. The Emperor addressed the Bohemians in a letter, half-rebuke for their turbulent proceedings, half-apology for his own unroyal weakness in surrendering Huss to his enemies. "It was with inexpressible grief, after having more than once threatened to leave Constance, only to avert the dissolution of the Council, that he had submitted to the decree of Christendom, represented by the whole hierarchy, and by the ambassadors of all Christian Sovereigns."[p]

But neither did the sacrifice of one victim satiate, nor the dread of the revolt of a whole kingdom arrest the severe determination of the Council to suppress by these terrible means the growing resistance to ecclesiastical rule. They would break the yoke under which

---

[p] "Neque etiam licuit nobis ulterius pro hoc negotio loqui, quia exinde concilium totaliter fuisset dissolutum." This most remarkable letter in the Appendix to L'Enfant.

themselves groaned, that of the Pope; but the more
resolute were they that their own yoke should not be
broken. Robert Hallam, Bishop of Salisbury, stood
almost alone in assertion of the great maxim, "God
willeth not the death of a sinner, but that he should be
converted and live." He almost alone condemned the
punishment of death for heresy.[q] The Emperor had
left Constance; had he remained, Jerome of Prague could show no safe-conduct on his part. Jerome of Prague. Jerome of Prague, to the short relief of the
more moderate, displayed not the stubborn courage of
John Huss. Four months of weary imprisonment, in
chains, in darkness, on meagre diet; the terror, as
himself owned, of the stake; sickness; the bland promises of some, the awful threats of others; the persuasions of weaker friends, broke his spirit. In a public
Session of the Council, Jerome of Prague appeared and made a full retractation of all Recants. Sept. 21. errors against the Catholic faith, especially those of
Wycliffe and John Huss.

Instead of opening the prison doors and sending
forth the strong man shorn of his strength; if insincere
or repentant of his weakness with the burthen of apostasy on his conscience; under the suspicion, if not the
contempt of his partisans, who could not but contrast
his pusillanimity with the unbroken resolution of Huss;
instead of placing him, as they might, in safe custody,
the Council, with vengeance not less impolitic than
unchristian, loaded itself with the crime of another
inhuman execution, and compelled Jerome of Prague
to a martyrdom hardly less noble than that of Huss.
It was asserted by his implacable enemies, Michael de

---

[q] Aschbach, p. 202, with authorities.

Causis and Stephen Palecz, that the recantation was ambiguous.

New articles were exhibited against him. The Cardinals of Cambray, Aquileia, Orsini, and Florence (Zabarella had drawn the form of retractation) withdrew in indignation from the commission of inquiry. But different Commissioners were named at the instigation of his two implacable adversaries. The Patriarch of Antioch and (it is sad to write) the Chancellor Gerson urged this virtual breach of faith.

<small>April 27.</small>

Fresh charges were accumulated. Thrice was Jerome again arraigned before a General Congregation. The last time he was permitted to pour forth a long declamation in his defence, he dwelt on all the great men who had been the victims of false accusation, Socrates, Seneca, Boethius, Plato, the Prophets, the Protomartyr Stephen. He ascribed his persecution to the hereditary unforgiving hatred between the Germans and Bohemians. He acknowledged some concern in the tumults in the University of Prague, when certain Germans had lost their lives. He confessed his flight from Constance, and still further, "I confess that, moved by cowardly fear of the stake, against my conscience, I have consented to the condemnation of the doctrines of Wycliffe and John Huss. This sinful retractation I now fully retract, and am resolved to maintain the tenets of Wycliffe and of John Huss to death, believing them to be the true and pure doctrine of the Gospel, even as their lives were blameless and holy."

<small>May 23.</small>

<small>May 24.</small>

<small>Recants his recantation.</small>

From that moment Jerome of Prague resumed all his calm intrepidity. He was speedily condemned as a relapsed heretic. The Bishop of Lodi, doubtless as supposed to be gifted with most im-

<small>May 30, 1418. Condemnation.</small>

pressive eloquence, was again called upon to preach the funeral sermon of the heretic. His text was, "He reproached their unbelief and hardness of heart." On his own charity and that of the Council, their charity to the heretic himself, and to the rest of Christendom, for whose sake heresy was to be extirpated, the preacher was unctuous and self-adulatory. He laid down as irrefragably just the ordinary, the rightful course of procedure against all commonly reputed heretics. There should be diligent inquisition for them; they should be apprehended, placed in strong prisons. Articles should be exhibited against them, witnesses admitted, even the most infamous,—usurers, ribalds, common prostitutes. The heretics should be sworn to speak the truth. If they refuse to speak, they are to be put upon the rack, and subjected to various tortures. None should be admitted to visit them, but under strong necessity; they ought not to be heard in public. If they shall recant, they are to find mercy. If obstinate, they are to be condemned and made over to the secular arm. This brief and frightful and authoritative statement of the dominant usage is contrasted by the preacher with the magnanimous mercy of the Council to Jerome of Prague.'

Jerome was permitted to answer; he answered with boldness bordering on scorn. He ended thus: "You are resolved to condemn me in this wicked and iniquitous manner, without having convicted me of any crime; but after my death I will be in your consciences an ever-gnawing worm. I appeal to the Supreme Judge, before

---

' The whole sermon is remarkable. It is in Von der Hardt, iii. p. 35. There was a lofty burst of feudal indignation, that two men, vile plebeians of the basest sort, of unknown birth, should have convulsed the whole kingdom of Bohemia.

whom ye will appear with me, ere a hundred years are passed."[a]

An accomplished Florentine, Poggio Bracciolini, present at the trial, has left an account of the demeanour of Jerome, which impressed him as a display of power and eloquence, almost unrivalled at any time. Emerging from a fetid dungeon, after the depression of a long confinement, with the weight of his recantation upon him, against an adverse Court, he stood his ground, with wonderful copiousness, fluency, and readiness of language, and with consummate dexterity, now deeply pathetic, now with playful wit or taunting sarcasm, confounding, bewildering, overpowering his adversaries. His voice was sweet, clear, sonorous, with a certain dignity; his gesture admirably fitted to express indignation, or to move that commiseration, which he neither sought nor cared to obtain. He stood fearless, intrepid, like another Cato, not only despising, courting death.[b]

His death was as surprising for its calmness and courage. Two days were left to permit him to retract again. The Cardinal of Florence attempted to persuade him to submission. His countenance was constantly not only composed but cheerful."[c] He was bound naked to the stake; he continued to sing hymns with his deep untrembling voice. The executioner offered to light the fire behind him, lest he should see it. "Light it before my face," said the martyr; "had I the least fear, I should not be standing in this place."

Execution.

There remained one case of criminal jurisprudence for the decision of this great Senate of Christendom.

---

[a] L'Enfant is inclined, I think on insufficient grounds, to doubt the authenticity of these last words.
[b] Poggio Bracciolini Oper.   [c] Von der Hardt, III. 64.

ALLEGED CRIMES OF JOHN XXIII.

Before the Council of Constance were arraigned, for different violations of the law of God and man, three persons, all, somewhat singularly, bearing the name of John. Pope John XXIII., according to the articles exhibited against him, and those articles supported by undoubted testimony, and so affirmed by the Council and put forth as the accredited foundation of their judgement, had been guilty from his youth, and during his whole life, of the foulest crimes, being a priest, of licentiousness which passes belief, promiscuous concubinage, incest, the violation of nuns; of the most atrocious cruelties, murder, massacre, the most grinding tyranny, unglutted avarice, unblushing simony. He had rarely celebrated the solemn rites of the Church, the Holy Sacraments, and then with contemptuous neglect and indifference.[a] Against some of these charges John made no defence; in some he seemed to acquiesce, only resting on the plea that they were no heresies, and that the Pope could be judged for heresy alone. John XXIII. was deposed from his Pontifical office, having fled from the Council in violation of his own most solemn protestations; he was ignominiously apprehended, and cast into prison; he was detained in dishonourable but not harsh captivity till the close of the Council. Afterwards, having ceased to be dangerous to the ruling Pope, and having humbled himself beneath his feet, he was permitted to close his days in peace, even

---

[a] "Unus Articulus qui fuit in ordine sextus plura vitia concludit sub hâc formâ. Item quod dictus Johannes fuit et est pauperum oppressor; justitiæ persecutor; iniquitatum columna; Simoniacorum statio; carnis cultor; vitiorum fex; a virtutibus peregrinus; infamiæ speculum et omnium malitiarum profundus admonitor; adeo et in tantum scandalizans ecclesiam Christi, quod inter Christi fideles vitam et mores cognoscentes vulgariter dicitur Diabolus Incarnatus."—Thus speaks a Council of a Pope! Gobelinus, p. 341.

in honour, for he was raised again to the rank of a Cardinal.

The second, John Huss, of life blameless to austerity, absolutely unimpeachable in his morals, charged only with some indirect connexion with turbulent proceedings in Bohemia, with an acquittal of all heresy from the Archbishop of Prague and the Grand Inquisitor, with a safe-conduct from the Emperor, was accused of erroneous belief in Transubstantiation and the Administration of the Cup to the Laity. These charges he distinctly denied, and repelled to the satisfaction of most present: he was likewise accused of having denounced the corruptions and vices of the clergy; yet his denunciations, not to speak of those of Nicolas of Clemangis, Henry of Hessia, Theodoric à Niem, Theodore de Vrie, could hardly have surpassed in severity those of men who sat in judgement upon him, Gerson and Peter d'Ailly Cardinal of Cambray. It is difficult to define or to apprehend the precise remaining delinquencies or errors of which he was found guilty, as having adopted and propagated the condemned doctrines of Wycliffe, treated with derision, or undermined the Power of the Keys, and the absolute irrepealable authority of the clergy, and making that authority dependent not on their succession or ordination, but on their personal holiness. For these offences, notwithstanding the Imperial safe-conduct, John Huss was seized, imprisoned, burned at the stake.

The third, Jean Petit, in an acknowledged, and published, and unambiguous writing, had vindicated as just and lawful a most foul and treacherous murder. In this vindication he had laid down principles utterly subversive of human society—principles which would let loose mankind upon each other, like wild beasts; principles in direct violation of one of the Commandments of God, and in plain, bold opposition to every precept and to the whole religion of Christ.[1]

Jean Petit had escaped by death all personal penalty.[2] The condemnation of his book by the Council of Constance, through the awe and influence of the Duke of Burgundy, was postponed, debated, at length eluded. For to condemn Jean Petit for his abstract propositions, was to condemn the act of the Duke of Burgundy. From the first the partisans of Burgundy, with the acquiescence, the servile admission of those who dared not be his enemies, acquitted the Duke of all personal participation in a crime of which all believed, all knew him to be guilty. But the Council of Constance, to its close, hesitated to pass that censure demanded and uttered by the shuddering abhorrence of mankind against the book of Jean Petit. A Council of Faith at Paris, under the Archbishop and the Grand Inquisitor, had condemned the Eight Verities asserted by Jean Petit. The Council of Constance would not affirm this censure; it was even annulled on account of informality by the Cardinal Orsini and others of the same rank. The world eagerly awaited the decree of the supreme authority in Christendom on the momentous question, the legality of murder. Session after session dragged out in illimitable length. Bishops, Abbots, theologians, the Bishop of Arras, the Abbots of Clairvaux and Citeaux, Jean de la Roche, a learned Dominican, did not scruple to undertake the contest, to allege every kind of captious objection, every subtlety of scholastic logic. These monstrous tenets were declared to be only moral and philosophical opinions, not of faith, therefore out of the province of

---

[1] See in Monstrelet the Eight Principles of Jean Petit, II. c. xxxix.
[2] He died 1411; it is said repenting of his book.

the Church and of the Council. Gerson, the prosecutor in the name of the University of Paris, not avowedly, though known to be in secret supported by the King of France, could not but perceive the monstrous incongruity between the condemnation of John Huss for his anti-hierarchical tenets as of Faith, and the dismissal of questions which concerned the first elements of religion and the Commandments, as beyond the province of Faith. Gerson himself was involved in charges of heresy by the advocates of Jean Petit, determined at all hazards to silence their powerful antagonist. With difficulty a condemnation was extorted of one broad and general proposition. "It is lawful and even meritorious in any vassal or subject to kill a tyrant, either by stratagem, by blandishment, flattery, or force, notwithstanding any oath or covenant sworn with him, without awaiting the sentence or authority of any judge."[a] Yet even this censure was annulled, as wanting in form, by the new Pope. Nothing could induce Martin V. to condemn in full Council either the propositions of Jean Petit, or kindred doctrines which had been published in Poland.[b] Even the memory of the third John escaped unscathed from any authoritative proscription by Council or by Pope. But Gerson, the learned, pious Gerson, dared not return to Paris, now in the power of Burgundy and the English; he lay hid for a time in Germany, lingered out a year or two at Lyons, and died a proscribed and neglected exile; finding his only consolation, no doubt full consolation, in the raptures of his Holy Mysticism.[c]

---

[a] Von der Hardt, iv. 442; L'Enfant, p. 408.
[b] L'Enfant, ii. 212; Gerson. Opera, v. 1014.
[c] "Synodo finitâ Joannes Gersonius, tot laborum suorum, insignisque pietatis, ac in justitiam ac verum ardentissimi amoris, non aliud præmium consecutus est, quam perpetuum exilium."—Dupin, Vit. Gerson. p. xxxvi.

CHAPTER X.

Close of the Council of Constance. Pope Martin V.

YET by these acts (the affair of Jean Petit dragged on to its close) the Council of Constance had only commenced its proper work, the Reformation of the Church and the election of a Pope. Nor had the Fathers approached the solution of the great difficulty, which of these was to take precedence. This question involved another perhaps of higher moment. Could the Church legally reform itself without a Pope? Was it complete, invested in full power of action, without a head? Nor, though John XXIII. was removed, was the ground clear for the election of a new Pope. There were still two Popes, who had not absolutely abandoned their claims; and whose ambassadors had been admitted by the Council. Gregory XII., friendless, worn out, made no resistance; indeed, before the election of the new Pope he had relieved the Council by his death. But the Spaniard, Benedict XIII., was impracticable. Month after month for above a year he fought with firmness which might have been admired in a better cause. The Emperor met at Perpignan the Kings of Arragon, Castile, and Navarre. Benedict refused a safe-conduct addressed to him only as a Cardinal; he would appear but as Pope in his Pontifical robes. He appeared, fled, appeared again. His demands were as exorbitant as if he still divided the world. He would have the Council of Pisa annulled, the Council of Constance broken up, a new and more impartial tribunal summoned. He would cede, and he would not cede; he would dictate, not receive laws of reform.

Nov. 2.
Again he fled to Collaria, a strong fortress near the sea. He was besieged by the deputies of the Spanish cities. He withdrew to the more impregnable Peniscola. At Narbonne certain capitulations were framed; according to which the Kings of Arragon, Castile, Navarre, and the Count de Foix renounced their obedience to Benedict. The Spaniards joined the Council, they formed a fifth Nation. Benedict, deserted by his Cardinals, cited again and again, declared contumacious, accused, condemned, deposed, to the last adhered to himself. Two Benedictine monks brought him the summons of the Council. "Are ye the ravens returned to the Ark? No wonder that the ravens gather where the dead body is!" He received the sentence with the utmost impatience, threw back on the Council the charge of schism, and broke out, striking his chair with violence, "Not at Constance, the Church is at Peniscola." He created two new Cardinals, maintained the forms of state, and not till some years after died at Peniscola as obstinate and unyielding as he had lived.

Dec. 13.

Jan. 1417.

March 8.
April 1.

The deposition of Benedict brought the two contending parties into direct conflict. On the all-important but undecided question, the Cardinals, on one side, insisted that no reform could be valid, authoritative, complete, unless by the Church in her full and perfect capacity, with a Pope at her head. The Emperor, supported by the Germans and English, was determined not to let slip the golden opportunity for reform, unembarrassed if not by the natural repugnance,

Divisions in the Council.

by all the forms and difficulties inseparable from the Papal assent. They maintained the imperious necessity of reform in the head as well as in the members. The Pope himself must submit to the salutary restrictions imposed on the rest of the hierarchy; and could that be expected, could it be extorted from an actual ruling Pope? Menacing and ominous signs of division began to appear. The Cardinals protested against pro- <small>August, September.</small> ceeding to any reform unauthorised by a Pope; the Germans and the English were accused of heresy, for promulgating such dangerous doctrines. <small>Sept. 11.</small> The Emperor took the strong measure of prohibiting the separate meetings of the Cardinals.

At this juncture, the death of Robert Hallam, Bishop of Salisbury, changed the whole state of affairs. <small>Sept. 4. Death of Robert Hallam.</small> On his wisdom, on his resolute firmness, the Emperor had relied; his authority held together the Germans and the English. The French, from hatred of the English, had somewhat cooled in their ardent zeal for reform; they had even contested the right of the English to vote, especially after the arrival of the Spaniards, as one of the Nations. In D'Ailly the Cardinal prevailed over the Reformer. Two of the more distinguished German Prelates were bought over. Wallenrod of Riga received the wealthy Bishopric of Liège, with its princedom, Abondi of Coire, the Archbishopric of Riga.* Only a few days after Hallam's death the English fell off to the Italian party; the Emperor was compelled to assent to the election of a Pope, upon the specious but precarious resolution that the Pope should stipulate to reform the Church before

---

* Von der Hardt, iv. 1432-1440. Probably, after the consent to the election, as a reward.

the dissolution of the Council. The angry feud between the Emperor and the Cardinals was allayed by the good offices of Beaufort, Bishop of Winchester (uncle of King Henry VI.), on his return from the Holy Land, and so invested with a kind of holy influence.

Great bodies are apt, when weary of the tardy and encumbered progress of affairs, to rush on in headlong precipitation, and to accomplish in reckless haste what might seem to require the most grave and slow deliberation. They waste years in debate, and then do desperately in a few days or hours the most important acts. The hard-wrung consent of the Emperor was given on the last day of September. The inevitable contests as to the form of election were over in one month. On the 30th of October (at its Fortieth Session) the Council made its last effort for independent life. It declared that it was not to be dissolved till the Pope had granted reform. On the 8th of November those who were to be joined with the Cardinals in the privilege of election (this concession the Council had demanded and obtained) were named. Twenty-three Cardinals and thirty Delegates of the Council entered the Conclave. The strife was sharp but short. On the 11th of November, an Italian, a Roman, a noble of the house of Colonna, had united the suffrages; the Cardinal Colonna, elected on St. Martin's day, took the name of Martin V.[b]

Election of Martin V.

The election of the Pope woke the whole Council to

[b] "Quod autem in Papam electus est ille, qui de Collegio Cardinalium obedientiæ Urbani Papæ descendit, Spiritus Sanctus quodam mysterio singulari egisse præsumitur; cum id quod prius ira, odium, insidiæ et protervitas et alto dubium facti temporis diuturnitate subortam, de Papatus justa possessione discerni non siverant, hoc jam totius mundi consensus simpliciter in cordibus veritatem et justitiam diligentium scintillaret."—Gobelinus, p. 344.

a paroxysm of joy. He was at once invested in the Papal robes, and placed on the altar, where eager throngs hasted to kiss his feet. The Emperor prostrated himself before the Pontiff, and paid that act of reverential homage. Throughout the rest of the ceremonial of the inauguration Constance vied with Rome in its pomp, and in its adherence to the ancient formularies, as far as could be done in a strange city. The immense multitudes, which might more fairly be supposed to represent Christendom, made up for the sacred emotions inseparable from Rome. If the Minster of Constance but poorly represented the time-hallowed Lateran, the fantastic S. Maria Maggiore, the Apostolic Church of St. Peter, yet the inexhaustible crowds of all nations, Kings, Princes, Burghers, Prelates, Clergy of all the kingdoms of Europe, might add even greater dignity to the ceremony than the so-called Consuls, Senators, Magistrates, and populace of Rome.

The Cardinal Otto Colonna was a man in elevating whom conflicting parties might meet without the humiliation of a compromise. Of the highest birth, irreproachable morals, with the reputation of learning in the Canon Law, in only two points he had departed from the most calm moderation, in both with the full sympathies of the Council. He had been strenuous for the condemnation of Huss; he had adhered to, had even followed Pope John in his flight; but this would find excuse as an act of generous fidelity to the ruling Pontiff and to a falling friend. In all other respects he had held a middle course with great dignity; no stern adversary of reformation, no alarming fanatic for change. He was courteous in manners, short and sententious in speech, quick and dexterous yet cautious in business, a strict and even ostentatious lover of justice. His enemies could only assert that much craft lurked under his moderation; later in life his prudence degenerated into avarice. The conduct of the Pope, until the dissolution of the Council, the dissolution of the Council without any great general measure of reform, while he avoided all serious offence to the Emperor or to the more formidable advocates of reform, display the great sagacity, the consummate policy of Martin V.

Yet in his first act Martin might seem to throw off his moderation, and to declare hastily and imperiously his determination to maintain all the existing abuses. The Papal chancery had been the object of the longest, loudest, and most just clamour. The day after the election, the Pope published a Brief confirming all the regulations established by his predecessors, even by John XXIII.[c] All the old grievances, Reservations, Expectancies, Vacancies, Confirmations of Bishops, Dispensations, Exemptions, Commendams, Annates, Tenths, Indulgences,[d] might seem to be adopted as the irrepealable law of the Church.[e] The form was

First act of Martin V.

---

[c] On the regulations of the Roman Chancery, see Eichhorn, iii. p. 511, note. To the Chancery belonged the preparation and expedition of all Briefs and Bulls, appeals, negotiations. The Dataria was originally a branch of the Chancery; from the Dataria came all grants, gifts, appointments to benefices. The head of the whole was the Protonotarius or Primicerius, called also Corrector of the Papal Letters. There was a College of Abbreviators, 12 de parco majori, 22 de parco minori (from these were the Rescribendarius, the Taxatores who fixed the price of Briefs or Bulls, and the Plumbator who held the seal); the rest, making up 72, might be laymen or married men, and were called examiners. The first wore the violet dress of bishops. There were three courts of justice, the Rota, the Signatura Justitiæ, and Signatura Gratiæ. All this vast incorporation was maintained by the fees of office.

[d] The decree is in Von der Hardt, I. p. 955 et seqq., L'Enfant, ii. 415–428 countersigned by the Cardinal Bishop of Ostia, Nov. 12, 1417, published, with severe penalties for its infringement, Feb. 26, 1418.

[e] The right of the Holy See to appoint to all benefices, out of which gradually grew up all these abuses of Reservations, Provisions, Dispensations,

not less dictatorial than the substance of the decree. It was an act of the Pope, not of the Council. It was

Annates, Commendams, Pluralities, was unknown till the twelfth century. The prerogative might seem necessarily vested in the universal Bishop, enabling him, by his higher episcopal authority, to place the worthiest men in every office or function of the Universal Church. Its first exercise appears to have been, when on the removal, the deposition, or degradation of any unfit, criminal, or heretical dignitary, the right might devolve* on the supreme arbiter (these were mostly cases of appeal) to substitute some worthier prelate. Hadrian IV. began to recommend spiritual persons to the bishops for preferment. These *prayers* with his successors grew into mandates: the haughty Alexander III. not merely issued those mandates, but sent his officers to enforce their execution.† It was an early usage, too, that when a prelate or high dignitary died at Rome, the Pope and the Roman Court in their abundant charity would send a successor from Rome for the consolation of the widowed Church.‡ Innocent III. first asserted for the Supreme Pontiff the plenary power of disposing of all benefices, for the advantage of such persons as should have deserved well of the See of Rome.§ From this time Bulls for the appointment of such prelates bear the significant words of "our plenary authority:" and the more sweeping "notwithstanding," which at once annulled all existing rights, privileges, prescriptions of rightful patrons. The Papal Legates were invested in the same high powers; ‖ in them, if they deemed it necessary to put forth their power, was the derivative authority to summon any ecclesiastic to any office or dignity. As yet it was the haughty assertion on special occasions only, and occasions in many cases such as might seem to justify the Papal interference and the exercise of this all-embracing prerogative. We have seen Stephen Langton seated on the throne of Canterbury by this title, in vain contested by the King, admitted by the world. Clement IV. fifty years later specially reserved for the Papal nomination all benefices of which the possessors died at Rome.¶ That which was a proud prerogative, exercised so far with some modesty, and with some respect for the high purposes for which it was assumed, with the Avignonese Pontiffs and their successors became a wanton and arbitrary authority, exercised for the aggrandisement of the Pope's power and the Pope's wealth. Already Clement V. reserved for himself, out of his love for his former see the archbishopric and certain abbeys in Bordeaux. John XXII. not only extended the special reservation to whole dioceses, Aquileia, Milan, Ravenna, Genoa, and Pisa, but as we have seen, pro-

* This was called "jus devolutionis." † See Eichhorn, III. p. 507. Preces, Mandata.
‡ "In consolationem de obitu defuncti."—Ibid. § Planck, iv. p. 721.
‖ "De officio Legati."—Regest. c. 6, E.
¶ "Licet . . . beneficiorum . . . plenaria dispositio ad Romanum spectetur Pontificem pertinere . . . collationem tamen . . . beneficiorum, apud Sedem Romanam vacantium, specialites cæteris antiqua consuetudo R. P. reservavit."—B. Clement, IV.

throughout the Pope who enacted and ordained; it was the absolute resumption of the whole power of Reforma-

claimed the Papal reservation of all beneficies vacated by promotions through the grace of the Roman See. We have seen, too, that John XXII. endeavoured by one sweeping edict to strip all pluralists of their execrable and unholy accumulation of preferments, and to secure their spoils, as Reserves, for himself and the Holy See. We have seen how out of the Reservations arose the *Expectatives*, granted with such lavish prodigality by the Italian Popes who succeeded to those of Avignon; with the not less lucrative creation of *coadjutorcies*.

With the reservation of benefices, and still more with the right of confirmation of bishops—a right asserted, and more or less rigidly exercised, since the twelfth century—was closely connected the right of the taxation of benefices. The tax assumed the name of Annates, as calculated on the annual revenue of the benefice. It was levied as a fee on consecration upon every bishop confirmed in Rome. At first it was confined to prelacies. Clement V. extended this privilege of paying a year's income to all benefices in England. John XXII. extended it throughout Christendom for three years only, on account of the pressing necessities of the Roman Church;" but those necessities ceased not to be urgent: the three years grew into a perpetuity.† Towards the end of the fourteenth century it became a tax, the fees on confirmation must be paid over and above. Thus the Papal Chancery held a roll of assessment of the value of almost all benefices in Christendom; this ecclesiastical valuation was raised from time to time, as not only th. annates, the first-fruits, but the tenths which were occasionally commanded or granted were collected according to this cadaster.‡ In the same manner the Pope seized, what Kings had claimed, the possessions left by the clergy, and the produce of vacant benefices.

The plenary power which could bestow, could *dispense* with the duties of all benefices. It could permanently unite contiguous and poor benefices: it could excuse, on the pretext of higher duties, the duties of the member of the Capitular Body, of the parish Priest, even of the Bishop. Who but the Head of the Church could judge what was for the benefit of the Church? If this could be done in benefices with cure of souls, how much more when it was only the rule of a monastery, the seat in or the presidency of a Chapter, the stately and almost inactive charge of the Abbot, or the regular and ritual duty of the Canon or the Prebendary? Here the Prior, there the Vicar, might go through with sufficient decency the scanty or the mechanical services in the church, dream in the cloister, chant in the choir. The Pope would therefore less scruple to accumulate such benefices on his Cardinals, his officers, his courtiers, his favourites, whom he

* Compare vol. vii. p. 435; Eichhorn, III. p 507.
† They were likewise called " servitia communia et minuta."
‡ Extravagant. Cap. ii. de Prebend.

tion, so far at least as the Papal Court, into his own hands. Whatever he might hereafter concede to the Church in general, or to the separate nations of Christendom, was a boon on his part, not a right on theirs. Did the secret of this bold measure really lurk in this—that it appeared to be and was received as a declaration against all reform?

The Council saw its fatal error. In creating a Pope of high character, it had given itself a master. It might dictate to a John XXIII., it must submit to a Martin V. The Emperor himself had fallen into the second rank; the Pope took his seat as of course President of the Council. They were at the Pope's mercy. Their only hope was that his magnanimity, his gratitude, or his zeal for religion might prevail over his jealous care of his supremacy, that precious trust which had been handed down by so many generations of Popes, the unlimited Vice-gerency of God.

Yet the Nations would not abandon or relax their strenuous efforts for reform. The Germans presented a strong memorial; it contained eighteen articles, limiting the number of Cardinals, placing the Papal power under severe restrictions as to collation of benefices, Annates, Reservations, Appeals, the abuses of the Chancery and the Penitentiary, Exemptions, Unions, Commendams.[f] The French had been at first the most bold and earnest in their denunciations against the abuses in the Church.

---

could commend to the formal election of the Chapter or the Monks, and permit to hold (in commendam), without once having visited the Convent or the Chapter, the Prebend, the Deanery, the portion of one or more monks, the Priorate, the Abbacy. Thus was all bound together in one complicated but subtly-interwoven system; and now wrested by the dexterous craft of Martin V. out of the hands of the spoiler.

[f] L'Enfant gives the articles, iii. p. 186 et seqq.

Gerson, the Cardinal D'Ailly, Nicolas Clemangis,[a] had uttered terrible truths in language hardly less violent than Wycliffe or Huss. They had entreated the Emperor to enforce reform. Sigismund bitterly replied, "When we urged that reform should precede the election of a Pope, you scorned our judgement and insisted on first having a Pope. Lo, you have a Pope, implore him for reform. I had some power before a Pope was chosen, now I have none."[b] The Spaniards even threatened to return to the obedience of Pope Benedict; but they exhausted all their indignation in violent satires, which obtained great currency and vogue, were laughed at, and forgotten.[c]

The Pope acted with perfect address. He seemed to yield in the amplest manner. He submitted to the Nations a counter plan of Reformation, each article of which might have occupied the weary Council for months

---

[a] De Clemangis, from Clemange, a village in the diocese of Chalons. See life prefixed to his Works, by Dupin, Gersoniana. Also his works passim, more especially his 'Declaratio de Corrupto Ecclesiæ Statu.' This must be read as a declamation. Clemangis begins with a golden age of the Church and of the world; as brilliant as their state in his own day was blackly coloured. His remorseless scourge spares neither Pope, nor Cardinals, nor Bishops, nor Priests, nor Monks, nor Friars, nor Nuns. No one can judge what things were written, and not by persiarchs, but by pious churchmen, who does not read this work of Clemangis, the scholar of Gerson. "Si quis hodie desidiosus est, si quis a labore abhorreas, si quis in otio luxuriari velms, ad sacerdotium con-
volat, quo adeptu, statim se cæteris sacerdotibus voluptatum sectatoribus adjungit, qui magis secundum Epicurum quam secundum Christum vivroles, et canposulas seduli frequentantes, potando, commessando, prandiando, conrivando, cum tesseris et pilâ ludendo tempora tota consumunt. Crapulati verò et inebriati pugnant, clamant, tumultuantur, nomen Dei et Sanctorum suorum pollutissimis labris execrantur. Sicque tandem compositi, ex meretricum suarum amplexibus ad divinum altare veniunt."—Oper. t, xvi. p. 16. See further on the corruption of French morals by the Papal court at Avignon; and the Pluralities of the Cardinals.

[b] Gobelinus Persona, vi. p. 345.

[c] L'Enfant, ii. p. 190.

of hot debate. In the mean time, on the old maxim of ruling by the division of the adverse forces, he entered into negotiations for separate Concordats with each of the Transalpine nations. Italy had acquiesced at once in the Papal autocracy. Each of the other Nations had its usages, its institutions, its national character; each Nation, therefore, ought to have its peculiar ecclesiastical regulations, as concerned its relations to the Papacy. Thus it was no longer Christendom, no longer the whole Church, no longer the Council, the representative of the Church, which was confronted with the Pope. Each kingdom stood alone to make the best terms in its power. So, too, the infringement, neglect, abrogation, of any of those articles, was no longer a breach of the great Canonical Law of Christendom, it became a matter of quarrel with one King, or one Nation, it concerned none other; it awoke no general indignation, was no breach of faith to the world at large. The League of Christendom for its common rights, common interests, common religion, was broken in pieces.

The Concordat with Germany (limited to five years) was vague, ambiguous, and left almost everything to the interpretation of the Pope. Cardinals were to be elected in moderate numbers. Some limitation was placed, but that indefinite, on the Pope's right of nominating to and confirming the larger vacant Benefices. Annates were to be levied according to the ancient taxation; Commendams were to be bestowed, Dispensations issued, Indulgences granted in more sparing and prudent measure.[k] *Concordat with Germany;*

That with England contained six even more meagre

---

[k] Art. de Indulgentiis. "Carebit Romanus Papa in futurum nimiam Indulgentiarum effusionem, ne vilescant."

articles. Two of these stipulated that the inferior Prelates were not to wear the decorations of the higher—the mitre and sandals; that Englishmen should be admissible to offices in the Roman Court.

with England.

Nor was that with France, though more diffuse, more full or unambiguous. No one of the nations by any authoritative act accepted these Concordats. France, by a royal edict, by a decree of her Parliaments, rejected hers with contempt.[m] It was presented by Martin, Bishop of Arras, before the Parliament of Paris, repudiated with unanimity.[n] The Parliament proclaimed the maintenance of the liberties of the Gallican Church, especially as to the collation of benefices, though prepared to contribute to the maintenance of the Popedom by moderate and necessary payments: it prohibited with the utmost rigour all payments whatever for Provisions, Annates, Vacancies, and such usurped powers.

with France.

It does not appear that the King or the Parliament of England deigned to notice the treaty passed in her name; her stern limitary laws stood unshaken, unrepealed.[o]

The work of the Council was done, or rather it had now no work to do. The Council was as anxious to be released from its weary imprisonment as the Pope to

---

[m] Preuves des Libertés de l'Eglise Gallicane, c. xiii. No. 16.
[n] Von der Hardt, iv. 1567.
[o] Compare the treatise of Clemangis, "De Annatis non Solvendis." He lays down the axiom, "Quia nullo statuto, privilegio, consuetudine, præscriptione, aut alio titulo potest induci, quod propter conferre aut consentire promotioni, aut electioni alicujus Monasterii vel Ecclesiæ Cathedralis, sive ut præficiatur administrationi prælaturæ, beneficio, sive Ecclesiæ, aliquid possit vel debeat peti vel exigi, eo quod secundum Apostolicas et Canonicas traditiones, clarissime foret Simoniacum." It is curious that there is frequent appeal to English usage.—Oper. p. 85.

release it. The Council felt itself baffled, eluded, fallen under the inextricable dominion of the Pope. The Emperor was conscious that he had sunk to a subordinate position; his majesty was eclipsed. On the occasion of his solemn farewell the bitterness of his heart seemed to creep out. He declared his full obedience to the Pope; his submission to all the decrees of the Council. But if the Council had fallen into error he disclaimed all concern in it.[p] These significant words would bear various meanings, and were variously interpreted as alluding to the execution of Huss, the refusal to condemn Jean Petit and John of Falkenburg who in Poland had asserted the same execrable doctrines, the failure in the reformation of the Church. That miserable failure was admitted in all quarters.[q] The Pope kept up to the last his grave and stately dignity. On Whitsunday he officiated in the Cathedral with high pomp; countless multitudes thronged all night around the Episcopal Palace to receive his benediction: he showered indulgences on the enraptured thousands. The next day he set off for Geneva escorted by the Emperor, the whole city, and all the hierarchy who had not already taken their departure. He had refused the Emperor's pressing invitations to remain longer in Germany. The Council of Constance was at an end.[r]

The Council of Constance threatened to shake, might seem to have shaken, the Papal supremacy to its foundations; but for a time it strengthened rather than enfee-

---

[p] Von der Hardt, iv. p. 1563. L'Enfant, ii. 248.

[q] "Sunt tamen quædam reformata, quamvis respectu conceptorum paucu, verbis quidem et scriptis quæ propter humanæ mentis mutabilitatem, divinitatis excusantem se sub umbrâ, hic inserere non præsumo."—Gobelinus Persona, p. 355.

[r] The Council had sat for three years and six months without a tumult in the streets, without rise in the price of provisions, without any epidemic or contagious malady.

bled its authority. It compelled the election of a Pope, whose character, irreproachable, if not imposing from learning and sanctity, recovered the waning reverence of Christendom. Nor was it till the next century, when the Popes had become powerful temporal sovereigns, when the Italian wars had almost quenched the last awe of religion, when the struggle for dominion between the great conflicting powers of Europe, France, the Empire, Spain, England, made Italy the battle-field of the world; it was not till then that the Popes sank again to the moral level, or lower than the level of Italian Princes or temporal potentates, and that an Alexander VI. could be endured on the throne of St. Peter. It had been established indeed that there was a tribunal which in extreme cases might depose a Pope. But then it must be during a schism among contending Popes, each with a doubtful title, or at farthest a Pope flagrantly defective in faith or morals. But the right in the Council to reform the Church in its head as well as its members, to impose restrictions on the all-enacting, all-abrogating, all self-executing power of the Popedom, this right, which there can be no doubt was asserted by the Council, remained a barren, abstract proposition, to be again asserted, but asserted in vain, in the Council of Basle. Still the Pope claimed, he exercised the prerogative of issuing Canons for the universal obedience of Christendom, and of giving to Papal Decrees the infallible authority of the Gospel, of God himself. Pope Martin quietly resumed all the unrevoked authority which the Christian world had yielded to Innocent III., or even to Boniface VIII. No single Canon, not one of the Extravagants of Boniface, not one even of the Clementine Decretals was annulled; every precedent remained in force. The Concordats granted by the will of the

Pope, feeble guarantees as they were for the liberties of national churches, or against abuses, might be abrogated or fall into desuetude. Of what force were they against what was averred to be the ancient, immemorial, irrevocable privileges of the Roman See?

The Council had given its sanction, its terrible sanction, to the immutability of the whole dominant creed of Christendom, to the complete indefeasible hierarchical system. It had declared implacable war against all who should revolt, not only from the doctrine but from the discipline of the Church. One part of the sacerdotal order might aspire to greater freedom, but the slightest emancipation of mankind from the rule of the sacerdotal order entered not into the thoughts, hardly into the apprehensions, of the Fathers of Constance. In the execution of Huss and Jerome of Prague there had been awful unanimity. Few foresaw, still fewer had they foreseen would have shrunk from, the horrors of the Bohemian war, in which it was first shown in a whole nation, how much more dreadful is the collision of hostile fanaticisms than the worst strife of temporal interests or principles. Bohemia as a province of the Christian world in insurrection against the unity of the Church, was even more beyond the pale of mercy than a heathen land. The Christian duty, the Christian justice, of enforcing belief in the Gospel on the wild and yet unconverted races in the North of Germany was debated, and with strong resistance, by the more tolerant. Few of those who fought, or drove others to fight, with Ziska and Procopius, doubted the holiness, the imperative obligation of battling against these heresiarchs to the death.

Martin V. travelled slowly through Italy. He accepted the splendid hospitalities of Florence, now at the height of her power, and proud to receive the Supreme Pontiff as her guest. The grateful, yet poor or parsimonious Pope, had no other return to make but the elevation of Florence to an Archiepiscopate. At Florence John XXIII. having, by the Pope's desire, been transferred from a German to an Italian prison, though he had once made his escape, now quieted the apprehensions of his rival by throwing himself at his feet, expressing the deepest contrition for all his sins, and abdicating his last hold on the Papacy in the most full and humiliating terms. Martin felt the policy as well as the generosity of mercy. Balthasar Cossa, after a few days of austere penance, was named Cardinal and the Head of the Sacred College. But his eventful life drew to its end: he died, worn out; it was said that his last humiliation preyed on his weary spirit. He was buried with great pomp at the expense of the Republic. His tomb is still seen under the noble dome of Florence. Benedict XIII. closed at length his stubborn career at Peniscola. He had still two partisans, whom he dignified with the name of Cardinals; faithful to the memory of their patron the two Cardinals proceeded to elect a successor, a canon of Barcelona. Martin was wise enough to dispel this phantom of a Pontiff by mild measures. The Antipope sank willingly into the Bishop of Majorca.

Martin was undisputed Pope; but in the Papal territory he was not master of a single city. Besides the kingdoms and dukedoms, Naples and Milan, the Republics, Venice and Florence, the independent lords of other cities, a new Power had arisen to still greater height—the Captains of the Free Companies, who had carved themselves out principalities, which they maintained by the bands of their mercenary followers. Braccio Montone occupied the greater part of the Papal dominions.' Pope Martin had recognised the title of Joanna II., the inheritress of the name, the throne, the licentiousness, the misfortunes of Joanna I., to the throne of Naples. In return the famous Condottiero, Ludovico Sforza, hereafter to be more famous, now at the head of his own bands and those of Naples, advanced as Gonfalonier of the Church to expel Braccio Montone from the territory of St. Peter. But Sforza, or rather Sforza's ally Tartaglia, whom he had seduced from Braccio, suffered a disastrous defeat; the Pope was compelled to make terms, through the mediation of Florence, with the triumphant Braccio.[t] To Florence Braccio came; the fickle city contrasted the magnificence, the frank bearing, the lavish expenditure, the feasts and tournaments of the adventurer, with the cold and severe dignity, the poverty of the Pontiff. Popular songs were current to the glory of the soldier, the shame of the Pope. The children sang two verses under the window, which taunted at once his worthlessness and his penury.[*] Martin made haste to reconcile the powerful Braccio with the Church. Braccio restored Orvieto, Narni, Terni, and Orta to the Pope; he held as a fief under

---

* Of Braccio Montone, Æneas Sylvius writes that one side of his body was palsied. He was eloquent and facetious. "Blandus eloquio, crudelis opere. De clavibus Ecclesiæ, de Christo, de Deo nihil timuit, ut qui animam cum corpore extingui Epicurea dementia crediditi."—Vit. Freder. III. apud Kollar, II. p. 1541.

[t] Muratori, sub ann. 1419. Braccio affected to become a sort of Cæsar. He was reported to have said that he would reduce Pope Martin so low that he would say six masses for a piece of silver. A Florentine reproached Braccio with this speech, "Six masses for a piece of silver! I would not give him a piece of copper for a thousand." See the account of his death and burial.—Æneas Sylvius, ibid.

[*] "Papa Martino, Non vale un quatirino." Pope Martin, Not worth a farthing. *Muratori, Ann. sub ann.*

the sovereignty of the Church Perugia, Assisi, Iesi, Todi, and other towns. He compelled Bologna to acknowledge the sovereignty of the Pope, and to admit a Papal garrison.

June, 1420.

It was not till late in the following year that Pope Martin ventured to return to his native city and to the palace of the Popes. The Roman and the Pope might behold with the profoundest sorrow the state of the Eternal City. It was difficult to say during many late years whether the presence or the absence of her Pontiffs had been most disastrous. On every side he beheld tottering houses, churches in ruins, deserted streets, the whole city a mass of filth and rubbish, the inhabitants wasting away with poverty and dearness of provisions.[a] The citizens looked like strangers, or like an immigration of the dregs of all people. An inundation of the Tiber, of more than usual height and violence, soon after his arrival, added to the wretchedness; the waters came up to the high altar of the Pantheon. If there were great discontents in the Papal territories at the heavy taxation; if the Pope was accused, and too justly accused, in his later days of avarice, and of having left a vast treasure in the hands of his kindred;[r] if he infringed,

Sept. 22, 1421.

Martin in Rome.

---

[a] Platina, Vit. Martini V.

[r] Voigt has printed, in the Historisches Taschenbuch for 1833, a very curious paper called "Stimmen aus Rom über dem Papstlichen Hof im 15ten Jahrhundert." It is compiled from more than 100 inedited letters from the ambassadors or procurators of the Teutonic Order at Rome. They were mostly written by persons who had long resided there, and are confidential, business-like, passionless letters. These ambassadors at first lived in great state; had 2000 ducats income; they had nine horses and a mule (the Cardinals were constantly borrowing their horses). In 1430 they were cut down to six, to the great diminution, as they remonstrate, of their influence. The ambassador of the Hospitallers had but three horses, and their affairs could not get on at all. The ambassador of the Teutonic Order was always in special connexion with

for the sake of filling the Papal coffers, on the Concordats extorted from him at Constance; in Rome if he treated the Cardinals with overbearing haughtiness, even harshness,* Martin V. was honoured during his life, and after a pontificate of fourteen years followed to his splendid sepulchre by the whole people of Rome, by the clergy of all ranks, lamenting the Father of the city. Rome under him had risen from her ruins, populous, prosperous, again the capital of the Christian world.

During the whole of this period the Colonna, of one of the old princely houses of Italy, the lord of a great

---

some one Cardinal, the protector of the Order (p. 89, &c.). The protector was to be propitiated and kept to his duty by perpetual and very costly presents in money, plate, jewels, horses. On those gifts there are many very curious particulars. So, too, on the venality of all, from the Pope and Cardinals downwards. One, after many others in like tone, sums up in one brief sentence: " Wer da mehr giebt der hat auch mehr recht" (p. 97). " 'How is it,' " writes one ambassador, " you inquire, 'that the Poles have every thing their own way?' Because they spend more money. This year" —1411, before the Council of Constance—" they have spent 20,000 ducats. .... The Pope has yearly from the Order 400 ducats." . . . In 1420 (Pope Martin is on the throne), "the Pope has said thrice to me, 'Come to me alone, without your Cardinal; I will be protector of the Order.' I knew well what he meant, and sent him a handsome present, as a welcome on his return to Rome. He took it most willingly" (p. 101). In 1429 the Pope claimed the right of appointing a Master of the Order, as every one saw, to bring more money to himself. "One or two Cardinals can do nothing; we must reach the Pope himself, which cannot be done without money and presents." The Pope was very jealous of the presentation to all the benefices in Prussia and Livonia possessed by the Order; he would have them or their worth in money. See, too, the list of Christmas-boxes to the Pope, Cardinals, and others (p. 107): —A blue velvet cloth for the Pope, 88 ducats; a gold cup, 64 ducats; 13 silver spoons for the Pope's chamberlains, 117 ducats . . . Comfits for the Cardinals and Auditors, 70 and 31 ducats . . . . for the Pope's groom, 3 ducats; a horse for a present, 30 ducats. Each Pope had his favourite, who was bribed at a higher price; with Martin V., first, the Patriarch of Grado—later, Herman, his Protonotary (p. 126). The whole correspondence is very unfavourable to Martin V., to his pride and rapacity (p. 171).

* See on, p. 377.

territory, the Pope, could not but be mingled up in the intricate, versatile, and treacherous politics of Italy. Martin, not more embarrassed than the other temporal sovereigns, or the ambitious Republics, by gratitude to allies or fidelity to treaties, in the renewed strife between the houses of Arragon and Anjou for the throne of Naples, in the long wars between the Visconti, Duke of Milan, and Venice and Florence, calmly pursued his own interests and those of his See. The Papal territories, if heavily burthened with imposts, at least escaped the ravages of foreign war, and were no longer desolated by the wanton pillage of the Free Companies. Bologna alone rose for her freedom; but the signal was not hailed by the neighbouring cities. The Bentivogli came into power, but were obliged to acknowledge at least the restricted lordship of the Pope. They were goaded to a second insurrection by the massacre of some of their house by the Legate, and a second time under Eugenius IV. reconciled to the Church.

Towards Transalpine Christendom Martin V., safe on his throne at Rome, resumed all the haughty demeanour and language of former Pontiffs. He interfered in the disposal of the wealthy benefices of Germany. In England he heard with indignation, and endeavoured by the most vigorous remonstrances to repress, the growing spirit of independence. The Church in England had plunged headlong into the wars of France. If the Primate Chicheley[*] did not instigate, he urged, he

---

[*] Archbishop Chicheley was ambassador to Gregory XII. at Sienna; at Lucca he was appointed by the Pope, by way of provision, Bishop of St. David's. He was at the Council of Pisa, and assenting to the degradation of Gregory XII. He was Archbishop of Canterbury, 1414. The Pope claimed the right of provision, but named the prelate designated by the crown, and elected by the Monks.—Life of Chicheley. London, 1789.

justified the iniquitous claim of Henry V. to the throne of France. The lavish subsidies of the Church were bestowed with unexampled readiness and generosity for these bloody campaigns. It was more than gratitude to the House of Lancaster for their firm support of the Church, and the statute for burning heretics; it was a deliberate diversion, a successful one, of the popular passions to a foreign war, from their bold and resolute aggressions on the Church.[b] What torrents of blood could be too deep, what amount of misery too great to avert such danger! But the Church in England had enough to do to look to itself; it could not be equally vigilant or self-sacrificing for the interests of the Pope. Henry V. like his predecessor, and his Parliament, held the law in their own hands. The nation fully concurred, or had rather enforced the constitutional opposition to the Papal power. The Statute of Præmunire remained among the laws of the realm. It could no longer be overlooked by the Church of Rome. To Chicheley, still Archbishop of Canterbury, Martin addressed a grave missive, reproving in the harshest terms his criminal remissness, his treacherous cowardice.[c] "By this execrable statute the King of England has so entirely usurped the spiritual jurisdiction, as if our Saviour had constituted him his Vicar. He makes laws for the Church and the Order of the Clergy; draws the cognisance of ecclesiastical causes

Statute of Præmunire.

---

[b] Shakespeare in the first scene of Henry V. speaks the language of the chronicles, the chronicles the language of history. The allusion to the famous petition, which the poet makes a bill (see vol. v. p. 527), is curious. Is there Parliamentary authority for this?—

"That self-same Bill is urged,
Which in the eleventh year of the last King's reign
Was like and had indeed against us passed,
But that the scambling and unquiet time
Did push it out of further question."
Henry V., Act I. Scene 1.

[c] Raynaldus, sub ann. 1426. Collier, E. H. B. vii. p. 633. Henry VI. was on the throne.

to the temporal courts; makes provision about clerks, benefices, and the concerns of the hierarchy, as if he held the keys of the kingdom of heaven, as if the administration of these affairs were with the King, not with St. Peter. Besides these hideous encroachments he has enacted terrible penalties against the clergy: Jews and Saracens are not treated with so much severity. People of all persuasions, of all countries, have the liberty of coming into England; except those who have cures bestowed upon them by the Supreme Bishop, by the Vicar of Christ Jesus. Those only are banished, arrested, imprisoned, stripped of their fortunes. Proctors or notaries charged with the execution of the mandates or censures of the Apostolic See, if they venture to set foot on English ground, and proceed in the fulfilment of their commission, are treated as the King's enemies, cast out of the King's protection, exposed to the extremest hardships. . . . . Is this a Catholic kingdom? If any discipline or Apostolic censure is urged against this usage it is treated as a capital offence." The Archbishop is reminded that he is the successor of the glorious martyr St. Thomas. In the following year the Pope addressed the Parliament of England; and in a second letter to the Archbishop accused him of having irreverently and wickedly declared in public that the Apostolic See sought the abolition of that statute only from sordid pecuniary motives.

A.D. 1427

But Martin V., perhaps inadvertently, had wounded the pride and infringed on the dignity of the Anglican Primate. Henry of Beaufort, it has been seen, the King's uncle, on his return from the Holy Land, had done good service at the Council of Constance [a]

Cardinal Beaufort.

---

[a] Dr. Lingard has inadvertently written Basil.—Hist. of England.

by his mediation between the conflicting parties. The Pope had rewarded him by creating him Cardinal of Winchester and Apostolic Legate in England. This usurpation on the Legatine power, of late held by Chicheley, and on the undisputed Primacy of the Archbishop of Canterbury, could not be tamely endured. Chicheley had obtained from Henry V. a prohibition to the Bishop of Winchester to exercise Legatine power in England. The Regency, during the minority of Henry VI., would not receive Beaufort with the honours due to his rank, and demanded that he should surrender his Bishopric of Winchester, vacated by his acceptance of the Cardinalate. This Churchman had been appointed Captain-General of a crusade against the Hussites in Bohemia. The iniquity of this act, the employment of such a man in such a service (what said the Lollards in England?), brought its own shame and punishment. Beaufort raised money and troops in England for the crusade.* By a scandalous and intricate fraud these troops were poured into France to consolidate, defend, or advance the progress of the English arms under the Duke of Bedford. The King of France sent the bitterest complaints to Rome; Pope Martin was compelled to condemn this act of the Cardinal as injurious to the cause of religion, highly dishonourable to the See of Rome;ᶠ but Henry of Winchester did after all better service in Bohemia than all the Princes and Generals of the Empire. The English churchman, by his courage, put to shame the whole panic-stricken host.ᵍ Beaufort returned to plunge into the politics of England, the implacable antagonist of him who was called the good Duke of Gloucester. Beaufort is that Cardinal

---

* Rymer.   ᶠ Compare Lingard, Hist. of England.   ᵍ See on, page 344.

consigned—in some degree perhaps unjustly consigned—to everlasting torment by a decree, as far as the estimation of mankind, more powerful than Papal. His death of despair, described by Shakespeare, painted by Reynolds, is indelibly imprinted on the mind of man.[b]

Archbishop Chicheley strove to maintain a middle course. He could not defy the Pope; he knew that he could not annul the law of England. He urged on a Parliament at Westminster the terrors of a Papal interdict on the land. The Parliament paid no further regard to these terrors than to petition the Pope to restore the Primate of England to his favour.[i]

Martin V. by no means openly rejected the yet imperious demand for reformation, which beyond the Alps had not relaxed its importunity; nor was he disposed altogether to elude that regular convocation of General Councils, at stated intervals, to which he had agreed before the dissolution of that of Constance. By the decree of Constance, confirmed by the Pope, Councils were to be held every five years. Pavia had been appointed as the seat of the next meeting.

Council of Pavia. A.D. 1423. Accordingly, in the year 1423, a Council opened at Pavia, but it was attended only by Italian Prelates. The Transalpines either were afraid or unwilling to trust themselves and their cause on Italian ground; or perhaps they had intimation of an affair, to them comparatively of less interest, but which the Pope

---

[b] Compare the House of Lancaster. The sensible author concludes in favour of Beaufort, "that he was not much better nor much worse than the other Romish dignitaries of the fifteenth century." This as regards England is not quite fair in the times of Wykeham and Hallam. I cannot in Chicheley forget the munificent founder of All Souls, Oxford.

[i] Wilkins, Concilia.—Collier, i. 658.

intended, as of more vital importance, at least to Papal Christendom, to supplant the general Reformation—the reunion of the Greek with the Latin Church. The Greek Emperor, pressed by the Ottoman Turks almost to the utmost, was inclined to buy the aid of the West by the surrender of his religious freedom: the Pope contemplated with lofty expectation the whole world reposing under his supremacy. Martin V. ere long evoked the Council of Pavia to Sienna: there he might take part in the proceedings, and urge on more vigorously the reconciliation of the Greeks. At Sienna appeared only five German prelates, from France six, from Spain not one; but even this Council, after renewing the condemnation of Wycliffe, Huss, and their doctrines, came to an unwelcome resolution, that internal Church union by reform ought to take precedence of external union. The suffrages of the Nations were so decidedly in favour of this decree that the Pope took alarm at the dangerous spirit of innovation universal throughout Christendom: "that the Supreme Pontiff should be called to account was a perilous thing."[k] Martin seized the specious pretext that so few Prelates could not pretend to represent the Church, as an occasion for the dissolution of the Council.[m] It was prorogued for seven years, then to meet in the German city of Basle.

Martin V. just lived to see the opening of the Council

---

[k] "Noverat oculatus Pontifex omnem multitudinem novitatis cupidam esse, iniqua in Romanos Pontifices judicia plebis, invidos patres, nihil periculosius quam maximi præsulatus reddere rationem. Arte igitur usus est," p. 34.—Æneæ Sylvii Comment. This work of Æneas Sylvius was first published at Rome by C. Fea, 1823. It is of great importance; I owe the use of it to my excellent friend the Chevalier Bunsen.

[m] Bull of Dissolution, March 12, 1424.

of Basle. An apoplexy carried him off suddenly, and left to his successor that conflict with the Council which might perhaps have been avoided or mitigated by the experience, dexterity, and conciliatory manners of Pope Martin.

CHAPTER XL.

Eugenius IV. The Hussite War.

MARTIN V., by the aggrandisement of his family, had not established a predominant influence in the Conclave for the house of Colonna, nor even for the Roman clergy. The Cardinals met; they had been unduly depressed as they thought, doubtless kept in stern subordination, by Martin V.[a] Their first business was to erect themselves into a standing Council, superior to the Pope, so that without their advice the Pope could do nothing. They solemnly pledged themselves, whoever should be elected to the Popedom, to reform the Roman Court, in its head and in its members, with the Council of the Cardinals; not to remove it from Rome; to hold a General Council at intervals according to the decree of Constance; not to create Cardinals, or to do any important act without the advice of the Cardinals; to the Cardinals was to be assigned one moiety of the whole Papal revenue. All took this oath without hesitation, and kept it as the Cardinals were wont to keep such oaths.[b] They then proceeded to the election.

---

[a] They (five Cardinals well disposed to the Teutonic Order, Orsini, Arles, De Comte, Rouen, Novara) dare not speak one word to the Pope but what he would willingly hear; for the Pope has so repressed the Cardinals that they never speak except according to his sentiments, and while they speak turn red and pale.—Volgt, Stimmen, p. 74. When Martin fled from Rome to Ferentino on account of the plague, he would not let a single Cardinal come near him.

[b] Raynald. sub ann. 1431.

The contest lay between a Spaniard and a French prelate. Neither would make concessions. Both parties threw away their suffrages on one whom none of the College desired or expected to succeed: their concurrent votes fell by chance on the Cardinal of Sienna.* Gabriel Condolmieri, Cardinal of Sienna, was the nephew, on a sister's side, of the abdicated Gregory XII.: he took the name of Eugenius IV.ᵈ Bred a monk of the rigid Cœlestino Order, Eugenius had the narrow virtues of a monk, austere morals, rigorous discharge of the offices of devotion. He had likewise the hardness, self-sufficiency, stubbornness of a monk. His sudden elevation gave him overweening confidence in his own judgement: he implicitly believed in his own supremacy, and that he was invested by that supremacy in wisdom to maintain it. This was to him his one great duty, one paramount virtue. He was not averse to the reformation of the Church; he would willingly have submitted the whole clergy to the same austere discipline to which he had subdued his own person; but it must be reformation issuing from himself, granted by himself, regulated by himself; nor would he make any concession which would detract from the Papal power, hardly from the Papal wealth. To this all considerations of policy, humanity, fidelity to engagements, must be subordinate. He had the singular praise that he religiously observed all compacts, except those which it was for the advantage of his See

March 3. 1431. Eugenius IV.

---

* Andreas Billius, Hist. Mediolan. Sismondi has represented Eugenius IV. as the most insignificant of all the Cardinals. Yet he had filled offices of high trust. He had been Legate to Romagna.—Platina, in Vitâ.

ᵈ The ambassador of the Teutonic Order deplores the parsimony of the Order, which will not enable him to vie in his gifts with other sovereigns. "The Venetians are used to gifts."— p. 110.

to violate.* In policy, indeed, Eugenius IV. was a Venetian. He broke up at once the alliance maintained so successfully, as regarded the peace of Rome and the Roman territory, with the Visconti and Milan, and joined Florence and Venice with all his power. To war against his own refractory subjects, or against the enemies of his allies in Italy, Eugenius IV. had no scrupulous aversion. His panegyrist acknowledges his love of war,[f] but it was above all war against heretics, an exterminating war, war which admitted of no treaty. Against heretics it was religion to annul, infringe, tread under foot any compact; against them cruelty was mercy, perfidy justice. Yet there were those who, to their admiration of the beauty of the person of Eugenius, added that of his virtue and his equanimity.[g]

Eugenius began his Pontificate with an act of resolute violence, perhaps unavoidable, but which ungraciously exposed the one great vice of his predecessor, and ended in the most offensive condemnation of his memory. The vast wealth accumulated by Martin was in the hands of the Colonnas, the Cardinal Prospero, Antonio Prince of Salerno, Edward Count of Celano. The Pope demanded the surrender of these treasures, the inalienable inheritance of the See. He stood in need of them, for all Romagna was in revolt; Perugia had driven out the Legate; Viterbo, Civita Castellana, Spoleto, Narni, Todi, were in arms. The Colonnas refused to disgorge their treasures. They fortified their castles; they proclaimed the Pope only

First acts of Eugenius IV.

---

* "Constans præterea in pactis servandis est habitus, nisi quid pollicitus fuisset quod revocare quam perficere malius esset."—Platina.

[f] "Bella autem ita amavit, quod mirum in Pontifice videbatur."—Vit. Eugen. apud Muratori, S. R. I.

[g] Antoninus of Florence; see also Æneas Sylvius, Europa, l. 48. Compare Weissenburg, ii. p. 280

a servile instrument in the hands of their enemies the Orsini; they broke with armed bands into the fiefs held by the Orsini, and laid all waste; but Rome was still in that state of loyal excitement which always followed for a short time the election of a new Pope. The love and reverence of Pope Martin were buried with him in his grave: it adhered not to his house. The Pope had power enough at his command to seize all the Colonnas in Rome. His vengeance was unscrupulous: he tortured Otho, the treasurer of Pope Martin, an aged man, till he expired; two hundred Roman citizens perished on the scaffold;[h] the palace of Martin V. was razed to the ground; his arms effaced from all public monuments. Florence and Venice, the new Pope's new allies, sent aid. The Prince of Salerno was attacked on all sides; his garrisons were ignominiously driven from the forts which he had seized; he was compelled to humiliating submission; all that remained of the treasures of Pope Martin, 75,000 golden florins, was surrendered to the Pope.[i] These vigorous measures secured to Eugenius the peaceable possession of Rome for two years, the last of which witnessed the coronation of the Emperor Sigismund.

Sept. 22, 1431.

This first success was followed by the subjugation of the Roman States. City after city yielded to the combined troops of the Free Companies in the pay of the Pope, of Florence, and of Venice, until the implacable and inexhaustible intrigues of the Duke of Milan raised again the banner of revolt. These triumphs at Rome were not likely to disenchant Pope Eugenius from his

---

[h] Muratori, Ann. d' Italia, sub ann. 1431; Vita Eugenii Papæ, S. R. I. iv.
[i] In the Stimmen aus Rom, Eugenius is favourably contrasted with Martin V. On the occasion of a favourable decree, the ambassador writes, "I must have paid Pope Martin 1000 ducats more for this."—p. 114.

full faith in himself and in his Pontifical power. So plunged he at once into that long irreconcileable contest with Transalpine Christendom, from which, however he might seem to emerge conqueror, and to bear down all resistance by stubborn resolution, his victory was dearly won, though its results might wait almost another century to come to maturity.

Now for the first time a Council beyond the Alps, that of Basle, stood up boldly on democratic principles, first against the Pope alone, afterwards against the Pope with a rival Council. At length the Transalpine Council set up its own Pope, and two Popes at the head of two General Councils distracted the worship and divided the obedience of Christendom.

The Hussite war had already almost filled the whole period of more than thirteen years, from the close of the Council of Constance to the opening of the Council of Basle. It lasted during all the Pontificate of Martin V., who contemplated it far aloof, if with horror and dismay, it is to be hoped, not without some commiseration, though he might think it his duty to stimulate it and keep it alive with all his authority. Safe in Rome, he heard but from a distance the thundering roll of Ziska's chariots, the shrieks of cities stormed, the wail of armies mowed down by the scythe. The war was still raging at the accession of Eugenius, and at the meeting of the Council of Basle.[a] They were years of terrible and fatal glory in the history of Bohemia, of achievements marvellous as to valour, military skill, patriotism, and the passion for civil and

A.D. 1418- 1431.

---

[a] Compare in Palacky (Geschichte Böhmens) references to the MS. Histories of John of Ragusa and John of Segovia, lii. p. 518. Also in Martene and Durand, viii. 48, the Articles placarded in Rome demanding the Council, as the only means of putting an end to the Hussite war.

religious freedom; to the Empire, to the Teutonic nation, beyond all precedent disastrous and ignominious. Had Bohemia possessed a race of native Sovereigns; were it not in the nature of profound religious fanaticism to awaken differences irreconcileable under the most favourable circumstances; could Bohemia have consolidated her own strength within herself, and not carried fire and sword into the Empire, she might have been the first nation which threw off the yoke of the Pope and of the hierarchy, the centre of Sclavonian independence. But that Sclavonian Reformation might perhaps have retarded, from the hostility of the two races, embittered by the long contest, the later, more successful, more irrevocable Teutonic emancipation.

Of all wars none was so horribly, remorselessly, ostentatiously cruel as this—a war of races, of languages, and of religion. It was a strife of revenge, of reprisal, of extermination considered to be the holiest of duties. On one side no faith was to be kept, no mercy shown to heretics: to cut off the spreading plague by any means was paramount to all principles of law or gospel. On the other, vengeance was to be wreaked on the enemies of God's people, and therefore the enemies of God; to root out idolatry was the mission of the Bohemians; mortal sin was to be cut off with the righteous sword; and the whole priesthood, all monks, friars, nuns, were so utterly depraved, according to their sweeping condemnation, that it was only to fulfil the Divine commandment to extirpate the irreclaimable Order. These terrible theories were relentlessly carried into more terrible practice. Kuttenberg, the second city in the realm, the rival of Prague, Catholic and German as Prague was Hussite and Bohemian, burned, beheaded, hanged all who would not retract their

Atrocity of the war.

opinions. They bought the prisoners taken in war for a few groschens a head (five times as much for a preacher as for a common man), and executed them without trial, without mercy. They are charged with having put to death sixteen hundred men.ᵐ The Hussites, wherever they could, perpetrated horrible reprisals; for so many of their brethren as were burned, they hanged as many monks or friars.ⁿ The names assigned to their fortresses, and assumed by the more fanatic Hussites, Taborites, Horebites—show from which part of the Bible they drew their prevailing principles. Some of the preachers proclaimed the approaching end of the world. Christ was already coming, already come. The enemies of truth were to be exterminated; the good alone preserved, and put in the five faithful cities.º Bohemia boasted, beyond all kingdoms of Europe, of her magnificent religious buildings, not in her cities alone, but in her villages. Fanaticism, maddened by persecution and by its own blind fury, warred on all that was splendid. The sky-aspiring churches, of vast length and width, on their pillars and arching vaults of stone, the stately altars, where the reliques of the saints were enshrined in gold and silver, the embroidered vestments inlaid with precious stones, the gorgeous vessels, the rich painted windows—all was demolished—all was ruin, havoc, desolation.ᵖ

ᵐ Palacky, iii. 74-5.
ⁿ For the atrocity of the war, see the revolting account of the taking of Prachalic by Ziska, Palacky, p. 171.
º Palacky, from Brezowa.
ᵖ Thus writes Æneas Sylvius who had visited Bohemia: "Nullum vero regnum ætate nostrâ in totâ Europâ tam frequentibus, tam augustis, tam ornatis templis ditatum fuisse quam Bohemicum reor. Templa in cœlum erecta, longitudine atque amplitudine mirabili fornicibus tegebantur lapideis; altaria in sublimi posita, auro et argento quo sanctorum reliquiæ tegebantur onusta; sacerdotum vestes margaritis textæ; ornatus omnis dives, pretiosissima supellex, fenestræ altæ atque amplissimæ vitro et admirabili opere lucem præbebant. Neque hæc tantum

The execution of John Huss and Jerome of Prague had aroused a general access of national as well as religious indignation. But so long as King Wenzel lived, the Bohemian insurrection had not attained its height. For Wenzel was a Bohemian in heart, as a Bohemian beloved by the people, and supposed, though he outwardly supported the old religion, not to be unfavourable to, at least he had taken no decided or violent part against the new doctrines. But on the death of Wenzel, the hereditary claim of Sigismund to the throne of Bohemia was undoubted —of Sigismund who had allowed his safe-conduct to be violated, and so was guilty of the death of the martyrs, even if he had taken no more active share in the murder. The act had been a breach of faith, an outrage to the Bohemian nation. Sigismund attempted to awe the reluctant kingdom to obedience. At Breslau he revenged an insurrection with such terrible severity, that Prague might stand aghast at the peril of resisting, or of receiving such a master. He burned without scruple all the heretical teachers that fell into his hands. John Kincha, a member of the town Council at Prague, was dragged at horses' tails, and, after all this savage usage, died on the scaffold with the recklessness of a martyr. Two days after this, the Pope's Legate, Ferdinand of Lucca, published the Bull for the Crusade.

Death of Wenzel Aug. 16, 1419.

Accession of Sigismund.

March 17, 1420.

Bohemia, following the example of Prague, rose at once and repudiated the sovereignty of Sigismund. She had no native Prince to fight her battles. Hussinetz,

---

in oppidis atque urbibus sed in villis quoque admirari licebat."—Hist. Bohemica, c. 36. Bohemia bears sad witness to this revolution. Except the | St. John Nepomuk on the Hradshin, all her churches are of the later Jesuit style.

who secretly aimed at the throne, perhaps fortunately for his country, died at an early period. Somewhat later the crown was accepted and worn by a Lithuanian Prince, Sigismund Korybert, finally deposed and expelled the land by the common consent of the nation.⁴ But the armies of Bohemia needed no royal leaders. We must pass with rapidity, we cannot altogether avert our eyes from those terrible but noble scenes, the victories of Ziska and Procopius. The first crusade ended with the disgraceful defeat, with the shameful flight of the Emperor from the walls of Prague,ᵉ and the disastrous battle of Wyschebrad.⁶ The second campaign saw the German army break up in panic flight from Saaz, with the now renowned and irresistible Ziska in the rear, bearing down whole squadrons, and revenging the unspeakable barbarities inflicted on his countrymen. The third year Sigismund advanced into Moravia at the head of the Hungarian forces; they too, fled at once at the approach of Ziska with his wild war-chariots; they were overtaken at Deutschbrod, and massacred rather than routed by the remorseless conqueror. Bohemia seemed to be severed, and for ever, from Latin unity. Conrad, the Archbishop of Prague, accepted, to the utter astonishment and dismay of the Church, the four articles of Prague.¹

Internal feuds were sure to break out immediately that the enemy was beyond the borders of Bohemia.

---

⁴ In 1427.
ᵉ Aschbach, lil. 47; compare his authorities with Palacky, lil. 91. The camp broke up July 30. Sigismund had gone through the idle ceremony of coronation.
ᶠ The spirited poem in Palacky taunts

Sigismund with personal cowardice:
"Wie ein Has vor Hunden lief er,
Hätte Fikael er bremen
Wär fürwahr er kurtzgehgewn;
Solch ein lapires Herre hatt' er,
Herr von sieben Königreichen."
—p. 162.

¹ Palacky, page 218.

VOL. VIII. 2 A

The wealthy burghers of Prague (the nobles had entered the strife with reluctance) would have accepted a moderate share of religious independence. The four articles of Prague stipulated, I. For freedom of teaching by their own ministers throughout the realm. II. Communion in both kinds. III. That the clergy should not hold estates, nor mingle in secular affairs. IV. The punishment of deadly sins by the magistrates, with the suppression of indulgences for money. Whoever should compel them to abandon either of these articles they declared to be a most cruel tyrant, an Antichrist." They were called the Utraquists, as insisting on the Eucharist in both elements. Ziska* and the Taborites had wilder and loftier views: the national independence, far harsher measures to the clergy. There were among them, millenarians, communists. They swept away every vestige of traditional religion; everything but the barest, most unadorned worship. But to the old creed they still adhered with stern fidelity. Martinet Hauska and his followers were burned by both parties for denying Transubstantiation, or the Real Presence.' But neither these divisions, nor the death of Ziska by the plague, weakened the indomitable resistance of the Bohemians to their foreign foes. No sooner had the crusading army again crossed the borders, than the nation was one; the din of polemic strife was silent. The moderate party followed the Taborites to the field under their new general, almost the equal of Ziska in military skill. The blind Procopius, the shaven Procopius,* had been a

Articles of Prague

Oct. 12, 1424.

---

* See Articles.—Palacky, 190.
* Laurent Brov. p. 175. The character of Ziska in Palacky (p. 360, &c.) is just and striking. He was as stern a bigot for Christian virtue as his enemies for their Christian creed or discipline.   * Palacky, 236.
* Palacky writes of Procopius:—

priest;[a] under him the old Taborites, and the Orphans, the followers of Ziska, their lost father, as well as his own peculiar religious and political faction, met together in fierce, unconflicting unity. Under him the third crusade, which had lingered on for two or three years, was discomfited in the final battle of Aussitz. So total was the rout, that the Germans, not without cause, dreaded the irruption of these formidable conquerors into their own territories. Erfurt, Jena, Halle, even Magdeburg, already saw the fierce Procopius, and heard the rattlings of his waggons under their walls.[b]

Procopius.

Battle of Aussitz. June 16, 1426.

Shame, indignation, terror, prudence, demanded a better-organised, better-disciplined army, than those which had been hastily raised in different parts of Germany. The banner of the Empire was unfurled. From the Danube and its Hungarian shores up to the Black Forest—from the Alps to the border of Flanders, contingents were required; temporal and spiritual powers, nobles and bishops, knights and burghers, crowded to the Imperial standard; 200,000 men were in arms.[c] A new Order was instituted; the banner bore the Virgin and the Infant Saviour.[d] All this magnificent preparation ended in almost incredible disgrace. The three divisions of the vast army, or rather the three armies, fled without striking a blow, abandoning all their treasures, munitions, carriages,

July 12 and following days. Great flight, Aug. 4, 1427.

---

[a] "Wenn er Ziska in kriegerischer Genialität nicht glich, ihm doch an Geist und politischem Umblick übertraf."—P. 432.

Procopius solemnly declared before the Council of Basle that he had never shed a drop of blood with his own hand. He had commanded in many battles: but Bohemia had been compelled to war by the Pope and the Cardinals: to them belonged all the guilt.

[b] Palacky, p. 414.
[c] Herman Corner, p. 1278.
[d] Raynald. sub ann. 1427. Palacky, p. 430.

cannon. Henry of Winchester alone, at the head of a band of English crusaders, endeavoured, but in vain, to arrest the utter rout.

The Crusades against the Hussites had made the Hussites what the Saracens had long been to the Christian world, and they became as Saracens to the whole of Germany. They would no longer wait to be assailed. They assembled on the White Mountain near Prague, 50,000 foot, 20,000 horse, with their impregnable waggons which they built up as a fortress at a few hours' warning, a garrisoned citadel in the enemy's land. On every side they broke out unresisted, except by the stronger cities. Austria, even as far as Hungary, Lausitz, Saxony, were a waste. Leipsic escaped only through her fortifications. Cobourg and Bayreuth were in flames. Nuremberg, Bamberg, closed their gates in terror. The Marquis of Brandenburg, the Bishop of Bamberg, bought the retreat of the Bohemians at great cost. Everywhere revenge, religious hatred, fierce fanaticism, marked their way with unspeakable horrors. They thought it but compliance with the Divine command to dispeople the lands of the Philistines, the Edomites, and the Moabites.

Bohemian invasion of Germany.

Sigismund at length attempted milder measures; pacific negotiations began, but the religious question could not be reconciled. The Emperor demanded the unqualified submission of the Bohemians to the decrees of a General Council, to which they were to be admitted in perfect freedom. The Taborites, who might well mistrust, would contract no such obligations. The Orphans, Ziska's section of the milder party, promulgated the new doctrine, that a free people needed no king.

Negotiations.

Nothing remained but a fifth crusade. An army of

100,000 men crossed the Bohemian frontier. In the battle of Taass the Bohemians won a victory no less signal and complete than on former fields. Again the Pope's Legate, the Cardinal Julian Cæsarini, alone conducted himself with courage; he was at last constrained to fly; he hardly escaped in the disguise of a common soldier, and left behind him the Papal Bull for the Crusade, his cardinal's hat, and his pontifical robes. These trophies remained in the church of Taass for two centuries; the banners were hung in the Tron Church in Prague.*

From Aug. 1 to 11. Battle of Taass, Aug. 14, 1431.

* There is a fair general view of these wars in Aschbach, Kaiser Sigismund, vol. iii.; but the more full, careful, and accurate one from MSS. as well as printed authorities in Palacky, Geschichte von Böhmen

CHAPTER XII.

Council of Basle.

SUCH was the state of the Hussite or Bohemian war on the opening of the Council of Basle under John of Polemar and John of Ragusa, delegates of the Cardinal Julian Cæsarini. On July 23 the Council held its first sitting; in the beginning of August was fought the crowning victory of Procopius, the battle of Taass. Bohemia might seem lost for ever to King Sigismund, to the Pope, to Latin Christianity. The Cardinal himself had witnessed the valour, with difficulty had fled out of the hands, of the unconquerable Taborites. The intelligence of the defeat struck the Council with the utmost consternation; the Fathers began to take even more serious views of the absolute and inevitable necessity of reformation in the Church.*

Eugenius IV. was obstinately ignorant, imperfectly informed, or contemptuously regardless of the state of affairs beneath the Alps. The calamities which Germany had suffered in this internecine war for nearly fourteen years were beneath the consideration of a Pontiff whose one principle was no peace with heretics. Eugenius had no intention to venture his sacred person beyond the Alps; but a Council not under his own immediate con-

A.D. 1431.

---

* "Quibus auditis, omnibus postpositis, consternati omnes patres de concilio . . . . recesserunt, multa in animo ruminantes, et nihilominus fortius accensi ad reformationem Ecclesiæ."—John de Ragusio, MS. quoted by Palacky, iii. 3, 6.

trol was a dangerous experiment, which he would, if possible, avert. Of all things he was affrighted by the manifest determination to enter into peaceful negotiations with the Hussites, with whom he had already declared all treaties null and void, with whom no treaties, on any account, ought to be respected, with whom to negotiate was to suffer a rehearing of questions already decided at Constance and at Sienna, and to admit the possibility that such heretics might have a good cause. A treaty with heretics (according to the language of the Pope's Bull) confirmed, as it was said to have been, with mutual oaths, was an insult to God, a blasphemy against the Pope's authority. Without faith salvation was impossible. The Pope therefore abrogated all such treaties, should they exist, in all their articles; he absolved from their oaths princes, prelates, knights, soldiers, magistrates of cities; he commanded them, notwithstanding any such treaty, to rise in a mass, and besiege, slay, exterminate heretics, so that their heresy might perish for ever.[b]

Without delay, without consideration, almost without consultation with the Cardinals, Eugenius issued his Decree, commanding the dissolution of the Council of Basle and the assembly of another after two years at Bologna. The reasons which he deigned to allege were that as yet but few prelates had appeared at Basle; that the roads to Basle were insecure on account of the war between the Dukes of Burgundy and Austria; above all, the greater convenience of the ambassadors from Constantinople. The Byzantine Empire, in its growing agony of dread at the approach of the Turks, had made still more urgent overtures to purchase aid from

---

[b] Raynald. p. 88, sub ann. 1431.

the West by the submission of the Greek Church to the Pope and to Latin Christianity.

The Legate, Julian Cæsarini, at first so far respected the decree of the Pope that he declined to take his seat as President of the Council. But Cæsarini was a wise and experienced man, he knew well the state of Germany. Even before the arrival of the final Papal mandate for the dissolution, he had addressed a remonstrance, remarkable for its firmness, vigour, dignity; above all, for its weighty and authoritative statement of the sound and just policy of maintaining the Council. "Germany is ready for another campaign in Bohemia; they only await aid and money from Rome. I thought you would have sold your crosses and chalices for such an object. I wait five months; instead of succour I receive an order to dissolve the Council, which is the only hope of union and success." Cæsarini's personal remonstrances to the Pope lest he should stand in the way of the reform of the clergy are most solemn and earnest—"he will be suspected of the grossest hypocrisy as to his own virtue."

Dec. 13, 1431. In his answer to the Bull,[e] the Cardinal Legate almost scornfully disposes of the reasons of the Pope for the prorogation of the Council. "There were few Bishops at the first session, now they are gathering from all quarters. The Emperor has declared the Council under his protection; the Dukes of Burgundy and Austria have suspended their feud, and grant safe-conduct to the Holy Fathers. The peace of Germany is not to be sacrificed for the old song, which has rung in the ears of Western Europe for three centuries and ended in nothing, the reconciliation of the Greek and

---

[e] These two letters are in the Works of Æneas Sylvius, at the close of his Hist. Consil. Basil.

Latin Churches. The Bohemians have been deliberately, formally invited to the Council; arms have been tried in vain; this is the only way in which they can be restored to the Church. What will the heretics say if the Council be dissolved? Will they not, in their insulting and warrantable pride, proclaim that the Church dares not confront them? Will it not be held a confession of weakness? 'Behold, their armies have fled (how often!) from before our face, and now the Catholic Church flies again before us.' Such will be their boast. They are unconquerable in controversy as in war; the hand of God is with them: they hold the truth, we falsehood.

"What will the world say? Council after Council and no reformation! The incorrigible clergy will submit to no amendment. The whole laity will fall upon us like the Hussites.[d] Terrible rumours are abroad. Men's minds are in travail; they are ready to vomit forth their deadly venom: they will think it a sacrifice to God if they shall murder or despoil the clergy. The priesthood will become odious to God and man; the slight reverence which now remains will die away. Already Magdeburg has expelled her archbishop and clergy, and is preparing waggons to wage war like the Hussites; it is rumoured that they have sent for a Bohemian general. It is greatly to be feared that Magdeburg is the head of a league among the neighbouring cities. Passau has expelled her Bishop, who was lord of the city; they are even now besieging his castle. In Bamberg there is war between the city and the Bishop and Chapter. Yet not only is the Council to

---

[d] "Propter quod valde timendum est, nisi se emendent, ne laici in more Hussitarum in totum clerum irruant ut publice dicant."—P. 68.

be prorogued to Italy, but to be adjourned for a year and a half. In a year and a half I fear that the whole clergy of Germany will be in a state of ruin. If the news spreads throughout Germany that the Council is dissolved, the whole clergy will be given up to pillage and massacre. 'We shall lose our temporalities.' So said the Jews, ' If we let him go, the Romans will come and take away our place and nation.' And thus say we, ' If we permit the Council to sit, the laity will come and take away our temporalities.' But as by God's justice the Jews, who would not let Christ go, lost their place, so by God's justice if we allow not the Council to sit, we shall lose, not our temporalities only, but our bodies and our souls." The Cardinal ends with earnest supplication that the Pope will at least wait till July, when the heretics were to appear, to frame some canons for the reformation of the German clergy. "If I refuse the Presidency," he concludes, "they will at once proceed to elect their own President."

Magdeburg, Passau, and Bamberg were not the only cities in which the burghers had risen against their bishops, or were prepared to rise. In Aix-la-Chapelle, Cologne, Erfurt, Spires, Wurtzburg, Strasburg, feuds were raging; the burghers called in the neighbouring princes who were ready to aid them in throwing off the ecclesiastical rule. Was then the crisis so perilous? If the Council of Basle had offered no resistance, and submitted at once to be prorogued to Bologna, is it possible that Germany (worn out by the long war, and exasperated at her own disgrace and misery, of which all would throw the blame on the clergy) might not have disdained to follow the guidance of Bohemia, that the Sclavonian might have become a Teutonic movement, and thus a Wycliffite Reformation anticipated by a century that of Luther, Melancthon, and Calvin? But the Council of Basle now boasted the avowed support of the Emperor and of the Duke of Milan, and scrupled not to send ambassadors to all the other courts of Europe. Their envoys asserted that the Council was lawfully assembled under the inspiration of the Holy Ghost; that all men, even the Roman Pontiff, were bound to render their obedience; that the dissolution of the Council by Eugenius IV. was absolutely null. The Bishop of Novara was sent to Charles King of France; the Bishop of Lodi to Henry of England; the Bishop of Parma to Poland and Prussia; the Abbot of S. Ambrogio in Milan to Alfonso of Arragon; the Abbot of Beauvale to Castile. The Abbot of Clairvaux was to address that great Prince, the Duke of Burgundy.

Council send ambassadors.

Already the Council began to administer the affairs of Christendom as the great Christian Senate. But at Basle there was a fatal departure from the usage established at Constance. The voting by nations was abrogated, partly, it should seem, in jealousy of the admission of England as the fifth nation;[*] Spain claimed to rank as the fourth. Four deputations were formed. I. Of faith. II. Of pacification. III. Of reformation. IV. Of other matters. Magistrates were appointed to examine and to distribute those who claimed the right of seat and suffrage among these deputations. No dignitary of the Church was rejected

Right of voting.

---

[*] There was great strife for precedence between the ambassadors of Spain and England. The Bishop of Parma writes to the Grand Master of the Teutonic Order: "Hic fuit magna discrep- tatio super modo sedendi inter ambasciatores regis Ispaniarum et regis Angliæ; tandem operante Deo, sedata est."—Compare Voigt, Stimmen, p. 64.

who was not a criminal or of evil fame. The result of this was the enormous preponderance of the German and French clergy: being nearer to Basle they poured in with overwhelming numbers. Comparatively few would undertake the long, perilous, and costly journey from Italy, Spain, England, Hungary. The second innovation was even more serious—the annulment of the dominant episcopal authority. The Bishops lost their prerogative, their influence. Bitter complaints were made that the meanest and most ignorant (the Universities, the Doctors of Canon and Civil Law do not appear prominently), the very dregs and lees of the clergy, carried all questions with a total forfeiture of dignity and utter confusion. It became a fierce democracy.[t]

Sigismund in Italy, A.D. 1431.   The Emperor Sigismund, abandoning for the present all hope of reconquering Bohemia, and wisely leaving the negotiations with the Council to work their effect, chose this time for a descent into Italy to receive the Imperial Crown. Philippo Maria Visconti had made magnificent promises of aid. The Duke of Milan now stood almost alone against Florence, Venice, and the Pope. Sigismund came down the Alps with not more than 2000 German and Hungarian horse. Milan welcomed him with a splendid display of feudal honours. He received the Iron Crown of Lombardy from the Archbishop of Milan in the Church of S. Am-

---

[t] "Sic turba inconsulta confusaque, cum docti atque indocti passim admitterentur, tantaque multitudo plebeiæ fæcis implevit synodum ut nulla vox esset, nullaque potestas episcoporum: quia non ratione sed numero vota congregationis æstimabantur." — Æneas Sylvius, Fra, p. 40. In a speech reported in Mansi, p. 231, it is said: "Inter Episcopos cæterosque patres conscriptos vidimus in Basilia coquos et stabularios orbis negotia judicantes." This is no doubt aristocratic, probably Italian exaggeration, but it shows the prevailing jealousies.

brogio. The Duke of Milan alone, notwithstanding his own words, stood aloof in sullen suspicion. He shut himself up in his castle of Abbiate Grossa. He remembered, perhaps, the seizure of his ancestors by the predecessor of Sigismund, the last Emperor who had entered Milan on his descent into Italy.

Sigismund passed onward to the south. If his allies looked on his progress with ungracious and inhospitable coldness, the Guelfic republics hardly abstained from molesting his march; but all parties were exhausted with the wars of the latter years. Sigismund reached Sienna, till then nowhere welcome; he hardly escaped being besieged in Lucca by the Free Companies in the pay of Florence. Sienna received him with some show of joy and pride. His father, Charles IV., had entered Sienna soon after his marriage; the Siennese hailed the Emperor as a fellow-citizen begotten within their walls. At first they were lavish in their contributions, but during eight long months of subtle negotiation with the Pope the weary city was overburthened with his costly and unprofitable maintenance.

And still the Council of Basle, emboldened by the controversy of Cæsarini with the Pope, emboldened by increasing numbers, went on rising in its loftier assumption of authority. The first act was to adopt the extreme assertion of the Council of Constance as to the supremacy of a General Council over the Pope. The doctrine of Gerson and of Hallam found a new, a bold, and an eloquent advocate in Nicolas of Cusa, a man of the most fervent piety and commanding blamelessness of life. The Council constantly received letters of adhesion from Kings, Princes, Bishops, Universities, Cities. The number of Prelates was steadily on the increase; Cardinals, not merely two or three from personal animosity to Eugenius IV., but in considerable numbers, began to fall away from the Pope, to approach, singly and at intervals;[a] though some still hesitated to appear in the Council. The Cardinal of St. Peter, John Cervantes, fled in the disguise of a servant from Amelia. At length not more than four Cardinals remained with the Pope. In vain Eugenius sent forth his inhibitory letters denouncing the Council as the Synagogue of Satan, declaring all excommunicate who went to the Council or aided others in going; that these infected sheep ought to be exterminated; that those would please God who should rise up against, plunder, slay these rebels against the Apostolic See, the fautors of schism, the abettors of division. "It is marvellous but true," that the more Eugenius threatened, the more all flocked to Basle; the inhibition of the Pope had more effect than the summons of the Council.[b] The Council, in this third Session, issued its citation to the Pope and to the Cardinals, and threatened them with further proceedings if they did not appear in three months. In a subsequent Session they declared that in case of the decease of Eugenius IV. the election of the Pope was in the Council. They prepared a Great Seal, they sent the Cardinal of S. Eustachio to take possession of Avignon and the Venaisin. The Pope's four Legates, who appeared with the Archbishops of Tarento and Colocza at their head, were not permitted to assume the Presidency. Their

April 20, 1432.

June 20.

---

[a] Voigt, Stimmen.

[b] Æneas Sylvius, Fea. "Nec pauciores, ut mea fert opinio, Eugenii prohibitio viros adduxit, quam vocatio conciliaris." The historian adds: "Quia vetitum quicquid est, magis optamus, insistimusque negatis."— P. 48.

protestations that all which had been done without the Pope's consent was null and void, were treated with contempt. On the Pope was thrown back the guilt of schism. On September 6 the Pope and seventeen Cardinals were proclaimed in contumacy, because they had not appeared, and because they had issued the Bull for the dissolution of the Council.

Sigismund was still at Sienna, in a situation at once proud and humiliating;[1] he was formidable, yet, as he described himself, through the treachery of the Duke of Milan, like a wild beast in a cage; a mediator without power to enforce his mediation; courted by all, yet fully obeyed by none; hoping to receive the Imperial crown, yet dependent on extorted or almost eleemosynary contributions for his daily subsistence. The Council looked up to him, yet not unjustly mistrusted him. The Pope feared, yet, until the coronation, had him to a certain extent in his power. Sigismund in honour and in interest could not abandon the Council; in honour, for he was a high-minded, generous man, pledged by years of consistent determination to the reform of the Church; in interest, for only through the conciliatory demeanour of the Council to the Bohemians could he regain the crown, which by the inflexible obstinacy of the Pope he must irrecoverably lose. The Pope had endeavoured to extort as the price of Sigismund's coronation (that coronation he could not, he dared not longer refuse) the dissolution of the Council of Basle. May 30, 1432 The coronation was celebrated at Rome in the spring; but the Emperor would not yield. The Reformation of the Church had been the declared, ostentatious object

---

[1] Aschbach, Kaiser Sigmund. The residence of Sigismund at Sienna is minutely detailed in Rancis, Hist. Senen. Muratori, S. R. I. v. xx. p. 48.

of his whole reign. All that the Pope could obtain was
the promised intercession of the Emperor with the
Fathers of Basle not to proceed to any harsh decree
against the Pope.ᵇ Sigismund returned over the Alps,
he descended towards Basle. The Council, even the
Cardinal Julian, would listen to no terms; Sigismund
must acquiesce no doubt, with but seeming reluctance.

At length Eugenius IV. was compelled to yield.
Already before the Emperor's coronation he had admitted, in a limited way, the legitimacy of the Council.
There was still much jealous, ungenerous, dilatory disputation as to the terms in which he should make the
concession. But at length, after more than two years'
strife and negotiation, the Council of Basle was declared
a lawful Œcumenic Council from its commencement.ᵐ
The Bull of Dissolution was absolutely revoked. Sigismund had the satisfaction, before
he left Basle,ⁿ to see the Council established in full
authority, and to take his place at its head.

Before the Emperor left the Council, he submitted
for the consideration of the Fathers the all-important
question, the marriage of the clergy. John of Lubeck
was to demand in the Emperor's name, in the name of
the public morals, the abrogation of their fatal celibacy.
John of Lubeck is described as a man of wit, indulging
in jests on every occasion. But nothing could be more
fearfully serious than the representation on this subject,
which John was to lay separately before each deputa-

ᵇ "Ne quid adversus eum durè decernerent."—Æneas Sylv. p. 54.

ᵐ "Decernimus et declaramus . . . Concilium Basiliense a tempore prædictæ inchoationis suæ legitimè continuatum fuisse et esse." The full recognition was no doubt influenced by the insurrection at Rome. See on.

ⁿ He was at Basle, almost without interruption, from Oct. 11, 1433, to April 12, 1434.

tion, and urge in the strongest manner. After centuries of strife, after all the laws of Hildebrand and his successors, the whole clergy are declared to be living with concubines, in adultery, or worse. They were hated by the whole laity as violating their marriage-beds; confession was become odious. There was strong fear lest the wealth of the clergy should be alienated to their legitimate children; even were it so, better the loss of wealth than of chastity. The Greek Church admitted marriage. The priests of the Old and New Testaments were married. The greater part of the Council were favourable to the change,⁰ except only some of the old, whose days of marriage had gone by, and the Monks, jealous lest the secular Clergy should have privileges denied to themselves. Yet one, a Cardinal, declared in the spirit, almost in the words, of old Paphnutius at Nicæa, that though himself aged, he earnestly desired that wives should be *restored* to the Priesthood.ᵖ The

---

* "Res erat complurimis accepta, sed tempori non conveniru."

ᵖ The Cardinal of St. Peter said: "Quamvis senio gravior, neque mentem habeo ad conjugium, sanctum tamen arbitror, uxores restitui sacerdotibus: quia non est omnibus gratia Dei concessa, ut legi lumborum resistant, ut de Paulo legimus." There is a very curious passage on this subject in the Nemus Unionis of Theodoric à Niem (Tr. vi. c. 35) about the clergy of Norway and Ireland. The Norwegians, both lay and clergy, were great drinkers of ale, and would drink against each other till neither could stand. But in both countries bishops and priests publickly kept their concubines: and when the bishops went on their visitations, the clergy insisted that they should take their own "amasiæ" with them, lest they should be tempted by the superior beauty of those of the clergy. If the clergyman had not a "focaria," he paid double procurations ("ut prævaricator paternarum traditionum Episcopo visitante proinde procurationes duplices ministrabat"). The wives (?) of the clergy in Ireland took rank: "Ac etiam presbyterorum amasiæ seu uxores in eisdem partibus, statu et gradu in ecclesiâ, in mensis, eundo, sedendo, et stando, cæteris dominabus *etiam militaribus* præponuntur." The same marriage or concubinage, with the advancement of the children ("ex fædo complexu nati") to beneficia, prevailed in Germany, Spain, and Portugal. It must be remembered that this is from Theodoric à Niem. I

question, as unsuited to the time, was eluded, postponed, dropped.⁹

The Council of Basle had thus obtained an unlimited recognition of its authority, but the Fathers of that Council could not but know that it was an extorted recognition, and that from a most reluctant Pope. For the Council of Basle stood in very different relation to the Pope from those of Pisa or of Constance. Pisa was a Council of Cardinals, driven into revolt by the tergiversations of the two rival Pontiffs; the Italians by the abominable cruelties of Urban VI. As Cardinals, these Prelates assumed at least the lead in the Council; declared their right to depose the two contesting Popes, and to fill the vacancy by a creation of their own. At Constance, the Fathers of the Council sat as arbiters between three contending Pontiffs, one of whom, a despised and almost forgotten exile, had with difficulty found refuge in his native land of Venice; one was shut up in a fortress in Spain; one had rashly delivered himself, bound hand and foot by the crimes of his former life, into their hands. He had tried, but in vain, to break his bonds; he was abandoned by all Christendom. No sooner was there a Pope, Martin V., than he was acknowledged by the Council and by the whole West. He resumed at once the full supremacy over the Church. But the Council of Basle, if summoned by a Pope, and duly convened according to the decrees of former Councils, sat on one side of the Alps, and the Pope on the other; neither had any force to compel submission to its decrees. Eugenius IV. had so far been in uncon-

---

shall hereafter refer to unanswerable evidence on this repulsive subject from records of Visitations.

⁹ "Vicit tamen sententia illorum

qui hoc tempore tantum opus aggrediendum negavere." See the whole very curious passage in Æneas Sylvius, Fea, p. 55.

tested possession of Rome and of the throne of St. Peter; if embroiled in Italian politics, with no apprehension that either the Italian potentates or the Italian clergy, still less that any formidable majority among the Cardinals, would take the part of the Council against the Pope.

A sudden insurrection had compelled Eugenius to fly in a mean disguise from Rome. The Romans had thrown his nephew, the Cardinal of Venice, into prison, chosen a Senate, installed magistrates. They sent an embassy to Basle to arraign Eugenius; "they had cast out the proud Tarquin." Rome, in their language, was a city of Bruti, Scævolæ, Horatii, Catones.[r] The Pope was received in Guelfic Florence. The Patriarch of Alexandria, John Vitelleschi, a ferocious and able Condottier (he had already hanged the famous Antonio of Pisa for violating the Papal territory), appeared with his terrible troops under the walls of Rome. Not a Brutus nor a Cato would lay down his life. The people submitted ignominiously to return to their allegiance. But the Pope, as a punishment for their unruliness, or in mistrust, now honoured Bologna as his residence.[s] Behind the strong walls of Bologna, secure in the succour of Venice and of Florence, he was beyond the reach of the intrigue or violence of his deadly enemy, Philippo Visconti of Milan; and he might watch with serene composure the proceedings at Basle, ready to seize every opportunity of advantage or of revenge.

The Council of Basle, on the other hand, might as yet pursue its deliberations in dignified security, but no

---

[r] This may be the classic irony of Æneas Sylvius, p. 61.
[s] Muratori, sub ann. 1436. Till this time he had remained in Florence.

more. There was no great monarch to espouse their cause or give weight to their decrees. The Emperor Sigismund's final act of imposing power was his appearance in the Council. The two last years of his reign were more than inglorious, ignominious. He was succeeded for two disturbed years by his son Albert. Frederick III., the new Emperor elected on the death of Albert, surrendered himself to the treacherous guidance of Æneas Sylvius Piccolomini, at first the bold asserter of ecclesiastical freedom in the Council, then skilfully preparing his own way, first to Bishoprics, Cardinalates, finally to the Popedom, by calming down Germany to an undignified neutrality. Charles VII. governed hardly half of France. The King of England for the time ruled in Paris, and that king was the feeble, devout Henry VI. The only sovereign who seemed to take much interest in the proceedings of the Council was Alfonso of Castile, in virtue of his Sicilian or Neapolitan connexions.

Feb. 2, 1440.

Thus, then, the Pope and Council sat at first in disguised, before long in open, oppugnancy, but their hostility was confined to Declarations and Acts which neither could maintain but by words. Each asserted his prerogative to the utmost; the Council its own supremacy over all Christendom, including the Pope— its function was to reform the Church in its head and in its members; the Pope averred that the Council sat only by his permission, derived from him its limited authority, was guilty of ecclesiastical treason by any invasion of the all-comprehending Papal supremacy.

If the Council of Basle was wanting in the presence or the support of the great royal powers, as an Ecclesiastical Senate it was august enough. Though the most learned Fathers of Constance had passed away—

D'Ailly, Gerson, Zabarella, the Cardinal of St. Mark, Hallam—it boasted representatives of the Church from almost every quarter of Christendom. Among these was the Cardinal Louis, Archbishop of Arles, the President after the secession of the Cardinal Julian Cæsarini to Ferrara. His lofty independence and resistance to the Papal See did not prevent his subsequent canonisation.¹ Among the Prelates from Spain was the Archbishop of Palermo. From France came Thomas de Corcelles; from Deventer in Holland, Nicolas de Cusa, whose fame stood almost the highest among the theologians of the day. Nicolas de Cusa, a conscientious zealot for the reform of the Clergy, was afterwards decoyed from the Council by the adroit flattery of Pope Eugenius. "His peerless learning was absolutely necessary to conduct the negotiations with the Greek Church, now returning into the bosom of Rome." He went to Florence; and once within the magic circle, he left not the Papal Court during the sittings of the Council." Last and most important was Æneas Sylvius Piccolomini, an Italian, the most elegant writer of Latin, the historian of the Council—at one time its ruling authority, at another its most dangerous, because secret, foe.

The Council of Basle stood firm on the unshaken ground of the established theology; not a whisper of suspicion attainted the doctrinal orthodoxy of its Fathers. The concessions to the Bohemian insurgents were avowedly extorted in order to save Germany from their inroads. It was a far-sighted policy, a policy conducted by the Fathers of Basle (especially the President Car-

---

¹ Æneas Sylvius describes Louis as "homo multarum parabolarum, liberalitate insignis, sed odio erga Eugenium veteri et novo accendissimos."—P. 67.

² I have read a prolix and laborious life of Nicolas of Cusa by G. M. Dux, Regensburg, 1847.

dinal Cæsarini) with dignity and moderation which might command the admiration and gratitude of Christendom. According to the compact of Eger the ambassadors of Bohemia appeared at Basle. The theological questions arising out of the four Articles of Prague were discussed on the whole with singular sedateness, and with an earnest, almost an affectionate desire for union. On the side of the Bohemians stood Rokycana, now the acknowledged head of the Utraquists; Peter Payne, the Englishman; the Priest-warrior Procopius, as ready in theological dispute as in battle; on the other the most learned theologians of France, Germany, some of Italy. Julian Cæsarini presided with gentle dignity. The occasional outbursts of irresistible scorn and oppugnancy were repressed by common consent.[a] The concession of Communion in both kinds seemed determined, at least to a certain extent. The other Articles were eluded or compromised.

But these concessions, and the long-protracted negotiations which ensued, were fatal to the unity, and so to the strength of Bohemia. Dissensions arose: they could not but arise. The concessions were ambiguous, variously interpreted, received with eagerness, rejected with passion. The dragon's teeth were sown, the armed men sprang up. Nobles and Burghers, Utraquists and Taborites, were in open, deadly feud, or in secret counter-working hostility. The war, never entirely discontinued, broke out again. The disastrous battle of Lepan broke for ever the spell of Bohemian invincibility. Procopius the Great fell in the field; with Procopius fell the military glory, the religious inflexibility of Bohemia. After some time Sigismund (he still

---

[a] Palacky, ii. 3, ch. ii.

lived) ascended the throne; he was received in Prague. Rokyçana was permitted to accept the barren dignity of Archbishop of Prague. The able Philip, Bishop of Coutances, then Legate of the Council of Basle, exercised the real ecclesiastical authority. On Sigismund's death, the crown of Bohemia was the object of a fierce contest between his son, the Austrian Albert, and Casimir of Poland. But it was a strife of Sclavonian and German. The religious interest, the religious passions, were well-nigh burnt out. Tabor, Sion, were besieged and fell. The great Sclavonian Reformation was at an end; it lived only in its impulses, its glorious reminiscences, its opinions, the clang of its debates, which still rang in European remembrance; hereafter disembarrassed of some of its wilder tenets, to wake to final victory in the more sober, steadfast, reflective Teutonic mind. The Council of Basle had perhaps averted doctrinal reformation for above a century.

The ostensible and paramount purpose of the Council of Basle was the Reform of the Clergy. From all quarters the solemn admonitions, the grave expostulations of the more devout and rigid, the bitter satire of the wits of the day, the denunciations of the enemies of the Clergy had been deepening since the Council of Constance had eluded this perilous question. Still there was no thought of a religious revolution; a revolution, in modern phrase strictly conservative, was its utmost aim. Its highest ambition was to reduce the arbitrary autocracy of the Pope to a constitutional monarchy, in order to strengthen not to overthrow that monarchy. The Pope was to take a solemn oath on his inauguration to respect certain rights and liberties of the Church: the College of Cardinals was to be restricted to a certain number, but they were to be the standing Council, in some degree an authoritative Council, to the Pope; the Senate of the Church. On the other hand, against the concubinage of the Clergy the Council were now as rigid as Gregory or Innocent. For the first conviction the offender incurred deprivation of all emoluments for three months; for obstinate disobedience, degradation.

Yet the reform of the hierarchy must begin with the Head. The immoderate taxation of the Roman Court; the Annates and other charges; the usurpations of the Popes as to the promotions to the richer benefices, lay at the root of many of the abuses. The axe must strike boldly and relentlessly at the heart of the evil. Here began the open, obstinate, irreconcileable collision. The Council on these points would not yield, the Pope would not for a moment relax his grasp. Against each usurpation, as he declared it, on the inextinguishable rights of the successors of St. Peter, so soon as the decree reached him he protested with the most uncompromising haughtiness. Papal power had never been advanced in more undisguised or peremptory language. In the Pope was the absolute right of conferring all benefices; from him emanated all spiritual power; he was the Bishop of Bishops, the sole fountain, the arbiter, the dispenser, the distributer, of ecclesiastical authority. So was war fully declared between the Pope and the Council; their utterly irreconcileable pretensions had come into direct conflict. The Council would limit the Pope; the Pope would endure no limitation.

CHAPTER XIII.

Council of Ferrara. The Greeks.

THE Pope had appealed to Christendom on his original inherent irresponsible autocracy, even before the affair of the reconciliation of the Greek Church, now become more urgent, gave him a special pretext for evoking the Council to some city of Italy. This act was in truth the dissolution of the Council of Basle. For the Teutonic Council of Basle with all its aspirations after freedom, the substitution of an Italian Council, if not servilely submissive, in interests and views closely bound up with the Pope, had been from the first the declared policy of Eugenius IV. And now the union of the Churches of the East and West, so long delayed, so often interrupted, might seem an inevitable necessity; it was imminent, immediate, at the will and the command of the West, which might dictate its own terms. The Emperor, and even the Patriarch of Constantinople seemed driven, in their death-pang of terror at the approach of the victorious Turks, to accept the aid of the West at any cost, at any sacrifice. The Emperor John Palæologus was hardly master of more than the Imperial city. Constantinople was nearly the whole Byzantine Empire.

Nothing, however, shows more clearly that the Council and the Pope divided the allegiance of Christendom than that ambassadors from the Eastern Empire appeared in Basle as well as in Rome. Nego-

Reconciliation of Eastern Empire.

tiations were conducted by the Emperor and Patriarch as well with the Council as with the Pope.* Legates from the Council as from the Pope were sent to Constantinople. Contracts were entered into for galleys, *Negotiations with Pope and Council* if not hired, promised both by Pope and Council to convey the Byzantine and his Clergy to the West. The crafty Greeks seemed disposed to bargain with the highest bidder, and with him who could give best security. The difficulties and advantages seemed singularly balanced. The Pope might admit the Easterns to unity, but Transalpine Christendom alone could pay the price of their laudable apostasy. Effective aid could be expected not from Italy, but from the Emperor (Sigismund was still on the throne) and from a crusade of all Europe. If the Greeks were unwilling to appear at Basle, the Council would consent to adjourn for this purpose to Avignon. And Avignon, it was thought, would purchase the high honour of becoming the seat of the Council for this glorious object, at the price of 70,000 pieces of gold for the convoy of the Emperor and his retinue. Avignon declined, or at least was not prompt in the acceptance of these terms.

The Pope during the preceding year had offered the choice of the great cities of Italy—Bologna, Ancona, Ravenna, Florence, Pisa, Mantua, even Rome. He now insisted on the alternative of Florence or of Udine in

---

* Syropulus (p. 17), the Greek, describes the Council as assembled to remedy the monstrous evils which had grown up in the West, and for the limitation of the Pope's power, and that of his court: ἐπὶ διορθώσει τῶν ἀτόπων τῶν ἐν τοῖς μέρεσι τῆς Ἰταλίας παρεισφθαρέντων, καὶ μά- λιστα ἐπὶ τῇ συστολῇ καὶ ὑποτυπώσει τοῦ Πάπα καὶ τῆς αὐλῆς αὐτοῦ. Of the three ambassadors to Basle, two were Demetrius, the great Stratopedarch, and Isidore, afterwards Metropolitan of Russia. See the account of their reception—Syropulus, p. 23 et seqq.

the Friulian province of his native Venice. Florence, his faithful ally, would open her own gates; Venice would admit a Council into her territory, not within her lagunes. If the reconciliation of the Greek and the Latin Church, the tardy and compulsory submission of Constantinople to the See of Rome, had been the one paramount, transcendant duty of Christendom,—if it was to swallow up and supersede all the long agitated questions of the reform in the hierarchy, the reinstatement of the sacerdotal Order not only in its power but in its commanding holiness—the Pope might urge strong reasons for the transplantation of the Council to Italy. The Greeks might well be alarmed at the unnecessary difficulties of a journey over the snowy Alps, the perils of wild roads, of robber chieftains. The Pope felt his strength in resting the dispute on that issue alone. At all events it might create a schism at Basle. The Transalpine party still adhered to Avignon, or some city of France. But if the Greeks also were to be considered, there could be no doubt of the superior convenience of Italy.[b]

The Papal Legate, the Archbishop of Tarento, appeared at Basle to propose the removal of the Council for this great end to Florence or to Udine. *(March 3, 1437.)* The President of the Council was still the Cardinal Julian Cæsarini. Up to this time Cæsarini had stood firm and unshaken on the rights of the Council, but now with other Italian Prelates inclined towards obedience to the Pope. But the large number of the Transalpine Clergy, especially of the lower clergy, knew

---

[b] On one occasion the Patriarch said with simplicity that he had no inclination to be food for fishes: ἐμὲ δὲ οὐκ ἄξιον κρίνετε φείδεσθαι ἑαυτοῦ, μήποτε καὶ ἐν τῷ πελάγει μιψέλη κατάβρωμα γένωμαι τῶν ἰχθύων.— Syropulus, p. 22. The unegolloquent Latin translator makes the fishes whales.

that, once evoked to Italy, the Council, as an independent assembly, was at an end. The debate was long and turbulent. They came to the vote. Above two-thirds of the Council rejected the prorogation to Florence or Udine. The Duke of Milan, still opposed to the Pope in Italian politics, on his part desirous of having the Council in his dominions, offered a third alternative, the city of Pavia. Æneas Sylvius, in an eloquent speech of two hours (it was a convenient resting-place for Æneas ere he passed from the interests of the Council to that of the Pope), urged this middle course. He wrought on the ambassadors of Castile, but the Council was obdurate; it would not pass the Alps. The decree of the majority was publicly read, ordered to be engrossed, and confirmed with the seal of the Council. To the indignation of most, a Bishop arose and published aloud the decree of the minority as that of the Council.[c] Nor was this all; at night the Bull of the Council was stolen from its box, the silken thread which attached the seal had been cut, the seal appended to the substituted decree of the Papal party. The fraud was openly charged, it was believed to be brought home to the Legate, the Archbishop of Tarento. His officer was treated with contumely, even with personal violence. The Archbishop with inconceivable effrontery avowed and gloried in the crime. He had advised, ordered, aided in the theft. He had done it, and would do it were it to do again. Must he not obey the Apostolic See rather than a rabble?[d] He fled from the city (he was

[c] Æneas Sylvius, p. 73. L'Enfant, t. p. 481, &c.

[d] "Tarentinus alti cordis vir, intrepidus, audax. Quid vos, inquit, tantopere factum vituperatis? Rectum est et laude dignum, quod reprehenditur. Semel ego rem, fieri mandavi, operam dedi, et nisi fecissem, hodie facerem. Apostolicæ Sedi magis quam vestræ turbæ obnoxius sum. Verum

threatened with imprisonment) under an armed escort. The Emperor heard of this unworthy artifice; he declared that the crime should not pass unpunished. Europe rang with the guilt of the Legate.

<small>July 4, 1437.</small>

Eugenius loudly protested against this insolent impeachment of his Legate. He denounced the violence threatened against his sacred person, the rude usage of the Archbishop's officer: he afterwards rewarded the Archbishop with the Cardinalate. His protest and denunciations were heard with incredulity or indifference at Basle.

The Pope was more successful in his dealings at Constantinople. The Assembly, he urged, was but a small knot of unruly spirits, usurping the name of a Council; their sole object was to diminish the power of the Pope, the Pope who alone had the right to summon a Council and control their proceedings. He warned the Byzantines against trusting to their promises; they had no money to transport the Greeks to the West, none for ulterior purposes. Venice had already prepared her galleys for the convoy of the Emperor. Of Venice the Greeks well knew the power and the wealth. Yet the crafty Greeks might well smile at the zeal of the Pope for the unity of the Church, which made him hold up their reconciliation as the one great object of Christendom, while in the West the unity was thus broken by the feud of Pope and Council.

That feud was growing more violent and irreconcileable. The Council issued their monition to the Pope and to the Cardinals to appear before them at Basle within sixty days, and answer for their

<small>July 31. Sept. 21.</small>

<small>ego decretum plumbavi, vos adulteri- | vi rapitur? nolo negare quod feci et num. Vi nos impediistis plumbare: | recte feci."—Æn. Sylvius, p. 74. cur arts non vindicabimus, quod nobis</small>

acts. They annulled his creation of Cardinals. At the
expiration of the sixty days they solemnly
declared the Pope contumacious. He had promulgated his Bull for the Council of Ferrara. That Bull they declared void and of none effect. After some delay they proceeded to the suspension of the Pope. Other resolutions passed, limiting appeals to the Roman See, abolishing expectatives, gradually unfolding and expanding their views of Church Reformation.

The union of the Greek and Latin Churches, as it was understood in the West by the Pope and the high Papalists, the unqualified subjection of the East to the successor of St. Peter, by the Council the subjection to the Western Church represented at Basle, seemed to acquire more paramount importance from the eager and emulous exertions of the Council and the Pope to secure each to itself the Imperial proselyte. The Emperor, John VI. Palæologus, might at first appear to balance with lofty indifference their conflicting claims; to weigh the amount and the certainty of their offers, in which they vied against each other; and to debate which would be the most serviceable ally against the terrible Ottoman, and therefore best reward the sacrifice of the religious freedom of the East. Those were not wanting who advised him to dismiss the ambassadors of both, and declare, "when you have settled your own quarrels it will be time for us to discuss the terms of union." Friar John, the Legate of the Council, as he began to despair of conducting the Emperor to Basle, would at all hazards keep him away from Italy. He urged this

---

* Laonicus Chalcondylas. By a great anachronism he antedates the election of the Antipope Felix by the Council at Basle, and makes it a contest between the rival Pontiffs.—lvi. p. 287. Edit. Bonn.

dignified course; the more important adviser, the Emperor Sigismund, gave the same counsel.[f] But the Byzantine was now resolutely, as far as a mind so feeble was capable of resolution, determined on his journey to the West. He could not hope to hold a Council in Constantinople in which the West would be but partially represented, if it condescended to be represented,—or in which his own Church dominant in numbers, if required to make the slightest concession, would render obedience. His fears and his vanity had wrought him to desperate courage. He could not but know that the Turks were still closing round his narrowing empire, though there was for the moment some delay or suspense in their movements. Amurath had hardly consented to a hollow and treacherous delay,[g] and who could know when they might be under the walls of Constantinople? Yet had Palæologus strange notions of his own grandeur. The West would lay itself at his feet; he might be chosen the successor of Sigismund, and reunite the great Christian commonwealth under one sovereign.[h]

But he had great difficulty in persuading the heads of his Church to embark on a perilous voyage to a distant and foreign Council, where their few voices might be overborne by multitudes. Joseph the Patriarch was old, infirm, of feeble character: he yielded with ungracious reluctance,[i] but scrupled not to compel the attendance of his more prudent and far-sighted clergy. They too found consolation to their vanity, food for their ambition.

---

[f] Syropulus, p. 57.
[g] The treaty in Phranza, p. 118.
[h] Syropulus, p. 86.
[i] See his speech (Syropulus, p. 16) in the time of Pope Martin, in which he predicts the inevitable humiliation from attending a Council in Italy, at the expense of the Westerns. ἐν τοῦν τῷ ἀπελθεῖν οὕτω καὶ ἐκδίχεσθαι καὶ τὴν ἡμερσίαν τροφὴν ἐξ ἐκείνων, ἤδη γίνονται δοῦλοι καὶ μισθωτοί, ἐκεῖνοι δὲ κύριοι.

"The barbarous and ignorant West would bow before the learning and profound theology of the successors of Basil, the Gregories, and Chrysostom." Nor were they without some vague notions of the prodigal and overflowing wealth of the West: they would return having achieved a victory by their irresistible arguments, and at the same time with money enough to pay their debts.[k] If the Latins should stand aloof in stubborn obstinacy, they would return with the pride of having irradiated Italy with the truth, and of having maintained in the face of Rome the cause of orthodoxy; at the worst, they could but die as glorious martyrs for that truth.[m] The Patriarch laboured under still more extravagant illusions. "When the Eastern Emperor should behold the pomp of the Pope, the lowly deference paid to their ecclesiastical superiors by the great potentates of the West, he would take lessons of humility, and no longer mistake the relative dignity of the spiritual and temporal Sovereign."[n] These strange and chimerical hopes blinded some at least to the danger of their acts, and even mitigated for a time their inextinguishable hatred of the Latins; for the Latin conquest of Constantinople still left its deep indelible animosity in the hearts of the Greek Churchmen. They had been thrust from their Sees; Latin Bishops speaking a foreign tongue had been forced upon their flocks; they had been stripped of their revenues, reduced to poverty and contempt. On the reconquest of Constantinople, the Cantacuzenes and Palæologi had resumed the full temporal sovereignty,

---

[k] Syropulus, p. 63. Καὶ ἀπελευσόμεθα καὶ ὑποστρέψομεν νικηταὶ τροπαιοῦχοι.
[m] Syropulus, ibid.
[n] Syropulus, p. 92. Καὶ διὰ τοῦ πάντα ἐφόδοις ἐλευθερῶσαι τὴν ἐκκλησίαν ἀπὸ τῆς ἐπιτεθείσης αὐτοῦ δουλείας παρὰ τοῦ βασιλέως. —κ. τ. λ.

but the Church had recovered only a portion of its influence, wealth, and power. Even in Constantinople, still more in many cities of the Empire, the Latin Bishops still claimed a co-ordinate authority, refused to be deposed, and, where the Franks were in force, maintained their thrones. There were at least titular Latin Bishops of most of the great Eastern Sees.

The Emperor and the Patriarch determined to accept the invitation of the Pope, and to reject that of the Council. Vague and terrible notions of the danger of surmounting the Alps, or of the interminable voyage to Marseilles, if Avignon should be the seat of the Council; the more doubtful, less profuse promises of money for the voyage from the Council; the greater dexterity and address of the Papal Legate, wrought powerfully on their minds. The fatal and insulting declaration of the Council—"They had subdued the new heresy of the Bohemians, they should easily subdue the old heresy of the Greeks"*—had been industriously reported, and could not be forgiven. More politic Rome made no such mistake: her haughtiness could wait its time, could reserve itself in bland courteousness till the adversary was in her power, at her feet. *Emperor accepts the offer of Rome.*

Eight Papal galleys, furnished in Venice and in Crete, entered the harbour of Constantinople. They had not long arrived when it was heard that the fleet of the Council was drawing near. The Council had at length prevailed on the city of Avignon to furnish the necessary funds; the ships had been hired and manned at Marseilles. The Roman Admiral, the Pope's nephew Condolmieri, produced his commission to burn, sink, or *Rival fleets.*

* Syropulus, p. 27.

destroy the hostile fleet. He gave orders to his squadron to set sail and encounter the insolent enemy. It was with great difficulty that the Emperor prevented a battle between the fleets of the Pope and of the Council:[p] an edifying proof to the Turks, who occupied part of the shores, of the unity of Christendom!—to the Greeks a significant but disregarded warning, as to the advantages which they might expect from their concessions to Western Christendom, itself in such a state of fatal disunion!

After nearly three months' delay—delay afterwards bitterly reproached by the Pope against the Greeks, as having involved much loss of time and needless expense—the Emperor and the Patriarch embarked on board the Venetian galleys. The Emperor was accompanied by his brother, the Despot Demetrius, whom it might be dangerous to leave behind at Constantinople; and attended by a Court, the magnificence of whose titles might make up for their moderate numbers. The Church made even a more imposing display. The Patriarch was encircled by the Bishops of the most famous Sees in the East, some of them men of real distinction. There were those who either held or were supposed to be the representatives of the three Patriarchates now under Moslem dominion—Antioch, Alexandria, Jerusalem; the Primate of Russia, whose wealth excited the wonder and envy of the Greeks; Bessarion Archbishop of Nicæa, and Mark of Ephesus, the two most renowned for their learning; the Prelates of Cyzicum, Heraclea, Nicomedia, Trebizond, Lacedæmon, and other famous names. The greater monasteries were represented by

---

[p] μάλις οὖν διὰ πολλῶν λόγων καὶ μηνυμάτων κατέπεισε τὸν ναύαρχον μόγις, καὶ ἡσύχασε.—Syropulus. | p. 55. The Papal Legates had persuaded the Greeks that the Council of Basle was dissolved.

some of their Archimandrites. The Patriarch was attended, in his person, by all the high officers and the inferior dignitaries of S. Sophia, the cross-bearers, the whole choir of singers, the treasurer, the guardian of the books, the guardian of the vestments, the guardian of those who claimed the right of asylum, the expounder of the Canon Law, and Syropulus, the Ecclesiast or the Preacher. The last avenged the compulsion laid upon him to follow his master to Ferrara and Florence by writing a lively and bold history of the whole proceedings.* The preparations, both of the Emperor and the Patriarch, made an incongruous display of pomp and poverty. The Emperor, that he might appear as the magnificent Sovereign of the East, to the indignation of the Church appropriated and lavished the sacred treasures, which had been sent as votive offerings by rich worshippers, on his own adornments, on a golden chariot, and cloth of gold for his bed. It was proposed that the Patriarch alone should appear in becoming state; the Bishops without their useless copes and dalmatics, in the coarse dress and cowls of simple monks. It was answered that the haughty Latins would scoff at their indigence. Notwithstanding the prodigies which remonstrated against their removal, the sacred vessels of S. Sophia were borne off, that the Patriarch might everywhere be able to celebrate Mass in unpolluted patens and chalices, and without being exposed to the contemptuous toleration of the Latins. When, however, on the division of the first Papal subsidy (15,000 florins), the Emperor assigned only the sum of 6000 to the clergy, the Patriarch resolutely declared that he would not

---

* This remarkable work of Syropulus is the chief and trustworthy authority for the voyage, personal adventures, and personal feelings of the Greeks.

proceed to the Council. The Emperor was no less stubborn: he gave the Patriarch 1000 for his own use, and distributed the 5000 among the clergy; to the richer less, to the poor more.[r]

An earthquake (dire omen!) shook the city as they set sail. The voyage was long, seventy-seven days. The timid landsman, the Ecclesiast, may have exaggerated its discomforts and perils. It was humiliating alike to the Emperor and to the Patriarch. As they passed Gallipoli they were saluted with showers of javelins from the Turkish forts. In another place, though there was no declared war, the Hagarenes would scarcely allow them to take in water. The Emperor hardly escaped falling into the hands of some Catalan pirates. The Patriarch, when he landed, had to endure the parsimonious courtesy and the niggard hospitality of the Latin Prelates who occupied Greek Sees on the coast.[s]

The voyage.

Nothing, however, could equal the magnificence of their reception at Venice. The pride of the Republic was roused to honour, no doubt to dazzle, so distinguished a guest. As they approached the Lagunes, the Doge rowed forth in the Buccutaur, with twelve other galleys, the mariners in silken dresses, the awnings and flags of silk, the emblazoned banners of St. Mark waving gorgeously above. The sea was absolutely covered with gondolas and galleys. "You might as well number the leaves of the trees, the sands of the sea, or the drops of rain." The amazement of the Greeks at the splendour, wealth, and populousness of Venice

Arrival at Venice.

---

[r] Syropulus, 63.
[s] See the voyage in Syropulus at length, with many amusing incidents by land and sea, 69 *et seqq.* Gibbon justly says that "the historian has the uncommon talent of placing each scene before the reader's eye."—Note c. lxvi. p. 99.

forcibly shows how Constantinople had fallen from her Imperial state:—"Venice the wonderful—most wonderful! Venice the wise—most wise! The city foreshown in the Psalm, 'God has founded her upon the waters.'"[a]

The respectful homage of the Doge to the Emperor was construed by the Greeks into adoration.[b] He was conducted (all the bells of the city loudly pealing, and music everywhere sounding) up to the Rialto. There he was lodged in a noble and spacious palace: the Patriarch in the monastery of St. George. The Patriarch visited the church of St. Mark. The Greeks gazed in utter astonishment at the walls and ceilings glittering with mosaics of gold and precious stones, and the carvings in precious woods. The great treasury, shown only twice a-year, flew open before them: they beheld the vast and incalculable mass of gold and jewels, wrought with consummate art, and set in the most exquisite forms; but amid their amazement rose the bitter thought, "These were once our own: they are the plunder of our Santa Sophia, and of our holy monasteries."[c]

The Doge gave counsel to the Emperor—wise Venetian counsel, but not quite in accordance with the close alliance of Venice with the Pope, or her respect for her

---

[a] Phranza, ii. 15, p. 181, 6. Edit. Bonn.

[b] Phranza says, προσεκύνησι τὸν βασιλέα καθήμενον.

[c] Syropulus. There was one splendid image wrought entirely out of the gold and jewels taken in Constantinople: τοῖς μὲν κεκτημένοις καύχημα καὶ τέρψις ἐγένετο καὶ ἡδονή, τοῖς δ' ἀφαιρεθεῖσιν εἰ τοῦ καὶ παρατυχοῦσιν, ἀθυμία καὶ λύπη καὶ κατήφεια, ὃς καὶ ἡμῖν τότε συνέβη. Syropulus is better authority than Ducas, and would hardly have suppressed, if he had witnessed the wonder of the Venetians at the celebration of the Mass by the Greeks according to their own rite. "'Verily,'" writes Ducas, "they exclaimed in wonder, 'these are the first-born of the Church, and the Holy Ghost speaks in them.'" —Ducas, c. xxxi.

mitred son, Eugenius IV.⁷ He might take up his abode in Venice, duly balance the offers of the Pope and the Council of Basle, and accept the terms most advantageous to himself or his Empire.

If the Emperor hesitated, he was determined by the arrival of Cardinal Cæsarini, deputed by the Pope, with the Marquis of Este, to press his immediate presence at Ferrara. Julian Cæsarini had now abandoned the Council of Basle: his desertion to the hostile camp might indicate that their cause was sinking towards desperation. He was now the Legate of the Pope, not that of the majority, it might be, but dwindling, more democratic, almost discomfited, majority at Basle.⁸

Jan. 9, 1438.

Early in March the Emperor set forward to Ferrara. He travelled (it was so arranged) partly by water, partly by land, with greater speed than the aged Patriarch, who was highly indignant, as the Church ought to have taken precedence. In the reception of the Emperor at Ferrara all was smooth courtesy. He rode a magnificent black charger; another of pure white, with trappings emblazoned with golden eagles, was led before him. The Princes of Este bore the canopy over his head. He rode into the courts of the Papal palace, dis-

The Emperor at Ferrara.

---

⁷ Syropulus, p. 85.

⁸ There is however considerable difficulty, and there are conflicting authorities as to the time, at which Julian Cæsarini, the Cardinal of St. Angelo, left Basle (see Fea's note to Æneas Sylvius, p. 128); and also whether, as Sanuto asserts, he appeared before the Emperor of the East, not as representative of the Pope, but of the Council. Cæsarini seems to have been in a state of embarrassment: he attempted to mediate between the more violent and the papalising parties at Basle. He lingered for some months in this doubtful state. Though accredited by the Pope at Venice, he may have given himself out as representing the sounder, though smaller part of the Council of Basle. This was evidently the tone of the Eugenians.

mounted at the staircase, was welcomed at the door of the chamber by the Pope. He was not permitted to kneel, but saluted with a holy kiss, and took his seat at the Pope's right hand. The attendants had indeed lifted up the hem of the Pope's garment, and exposed his foot; but of this the Greeks took no notice. The Patriarch moved more slowly: his barge was splendidly adorned,[a] but there ended his idle honours. March 4.
He had still cherished the fond hope that the Pope would receive him as his equal. He had often boasted that the Patriarchate would now be delivered from its base subjection to the Empire. He was met by a messenger with the tidings that the Pope expected him to kneel in adoration and kiss his foot. March 8. A.D. 1438.
This degrading ceremony his own Bishops had declined.[b] "If he is the successor of St. Peter," said the Patriarch in his bitterness, "so are we of the other Apostles. Did they kiss St. Peter's feet?" No Cardinals came out to meet him, only six Bishops, at the bridge. His own Bishops, who were with him, reproached the Patriarch: "Are these the honours with which you assured us we were to be received?" The Patriarch threatened to return home. The Pope, disappointed in the public humiliation of the Patriarch at his feet, would grant only a private audience. In the morning they all mounted horses furnished by the Marquis of Este, and rode to the gates of the Papal palace. All but the Patriarch alighted. He rode through the courts to the foot of the staircase. They passed through a suite of chambers, through an array of attendants with silver wands of office. The doors closed behind them. They were admitted only

---

[a] Phranza compares it to Noah's Ark. He was astonished with its sumptuousness and accommodation.—P. 189. [b] Syropulus, p. 95.

six at a time to the presence of the Pope. Eugenius was seated with only his Cardinals around. He welcomed the Patriarch with a brotherly salute. The Patriarch took his seat somewhat lower, on a level with the Cardinals. His cross-bearers did not accompany him: they came last, and were permitted to kiss the hand and the cheek of the Pope. Now as afterwards, in their more private intercourse, the Pope and the Patriarch being ignorant, the one of Greek, the other of Latin, discoursed through an interpreter.[c]

Discontent of the Greeks. The Greeks had not been many days at Ferrara ere they began to suspect that the great object of the Pope was his own aggrandisement, the strengthening of his power against the Council of Basle. They looked with jealousy on every artful attempt to degrade their Patriarch from his absolute coequality with the Pope, on his lower seat, and the limitation of the honours paid to him; they reproached the Patriarch with every seeming concession to the Papal pride.[d] Before they met in the Council, they had the prudence curiously to inspect the arrangements in the great church. They found a lofty and sumptuous throne raised for the Pope in the midst: the rest were to sit, as it were, at his feet. Even the Emperor was roused to indignation. After much dispute it was agreed that the Pope should occupy a central throne, but slightly elevated. On his right, was a vacant chair for the Emperor of the West, then the Cardinals and dignitaries of the Latin Church; on his left, the seat of the Eastern Emperor, followed by the Patriarch and the Greek clergy. But the affairs dragged languidly on. The Pope affected to expect the

---

[c] Syropulus, p. 96.
[d] The Bishop of Trebizond was usually the spokesman. Syropulus, p. 160.

submission of the Fathers of Basle. The Italian Prelates were by no means imposing in numbers; of the other Latin clergy were very few. The only ambassadors, those of the Duke of Burgundy. The Greeks perhaps knew not in what terms the Western clergy had been summoned. " If the Latins had any parental love they would hasten to welcome the prodigal son, the Greek Church returning to his father's home." The appeal to the charity of the Latins had no great result. The Patriarch had joined with the Pope at the first Session in an anathema, if they should contumaciously remain aloof from this Council. Awe was as powerless as love.

The Emperor retired to a monastery about six miles from Ferrara, and abandoned himself to the pleasures of the chase. The husbandmen in vain remonstrated against his wanton destruction of their crops, the Marquis of Ferrara[e] against his slaughter of the pheasants and quails which he had preserved at great cost.[f] The Patriarch and the clergy were left to suffer every kind of humiliating indignity, and worse than indignity. They were constantly exposed to endure actual hunger; their allowance in wine, fish, meat, was scanty and irregular; their stipends in money always many months in arrear. They were close prisoners;[g] rigid police watched at the gates of the city: no one could stir without a passport.[h] The Bishop of Ferrara refused them one of the great

---

[e] Nicolas III. of Este. Laonicus Chalcondylas takes the opportunity of telling of the Marquis the dreadful story which is the groundwork of Lord Byron's " Parisina."—P. 288, &c.

[f] Raynald. sub ann.

[g] This ancient Italian usage, that no one could leave a city without a passport from the authorities, astonished the Greeks.—Syropulus, p. 141.

[h] Syropulus, Ibid. He is indignant: οὕτως ὁ Πνευματικὸς ἀνὴρ τιμᾶν ἔγνω τοὺς τοῦ ἁγίου Πνεύματος ὑπηρέτας.

churches to celebrate Mass according to their own rite: he would not have his holy edifice polluted. Three of them made their escape to Venice, and were ignominiously brought back. A second time they contrived to fly, and found their way to Constantinople. The indignant Patriarch sent home orders that the recreants should be suspended from their office, and soundly flogged.[1] Tidings in the mean time arrived, fortunately exaggerated, that the Ottoman who had condescended to grant a precarious peace, threatened Constantinople; the Pope evaded the demand for succour. He, indeed, himself was hardly safe. The bands of Nicolas Piccinino, Captain of a terrible Free Company, had seized Forlì and Bologna.

The miserable Greek clergy urged the Patriarch, the slow and irresolute Patriarch at length urged the Emperor, too well amused with his hunting, to insist on the regular opening of the Council. "We must wait the arrival of the ambassadors from the Sovereigns and Princes, of more Cardinals and Bishops; the few at present in Ferrara cannot presume to form an Œcumenic Council." Autumn drew on; with autumn the plague began to appear. Of the eleven Cardinals only five, of the one hundred and sixty Bishops only fifty remained in Ferrara. The Greeks escaped the ravage of the pestilence, all but the Russians: they suffered a fearful decimation.[2]

Not, indeed, that the whole of this time had been wasted in inactivity. Conferences had been held: private Synods, not recognised as formal acts of the Council, had defined the four great points of difference between the Greek and Latin Churches. Scandalous

---

[1] Syropulus, p. 125.   [2] Id. p. 144.

rumours indeed were disseminated that the Greeks were guilty of fifty-four articles of heresy; these charges were disdained as of no authority; but the Greeks were not less affected, and not less despised and hated by the mass of the people for such disclaimer. The Council was at length formally opened; but throughout it was skilfully contrived that while there was the most irreverent confusion among the Greeks, the Patriarch was treated with studied neglect, the Emperor himself, with reluctant and parsimonious honours; the Pope maintained his serene dignity; all the homage paid to him was skilfully displayed. The Greeks were jealous of each other; the courtly and already wavering Prelate of Nicæa was in constant collision with the ruder but more faithful Mark of Ephesus; they could not but feel and betray, they knew not how to resent, their humiliation.* Their dismay and disgust was consummated by news of the intended adjournment of the Council to Florence. They would not at first believe it; the Emperor was obliged to elude their remonstrances by ambiguous answers. The terrors of the plague, which Syropulus avers had passed away for two months; the promises of better supplies, and more regular payments in rich and fertile Tuscany; the neighbourhood of commodious havens, where they might embark for Greece; above all, starvation, not only feared, but almost actually suffered: all were as nothing against the perils of a journey over the wild and unknown Apennines, perhaps beset by the marauding troops of Piccinino, the greater distance from Venice, and, therefore, from their home. Already the Bishop of Heraclea, the homophylax, and even Mark of Ephesus, had attempted flight, and had

---

* See all the latter part of the 6th section of Syropulus.

been brought back by actual force or by force disguised as persuasion.*

Journey to Florence. The clergy with undissembled reluctance,* or rather under strong compulsion, the Emperor with ungracious compliance, yielded at length to the unavoidable necessity. The Emperor and the Patriarch, the Pope and his Cardinals found their long way to Florence, not indeed by the ordinary roads, for the enemy occupied Bologna, but, according to the Greeks, with the haste and secrecy of flight; to the Latins, with the dignity of voluntary retirement. The Pope travelled by Modena; the Emperor and the Patriarch by Faenza, and thence in three days over the savage Apennines to Florence.*

Basle. In Basle, meantime, the Nations continued their sessions, utterly despising the idle menaces of the Pope, and the now concurrent anathemas of the Greeks. The Cardinal Louis Archbishop of Arles, a man of all-respected piety and learning, had taken the place as President, on the secession of Cardinal Julian Cæsarini. But not only Cæsarini, the Cardinal of St. Peter's and many others had fallen off from the Council; the King of Arragon, the Duke of Milan menaced away their Prelates. None, it was said, remained, but those without benefices, or those from the kingdoms of which the Sovereigns cared nothing for these religious disputes. Amadeus of Savoy compelled his Bishops to join the Council, to make up

---

* Syropulus, 151.
* Καὶ πάντες τὸ τῆς μεταβάσεως βάρος ὁμονόως ἐκτραγῳδοῦντες καὶ ἀνοσευόμενοι, καὶ πρὸ ἐμποδισμὸν ταύτης πάντα ὅσα ἐνῆν λέγοντες.—Syropulus, p. 184.

* There is now a noble road from Forli to Florence; but before this road was made it must have been a wild and terrific journey, especially to the sedentary Greek of Constantinople.

a sufficient number to depose the Pope.¹ The death of the Emperor Sigismund, whose presence in the Council had no doubt raised its credit in the minds of men, was a fatal blow to the cause of Reformation. His son-in-law, Albert, was chosen at Frankfort King of the Romans; but Albert's disposition on this momentous subject was undeclared; his power not yet confirmed. The German Diet now took a lofty tone of neutrality; they would not interfere in the quarrel (it had sunk into a quarrel) between the Pope and the Council. In vain the Archbishop of Palermo, in the name of the Council, urged that it was the cause of ecclesiastical freedom, of holy religion. Even the great German Prelates heard in apathy.²

<small>Dec. 9, 1437.</small>

<small>At Frankfort, A.D. 1438.</small>

Not so the kingdom of France. On the 1st of May the Gallican Hierarchy, at the summons of the King, assembled in a national Synod at Bourges. The Kings and the clergy of France had seldom let pass an opportunity of declaring their own distinctive and almost exclusive independence on the Papal power. At the same time that they boasted their titles, as inherited from Pepin or Charlemagne as the defenders, protectors, conservators of the Holy See, it was with reservation of their own peculiar rights. They would leave the rest of the world prostrate at the Pope's feet, they would even assist the Pope in compelling their prostration; in France alone they would set limits to, and exercise control over, that power.

<small>France. Pragmatic Sanction.</small>

---

¹ Æneas Sylvius, p. 76.
² These verses are of the time:—
"Ut primum magni cœpit discordia cleri
Incipit Germani, non sibi parte summa,
Hoc ubi non rectum docti docuere magistri
Suspendunt animos, guttura non aperiunt."

Even St. Louis, the author of the first Pragmatic Sanction, in all other respects the meekest Catholic Christian, was still King of France. The King, or rather the King's advisers, the Legists and the Counsellors in the Parliament, saw that it was an inestimable occasion for the extension or confirmation of the royal prerogative. The clergy, though they had attended in no great numbers, were still in general adherents of the Council of Basle. The doctrines of Gerson and of the University of Paris were their guides. At the great Synod of Bourges the King proposed, the clergy eagerly adopted the decrees of the Council. Yet though they fully admitted the Assembly of Basle to be a legitimate Œcumenic Council, to which all Christians, the Pope himself, owed submission, they virtually placed themselves above Pope or Council. They did not submit to the Council as Legislator of Christendom; their own consent and re-enactment was necessary to make the decree of Pope or Council the law of the realm of France. The new Pragmatic Sanction, as now issued, admitted certain of the decrees in all their fulness, from the first word to the last; others they totally rejected, some they modified, or partially received. The Synod of Bourges assumed to be a co-ordinate, or, as regarded France, a superior Legislature. It asserted the rights of national churches with plenary authority, a doctrine fatal to the universal monarchy of Rome, but not less so to the unity of the Church, as represented by the Pope, or by a General Council. The Pragmatic Sanction encountered no opposition. It enacted these provisions: the Pope was subject to a General Council, and such General Council the Pope was bound to hold every ten years. The Pope had no power to nominate to the great ecclesiastical benefices,

Synod at Bourges. A.D. 1438.

except to a few specially reserved; the right of election devolved on those to whom it belonged. The Court of Rome had no right to the collation to inferior benefices; expectatives or grants of benefices not vacant were absolutely abolished. Appeals of all kinds to Rome were limited to very grave cases. No one was to be disturbed in his possession who had held a benefice for three years. It restricted the number of Cardinals to twenty-four, none to be named under thirty years of age. Annates and first-fruits were declared simoniacal. Priests who retained concubines forfeited their emoluments for three months. There were some regulations for the performance of divine service. The Mass was to be chanted in an audible voice: no layman was to sing psalms or hymns in the vulgar tongue in churches. Spectacles of all sorts, plays, mummeries, masques, banquets in churches were prohibited. The avoiding all commerce with the excommunicated was limited to cases of great notoriety. The interdict was no longer to confound in one sweeping condemnation the innocent and the guilty.*

Thus, then, while Germany receded into a kind of haughty indifference, France, as far as France, had done the work of the Council. The Pragmatic Sanction was her reform; the dissolution of the Council by the Pope, the deposition of the Pope by the Council, she did not condescend to notice. England, now on the verge of her great civil strife, had never taken much part in the Council, she had not even resented her non-admission as a Nation. Even Spain and Milan had

---

* Concilium Rituricense, apud Labbe. Ordonnances de France, iii. p. 287, 291. L'Enfant, Hist. du Concile de Bâle. Compare Sismondi, Hist. des Français, xli. p. 327.

to a certain extent withdrawn their sanction. But still the Council of Basle maintained its lofty tone; it must have had deep root in the reverence of mankind, or it must have fallen away in silent, certain dissolution.

CHAPTER XIV.

The Council of Florence.

FLORENCE received the strangers from the East with splendid hospitality. The Emperor, after some contest allowed the Church on this occasion her coveted precedence.[a] The Patriarch arrived first; he was met by two Cardinals and many Bishops. But at Florence curiosity was not highly excited by the arrival of an aged Churchman: he passed on almost unregarded. Three days after came the Emperor; the city was in a tumult of eager wonder; the roofs were crowded with spectators; trumpets and instruments of music rang through the streets; all the bells pealed; but the magnificence of the pomp (so relates the Ecclesiast, not without some ill-suppressed satisfaction) was marred by deluges of rain.[b] The gorgeous canopy held over the Emperor's head was drenched; he and all the spectators were glad to find refuge in their houses.

The Council of Florence began with due solemnity its grave theological discussions, on the event of which might seem to depend the active interference of the West to rescue her submissive and orthodox brethren

---

[a] Laonicus Chalcondylas describes Florence as the greatest and richest city after Venice. Ἡ δὲ Φλωρεντία πόλις ἐστὶν ὀλβιωτάτη μετά γε τὴν Οὐενετῶν πόλιν, ἐπὶ ἐμπορίαν ἅμα καὶ γεωργοὺς παριχομένη τοὺς ἀστούς. This union of agriculture with trade is, I presume, to distinguish them from the Venetians. He enters into the constitution of Florence.

[b] Syropulus, p. 213.

from the Mohammedan yoke, or the abandonment of the rebellious and heretical race to the irresistible Ottoman. It began with solemn order and regularity. The champions were chosen on each side; on the Latin, the most distinguished were the Cardinal Julian Cæsarini, the late President of the Council of Basle, not less eminent for learning than for political wisdom; and John, the Provincial General of the Dominican Order in Lombardy, esteemed among the most expert dialecticians of the West. On the side of the Greeks were Isidore of Russia, the courtly Bessarion, who might seem by his temper and moderation (though not unusual accompaniments of real learning) not to have been without some prophetic foresight of the Cardinalate and the quiet ease of a Western Bishopric; and Mark of Ephesus, whose more obstinate fidelity aspired to be the Defender, the Saint, the Martyr of his own unyielding Church. If legend were to be believed (and legend is still alive, in the full light of history) the Greeks were indeed incorrigible. Miracle was wasted upon them. St. Bernardino of Sienna is said to have displayed the first recorded instance of the gift of tongues since the Day of Pentecost; he disputed fluently in Greek, of which he could not before speak or understand one word.[c]

Already at Ferrara the four great questions had been proposed which alone were of vital difference to the Greek and Latin Churches. I. The Procession of the Holy Ghost, whether from the Father alone, or likewise from the Son. II. The use of leavened or unleavened bread in the Eucharist. III. Purgatory. IV. The Supremacy of the Pope. At Ferrara the more modest discussion had chiefly confined itself to the less momen-

---

[c] Raynaldus sub anno.

tous questions, those on which the passions were less roused, and which admitted more calm and amicable inquiry, especially that of Purgatory. At Florence they plunged at once into the great absorbing difficulty, the procession of the Holy Ghost. This, though not absolutely avoided at Ferrara, had been debated only, as it were, in its first approaches. Yet, even on this point,[a] where the object with the Latins, and with the more enlightened and best courtiers of the Greeks, was union not separation, agreement not stubborn antagonism, it began slowly to dawn upon their minds that the oppugnancy was in terms rather than in doctrine; the discrepancy, as it was calmly examined, seemed to vanish of itself. The article, however, involved two questions, one of the profoundest theology, the other of canonical law. I. Which was the orthodox doctrine, the Procession of the Holy Spirit from the Father alone, or from the Father and the Son? II. Even if the latter doctrine were sound, by what right had the Latin Church of her sole authority, in defiance of the anathema of one or more of the four great Œcumenic Councils, presumed to add the words "and the Son" to the creed of Nicæa? Which of these questions should take precedence was debated with obstinacy, not without acrimony. The more rigid Greeks would stand upon the plain fact, which could hardly be gainsaid, the unauthorised intrusion of the clause into the Creed. To the Latins, the Procession of the Holy Ghost from the Father alone (the Greek doctrine) was an impious disparagement of

---

[a] The Greeks were manifestly bewildered by the scholastic mode of argument, the endless logical formularies of the Latins (Syropulus, passim). They were utterly unacquainted with the Latin Fathers; could not distinguish the genuine from spurious citations; or even understand their language.—Syropulus, p. 218.

the co-equal, co-eternal Godhead of the Son; to the Greeks the Procession of the Holy Ghost from the Son also, was the introduction of two principles—it ascribed the incommunicable paternity of the Father to the Son.* It was discovered at length that neither did the Latins intend to deny the Father to be the primary and sole fountain of Godhead, nor the Greeks absolutely the Procession of the Holy Ghost from the Son. They all acquiesced in the form "of the Father through the Son;" yet on the different sense of the two Greek prepositions, "from and through," Mark of Ephesus and the rigid Greeks fought with a stubborn pertinacity as if their own salvation and the salvation of mankind were on the issue.' But the real difficulty was the addition to the Creed. As a problem of high speculative theology, the article might be couched in broad and ambiguous terms, and allowed to sink into reverential silence. The other inevitable question forced itself upon the mind, the popular mind as well as that of the clergy, almost in every service. Whenever the Nicene Creed was read or chanted, the omission of the words would strike the Latins with a painful and humiliating void; it was an admission of their presumption in enlarging the established Creed—the abasing confession that the Western Church, the Roman Church, had transcended its powers. To the Greek the unusual words jarred with equal dissonance on the ear; the compulsory repetition was a mark of galling subjection, of the cowardly abandonment of the rightful independence of his Church, as well as of truth and orthodoxy.

---

* The Latin argued, εἰ δὲ ὁμολογοῦντες ἡμεῖς οἱ Λατεῖνοι μίαν ἀρχὴν καὶ αἰτίαν καὶ πηγὴν καὶ ῥίζαν τὸν Πατέρα τοῦ υἱοῦ καὶ τοῦ πνεύματος, μὴ ποιοῦντες δύο ἀρχάς, τίς ἡ χρεία τοῦ ἀπαλείφειν προσθήκην.—Ducas, c. xxxi.

' Syropulus, p. 237.

On this point the Latins suffered the humiliation of having produced a copy of the Acts of the Second Council of Nicæa, which included the contested words. It was a forgery so flagrant that they were obliged to submit to its rejection without protest.ᵃ The Greeks drew the natural conclusion that they would not scruple to corrupt their own documents.ʰ The Latins were more fortunate or more skilful in some citations from S. Basil and other writers of authority. Their authenticity could not be disproved without awaiting the arrival of other copies from Constantinople. Throughout, the dispute rested on the Greek Fathers; the Greeks somewhat contemptuously avowed their ignorance of the Latin saints.

The Latins had the strength of strenuous union, the Greeks were weakened by discord. Already at Ferrara the more rigid Greeks had seen the accomplished Bessarion of Nicæa desert the faithful Mark of Ephesus. On the question of Purgatory they had differed more widely than the conflicting Churches. Their quarrel now degenerated into coarse and personal altercation. "Why do I dispute any longer" (Bessarion so far forgot himself) "with a man possessed by an evil spirit?"ⁱ Mark, in return, denounced Bessarion as a bastard and an apostate.

The Pope and the Emperorᵏ were resolutely determined upon the union. Every art, all influence and

---

ᵃ The interpolation was traced up to the time of Charlemagne, no higher.

ʰ ἐλέγομεν γὰρ καὶ ἐν τούτῳ, ὡς ἤδη ἔχομεν ἐλέγχειν αὐτοὺς ἐκ τοῦ τόπου, ὅτι ἐνοθεύθησαν καὶ τὰ ῥητὰ τῶν ὁντινῶν ἁγίων.—Syrop. p. 171.

ⁱ Syropulus, p. 257.

ᵏ The Emperor burst out into a furious invective against the Bishop of Heraclea, who had presumed to refute the Imperial arguments: οὕτω καὶ νῦν ἀναισχυντῶν λέγεις ἅπερ σοὶ οὐκ ἔξεστι. διότι ὑπάρχεις ἰδιώτης ἄνθρωπος, καὶ ἀπαίδευτος καὶ βάναυσος καὶ χωρίτης.—P. 224.

authority, were put forth to compel the more refractory to obedience. If the Cardinalate was not yet bestowed or promised to the more obsequious Prelates, Bessarion of Nicæa and Isidore of Russia, the appointments and allowances to the more pliant were furnished with punctuality and profusion, those to the contumacious parsimoniously if at all. The arrears of the disfavoured again extended to many months; they were again threatened with starvation. Christopher, the Pope's former Legate at Constantinople, proposed altogether to withdraw the allowance from Mark of Ephesus, the Judas who ate the Pope's bread and conspired against him." Rumours were spread that Mark was mad. It was skilfully suggested, it was plain to the simplest understanding, that the liberties of the Greeks, perhaps their lives, in a foreign land, were not their own; their return depended on the mercy or the generosity of their antagonists. They might be kept an indefinite time, prisoners, despised, starving prisoners. Their own poor resources had long been utterly exhausted; the Emperor, even the Patriarch, could make or enforce no terms for refractory subjects, who defied alike temporal and spiritual authority.

The Greeks met again and again in their private synod. The debates were long, obstinate, furious; the holy councillors were almost committed in personal violence; the Emperor mingled in the fray, overawing some to adulatory concessions, but not all." The question of the Procession of the Holy Ghost was proposed for their accordance in the mildest and most disguised form; that of the addition

---

" Syropulus, p. 251.
" The Bishops of Mitylene and Lacedæmon almost fell tooth and nail on Mark of Ephesus: καὶ μόνον οὐκ ὀδοῦσι καὶ χέρσιν ὁρμὴν διασπαράξαι αὐτόν.—P. 236.

to the Creed altogether eluded. There were twenty who declared themselves in favour of the union, twelve not content. But in subsequent meetings (every kind of influence was used, menaces, promises were lavished to obtain suffrages) the majority was gradually swelled by the admission of certain "Grammarians" to vote: the minority dwindled away by the secession of some Bishops through fear or favour, the disfranchisement of three of the cross-bearers and some obstinate monks, as not in holy orders. The Emperor determined that suffrages belonged only to Bishops and Archimandrites.[o] At length Mark of Ephesus stood alone, or with one partisan, Sophronius of Anchialus; even Sophronius seems to have dropped away; but in vain the Patriarch wasted all his eloquence on the adamantine Ephesian.

Yet the Emperor would not surrender the liberties of his Church without distinct stipulations as to the reward of his compliance.[p] His sole motive for submission had been the security of his empire, of Constantinople now almost his whole empire.[q] A treaty, negotiated by Isidore of Russia, was duly ratified and signed with these articles. I. The Pope bound himself to supply ample means, ships and provisions, for the return of the Emperor and the Greeks. II. The Pope would furnish every year two galleys and three hundred men-at-arms for the defence of Constantinople. III. The ships which conveyed the pilgrims to the Holy Land were to touch at Constantinople. IV. In the Emperor's need the Pope should furnish twenty galleys for six

---

[o] 'Ηγούμενοι.
[p] Gibbon has noted with his usual sarcasm the protest of the Emperor's dog, who howled fiercely and lament- ably throughout his master's speech.— Syropulus, 266.
[q] Syropulus, 261.

months or ten for a year. V. If the Emperor should require land forces, the Pope would use all his authority with the Princes of the West to supply them.

The temporal treaty was signed. With weary haste they proceeded to perfect, to ratify, and to publish the spiritual treaty, which pretended to unite the East and West in holy communion. The Patriarch, who had long been suffering from age and sickness, just lived to see and to sign this first article of his great work. He died suddenly, almost in the act of urging his followers to submission. He had already sent off some of his effects to Venice, and hoped to return (happily he did not return) to Constantinople. His obsequies were celebrated with great pomp; and in the Baptistery of Florence the stranger wonders to find the tomb of a Patriarch of Constantinople.

June 9.

The strife seemed to be worn out with this more momentous question. The discomfited and discordant Greeks had no longer courage or will to contest further.' The three other points had already been partially discussed; even that perilous one, the supremacy of the Pope, was passed, reserving only in vague and doubtful terms the rights of the Eastern Patriarchate. Death had silenced the remonstrant voice of the Patriarch. The final edict was drawn by common consent. One only difficulty remained which threatened seriously to disturb the peace. In whose names, on whose authority, should it address the world, as a law of Christendom, that of the Emperor the heir of Justinian, or the Pope

---

' There is a remarkable passage, in which Bessarion of Nicæa took the opportunity, to the perplexity and astonishment of the Greeks, of asserting their absolute unity with the Latins as to the sole power of the hierarchy to consecrate the Eucharist and to ordain the clergy.—Syropulus, p. 295; but compare p. 278.

the successor of St. Peter? The Emperor yielded to a compromise, which seemed to maintain his dignity. It spoke in the name of the Pope Eugenius IV. with the consent of his dear son John Palæologus, Emperor of the Romans, and the representatives of his venerable brethren the Patriarchs. Earth and heaven were summoned to rejoice that the wall had fallen which had divided the Churches of the East and West. The Greeks and Latins are now one people. I. The Holy Ghost proceeds from the Father and the Son, but as from one principle, by one operation. The words "from the Son" have been lawfully and with good reason inserted in the Creed. II. In the use of leavened or unleavened bread, each Church might maintain its usage. III. The souls of those who die in less than mortal sin are purified in purgatory, by what fire was not determined, but their sufferings may be shortened or alleviated by the prayers and alms of the faithful. IV. The Roman Pontiff, as successor of St. Peter, has a primacy and government over the whole Catholic Church, but according to the Canons of the Church.[*] The rights and privileges of the other four great Patriarchs, Constantinople, Alexandria, Antioch, Jerusalem, are inviolate and inviolable.

The Acts of the Council of Florence boast the signatures, on the part of the Latins, of the Pope, eight Cardinals, two Latin Patriarchs, of Jerusalem and Grado, two Bishops, Ambassadors of the Duke of Burgundy, eight Archbishops, forty-seven Bishops, four Heads of Orders, forty-one Abbots, and the Archdeacon of Troyes. Among the Greeks were the Emperor, the Vicars of

[*] About this there was a dispute, on which the Emperor threatened to break off the treaty. The Pope proposed "according to Scripture and the writings of the Saints."—P. 282.

the Patriarchs of Alexandria, Antioch, Jerusalem, nineteen Archbishops and Bishops by themselves or by their proctors, the great Dignitaries of the Church of Constantinople, the Head of the Imperial Monastery, and four Abbots. Of these some were compelled to set their hands, the Ecclesiast fairly owns, speaking no doubt of himself among others, from fear. Such were the representatives of the Christian world. The Despot Demetrius still sternly refused: he was to reap his reward in popularity, hereafter to be dangerous to his brother's throne. He retired to Venice in sullen dignity.

The Act was published with imposing solemnity in the Cathedral of Florence. Nothing was wanting to the splendour of the ceremony, to the glory of the Pope. After Te Deum chanted in Greek, Mass celebrated in Latin, the Creed was read with the "Filioque." Syropulus would persuade himself and the world that the Greeks did not rightly catch the indistinct and inharmonious sounds. Then the Cardinal Julian Cæsarini ascended the pulpit and read the Edict in Latin, the Cardinal Bessarion in Greek. They descended and embraced, as symbolising the indissoluble unity of the Church. The Edict (it was unusual) ended with no anathema. Bessarion and Isidore, with the zeal of renegades, had urged the condemnation of their contumacious brethren: they were wisely overruled. Even Mark of Ephesus, whom the Pope would have visited for his stubborn pride (the brave old man adhered to his convictions in the face of the Pope and his Cardinals), was protected by the Emperor. The service in the Cathedral of Florence was in the Latin form, the Pope was on his throne, with his Cardinals, in all his superiority. Greek vanity had expected to impress the

Latins by the more solemn majesty of their rites.[1] They proposed the next day a high Greek function, with the Pope present. The Pope coldly answered, that before they could be permitted in public, the rites must be rehearsed in private, in order that it might be seen whether there was anything presumptuously discordant with the Roman usage. The Greeks declined this humiliating mode of correcting the errors and innovations of the Roman ritual.[a]

Five copies of these Acts were made, and duly signed, that authentic proof of this union might never be wanting to perpetuate its memory to the latest time.

Thus closed the first, the great, Session of the Council of Florence. The Emperor with the Greek Clergy returned to Venice, and, after a long and fatiguing navigation, to Constantinople[x] there to be received, not as the Saviour of the empire from the sword of the Turks, not as the wise and pious reconciler of religious dissension and the peacemaker of the Church, but as a traitor to his own imperial dignity, as a renegade, and an apostate. Already in Venice signs of rebellion had appeared. The Bishop of Heraclea and the Ecclesiast, compelled to officiate in St. Mark's, revenged themselves by chanting the Creed without the obnoxious interpolation, and by refusing to pray for the Pope.[y] During the voyage the Emperor encountered bitter complaints from the Greeks of the tyranny and exultation of the

---

[1] The only superiority which the Latins seemed obliged to own, was the splendour of the Greek dresses of silk. "A la maniera degli abiti Greci, parera assai più grave, e più degna che quella de' Prelati Latini."—Vespasiano, Vit. Eugen. IV. Muratori, xxv. p. 201.

[a] ἡμεῖς ἐθαρροῦμεν διορθῶσαι πολλὰ σφάλματα τῶν Λατινῶν.— Syropulus, p. 299.

[x] He embarked Oct. 19; arrived in Constantinople Feb. 1.

[y] Syropulus, p. 315.

Latin Clergy. In Constantinople it was eagerly inquired whether they had returned victorious. They confessed with humble and bitter self-reproach that they had sold the faith; that they had yielded in base fear to the Franks.[a] Had they been scourged, imprisoned, put to the torture? they could not plead this excuse. It was openly said that, Judas-like, they had received money and sold the Lord. The Archbishop of Heraclea declared that he had been compelled to the base apostasy, and confessed his bitter remorse of conscience; he had rather his right arm had been cut off than that he had subscribed the union. At once the Monks and the women broke out into unrestrained fanaticism against the impious Azymites, who had treated the difference of leavened or unleavened bread as trivial and insignificant. The obsequious Bishop of Cyzicum, promoted to the Patriarchate, could not command the attendance of his own dignitaries without the mandate, without threats of severe punishment from the Emperor.[b] He stood even then, in the midst of his sullen retinue, in Santa Sophia, with hardly a single worshipper.[b] The churches where the clergy officiated who had favoured the union, not merely in the metropolis but in the villages around, were deserted by their flocks.[c] The Despot Demetrius raised the standard of Greek orthodoxy in direct rebellion against his brother. His partisans excited the people everywhere, if to less violent, to as stubborn rebellion. Bold had been the Priest who had dared to interpolate the Creed with the hated clause. Even in Russia, the Cardinal Isidore (the wiser Bessarion re-

---

[a] Ducas, c. xxxi.
[b] Syropulus.
[b] He demanded the reason of this from some of his refractory flock. διοτι ἠκολούθησαι καὶ σὺ τῷ πατριάρχῃ καὶ ἐλατίνισαι.—P. 337.
[c] Phranza, p. 194. Laonicus Chalcondylas. Ducas, c. xxxi.

turned to peace and honour in the West) was met with the same contemptuous, inflexible resistance.

A few short years had entirely obliterated all signs of the union in the East, excepting the more embittered feeling of estrangement and hatred which rankled in the very depths of their hearts towards the Latin Church; and these feelings were only quenched in their blood. For, as they thus indignantly repudiated all connexion with Rome, all subjection to Latin Christianity, the Pope and the Princes of Western Christendom thought no more of their treaty of succour and support against the Turks.

Only fifteen years after the return of the Emperor John Palæologus to the East, Constantinople was a Mohammedan city. S. Sophia, which disdained to be polluted by the "Filioque" in the Creed, resounded, unrebuked, with the Imaum's chant, "There is but one God, and Mohammed is his Prophet."

The sole lasting consequence of the Council of Florence, even in the West, was the fame acquired by Pope Eugenius, which he wanted neither the art nor the industry to propagate in the most magnificent terms. He, of all the successors of St. Peter, had beheld the Byzantine Emperor at his feet, had condescended to dictate terms of union to the Greeks, who had acknowledged the superior orthodoxy, the primacy of Rome. The splendid illusion was kept up by the appearance of ecclesiastical ambassadors—how commissioned, invested with what authority, none know, none now know—from the more remote and barbarous churches of the East, from the uttermost parts of the Christian world. The Iberians, Armenians, the Maronites and Jacobites o. Syria, the Chaldean Nestorians, the Ethiopians, successively rendered the homage of their allegiance to the one Supreme Head of Christendom.

CHAPTER XV.

Continuation of Council of Basle. Pope Felix.

The Council of Basle, frustrated in its endeavours to secure the advantage to itself of the treaty with the Eastern Emperor, looked on the negotiations at Ferrara and Florence with contemptuous disregard. Its hostility might seem embittered by the success of the Pope in securing the recognition of the Emperor and the Greek Clergy. It was some months before the time when Eugenius triumphantly announced his union with the Byzantine Church, that the Council determined to proceed to the deposition of the Pope. They would before long advance to the more fatal and irrevocable step—the election of his successor.

The Council might seem, in its unshaken self-confidence, to despise the decline in its own importance, from the secession of so many of its more distinguished members, still more from the inevitable consequences of having raised vast expectations which it seemed utterly unable to fulfil. It affected an equable superiority to the defection of the great temporal powers, the haughty neutrality of Germany, and the rival synod of France at Bourges. Even the lesser temporal princes, who had hitherto supported the Council, the Spanish Kings, the Duke of Milan, seemed to shrink from the extreme and irrepealable act—the deposition of the Pope. They began to urge more tardy, if not more temperate, counsels. The debates in the Council became stormy and tumultuous; the few great prelates encountered in bitter altercation. The Archbishop of Palermo, the representative of the King of Arragon, urged delay; he was supported by the Archbishop of Milan, and by others of rank and name. He endeavoured to counteract the growing democratic tendencies of the Council, by asserting the sole and exclusive right of the Bishops to suffrage. This preliminary debate was long and obstinate.* At its close, after the speech of the Cardinal of Arles, a violent collision took place. The old Archbishop of Aquileia arose, and rashly said, "You do not know us Germans; if you go on thus, you will hardly come off without broken heads." The Archbishop of Palermo, Louis the Papal Prothonotary, and others, rose, and, with one voice, exclaimed that the liberty of the Council was threatened. He called on the Count of Thierstein, the Emperor's representative, who still had his seat in the Council, for his protection. The Count solemnly declared that the peace should be maintained. He was supported by the magistrates and citizens of Basle, who were proud that their town was the seat of the Council, and declared that it should not be disturbed. Still, as the President went on to read the decree, he was interrupted by shouts and unseemly noises. "A miracle!" exclaimed the Archbishop of Lyons; "the dumb speak, Bishops who never uttered a word before are now become loquacious." The Cardinal Archbishop

---

* See the whole in Æneas Sylvius. Comment. lib. l. Opera, p. 23. The speech of the Cardinal of Arles is of many folio pages. He rashly said that the Archbishop of Milan, though a prelate of the greatest weight and dignity, was no great orator. "As good an orator as you a president," burst in the indignant Lombard. The Cardinal of Arles bore the interruption with patience, and went calmly on (p. 26). He soothed the Bishops with great skill, who were jealous of the suffrages of the inferior clergy. He compared the Council to the Spartans at Thermopylæ.

of Arles, the President, stood quite alone of his Order, almost alone among the Prelates of the highest rank, in his inflexible fidelity to the Council. His dignity, his unalterable temper, his promptitude and eloquence, which excited the most unbounded admiration, his consummate ability, by which, though a Frenchman, he outmanœuvred the subtle Italians, still maintained his sway. His chief supporters, though of inferior rank, were men of fame for learning. He always happily chose his time: on the second meeting, he carried his point against the Archbishop of Palermo and all the Spanish and Milanese Prelates, who withdrew angry but baffled. "Twice," said the Archbishop in Italian, meaning, twice we have been beaten, or twice overreached.

As the session drew on which was to determine the question of deposition, the Bishops—some from timidity, some from dislike of the proceeding—shrunk away. Of the Spanish Prelates there was not one; from Italy one Bishop and one Abbot; of mitred Prelates from the other two kingdoms (England took no part in the Council) only twenty; their place was filled by clergy inferior in rank, but, according to Æneas Sylvius, much superior in learning. The Cardinal of Arles was embarrassed, but not disheartened, by this defection. The reliques of many famous Saints were collected, borne by the Priests of his party through the city, and actually introduced into the hall of council in the place of the absent Bishops.[b] At the solemn appeal to the Saints in bliss, a transport of profound devotion seized the assembly; they all burst into tears. The Baron, Conrad of Winsperg, the Imperial Commissioner,

May 16.
A.D. 1439.

---

[b] "Plurimasque sanctorum reliquias totâ urbe perquiri jussit, ac per sacerdotum manus in sessione portatas, absentium Episcoporum locum tenere." Æneas Sylvius, lib. ii. p. 43.

wept the loudest, and declared that he derived ineffable consolation in the execution of his arduous duty. Though so few Bishops were there, never were the seats so full. Proctors of Bishops, Archdeacons, Provosts, Priors, Presbyters, sat to the number of four hundred or more. Nor did the Council ever proceed with such calm and dignified decency. There was no word of strife or altercation, only mutual exhortation to defend the freedom of the Church.[c]

The edict passed almost by acclamation. This act for the deposition of Eugenius condemned the Pope, who was now boasting the success of his inappreciable labours for the union of the whole Church, as a notorious disturber of the peace and unity of the Church, as guilty of simony and perjury, as an incorrigible schismatic, an obstinate heretic, a dilapidator of the rights and possessions of the Church.[d] All Christians were absolved from their oaths and obligations of fealty, and warned that they must neither render obedience nor counsel nor receive favour from the deprived Gabriel Condolmieri. All his acts, censures, inhibitions, constitutions, were declared void and of none effect. The decree of course abrogated all the boasted acts of the Council of Florence. To the astonishment of the Council itself, the ambassadors of the Emperor and of the King of France, the Bishop of Lubeck and the Archbishop of Tours, made almost an apology for their absence in their master's name, approved the act of the Council

---

[c] "Quae inter nullum unquam probrum, nulla rixa, nulla unquam contentio fuit: sed alter alterum in professione fidei hortabatur, unanimisque omnium esse consensus ad defendendam Ecclesiam videbatur."—Ibid.

[d] The decree is dated May 26.—Labbe. According to the Continuator of Fleury (see Patrici. Act. Concil. Basil.), June 25; the very day on which was announced the union of the Greek and Latin churches.

and declared Pope Eugenius IV. an enemy to the truth.*

It was thought but decent to interpose some delay between the act for the deposition of Eugenius and the election of his successor. It was determined to wait two months. During those two months the plague, which had raged in the Pope's Council at Ferrara, with impartial severity broke out at Basle. The mortality, not in Basle alone, but in many cities of Southern Germany, was terrible.ᶠ In Basle the ordinary cemeteries were insufficient; huge pits were dug to heap in the dead. Many of the Fathers died, protesting in their death, with their last breath, and with the Holy Eucharist on their lips, their fearless adhesion to the Council, and praying for the conversion of those who still acknowledged Gabriel for the Pope.ᵍ The aged Patriarch of Aquileia rejoiced that he should bear into the other world the tidings of the deposition of Eugenius. Æneas Sylvius was among the rare examples of recovery from the fatal malady. But the Fathers stood nobly to their post; they would not risk the breaking up of the Council, even by the temporary abandonment of the city. The Cardinal of Arles set the example; his secretary, his chamberlain, died in his house. The pressing entreaties, prayers, remonstrances of his friends, who urged that on his safety depended the whole influence of the Council, were rejected with tranquil determination. The malediction fulminated against the Council by Eugenius at Florence disturbed not their equanimity. Even at this hour they quailed not. They were de-

---

* Sermon XXXIV. apud Labbe, sub ann. 1439.
ᶠ The Bishop of Lubeck died between Buda and Vienna; the almoner of the King of Arragon in Switzerland; the Bishop of Evreux in Strasburg; a great Abbot in Spires.
ᵍ Æneas Sylvius, lib. B. p. 47.

scribed as a horde of robbers; "at Basle all the devils in the world had assembled to consummate the work of iniquity, and to set up the abomination of desolation in the Church of God." All Cardinals, Prelates, were excommunicated, deposed, menaced with the fate of Korah, Dathan, and Abiram. All their decrees were annulled, the brand of heresy affixed on all their proceedings. Against this furious invective the Fathers at Basle published an apology, not without moderation.

The plague had mitigated its ravages; the two months had fully expired; the Council proceeded to the election of a new Pope. The Cardinal of Arles was alone entitled by his rank to be an Elector; in his name there was unanimous assent. It was proposed that three persons should nominate thirty-two, who with the Cardinal should form the Electoral College. The triumvirate were men whose humble rank is the best testimony to their high estimation. John, called the Greek, the Abbot of an obscure Cistercian convent in Scotland; John of Segovia, Archdeacon of Villa Viciosa, Thomas de Corcelles, Canon of Amiens. Lest the most important Nation, the Germans, should take offence at their exclusion, they were empowered to choose a fourth: they named Christian, Provost of St. Peter's of Brun in the diocese of Olmutz, a German by birth.

These theological triumvirs with their colleague named twelve Bishops, seven Abbots, five distinguished divines, nine Doctors of Canon or Civil Law.[b] They were im-

---

[b] The numbers in Æneas Sylvius are perplexing. The twelve Bishops, including the Cardinal, were to represent the twelve Apostles. But he names many more. The account in the Acts of Patricius varies in many but not very important particulars. According to Voigt, seven Savoyard, two Spanish, one French, the Bishop of Basle with the Cardinal Archbishop of Arles.—L. 172.

partially chosen from all the four Nations, Germany, France, Spain, Italy. England alone, unrepresented in the Council, was of course unrepresented in the Conclave. The Conclave was conducted with the utmost regularity and a studious imitation of the forms observed by the College of Cardinals. The election, after not many days, was without serious strife; it struck Christendom with astonishment. It was not a Prelate whose vigour and character might guarantee and conduct the reformation in the Church, on the expectation of which rested all the confidence of the world in the Council of Basle; not a theologian of consummate learning, not a monk of rigid austerity, it was not even a Churchman of tried and commanding abilities. It was a temporal sovereign, who, weary of his crown, had laid it down, but was not unwilling to plunge again into the more onerous business of a Pope: who had retired not into the desert, but to a kind of villa-convent on the beautiful shores of the Lake of Geneva, and whose life at best decent and calmly devout, if not easy and luxurious, had none of the imposing rigour of the old founders of monastic orders. Amadeus of Savoy was summoned from his retreat at Thonon to ascend the Papal throne.[1]

---

[1] Æneas Sylvius (but we must begin to hear Æneas with more mistrust) attributes the elevation of Amadeus to a deep-laid plot. "Amadeus qui se futurum Papam sperabat" (p. 78). "Sapientiâ præditos dicebatur qui annis jam octo et amplius simulatam religionem accepisset, ut papatum consequi posset." He makes Amadeus too far-sighted. Æneas assigns a curious speech to Cardinal Cæsarini. "I was afraid that they would have chosen a poor and a good man; then there had been indeed danger. It is that which stirs the hearts of men and removes mountains. This man hopes to accumulate the wealth of Pope Martin,"—Martin's wealth had passed into a proverb,—"not to spend his own money." The election, Nov. 5; confirmed, Nov. 17.

Objections were raised that Amadeus of Savoy was not in holy orders; that he had been married and had children. These difficulties were overruled, and yielded easily to the magnificent eulogies passed on the piety, charity, holiness of the hermit of Ripaille. Some of the secret motives for this singular choice are clear enough. The Pope of Basle must be a Pope, at least for a time, without Papal revenues. Italy, all the patrimony of St. Peter which acknowledged the Pope, was in the possession of Eugenius, and showed no inclination to revolt to the Council. If any of the Transalpine sovereigns would recognise the Antipope, none was likely to engage in a crusade to place him on the throne in the Vatican. The only means of supporting his dignity would be the taxation of the Clergy, which his poor partisans could ill bear; the more wealthy and powerful would either refuse, or resent and pass over to the opposite camp. Amadeus, at first at least, might maintain his own court, if not in splendour, in decency. This, however, was a vain hope. The first act of the Council after the election was the imposition of a tax of a fifth penny on all ecclesiastics, for the maintenance of the state of the new Pope. Perhaps the unpopularity of this measure was alleviated by the impossibility of levying it. It was an idle display of unprofitable generosity. If Christendom had been burthened with the maintenance of two Popes it would have wakened up from its indifference, coalesced in favour of one, or discarded both.

A deputation of the most distinguished Churchmen in Basle, the Cardinal of Arles at their head (he was attended by the Count of Thierstein, the Imperial Commissioner), proceeded to the royal hermitage, there to announce to Amadeus his elevation to the Papal See.

Amadeus assumed, if he did not feel, great reluctance. If his retirement and seclusion had not been mere weariness of worldly affairs, and if he was not by this time as weary of his seclusion as he had been of the world, when Amadeus looked down on the shadow of his peaceful retreat, reflected in the blue and unbroken waters of the lake below, he might have serious misgivings in assuming the busy, invidious, and, at least of old, perilous function of an Antipope.[k] He had to plunge into an interminable religious war, with the administration, though without power, of the spiritual affairs of half Christendom, the implacable hatred of the other half. Some difficulties were raised, but not those of a deep or earnest mind. He demurred about the form of the oath, the change of the name, the loss of his hermit's beard. He yielded the two first points, took the oath, and the name of Felix V.;[m] the last only on finding out himself, when he appeared as Pope in the neighbouring town of Thonon, the unseemliness of a thick-bearded Pope among a retinue of shaven ecclesiastics.

Though enthroned in the Church of St. Maurice, some months elapsed before his triumphant progress through Switzerland to his coronation at Basle. He had created five Cardinals, who assisted the Cardinal of Arles in the imposing ceremony first of his consecration as Bishop, afterwards his coronation as Pope; his two sons, the Duke of Savoy and the Count of Geneva, an unusual sight at a Papal inauguration, stood by his side. Fifty thousand spectators beheld the stately cere-

June 24, 1440.

---

[k] It was his avarice which caused the delay, says the unfriendly Æneas. Yet it was natural in him to say, "You have passed a decree suppressing Annates; how is the Pope to be maintained? Am I to expend my patrimony, and so disinherit my sons?"— Fea, p. 78. [m] Acxpta, Dec. 17.

mony: the tiara which he wore was of surpassing cost and splendour, said to be worth 30,000 gold crowns.*

So then for the last time Christendom beheld the strife of Pope and Antipope, each on their respective thrones, hurling spiritual thunders against each other. The indignation of Eugenius knew no bounds. His denunciations contained all and more than all the maledictions which were laid up in the Papal armoury against usurping rivals. The Fathers of Basle repelled them, if with less virulent, with not less provoking contempt.

But Christendom heard these arguments and recriminations with mortifying indifference. That which some centuries ago would have arrayed kingdom against kingdom, and divided each kingdom within itself, the sovereigns against the hierarchy, or the hierarchy in civil feud, now hardly awoke curiosity. No omen so sure of the decline of the sacerdotal power; never again had it vital energy enough for a schism.

The Transalpine kingdoms indeed took different parts but with such languid and inactive zeal, that as to the smaller states it is difficult without close investigation to detect their bias. France had already in her synod at Bourges declared in favour of the Council, but expressed cold and discouraging doubts as to its powers of deposing Pope Eugenius and electing another Pontiff. The King spoke of Felix V. as of Monsieur de Savoye, suggested the summoning another Council in some city of France, but took no measure to enforce his suggestion. England was occupied, as indeed was France, with its own internal contests. The King of Arragon alone took an active part, but on both sides, and for his own ends. The kingdom of Naples was his sole object; he would

---

* Æneas Sylvius, Hist. Concil. Basil. l. ii.

wrest that realm from the feeble pretensions of René of Anjou. At first the devoted ally of Felix, he would transport the Antipope to the shores of Naples, having subdued the kingdom to himself under the Papal investiture, march to Rome with his triumphant forces, and place the Antipope in the chair of St. Peter. Amadeus wisely shrunk from this desperate enterprise. The King of Arragon, in a year or two, had changed his game. The Pope Eugenius scrupled not, at the hazard of estranging France, to abandon the helpless Angevine. Alfonso of Arragon became convinced of the rightful title of Eugenius to the Pontificate.

Germany maintained the most cool and deliberate apathy. At three successive Diets at Mentz,* at Nuremberg, at Frankfort, appeared the envoys of Basle and of Rome, of Felix and of Eugenius, men of the most consummate eloquence. At Mentz John Bishop of Segovia on the part of Basle, Nicolas of Cusa on the part of Rome, pleaded the cause of their respective masters: they cited authorities which of old would have commanded awful reverence, precedents which would have been admitted as irrefragable, but were now heard with languid indifference. At Nuremberg with Nicolas of Cusa stood the Archbishop of Tarento and the famous Dominican Torquemada, on the side of Basle the Patriarch of Aquileia. At Mentz[p] again Nicolas de Cusa took the lead for the Pope, the Archbishop of Palermo for the

Nov. 30, 1440.

A.D. 1441.

---

* Mentz, Feb. 1440. At Mentz the Diet, before the election of the Emperor Frederick III., in the disdainful assertion of their neutrality, published a declaration in which they sedulously avoided the word Pope. They spoke of Ecclesia Dei, Ecclesia Romana, Sedes Apostolica, as the "cui facienda est adhæsio."—Dax, Nicolas von Cusa, p. 223.

[p] Dax has given Nicolas de Cusa's speech at length. His speech and that of the Archbishop of Palermo are in Wurdtwein.

Council. The Diet on each occasion relapsed into its ostentatious neutrality, which it maintained at subsequent meetings.[q] Even the aggressive measure ventured at length by Eugenius, the degradation of the Archbishops of Cologne and Trèves, as adherents of the heretical Council, and the usurping pseudo-pope, might have passed away as an ineffectual menace; no one would have thought of dispossessing these powerful Prelates. If he might hope to raise a strife in Germany by appointing Prelates of noble or rich German houses, there was danger lest the nation might resent this interference with the German Electorate; it might lead to the renunciation of his authority. He must look for other support. To Cologne he named the nephew, to Trèves the natural son, of the Duke of Burgundy.

A.D. 1443.

The Schism seemed as if it would be left to die out of itself, or, if endowed with inextinguishable, obstinate vitality, be kept up in unregarded insignificance. Some of the Fathers of Basle still remained in the city, but had ceased their sessions.[r] The Council of Florence was prorogued to Rome. Eugenius was in undisturbed possession of Italy; Felix in his court at Lausanne, or Geneva. The Popes might still hate, they could not injure, hardly molest each other; they might wage a war of decrees, but no more.

---

[q] The speech of Nicolas of Cusa shows the course of argument adopted to annul the pretensions and blast the character of Felix. The whole is represented as an old and deep-laid conspiracy on his part. The Council, the Conclave had been crowded with his obsequious vassals (the four Italian Bishops were, it is true, those of Vercelli, Turin, Aosta, and another); his reluctance to assume the tiara was hypocritical effrontery; even his former abdication of his throne a base simulation of humility. The proceedings of these Diets may be read at some length in Voigt, Pius II. L pp. 157-166.

[r] Last session. The 44th. May, 1439.

One man alone by his consummate address and subtlety, by his indefatigable but undiscerned influence, restored the Papacy to Italy, never but for one short reign (that of Adrian VI. of Utrecht) to depart from it, himself in due time to receive the reward of his success in nothing less than the Popedom. Eugenius and his successor Pope Nicolas V. enjoyed the fame and the immediate advantage of the discomfiture of the Council of Basle, of its inglorious dissolution. But the real author of that dissolution, of its gradual degradation in the estimation of Europe, of the alienation of the Emperor from its cause; he who quietly drove Pope Felix to his abdication, and even added firmness and resolution to the obstinate and violent opposition of Pope Eugenius, was Æneas Sylvius Piccolomini.

CHAPTER XVI.

Æneas Sylvius Piccolomini. Dissolution of Council of Basle.

THE life of Æneas Sylvius is the history of the dissolution of the Council of Basle; and not only so, but as an autobiography of an Italian, a Churchman, a Cardinal, at length a Pope, the most valuable part of the Christian history of his times—that of the opinions, manners, judgements, feelings of mankind. Contrast it with the rise of high ecclesiastics in former times!

The house of Piccolomini had been among the noblest of Sienna, lords of fortresses and castles. On the rise of the popular government in that city, the Piccolominis sank with the rest of the nobles. Yet the grandfather of Æneas possessed an ample estate. He died early, leaving his wife pregnant. The estate was dissipated by negligent or improvident guardians; the father of Æneas married a noble virgin, but without dowry, except the burthensome one — extraordinary fertility. She frequently bore twins, and in the end had twenty-two children. Ten only grew up, and Piccolomini retired to the quiet town of Corsignano, to bring up in humble condition his large family. The plague swept off all but Æneas Sylvius and two sisters.

Æneas Sylvius was born October 18, 1405. His third baptismal name was Bartholomew, that of the Apostle of India. His infancy was not uneventful: at three years old he fell from a wall, was taken up, as supposed, with a mortal wound in his head; at eight was tossed by a bull. At the age of twenty-two he left his father's house, heir to no more than his noble name, went to Sienna, was maintained by his relations, and studied law and letters. The war between Florence and Sienna drove him from his native city to seek his fortunes. Dominico Capranica, named as Cardinal by Pope Martin V., rejected by Pope Eugenius, espoused the cause of the Council of Basle. He engaged the young Piccolomini as his secretary. After a perilous voyage Æneas reached Genoa, travelled to Milan, where he saw the great Duke Philippo Maria, and passed the snowy St. Gothard to Basle. Capranica, though he resumed his Cardinalate on the authority of the Council, was too poor to keep a secretary. Æneas found employment in the same office, first with Nicodemo Scaligero, Bishop of Freisingen, son of the Lord of Verona; him he accompanied to Frankfort: afterwards with Bartolomeo Visconti, Bishop of Novara. With the Bishop of Novara he returned to Italy; by his own account, through his eloquence he obtained the Rectorship of the University of Pavia for a Novarese of humble birth, against a Milanese of noble family and powerful connexions. With the Bishop of Novara he went to Florence, to the Court of Pope Eugenius: he visited the famous Piccinino, and his own kindred at Sienna. On his return to Florence he found his master, the Bishop of Novara, under a charge of capital treason.[a] This Bishop and his secretary Piccolomini found refuge under the protection of the Cardinal of Santa Croce (Albergata). The Cardinal

---

[a] Voigt, Leben Æneas Sylvio, p. 80 (Berlin, 1856), has attempted to unravel a deep plot against Eugenius IV. It is questionable whether the Bishop of Novara was not treacherous both to the Pope and to the Visconti, in whose favour he was reinstated.

was sent as Legate to France, to reconcile the Kings of
France and England, Charles VII. and Henry VI. In
attendance on the Cardinal Æneas passed a third time
through Milan, crossed the St. Bernard, and descended
on the Lake of Geneva. At Thonon he saw Amadeus
of Savoy, afterwards the Pope Felix V. of the Council
of Basle, in his hermitage, living, as he says, a life of
pleasure rather than of penance.[b] They proceeded to
Basle, not yet at open war with Pope Eugenius, dropped
down the Rhine to Cologne, took horse to Aix-la-Chapelle, Liège, Louvain, Douay, Tournay, to Arras. The
Cardinal of Santa Croce began his difficult function of
mediating between the French, the English, and the
Burgundians.

Æneas was despatched on a special mission to Scotland, to restore a certain prelate to the favour of the
King. He went to Calais. The suspicious English
would not permit him to proceed or to go back. Fortunately the Cardinal of Winchester arrived from Arras,
and obtained for him permission to embark. But the
English looked with jealousy on the secretary of the Cardinal of Santa Croce, whom they accused of conspiring
to alienate Philip of Burgundy from their cause. He
was refused letters of safe-conduct; he must be employed
in some hostile intrigue with the Scots. During this
delay Æneas visited the wonders of populous and most
wealthy London. He saw the noble church of St. Paul's,
the sumptuous tombs of the kings at Westminster, the
Thames, with the rapid ebb and flow of its tide, and
the bridge like a city.[c] But of all things, the shrine of
St. Thomas at Canterbury most excited his amazement,

---

[b] "Magis voluptuosam quam pœnitentialem."
[c] He saw also a village, where men were said to be born with tails.

covered with diamonds, fine double pearls,⁴ and carbuncles. No one offered less than silver at this shrine. He crossed to Flanders, went to Bruges, took ship at Ecluse, the most frequented port in the West, was blown towards the coast of Norway, encountered two terrible storms, one of fourteen hours, one of two nights and a day. The sailors were driven so far north that they did not know the stars. The twelfth day a lucky north wind brought them to Scotland. In a fit of devout gratitude Æneas walked barefoot ten miles to Our Lady at Whitchurch, but suffered so much from exhaustion and numbed feet that he hardly got to the court. He was received by the King with great favour, obtained the object of his mission, his expenses were paid, and he was presented with fifty nobles and two horses for his journey.

The Italian describes Scotland as a cold country, producing little corn, almost without wood. "They dig out of the earth a kind of sulphurous stone, which they burn." Their cities have no walls, their houses are mostly built without mortar, the roofs of turf, the doors of the cottages bulls' hides. The common people are poor and rude, with plenty of flesh and fish; bread is a delicacy. The men are small and bold; the women of white complexion, disposed to sexual indulgence.⁶ They had only imported wine.⁷ They export to Flanders hides, wool, salt-fish and pearls.⁸ The Scots were delighted by nothing so much as abuse of the English. Scotland was

---

⁴ Unionibus.

⁵ And in his cup an union shall be throw
Richer than that which four successive
kings
On Denmark's throne have worn."
Hamlet, v. 2.
—See Nares' Glossary.

⁶ Æneas adds that kissing women in Scotland meant no more than shaking hands in Italy. Like Erasmus later in England, he drew Italian conclusions from Northern manners.

⁷ Their horses were small hackneys, mostly geldings. They neither curried nor combed them. They had no bridles!

⁸ Margaritas.

divided into two parts: one cultivated (the lowlands); one forest (the highlands) without corn-fields. The forest Scots spoke a different language, and lived on the barks of trees.[b] During the winter solstice, the time when Æneas was there, the days were only four hours long.

Æneas had suffered enough in his sea voyages; he determined to run all hazards, and find his way through England. He was fortunate in his resolution: the ship in which he was about to embark foundered at the mouth of the haven. The captain, who was returning to Flanders to be married, with all the passengers and crew, were drowned in sight of shore. Æneas set off disguised as a merchant. He passed the Tweed in a boat, entered a large town about sunset, found lodging in a cottage where he was housed and supped with the parish priest. He had plenty of broth, geese and fowls; neither wine nor bread. All the women of the town crowded to see him, as to see a negro or an Indian in Italy. They asked who he was, whether he was a Christian. Æneas had been warned of the scanty fare which he would find on his journey, and had provided himself in a certain monastery (there no doubt alone such luxuries could be found) with some loaves of bread and a measure of red wine. This heightened the wonder of the barbarians, who had never seen wine nor white bread. Some women with child began to handle the bread and smell the wine. Æneas was too courteous not to gratify their longings, and gave them the whole. The supper lasted till the second hour of the night, when the priest, his host, and his children, and all the men,

---

[b] He says also that there were no woods in Scotland. Rooks (*cornices*) were newly introduced, and therefore the trees whereon they built belonged to the King's Exchequer!

took leave of Æneas, and said that they must retire to a certain tower a long way off for fear of the Scots, who, on the ebb of the tide, were wont to cross over and plunder. No entreaties could induce them to take Æneas with them, nor any of their women, though many of them were young girls and handsome matrons. The enemy would do them no harm: the borderers' notions of harm were somewhat peculiar.[1] The Italian remained with his two servants, a single guide, and a hundred women, who sat round the fire all night spinning hemp and talking with his interpreter. After great part of the night was passed, there was a violent barking of dogs and cackling of geese. The women ran away, the guide with them, and there was as great confusion as if the enemy were there. Æneas thought it most prudent to stay in his chamber (it was a stable), lest, being quite ignorant of the ways, he might run into the arms of the mosstroopers. Presently the women and the guide returned: it was a false alarm.

Æneas set out the next morning. When he arrived at Newcastle (said to be a work of the Cæsars) he seemed to have returned to the habitable world, so rugged, wild and bleak, was the whole Border. At Durham he visited the tomb of the venerable Bede. At York, a large and populous city, there was a church famous throughout the world for its size and architecture, with a most splendid shrine, and with glass walls (the rich and large windows) between very slender clustered pillars. (Had Æneas seen none of the German or Flemish Gothic cathe-

---

[1] "Qui stuprum inter mala non ducunt." It must be remembered that Æneas picked up all he learned through an interpreter, probably a man who knew a few words of bad Latin. I owe perhaps an apology for inserting this scene, so irresistibly characteristic, if not quite in its place. Walter Scott, if I remember, had seen it in his multifarious reading.

drals?) On his way southward he fell in with one of the judges of the realm, returning to his court in London. The judge began to talk of the business in Arras, and, not suspecting who Æneas was, to abuse the Cardinal of Santa Croce as a wolf in sheep's clothing. In the company of the judge, who, had he known who he was, would have committed him to prison, he arrived safe in London. There he found a royal proclamation that no foreigner should leave the realm without a passport, which he cared not to ask for. He got away by bribing the officers; a matter of course, as such personages never refuse hard money. He crossed from Dover to Calais, thence to Basle and to Milan. Finding that the Cardinal of Santa Croce had been sent back from Florence, and had passed by the Valley of the Adige, and over the Arlberg to Basle, he returned over the Alps by Brig, and joined his master at Basle.

Æneas was an Italian in his passions, and certainly under no austere, monkish self-control. His morals were those of his age and country. His letters are full of amatory matters, in the earlier of which, as he by no means counsels his friends to severe restraint, he does not profess to set them an example. Licentiousness seems to be a thing of course. He was not yet in holy orders: to do him justice, as yet he shrank from that decided step, lest it should involve him in some difficulties.[k] His confessions are plain enough; he makes no boast of constancy.[m] But the most unblushing avowal of his loose notions appears in a letter to his own father, whom he requests to take charge of a natural son. The

---

[k] "Cavi ne me maser ordo involveret."—Epist. l.

[m] "Ego plures vidi amavique fœminas, quarum exinde potitus, magnum tædium suscepi."—Epist. xlvi. Compare the coarse pleasantry, Epist. lxii. He was averse to German women; he could not speak German.

mother of his son was an Englishwoman whom he met at Strasburg, of no great beauty, but who spoke Italian with great ease and sweetness. "It was the beauty of her eloquence by which Cleopatra enthralled not Mark Antony only, but Julius Cæsar." He anticipates his father's objection to the sinfulness of his conduct, in being a parent without being a husband. He had done only what every one else did. God had made him prone to desire: he did not pretend to be holier than David, or wiser than Solomon. He borrows the language of Terence—"Shall I, weak man that I am, not do that which so many great men have done?" But his examples are not the gods of the heathen lover in the comedy, but Moses, Aristotle, and some good Christians.[a] Let us hastily despatch this, if not the least curious, not the most edifying passage in the life of the future Pope. Later in life he was seized with a paroxysm of virtue, and wrote some letters on such subjects in a more grave and ecclesiastical tone. In an epistle written at the approach of Lent, he urges his friend to flee all womankind, as a fatal pestilence. When you look on a woman you look on the devil. He had himself erred often, too often; and he acknowledges that he had become more correct, not from severe virtue, but from the advance, it must have been, of premature age. He consoled himself, however, for one vice which he could not indulge, by another. The votary of Venus (his own words) had become the votary of Bacchus. To his new

---

[a] "Meccmque quis reprehendit, inquam, si ego humuncio faciam, quod maximi viri non sunt aspernati. Interdum Moysen, interdum Aristotelem, nonnunquam Christianos in exemplum sumebam."—Epist. xv. The publication, or at least the admission of this letter into a collection published after the Popedom of Æneas, is singular enough. But even this letter is modesty compared to Epist. xxiii.

god he will be faithful to death. Æneas must then have been between thirty-five and forty years old.*

He was forty when he wrote his celebrated Romance, 'Euryalus and Lucretia,' a romance with neither incident nor invention;ᵖ in its moral tone and in the warmth of its descriptions, as in its prolixity, a novel of Boccaccio, but without his inimitable grace; yet Æneas no doubt thought that he infinitely surpassed Boccaccio's vulgar Italian by his refined and classical Latinity. In the penitential Letter on this subject, in later life (after he was Pope!) the lingering vanity of the author still struggles with his sense of decency.ᵠ

So, then, the Siennese adventurer had visited almost every realm of Northern Europe, France, Germany, Flanders, Scotland, England; he is in the confidence of Cardinals, he is in correspondence with many of the most learned and influential men in Christendom.

No sooner was Æneas fixed at Basle, than his singular aptitude for business, no doubt his fluent and perspicuous Latin, his flexibility of opinion, his rapidly growing knowledge of mankind, his determination to push his fortunes, his fidelity to the master in whose service

---

* "Tum quoque et illud verum est languescere vires meas, canis aspersus sum, aridi nervi sunt, ossa cariosa, rogis corpus aratum est. Nec ulli ego fæminæ possum esse voluptati, nec voluptatem mihi afferre fæmina potest. Baccho magis quam Veneri pareto: vinum me alit, me juvat, me oblectat, me beat; hic liquor snavis mihi erit usque ad mortem. Namque ut fateor, magis me Venus fugitat, quam ego illam horreo." The letter (Epist. xcii.) is written to John Freund, Prothonotary of Cologne, not long after the diet of Nuremberg, A.D. 1442.

ᵖ The disgraceful history is probably a true one.

ᵠ Epist. ccxiv. There were two things in the book, a too lascivious love story and an edifying moral. Unhappily many readers dwelt on the first; hardly any, alas! attended to the latter. "Ita Impuratum est atque obfuscatum infelix mortalium genus." He adds, "Nec privatum hominem pluris facit quam Pontificem; Æneam rejicit, Pium suscipite."

he happened to be, opened the way to advancement; offices, honours, rewards crowded upon him. He was secretary,[r] first reporter of the proceedings, then held the office as writer of the epistles of the Council.[s] He was among the twelve Presidents chosen by the Council. The office of these duodecimvirs was to prepare all business for the deliberation of the Council; nothing could be brought forward without their previous sanction, nor any one admitted to the Council till they had examined and approved his title. He often presided over his department, which was that of faith. The leaden seal of the Council was often in his custody. During his career he was ambassador from the Council three times to Strasburg, twice to Constance, twice to Frankfort, once to Trent, later to the Emperor Albert, and to persuade Frederick III. to espouse the cause of the Council.

His eloquence made him a power. His first appearance with a voice in the Council seems to have been in the memorable debate on the prorogation of the Council to Italy. We have heard that, while the Pope insisted on the removal of the Council to Florence or Udine, the Council would remove only to Avignon. The Duke of Milan, by his ambassadors, urged the intermediate measure, the adjournment to the city of Pavia. But his ambassador, Isidore Bishop of Rossano, was but an indifferent orator. He talked so foolishly that they were obliged to silence him. Æneas had been twice or three times at Milan; he was not averse to make friends at that powerful Court; nor was he disinclined by taking a middle course to wait the issue of events. He obtained permission of the President, the Cardinal Julian Cæsarini, and urged in a speech of two hours, which excited the

---

[r] "Scriba."   [s] "Abbreviator major."

greatest admiration, the claims of Pavia against Florence, Udine, and Avignon. His zeal was not unrewarded. The Archbishop presented him to the Provostship of St. Laurence in Milan. His rival Isidore remonstrated against the appointment of a stranger. He protested before the Council; the Council was unanimous in favour of Æneas. He went to Milan, but found that the Chapter had already elected a Provost of the noble house of Landriano, whom he found in actual possession. But the Duke, the Archbishop, and the Court were all-powerful; the intruder was expelled. At Milan Æneas was seized with a fever, which lasted seventy-five days, and was subdued with great difficulty.[1] On his return to Basle, he recovered his health so far as to be able to preach the commemoration sermon on the day of St. Ambrose, Bishop of Milan. This sermon by one not in orders was opposed by the theologians, but met with great success.

The war had now broken out between the Pope and the Council; there was no middle ground; every one must choose his side. None, so long as he was in the service of the Council, and the Council in the ascendant, so bold, so loyal a partisan, or with such lofty conceptions of the superiority of the Council over the Pope, as Æneas Piccolomini. As historian of the Council, he asserts its plenary authority. The reasons which he assigns for undertaking this work are characteristic. He had begun to repent that he had wasted so much time in the idle and unrewarded pursuits of poetry, oratory, history. Was he still to live improvident as the birds of the air or the beasts of the field?

---

[1] He relates that a certain drug was administered, which appeared to fail in its operation. He was about to take a second dose, when the first began to work: "ut nonaginta vicibus assurgere cogeretur."

Was he never to be in possession of money, the owner of an estate? The true rule of life is, that a man at twenty should strive to be great, at thirty prudent, at forty rich. But, alas! the bias was too strong: he must write history.

Throughout that history he is undisguisedly, inflexibly, hostile to Eugenius IV.[a] He sums up with great force and clearness, irrefragably, as he asserts, to his own mind, irrefragably it should be to the reason of men, the whole argument for the supremacy of the Council over the Pope. Words are wanting to express his admiration of the President of the Council, the Cardinal Archbishop of Arles: his opponents are secret or timid traitors to the highest Church principles. Eugenius IV. sinks to plain Gabriel Condolmieri.[a] Æneas does not disguise his contempt. He reproaches the Pope with perfidy, as seeking either to dissolve the Council or to deprive it of its liberty. He is severe against the perjury of those who had deserted the Council to join the Pope. Nicolas of Cusa, the *Hercules* of the apostasy, is guilty of schism. So he continues to the end: still he is the ardent panegyrist of the Cardinal of Arles, after the declaration of the heresy of Pope Eugenius, after the deposition of that Pope, even after the election of Pope Felix.

On the death of the Emperor Sigismund, Albert of Austria, elected King of the Romans, hesitated to accept the dignity. The Hungarians insisted that he had been raised to the throne of Hungary on the express condition that he should not be promoted to the Empire. Barto-

---

[a] The reader must not confound two distinct histories; one, that published in Brown, Fasciculus, and in his Works; the other by Fea, in Rome, as late as the year 1822. I cite this as "Fea."

[a] "Quocirca mentita est iniquitas Gabrieli, et perdidit eum Dominus in malitiâ suâ."—Lib. II. sub init.

lomeo, Bishop of Novara, the ambassador of Philip Duke of Milan to Vienna, persuaded Æneas, either as empowered, or thought to be empowered, by the Council, to accompany him on this important mission. An address, drawn by Æneas, not only induced Albert to accept the Imperial Crown, but won over the Hungarians, more than to consent, even to urge their King to this step. The grateful thanks of the Diet were awarded to Æneas. But Æneas took great dislike to Vienna, where he was afterwards to pass so many years: he returned to Basle. A.D. 1438.

He returned at a fearful time. During the sixty days, it has been said, between the deposition of Eugenius IV. and the election of his successor, the plague raged at Basle. Some of the dearest friends of Æneas fell around him. He was himself among the few who had the malady and recovered. He might well ascribe his cure to Divine goodness. Æneas preferred piety to science. There were two famous physicians, one a Parisian of admirable skill without religion, the other a German, ignorant but pious. The nature of a certain powder administered to Æneas (the rest of the mode of cure is fully detailed [7]) the pious doctor kept a profound secret. The patient was in a high fever, delirious, and so far gone as to receive extreme unction. A rumour of his death reached Milan; his Provostship was given away; on his recovery he found great difficulty in resuming it. He wrote to his patron the Duke, urging that the fact of his writing was tolerably conclusive proof that he was alive.

Æneas was not without his place of honour in the

---

[7] The bubo was in the left groin, the vein of the left foot therefore was opened. He was not allowed to sleep. He took the powder; cataplasms alternately of green radish and of moist chalk were applied to the sore.

great affair of the election of the new Pope. He might indeed have been an Elector. There were but few Italians in the Conclave. The consent of more was earnestly desired. Æneas was urged to accumulate the minor orders, with the subdiaconate and diaconate, which might qualify him for the suffrage. He was still unwilling to fetter himself with the awful sanctity of Holy Orders. He was first employed in the difficult negotiations as to the appointment of the Electors. He was afterwards one of the two Masters of the Ceremonies. He now describes himself as Canon of Trent. This canonry had been granted to him by the grateful Council, and was held with his Provostship of St. Laurence in Milan. On the ceremonial of the Conclave he is full and minute, as one who took no small pride in the arrangements. To his office was attached the duty of standing at the window to receive from the Vice-Chamberlain the food for the use of the Conclave, and to take care that no letters or other unlawful communications were introduced. No doubt his particular account of the kinds of food, in which the Electors indulged, is faithful and trustworthy. He takes care to inform us of the comical anger of the Archdeacon of Cracow, who was allowed to have his dishes of mutton or lamb, but complained bitterly that he might not have his poultry or game, or perhaps small birds.[1]

Æneas hailed the election of Amadeus of Savoy with the utmost satisfaction; he had forgotten the Epicurean life of the hermit which he had witnessed at Ripaille. The intrigues and the parsimony of Amadeus darkened on his knowledge at a later period. The splendid eulogy, which he makes a nameless Elector pronounce,

---

[1] "Aviculas."

might seem to come from the heart of Æneas, as far as his eloquence ever did proceed from the heart. Pope Eugenius is still the odious and contemptible Gabriel. In a letter to his friend John of Segovia, he describes in rapturous terms the coronation of Felix V., the gravity, majesty, ecclesiastical propriety of his demeanour: "the demeanour of him who had been called of God to the rule of his Universal Church."[a] Fifty thousand spectators rejoiced, some wept for joy. The vain Æneas will not be silent as to his own part in this splendid ceremonial, though it bordered on the ludicrous. The Cardinal of Santa Susanna chanted the service; the responses were given by the advocates and notaries[b] in such a dissonant bray, that the congregation burst into roars of laughter. They were heartily ashamed of themselves. But the next day when the preachers were to make the responses, Æneas, though quite ignorant of music (which requires long study), sang out his part with unblushing courage.[c] Æneas does not forget the tiara worth 30,000 pieces of gold, the processions, the supper or dinner to 1000 guests. He is as full and minute as a herald, manifestly triumphing in the ceremonial as equalling the magnificence, as well as imitating to the smallest point that of Rome.

The Antipope was not ungrateful to his partisan, whose eloquent adulation published his fame and his virtues to still doubtful and vacillating Christendom. Æneas became the Secretary of Pope Felix, he was not only his attendant in public, he became necessary to him, and followed him to Ripaille, Thonon, Geneva, Lausanne.

---

[a] Epist. ad Joann. Segoviens. Opera, 61, 3. [b] "Advocati et scriniarii."
[c] "Cantitare meum carmen non erubui."

Frederick III. had now succeeded to the Imperial throne. On his adhesion or rejection depended almost entirely the fate of the rival Popes. Who so able, who (might Felix suppose) so true and loyal, who with such consummate address to conduct his cause before the King of the Romans, who so deeply pledged to the justice and holiness of that cause, as his faithful Secretary? Æneas is despatched by Pope Felix to the Imperial Court at Frankfort.

A.D. 1440.

At the Court of Frederick the eloquent and dexterous Italian made a strong impression on the counsellors of the young Emperor, Silvester Bishop of Chiemsee, and James Archbishop and Elector of Treves. Frederick was urged to secure the services of a man so experienced in affairs, so gifted, so accomplished. Nothing could be more skilful than the manner in which the Emperor was recommended to secure his attachment. Of all his accomplishments, Æneas was most vain of his poetry. The Emperor appointed him his Laureate;[d] to his letters Æneas for some time prefixed the proud title of Poet. He says, that he did this to teach the dull Viennese, who thought poetry something mischievous and abominable, to treat it with respect.[e]

Æneas were tary to Frederick III.

Yet he made some decent resistance; he must return to Basle and obtain his free discharge from Felix. He wrung with difficulty, and only by the intervention of his friends, the reluctant assent of the Antipope. On the arrival of the Emperor at Basle, he was named Imperial Secretary, and took the oaths of fidelity to Frederick III.; he accompanied his new Lord to Vienna. Æneas saw the turning-point of his

Nov. 1442.

---

[d] The diploma of poet, dated July 27, 1442.   [e] Epist. c.

fortunes, and never was man so deliberately determined to push forward those fortunes. "You know," he writes to a friend not long after his advancement, "that I serve a Prince who is of neither party, and who by holding a middle course seeks to enforce unity. The Servant must have no will but that of his Master."[1] Æneas hopes to obtain a place for his friend at Vienna. "How this may be I know not. In the mean time I shall insinuate myself into the King's graces: his will shall be mine, I will oppose him in nothing. I am a stranger. I shall act the part of Gnatho: what they affirm, I affirm; what they deny, I deny.[2] Let those that are wise have their fame, let those that are fools bear their own disgrace; I shall not trouble myself about their honour or their discredit. I shall write, as Secretary, what I am ordered, and no more. I shall hold my tongue and obey: if I should do otherwise, it would not be for my interest, and my interest, you will allow, should be my first object." It will soon appear how much stronger was the will of the subtle Italian than that of the feeble and irresolute Emperor.

Æneas was for a time not unfaithful to the Council. Already indeed, before he left Basle, he had made the somewhat tardy discovery that their affairs were not altogether governed by the Holy Ghost, but by human passions. He began to think neither party absolutely in the right. He was gently, but rapidly veering to the middle course, then held by his master the Emperor.

---

[1] There is something curious in his observation about the Archbishop of Palermo, who was labouring hard at Frankfort about his writings. "Stultus est qui putat libellis et codicibus movere reges." Æneas is learning to know more of kings.

[2] "Ego peregrinus sum: consultum mihi est Gnathonis offensum (officium?) suscipere, aiunt aio, negant nego." Epist. xlv. p. 531.

Yet he treated the arguments of John Carovia, orator of Pope Eugenius, with sufficient disdain. "You say that the Pope has made more ample concessions to the Princes of Germany, and has humbled himself more than was ever heard of Roman Pontiff. This stuff may pass with peasants and those who are utterly ignorant of history." God alone, Æneas still asserts, is superior to a General Council. "You and your party desire unity; that is, on your own terms; if your Pope remain Supreme Pontiff." He more than hints the abdication of Eugenius. "He deserves greater praise not who clings to his dignity, but who is ready to lay it down. Of old holy men were with greater difficulty prevailed on to be elevated to the Popedom than they are now removed from it. A good disposition and a gentle spirit would not seek in what manner—but how speedily, he might resign."[b] "In truth," he adds, "the quarrel is not for the sheep but for the wool; there would be less strife were the Church poor."

Æneas at first, notwithstanding his prudential determinations, was an object of much jealousy at the Court of the Emperor. William Taz, a Bavarian, was acting as Imperial Chancellor, in the absence of Gaspar Schlick, who had filled that high office under three Emperors, Sigismund, Albert, and Frederick. The Bavarian hated Italians; he thwarted Æneas in every way. The Secretary bore all in patience.[i] Better times came with the return of Gaspar Schlick to the Court. At Sienna Gaspar had received some civilities, and made friendship with certain kinsmen of the Piccolomini. The enemy of Æneas, William Taz, who had trampled on

---

[b] Epist. xxv.
[i] "Auriculas declinavi, ut iniquæ mentis asellus;" so Æneas writes of himself.

the Secretary, began humbly to truckle to him. Tnz, however, soon left the Court. His other adversaries, as he rose in favour with the Emperor, became his humble servants. He was one of the four distinguished persons appointed to hear at Nuremberg the debate before the Diet.

Æneas, his young blood no longer remonstrating against his committing himself to Holy Orders, now entered into the priesthood. His orders of subdeacon, deacon, priest, followed rapidly on each other. He had ceased to dread the sacred office. He no longer desired to indulge the levity of a layman; his whole delight was henceforth to be in his holy calling.[k] He was not long without reward for this decided step. His first benefice, obtained through the Emperor's interest, was a singular one for an Italian born in sunny Sienna, and whose life had been passed in journeys, councils, and courts. It was the parochial cure of a retired valley in the Tyrol. It was worth sixty gold pieces a year. It was accessible only up one wild glen, covered with snow and ice three parts of the year. The peasants during the long winter were confined to their cottages, made boxes and other carpenter's work (like the Swiss of Meyringen and elsewhere), which they sold at Trent and Botzen. They passed much time in playing at chess and dice, in which they were wonderfully skilful. They were a simple people, knew nothing of war or glory or gold. Cattle was their only wealth,

Æneas to Holy Orders.

---

[k] "Jam ego subdiaconus sum, quod olim valde horrebam. Sed recessit a me illa animi levitas, quæ inter laicos crescere solebat. Jamque nihil magis amo quam sacerdotium." Epist. xciii. This letter is in unfortunate juxtaposition with the one (Epist. xcii.) in which he gives so much good advice to his friend, makes such full confession of his own former frailties, with the resolution to abandon Venus for Bacchus. See above.

which they fed with hay in the winter. Some of them had never tasted any liquor but milk. Some lived a great way from the church: if they died their bodies were laid out and became frozen. In the spring the curate went round, collected them into one procession, and buried them altogether in the churchyard. There was not much sorrow at their funerals. Æneas does not flatter the morality of his parishioners (he did not do much to correct it). They would have been the happiest of mankind had they known their blessings and imposed restraint on their lusts. As it was, huddled together night and day in their cottages, they lived in promiscuous concubinage; a virgin bride was unknown. Æneas had some difficulty (every one seems to have had difficulty where the rights of patrons were in perpetual conflict, and the Pope and the Council claimed everything) in obtaining possession of his benefice. Small as was its income, with his canonry it furnished a modest competency, two hundred ducats a year, with which he was fully content. He was anxious to retire from the turbulent world; to secure, as he had passed the meridian of life, a peaceful retreat where he might serve God.[m] We read in the next sentence in his Commentaries that he had given up his happy valley for a better benefice in Bavaria, that of Santa Maria of Auspac, not far from the Inn, which was given him by the Bishop of Passau.

As yet we do not see (when shall we see?) much indulgence of this unworldly disposition: in this respect it is impossible to deny the rigid self-denial of Æneas. In a letter to Gaspar Schlick, the Chancellor, the Italian

---

[m] "Vellem aliquando me sequestrare ab hujus mundi turbinibus, Deoque servire et mihi vivere." Epist. liv. It was the Sarontana vallis?

opens his whole mind. He does not attempt to conceal his own falsehood; he justifies it as of necessity. "Where all are false we must be false too; we must take men as they are." He adduces as authority for this insincerity (I hardly venture to record this) what he dares to call a departure from truth in Him that was all truth.[a] This letter embraces the whole comprehensive and complicated range of Imperial politics, Austria, Bohemia, Hungary. In the great question Æneas has become a stern neutralist. The plan proposed by Charles of France, at the close of 1443, to compel the Council and the Pope to union, now appears the wisest as well as the most feasible measure. "Let the temporal Sovereigns hold their Congress, even against the will of the Clergy, union will ensue. He will be the undoubted Pope, to whom all the Sovereigns render obedience. I see none of the Clergy who will suffer martyrdom in either cause. We have all the same faith with our rulers; if they worshipped idols we should likewise worship them. If the secular power should urge it, we should deny not only the Pope but Christ himself. Charity is cold, faith is dead: we all long for peace: whether through another Council or a Congress of Princes I care not."[b]

In the Diet of Nuremberg nothing was done in the momentous affair. Germany and Frederick III. maintained their cold neutrality. Æneas had sunk to absolute indifference. Another letter to the Pope's Orator Carvajal is in a lighter tone: "You and I may discuss such matters, not as angry theologians, but as calm philosophers. I am content to leave such

---

[a] "Sed fingendum est, postquam omnes fingunt. Nam et Jesus finxit se longius ire. Ut homines sunt Ita utamur." Æneas should have stuck to his Terence.—liv. p. 539.

[b] Epist. liv.

things to divines, and to think as other people think." He does not speak with much respect of the Diet.

<small>Oct. 1444.</small> "What has it done?—it has summoned another. You know my saying: 'No Diet is barren: this will be as prolific as the rest: it has another in its womb.'"[p]

But the tide now turned. Alfonso II., King of Arragon, his most obstinate and dangerous enemy, made peace with Eugenius. Philippo Maria, Duke of Milan, made peace with Eugenius. All Italy acknowledged Eugenius. The Italian Æneas had no notion of condemning himself to perpetual, if honourable, exile in cold, rude Germany. The churchman would not sever Christendom from Rome, or allow an Ultramontane Papacy to proclaim its independence, if not its superiority. Yet beyond the Alps to less keen eyes never might the cause of Eugenius appear more desperate. The Council, in its proclamations at least, maintained its inflexible resolution. Writings were promulgated throughout Germany, among others a strong manifesto from the University of Erfurt, calling on the German nation to throw off its inglorious neutrality, and at once to espouse the cause of religious freedom and the Council of Basle. The violent act of Eugenius <small>A.D. 1446. Bull of actual deposition. Feb. 9, 1446.</small> in threatening to depose the Archbishops of Cologne and Treves had awakened the fears and the resentment of many among the haughty Prelates of Germany, and had excited high indignation in the German mind. But Æneas knew his own strength, and the weakness of the Emperor. Frederick determined, or rather imagined that he acted on his own determination, to enter into negotiations. And now

<small>[p] Epist. lxxli. Compare Æneas Sylvius (Fea), p. 84.</small>

again who so fit to conduct those negotiations as his faithful Secretary? who but an Italian, so intimately acquainted with the interests of Germany, so attached to the Emperor, so able, so eloquent, could cope with the Prelates and Cardinals of Rome?[q] Æneas was more true to his Imperial than he had been to his Papal patron; being true to the Emperor he was true to himself.

Æneas arrived at his native Sienna. His kindred, proud no doubt of his position, crowded round him. They entreated him not to venture to Rome. Eugenius was cruel, unforgetful of injuries, bound by neither pity nor conscience.[r] A man so deeply committed in the affairs of the hostile Council might expect the worst. Æneas boldly answered that the ambassador of the Emperor of Germany must be safe everywhere. He did not betray a more important secret, that already he had obtained through two friendly Cardinals, Carvajal and Landriano, pardon for all that he had done at Basle.

Æneas in Italy.

He entered Rome: he was admitted to the presence of the Pope, beside whom stood the two friendly Cardinals. He was permitted to kiss the foot, the cheek of the Pontiff. His credentials were in his hand. He was commanded to declare the object of his mission. "Ere I fulfil the orders of the Emperor, allow me, most holy Pontiff, a few words on myself. I know that many things have been brought to the ears of your Holiness concerning me, things not to my credit, and on which it were better not to dwell: neither

At Rome.

---

[q] To this visit to Rome belong the observations he makes in a letter to his patron the Bishop of Passau. Epist. xcviii. The Cardinals, he says, are by no means so rich as of old.

[r] "Aiebant Eugenium crudelem, injuriarum memorem, nullâ pietate, nullâ conscientiâ teneri."—Apud Fea, p. 88

have my accusers spoken falsely. At Basle I have written much, spoken much, done much; but my design was not to injure you, I sought only the advantage of the Catholic Church. I have erred, who will deny it? but with neither few nor undistinguished men: Julian, the Cardinal of St. Angelo, the Archbishop of Palermo, Pontanus the Protonotary of your Court, men esteemed in the eyes of the law, masters of all truth. I speak not of the Universities and Schools throughout the world, almost all adverse to your cause. With such authorities who had not erred? I must confess, that so soon as I detected the errors of those at Basle, I did not, as most others did, fly to you. But fearing to fall from error to error, from Scylla to Charybdis, I would not, without consultation and delay, rush from one extreme to the other. I sided with those called neutrals. I remained three years with the Emperor, heard the discussions between your Legates and those of Basle, nor could longer doubt that the truth was on your side; not unwillingly therefore I accepted this embassy from the Emperor, hoping thereby, through your clemency, to be restored to your favour. I am in your hands: I have sinned in ignorance, I implore pardon. And now to the affairs of the Emperor."* The Pope, no doubt well prepared for this address, had his answer ready. The Ambassador of the Emperor, a man of the ability and importance of Æneas, was not to be repelled even by the stubborn Eugenius. "We know that you have erred, with many others; we cannot deny pardon to one who confesses his errors. Our holy Mother, the Church, withholds mercy from those only who refuse to acknowledge their sins You are now in

---

* Commentar. Nov. p. 11.

possession of the truth, look that you do not abandon it. Show forth the divine grace in your good works. You are in a position to defend the truth, to do good service to the Church. We shall forget all the wrongs committed against us; him that walketh uprightly we shall love!" Of the Cardinals, only the virtuous Thomas of Sarzana, afterwards Nicolas V., looked coldly on the renegade, and Æneas as haughtily refused to humiliate himself. "O ignorance of man," writes Æneas, "had I known that he would be Pope, what would I not have borne!"[t] But Æneas fell ill, and Thomas of Sarzana sent a common friend to console him, and to offer aid for the payment of his physicians. John Carvajal, the Pope's Legate in Germany, visited him every day. He recovered, returned to Sienna, saw his father for the last time, and went back to Germany. He was followed by a message from the Pope, appointing him his Secretary. "Wonderful and unparalleled grace of God" (so writes his biographer, probably Æneas himself), "that one man should be Secretary to two Popes" (he was continued in the office by Nicolas V.), "to an Emperor and an Antipope."[u] Æneas humbly ascribes the glory to God, as if his own craft and tergiversations had no share in the marvel.

Germany began slowly to feel and to betray the influence of the wily Italian. He ruled the irresolute Emperor.[x] Yet even now affairs looked only more

---

[t] "Si scisset Æneas futurum Papam, omnia tolerâsset."—Fea, p. 89.

[u] So too in Epist. clxxxviii. p. 760. "Apud tres Episcopos et totidem Cardinales dictandarum Epistolarum officium exercui. Hi tres quoque Pontifices maximi secretariorum collegio me ascripserunt Eugenius, Nicolaus, Felix, quamvis hunc adulterum dixerit. Apud Cæsarem non secretarius modo, sed consiliarius et principatus honore sanctus sum. Neque ego istæ fortunæ imputo, quamvis nescio cuinam, sed ipsius rectori et dominatori omnium Deo." Thus writes Æneas in his own person.

[x] There were negotiations, perhaps

menacing and dangerous to Pope Eugenius. After due deliberation he had peremptorily refused the Emperor's demand to convoke another Council in Germany. Not only were the two Archbishop Electors under sentence of deposition, new Electors[y] had been named on his sole authority; not even Germans, but near relatives of the powerful Philip of Burgundy, sworn to place them on their thrones. Six of the Electors entered into a solemn league, that if Eugenius did not immediately annul his Bull of deposal against the Archbishops, limit the ecclesiastical burthens on the Empire, and submit to the decree of Constance, which asserted the supremacy of General Councils, they would cast aside their long neutrality, and either summon a new Council or acknowledge the Council of Basle and Pope Felix V.[z] They sent an embassy to communicate this secret covenant to the Emperor and to six only of his Privy Councillors, and to demand his adhesion to the League. The Emperor admitted the justice of their demands as to the rehabilitation of the deposed Prelates, but refused to join the League, "it was impious to compel the Pope to terms by threatening to revolt from his authority."[a] The Emperor, not sworn to secrecy, confided the whole to Æneas, by him at his discretion to be communicated to Rome. Æneas was ordered again to Rome to persuade the Pope to cede the restitution of the Archbishops.

Frankfort. March 21, A.D. 1446.

a private treaty, between King Frederick and Eugenius. Carvajal was at Vienna.—Voigt, c. 6.

y They were Bishop John of Cambray, Philip's natural brother, to Treves; to Cologne, Prince Adolph of Cleves, his sister's son. Schmidt, vii.

19, p. 338.

z Apud Goden. iv. 290; Schmidt, p. 339.

a There is some slight discrepancy here between the Commentaries and the history.

He went round, it seems, by Frankfort, where the Electors held or were about to hold their diet.[b] At Frankfort he found, perhaps it was his object there, the Papal Legates, Thomas of Sarzana (Bishop of Bologna), and John Carvajal. They were in dire perplexity. One must hasten to Rome for further instructions, Carvajal was ill, Æneas set off in the company of Thomas of Sarzana. It was spring, the bridges were broken down. They crossed the Alps in three days by paths only known to mountain guides over precipices and glaciers.

At Rome the Pope took the counsel of Thomas of Sarzana. Before he admitted the Ambassadors of the Electors, he had a private interview with Æneas Sylvius. Æneas at his last visit had brought himself, he now brought the Emperor, to the feet of Eugenius. The only concession urged on the Pope was the revocation of the fatal step, and the restoration of the deposed Electors. The Emperor could not endure French Electors. For once the obstinate Eugenius bowed himself to the wiser yielding policy; Æneas had imparted his own pliancy to the Pope. There was but one difficulty, how to appease Philip Duke of Burgundy, who might resent the dismissal of his kindred, his nephew and natural brother, the intruded Archbishops of Cologne and Treves. The Papalists had tempted, flattered, bribed the pride and ambition of one of the proudest and most ambitious of men; they must allay that pride and ambition. Thomas of Sarzana was entrusted with this delicate mission: Æneas was to return to Germany, to manage the Emperor and the Empire. The

---

[b] I doubt this Frankfort journey, the Legates were probably at the Court of Frederick.

Pope then admitted the Ambassadors of the six Electors. At the head of these was Gregory of Heimburg, a bold, free-spoken, fearless man, the most learned lawyer in the Empire, but described by Sylvius as of coarse manners; a genuine German of his age unfavourably contrasted in his own judgement with the supple Siennese. Heimburg's address to the Pope was intrepid, haughty: "Germany was united; it was embittered by the deposition of the Bishops—the Princes were resolved to assert the authority of General Councils." The Pope's answer was cold and brief: He had deposed the Archbishops for good reasons: he had never shown disrespect to Councils, but had maintained the dignity of the Apostolic See. He would prepare a written reply. He detained them in Rome in sullen indignation at their delay in the hot ungenial city.[o]

Æneas set forth on his return with Thomas of Sarzana. They travelled together, though Æneas was suffering from the stone, by Sienna, Pistoia, Lucca. Æneas entered Florence, the Bishop of Bologna was not allowed to do so. Æneas was obliged to leave the Bishop ill at Parma. He hastened by Mantua, Verona,

---

[o] "Hic orationem arrogantiæ plenam habuit; dixit Germaniæ principes unitos esse, eadem velle et sapere, depositionem Episcoporum amaroleato tulisse animo, petere ut cæsetur annulleturque, ut auctoritas conciliorum approbetur, ut natival opportuné concedatur. . . . Eugenius ad hæc suo more pauca et graviter respondit."—Hist. Freder. III. apud Kollar. p. 123. See the curious account of Gregory's behaviour, "In terras legati Electorum affecti tædio murmurabant, neque sine timore fuerunt quod nimis rigidè se locutos sentiebant. Gregorius juxta Montem Jordanum post vesperas deambulare, caloribus exæstuans, quasi et Romanos et officium suum contemneret, dimissis in terram caligis, aperto pectore, nudo capite, brachia disuperiens, fustibandus incedebat, Romanosque et Eugenium et Curiam blasphemabat, multaque in calores terræ ingerebat mala. Est enim aër Romanus Theutonicis infestissimus, . . . quia plus sanguinis habent quam Italici, et plus merum ebibunt, plus calore cruciantur."—Ibid. 124.

Treut, Memmingen, Ulm.[d] At Ulm he was stopped by fear of robbers, who infested the whole road to Frankfort. He fell in with the Bishops of Augsburg and Chiemsee, and the Chancellor Gaspar; with them he reached Frankfort in safety.

At Frankfort the Diet had met in imposing fulness. The Emperor was represented by the Chancellor, the Bishops of Augsburg and Chiemsee, the Marquises of Baden and Brandenburg, and by Æneas Sylvius. The Electors were all present. The Pope's Legates were John de Carvajal and Nicolas de Cusa. Thomas of Sarzana did not arrive till he had successfully fulfilled his mission to the Duke of Burgundy. Louis, Cardinal of Arles, John de Lysura and others appeared for the Council of Basle and the Antipope. Louis of Arles claimed to have the cross borne before him, and to celebrate the first mass before the Diet as Papal Legate. His claim was supported by the Electors, fully determined to maintain the rights of the Council. The Emperor's Ambassadors remonstrated; Germany was yet pledged to strict neutrality. The citizens of Frankfort were on that side; they had sworn allegiance to the Emperor, not to the Electors; the Cardinal of Arles was forced ungraciously to submit.

Sept. 1, 1446. Diet at Frankfort.

The session was opened by Gregory of Heimburg, who reported the reception of his mission at Rome. He described the Court of Rome as implacably hostile to Germany; Eugenius as harsh, haughty, repulsive. The Cardinals he turned into ridicule, especially "the bearded old goat," the Cardinal Bessarion. Æneas replied, rebuking the unfairness of

Altercation.

---

[d] Comment. 94. Compared with other documents.

the German, and labouring to bring out the milder and more courteous points in the demeanour and language of the Pope. Æneas had to encounter some unpleasant altercation. The Cardinal of Arles reproached him with his tergiversations. "It is not I," answered Æneas, "who have changed, but the Council; they once offered to remove the Council from Basle, now they refuse; as if all truth were contained within the walls of Basle." John de Lysura was even more pointed and personal. "Are you come from Sienna to legislate for Germany? You had better have stayed at home and left us to settle our own affairs." Æneas kept prudent silence.

The reports from Rome had made a deep and unfavourable impression. Basle appeared to triumph; the Electors seemed determined to declare for the Council and for Felix V. But the resources of Æneas were not exhausted; he boldly summoned to his aid two irresistible allies—in plain language, bribery and forgery. All things, Æneas had said in his Antipapal days, are venal with the Court of Rome; the imposition of hands, the gifts of the Holy Ghost are openly sold.* Rome could buy as well as sell; and the severe virtue of Germany was not proof against pontifical gold. No less a person than the Archbishop of Mentz sold himself to Eugenius: meaner men could not hesitate with such an example. The Archbishop did not actually take the money with his own hands, but two thousand Rhenish florins were distributed among his four chief Counsellors.†

<small>* "Nihil est quod absque argento Romana Curia dedit. Nam et ipsæ manus impositiones, et Spiritûs Sancti dona venundantur."—Epist. lxvi.

† "Cumque res diu inutiliter tractaretur, ad pecuniam tandem recurrere oportet, cui rarus non obaudiunt aures, hæc domina coriarum est, hæc aures omnium aperit: huic omnia serviunt: hæc quoque Moguntinum expugnavit."</small>

But the Archbishop Elector would maintain decency. He could not veer round without some specious excuse. Æneas boldly took in hand the Ambassadors' instructions; he dressed them up, quietly discarding every hard or offensive word, insinuating milder and more conciliatory expressions; and with deliberate effrontery presented these notes, as authorised by Pope Eugenius.* He ran the risk of being disclaimed by the stubborn Pontiff, and exposed as the Forger of official documents. The notes declared the assent of the Pope to the restoration of the deposed Archbishops, vaguely recognised the independence of the German nation, saved the authority of General Councils. Æneas had calculated with his usual sagacity. These notes were accepted, and presented to the Diet, signed by the Elector of Mentz, the Marquis of Brandenburg, the Grand Master of Prussia, the Archbishops of Saltzburg and Magdeburg, and many other Princes. The Elector of Treves and the Duke of Saxony alone opposed; the Elector Palatine wavered. The Electoral League was paralysed, a new League formed between the Emperor, the Electors of Mentz, Brandenburg, and the rest. The Diet broke up, the three Electors departed in indignation; the Ambassadors of Basle in sorrow and discomfiture.

These are the words of Æneas Sylvius himself in his Hist. Frederic. III. published by Kollar, vol. ii. p. 127. The Emperor advanced the money; it was afterwards paid by Nicolas V. Compare also Fea, p. 100.

* "Cum Legati Cæsaris non possent menti Pontificis satisfacere, Æneas modum commentus est, qui, receptis notulis, secundum quas as Principes obligaverant, nisi Eugenius illas admitteret, vellet se eum deserere, omne venenum ex eis ademit, novasque notulas componit, per quas et Archiepiscopi deprivati restituerentur, et nationi opportune provideretur et auctoritas Conciliorum salvaretur, Illasque dixit sua opinione Eugenium non negaturum."—Vit. Fred. III., p. 129.

Æneas and Procopius Rubensteyn, a Bohemian Noble, were despatched to Rome as Imperial Ambassadors to obtain the Pope's assent to the terms thus framed. On his assent the Emperor and most of the German Princes would forswear their neutrality and acknowledge him for Pope. Letters had been previously sent; the College of Cardinals was divided; the more rigid theologians would admit no concession. Pope Eugenius was advised to create four new Cardinals, the Archbishop of Milan, the Abbot of St. Paul, Thomas of Surzana Bishop of Bologna, John Carvajal. At Sienna the Imperial Ambassadors encountered others from the Archbishop of Mentz and the German Princes. The representative of Mentz was no less than John of Lysura, but a few days before so stern a Basilian, who had been so offended by the apostasy of Æneas, and had now trimmed his sails to the wind.

They were received with joyous welcome, as bringing the submission of Germany to the Papal See.[b] The third day they were introduced into the private consistory. Æneas spoke; all heard with rapture. No voice was silent in his praise! That very day the Pope was seized with mortal sickness. The physicians said that he could not live ten days. Would he live long enough to ratify the Treaty? The Ambassadors were only commissioned to Eugenius: delay might be fatal, a new schism might arise. "If," said John of Lysura, "the little toe of his left foot is alive, it is enough." The Pope not only lived to issue the Apostolic Bulls, but to reward the invaluable services of Æneas Sylvius. A vacancy in the Bishopric of Trieste was announced,

---

[b] " Erat enim ingens gaudium propa sexdecim annos Germaniam perditam recuperatam."—Fea, p. 105.

DEATH OF EUGENIUS.

the Pope at once appointed Æneas to the See. The rejoicings at Rome were like those at a great victory; bonfires blazed, the city was illuminated, the noise of trumpets, the pealing of bells rang through the streets. After fourteen days died Pope Eugenius; his stubborn pertinacity might seem to have won a glorious triumph: he had deluded the Germans by some specious concessions, of which he himself well knew the hollow value (the Apostolic Bulls were called Concordats); he had almost reconquered the allegiance of Christendom. But he is said to have exclaimed on his deathbed, "Oh Gabriel, better had it been for your soul, if you had never been Cardinal, never Pope, but continued to practise the religious discipline of your monastery!"[1] The Pope was dead, the Monk still lived.

Feb. 23, 1447.

---

[1] Palatii Gesta Pontificum apud Weissenberg, p. 465. The character of Eugenius changes in the writings of Æneas with the changes in Æneas himself. We have seen some illustrations of this. In the Hist. Concil. Basil. "Eugenius is a reed shaken by the wind" (no very apt similitude), an object of dislike, even of contempt. In his Dialogus de Auctor. Concilii, alluded to in his Retractation, his praise of Felix passes into adulation. There is no grace or virtue which is not heaped upon him. In Eugenius the defiance darkens into vituperation: "Vexator ecclesiæ, non solum laude indignus, sed detestatione et execratione totius humani generis dignos proculdubio est." So says one of the interlocutors, unrebuked by Æneas. Compare on the other side the high character in the De Europâ, p. 458. So too in Vit. Frederic. III., p. 135. "Fuit autem Eugenius alti animi, injuriarum tenax, delatoribus aurem præbuit, avaritiam caluavit, honoris cupidus fuit: ubi sententiam imbuit, non facile mutari potuit: religiosis viris admodum favit." In another passage— "alti cordis fuit, sed nullum in eo vitium fuit, nisi quia sine mensurâ erat, et non quod potuit, sed quod voluit, aggressus est." This heightens our opinion of the boldness and sagacity of Æneas in persuading such a man to accept as his own, instructions which he had not given.

CHAPTER XVII.

Nicolas V.

The Pontificate of Nicolas V. is the culminating point of Latin Christianity. The Papal power indeed had long reached its zenith. From Innocent III. to Boniface VIII. it had begun its decline. But Latin Christianity was alike the religion of the Popes and of the Councils which contested their supremacy. It was as yet no more than a sacerdotal strife whether the Pope should maintain an irresponsible autocracy, or be limited and controlled by an ubiquitous aristocratic Senate. The most ardent reformers looked no further than to strengthen the Hierarchy. The Prelates were determined to emancipate themselves from the usurpations of the Pope, as to their elections, their arbitrary taxation by Rome, the undermining of their authority by perpetual appeals; but they had no notion of relaxing in the least the ecclesiastical domination. It was not that Christendom might govern itself, but that themselves might have a more equal share in the government. They were as jealously attached as the Pope to the creed of Latin Christianity. The Council, not the Pope, burned John Huss. Their concessions to the Bohemians were extorted from their fears, not granted by their liberality. Gerson, D'Ailly, Louis of Arles, Thomas of Corcelles, were as rigid theologians as Martin V. or Eugenius IV. The Vulgate was their Bible, the Latin service their exclusive liturgy, the Canon Law their code of jurisprudence.

Latin Christianity had yet to discharge some part of its mission. It had to enlighten the world with letters, to adorn it with arts. It had hospitably to receive (a gift fatal in the end to its own dominion) and to promulgate to mankind the poets, historians, philosophers of Greece. It had to break down its own idols, the Schoolmen, and substitute a new idolatry, that of Classical Literature. It had to perfect Christian art. Already Christian Architecture had achieved some of its wonders. The venerable Lateran and St. Paul's without the Walls, the old St. Peter's, St. Mark's at Venice and Pisa, Strasburg and Cologne, Rheims and Bourges, York and Lincoln, stood in their majesty. Christian Painting, and even Christian Sculpture, were to rise to their untranscended excellence.

The choice of Nicolas V. was one of such singular felicity for his time that it cannot be wondered at if his admirers looked on it as overruled by the Holy Spirit. "Who would have thought in Florence," so said Nicolas to his biographer Vespasiano, "that a priest who rang the bells should become Supreme Pontiff?"[a] Yet it seems to have been a happy accident. Eighteen Cardinals met in the Conclave. Ten voices were for the Cardinal Colonna; two more would give him the requisite majority. Alfonso, King of Arragon and Sicily, encamped at Tivoli, favoured the Colonna. Already, to end the strife, the Cardinal of Bologna had risen to add his suffrage. He was checked and interrupted by the wise Cardinal of Tarento. "Whom, then," said he, "do you nominate?" "The Cardinal of Bologna!" A sudden light seemed to flash on the Conclave: Thomas of Sarzana, Cardinal of Bologna, was Pope.[b]

Nicolas V.
March 4, 1447.

---

[a] Apud Muratori, p. 279.   [b] Vit. Nicolai V., a Dominico Georgio, p. 4.

Had a turbulent, punctilious, obstinate Pope, another Eugenius, succeeded Eugenius IV., all might again have been strife and confusion. The consummate diplomatic skill of Æneas Sylvius had extorted some concessions on his deathbed even from that impracticable Pope. Some questions had been designedly left in decent vagueness.

The Cardinal of Bologna was forty-eight years old. His rise to honours had been rapid—Bishop, Cardinal, Pope, in three successive years.[c] He was known as a lover and liberal patron of letters. As Legate he had been singularly active, conciliatory, popular, and therefore successful. He had seemingly personal friendship for Æneas Sylvius, and could fully appreciate his wise and dexterous management. He left the German negotiations in those able hands; but a speech attributed to him was well-timed. "The Bishops had too little, rather than too much power: he had no design to encroach on their lawful authority."[d] This is more remarkable, as in all business he had the most perfect self-confidence: nothing was well done which he did not do himself.[e]

Dissolution of Council of Basle. A.D. 1449.
Two years had hardly elapsed when Nicolas V. (so well had Æneas Sylvius done his work in Germany) was sole and undisputed Pope. The Council of Basle, disowned, almost forgotten, had dissolved itself. Felix V. was again Amadeus of Savoy, in his peaceful retreat at Ripaille. The Council had the wisdom to yield, the Pope the greater wisdom

---

[c] 1445, 1446, 1447.
[d] Weissenberg.
[e] See the elaborate character of Nicolas V. by Æneas Sylvius,—Fea, p. 139. He was hasty, but placable; friendly, but there was no friend with whom he was not at some time angry. "Nimium de se credidit, omnia per se facere voluit. Nihil bene fieri putavit, nisi interesset. Injuriarum neque ultor, neque oblitus est."

to admit the Council to an honourable capitulation. The Fathers at Basle appeared to submit to the friendly urgency of the Kings of France and England. They maintained prudent silence on the abandonment of their cause by the Emperor Frederick III. and his as yet ambiguous and disguised menaces of compulsory dissolution. The Prince-Pope was permitted to retire, not without dignity. Nicolas demanded not that insulting humiliation which had been enforced by his predecessors on their discomfited rivals. Felix V. sank into a Cardinalate, and that Cardinalate next in honour to the Pope. Louis of Arles was restored to his rank. Three out of the Cardinals named by Felix were advanced by Nicolas; the rest were dead or content to abdicate. All the Papal censures against the Pope and the Council were annulled; the Acts of the Council, as far as promotions and appointments, confirmed.

Abdication of Felix.

So ended the last Antipope,[f] so closed the last Council which claimed co-equal authority with the Pope. The peaceful treaty showed a great advance in Christian courtesy, in Christian forbearance, in the majesty of Christian gentleness; but some decay, too, in the depth and ardour of Christian zeal. To have been an Antipope was no longer an odious and inexpiable crime—a crime to be forgiven only after the most contumelious abasement, or as an ostentatious act of mercy. Felix may have owed something to his princely rank, more to the times and to the sagacious character of Nicolas V. Basle saw the last Council which could pretend to the title of Œcumenic: that of Trent was a Council of Papal Christendom, and by no means the whole of Papal

---

[f] Amadeus lived only to Jan. 1, 1451. Muratori, sub ann. 1449.

Christendom. All that had severed itself from Latin Christianity, part which was still in union, stood aloof from an assembly chiefly gathered from two nations, Spain and Italy.

Nicolas V. retired into his serene and peaceful dignity: not so his restless colleague in all his negotiations and in his journeys. Æneas Sylvius had still years of busy life before him. Among the first acts of Pope Nicolas had been the confirmation of Æneas in his Papal Secretaryship and in his Bishopric of Trieste. It was singular enough that, as Bishop of Bologna, Thomas of Sarzana had been honoured everywhere but in his own See. Bologna would not admit him within her walls. The Church of Trieste, at first refractory, could not but receive a Bishop commended by the Emperor and the Pope.

Æneas Sylvius.

The Bishop of Trieste returned to Germany. No affair of Frederick III. could be conducted without his aid. He was first sent to the Diet of Aschaffenburg, which, under the Archbishop of Mentz, accepted the Bulls of Pope Eugenius and acknowledged Pope Nicolas. Duke Philippo Maria, the last of the Visconits, died,[f] Milan was in confusion.[h] The Emperor, among the competitors for the Dukedom,[i] as an escheated fief of the Empire, would, beyond that, put in his claim as actual Ruler. Æneas was among his ambassadors. Milan would own the suzerainty of the Emperor, but at the same time maintain her freedom. The Embassy

July 19, 1447.

---

[a] In the castle of Porta Zobbia, Aug. 15, 1447.

[h] "Incredibile allora fu la revolusion dello Stato de Milano; tutto si reimpiè di sedizioni, ed ognuno prese l' armi."—Muratori, sub ann.

[i] Charles, Duke of Orleans, in right of his mother, Valentina, sister of the late Duke; Alfonso, King of Naples and Arragon, by the will of the late Duke; Francis Sforza, husband of the natural daughter of the late Duke.

returned, having effected nothing, from the impracticable city.[k] Æneas attributes their failure to the grasping ambition of his German colleagues in the Embassy: demanding too much, they lost all; his more subtle policy would have succeeded better. He returned to Vienna, was consecrated Bishop of Trieste, visited his diocese, was received with cordial welcome, and celebrated mass. But he was not long occupied with his peaceful duties. He was called upon to settle a question of frontier in Istria between the Emperor and the Venetians. On his return to Trieste he found a Count Rupert warring on the city, wasting the estates of the Church. He laid his complaints before the Emperor, but himself hardly escaped from the hands of the noble freebooter. On his return to Vienna he found his power in the Council somewhat in danger. His friend and patron Gaspar Schlick was in disgrace. He died July 16, 1449. As of the Chancellor's faction Æneas fell under suspicion. With his usual dexterity he steered his course, not absolutely renouncing his friend, yet not offending the Emperor. He received another benefice, a rich parish church in the neighbourhood of Vienna.

Milan again besieged by Francis Sforza made overtures to the Emperor. Again the indefatigable Æneas crossed the Worm Alp, descended into the Valteline, and found the Lake of Como and its shores overrun by the troops of Sforza; he reached Como with difficulty. That city was beset on all sides; Sforza eagerly desired to seize the Imperial Ambassadors. At the head of a few soldiers, Æneas dashed through by night and reached Milan.[m] Notwithstanding the open and the secret opposition of Sforza's partisans,

July, 1449.

---

[k] Commentar. Pii II., &c., pp. 19, 25.   [m] Vit. Frederic. III., p. 147.

he assembled and harangued the people. Three gates (quarters) of the city would have proclaimed the Emperor without condition, one more had been a majority.[a] Terms were however framed, on the whole favourable to the Emperor, but such as Æneas had no authority to accept. Charles Gonzaga proposed to Æneas to seize the city by force. This Æneas declined as unbecoming his ecclesiastical character. The scheme was full of dangers, and of very doubtful issue! Æneas returned to the Emperor. Frederick, however, needed not only dexterous Ambassadors, but well-appointed armies and able Generals to occupy and protect Milan: he had neither. Milan opened her gates to Sforza; Sforza was Duke of Milan.[b]

From Feb. 26
to March 22,
1450.

In the first year of Sforza's dukedom, that of the Jubilee, Æneas was engaged on a more peaceful mission, to settle the contract of marriage between the Emperor and Leonora, sister of the King of Portugal. The agreement was readily made at Naples with the Ambassadors of Portugal. Æneas saw Rome at the height of the Jubilee, his friend and patron, Nicolas V., receiving the homage, the well-deserved homage, and the tribute of the world.

In Nicolas V., in three short years, the Pope had become again a great Italian Potentate. Not that Nicolas V. was of one of the famous houses, or aspired to found a family of Princes. He was superior to, or not tempted to that Nepotism, which had already made some advances, some initiatory efforts, to invest the

---

[a] Vit. Frederic. III., p. 149.

[b] " Qui etiam insignia ducalia, tradente populo, suscepit, quæ res neque vim neque colorem habuit justitiæ."—P. 162. Muratori, sub ann. i. 450. For the personal adventures of Æneas Sylvius, see the Commentaries and Life of Frederick III. apud Kollar, p. 140 et seq.

descendants or kinsmen of Popes in territorial honours or titles. Hitherto these families had taken no root, had died out, sunk into obscurity, or had been beaten down by common consent as upstart usurpers. Nicolas V. laid the foundation of his power, not so much in the strength of the Roman See as a temporal Sovereignty, as in the admiration and gratitude of Italy, which was rapidly reported over the whole of Christendom. He kept in pay no large armies, his Cardinals were not Condottieri generals; he declared that he would never employ any arms but those of the Cross of Christ.* But he maintained the Estates of the Church in peace, he endeavoured (and the circumstances of the times favoured that better policy) to compose the feuds of Italy, raging at least with their usual violence. He was among the few Popes, really a great Pacificator in Italy. Four mighty Powers were now mingled in open war, or in secret intrigue. Alfonso, King of Arragon and the two Sicilies, the Dukes of Milan, the Venetians and the Florentines. Eugenius had had the wisdom, or good fortune, to abandon the French pretensions to the throne of Naples, that fatal claim by which the Popes had for centuries entailed the miseries of war upon Italy, and servitude upon themselves. The strife for the Dukedom of Milan, notwithstanding the pretensions of the Emperor, and all the arts of Æneas Sylvius, the claims of the King of Arragon, and of the House of Orleans, had terminated in the establishment of the Sforzas. Pope Nicolas almost for the first time entered openly into Italian politics, as a true Mediator—not as a partisan—and, so doing, was for the first time (to a certain extent at least) successful in his mediation. Even in the wars

---

* Vespasiano, p. 279.

of these powers Romagna was respected and escaped devastation. The warlike chieftains who had usurped the cities and domains of the Church, were glad to become her subjects. The Malatestas accepted the recognition of their title as Lords of Rimini, Fano, and other cities of Romagna, and from their tribute the Pope received a revenue, if not equal in amount, more sure and less invidious than his own taxation. The retrenchments insisted upon by the Council of Basle were eluded by a Concordat, drawn with all the subtlety of Æneas Sylvius, and received by his obsequious master Frederick. In remote regions there were still deep murmurs at the avarice, the venality of Rome; Nicolas and his Court escaped not, and did not deserve to escape, the common charge of rapacity; but such murmurs died away in those distant quarters, or had lost their effect.[q]

All this was not done, but it was well begun before the Jubilee; and no Jubilee had been more splendid, more peaceful, attended by greater numbers,[r] productive of more immense wealth.[s] A new coin for the Jubilee was struck. From every part of Europe came pilgrims

---

[q] Stimmen, p. 115. The ambassador, credited with 1225 ducats, is instructed to give 1000 ducats either in gold or in some rich present—225 are for the Cardinal patron. But if the Pope is not content with the 1000, he must have it all, and the Protector wait. The close of the affair is even more discreditable to the Pope. It is a very curious detail on the process of Papal bribery. In 1449, a collector and vendor of Indulgences levied in Prussia 7845 marks: for Indulgences, 3241; for Peter's Pence, 4604.—P. 137.

[r] "Dopo il primo Giubileo del Anno 1300 forse non fu mai veduto sì gran flusso e riflusso di gente in Roma, di modo che le strade Maestre d' Italia parevano tante Fiere."—Muratori, Ann., sub ann. "Licet quadringenta et amplius millia diebus singulis per urbem templa forumque vaderent,"—Vit. Freder. III., p. 172.

[s] The Teutonic Order tried to suppress the Bull, and to discourage the wasteful journey to Rome. The Pope was furious, and only appeased by a great offering.—Stimmen, p. 140.

of the highest rank, strangers swarmed like ants in the streets of Rome and Florence. The throng was so great that above 200 persons were crushed to death on the bridge of St. Angelo.¹ The Bank of the Medici alone had 100,000 florins belonging to the Church,² and during the whole time poured in riches, which aided in the restoration of the dilapidated finances of the Popedom. The Pilgrims carried back throughout Europe accounts of the resuscitated majesty of the Roman Pontificate, the unsullied personal dignity of the Pope, the reinthronement of religion in the splendid edifices, which were either building or under restoration.³

Among those who would disseminate the fame of Nicolas V., none would be more loud, as none had stronger reasons to be grateful, than Æneas Sylvius. He had just reached the Alps on his return from Rome (he had hardly escaped drowning in a swollen stream), when he was overtaken by the pleasant intelligence that he had been named by the Pope Bishop of his native city of Sienna. Æneas had never contemplated the passing the rest of his life in the cold ungenial region of Germany. "I yearn," he writes, "for my

---

¹ Infessura, Chron. de Rimini; Æneas Sylvius, Vit. Frederic., p. 172.
² Vespasiano, Vit. Nicol. V.
³ The Jubilee was interrupted by the plague, the fear of which had driven many in devotion to Rome (Sanuto says 60,000 died in Milan; hardly a man was left alive in Piacenza).—Muratori. The Cardinals, the Pope himself, were obliged to fly from Rome. "His Holiness goes from one castle to another with a small Court, and very few followers, seeking to find anywhere an uninfected place.

His Holiness is now in a castle called Fabriano, where he was last year for some time; and it is said has forbidden, under pain of death, that any one, of any rank whatever, who is at Rome, shall come secretly or openly to Fabriano, or within seven miles of it: the Cardinals alone are excepted, who are limited to four servants."—Voigt, from the Despatches of the Teutonic Knights. Stimmen, p. 70. This is not a very high view of the Pope's courage.

native Italy; I dread nothing so much as to lay my bones in a foreign land, though the way to heaven or to hell lies open alike from both. But it would be less painful, I know not why, to die in the arms of brothers, sisters, sons, grandsons."[y] It should seem[z] that he turned back, saw the Pope again, entered Sienna, was welcomed with the joyful acclamations of the inhabitants, proud to receive a native Siennese as their Bishop. But the Bishop of Sienna returned to his Imperial Master: Germany must still be held in its close alliance with Rome. His next embassy, in the following year, was into Bohemia. Both on his journey towards Prague and on his return, he was hospitably received in Tabor, the city of the most extreme disciples of John Huss. In a letter to John Carvajal,[a] the Cardinal of St. Angelo, he gives a striking description of that inexpugnable fortress. Over the gates were two shields: on one was painted an Angel with the Sacramental Cup; on the other the blind old Ziska, their leader in war while alive, whose skin, stretched on a drum, after his death, had inspirited them to certain victory. The Bishop of Sienna had strong misgivings in entering this headquarters of Satan. The Churchman held the audacious sectaries, who disdained the Primacy of Rome (the head of their offending, which included all other heresies), in the devoutest horror. "The Emperor Sigismund, instead of granting terms of peace to this most wicked and sacrilegious race, ought to have exterminated them, or reduced them to hewers of stone for the rest of mankind." Æneas had forgotten the irresistible valour, the splendid years of victory, which had extorted these terms from the Emperor. But the rude, poor Taborites treated

---

[y] Epist. lxv.   [z] The account is not clear.   [a] Epist. cxxx.

the Bishop with perfect courtesy. At a town about twenty-five miles from Prague (a pestilence was raging in Prague, and to his regret he dared not approach that ancient and noble city), he met the heads of the Bohemian nation. The object of his mission was soon despatched; the summons of a general Convention in the following year, with the Ambassador of the Emperor, and the Pope's Legate, at Leutmeritz. In that city he held a long theological discussion with George Podiebrad; a second at Tabor with Nicolas, the Bishop of the sect. He acknowledged that all his eloquence made no impression on the stubborn Utraquists. The Taborites stuck to the Scripture, Æneas to the power of the Church; no wonder that they came to no conclusion. But whatever might be the secret thoughts of each party as to the fate of his antagonist on the Day of Judgement, they parted with seeming mutual respect.

Nicolas V. was to behold, as it were, the final act of homage to the Popedom, from the majesty of the Empire. He was to be the last Pontiff who was to crown at Rome the successor of Charlemagne; Frederick III. the last Emperor who was to receive his crown from the hands of the Pope.[b] Æneas Sylvius is again in Italy: he is the harbinger of the Emperor, who is about to descend into Italy to meet his Portuguese bride, to consummate his marriage, and at the same time to celebrate his Coronation at Rome. The Free cities were always troubled, and were thrown into a tumult of intrigue, if not of feud, by the appearance of the Emperor in Italy. Guelf turned pale, Ghibelline brightened. Sienna was under popular government. Would the Emperor's favourite, the favourite of the

---

[b] Charles V. was crowned, but at Bologna.

Pope, the heir of the proud but fallen house of Piccolomini, now their Bishop, forego the opportunity of seizing for his own family the lordship of the city?* Sienna, which the year before had thronged out to meet Æneas, received him in sullen silence; no one visited him, his name was heard muttered with low curses in the streets. Æneas, as he says, smiled at the sudden change (did not his vanity magnify his own unpopularity, and the jealousy of the city?). He assembled the Senate, assured them of the peaceful and unambitious views of himself, his family, and of the Emperor. The Sienneso suppressed, but could not conceal their mistrust. Æneas having splendidly buried his colleague in the Embassy, who died at Sienna, thought it most prudent to go down to Telamona, in order to be in readiness to receive the Portuguese Princess.

Pope Nicolas himself began to look with alarm at the approach of the Emperor. There were suspicious movements at Rome: more than suspicions, of the dire designs of Stephen Porcaro and his partisans, which broke out during the next year.

The pride and the felicity of Nicolas V. was in the undisturbed peace of Italy, at least of Roman Italy; who could foretell what strange or unexpected tumults might arise at the appearance of the Emperor? He sent to delay the march of Frederick, at least till the summer; he urged the want of provisions, of preparation, the dangers of a winter journey. Æneas was indignant at this timid vacillation of the Pope; "it became not the supreme Pontiff to say one thing to-day, another to-morrow." He assured Pope Nicolas of the pacific intentions of the Emperor. He appealed to the conduct

---

* Vit. Frederic. III., p. 244.

of the Emperor to the Church; if he had been an enemy to the Church, the whole majesty of the Clergy had been crushed; we had not had the joy of beholding you in your present state of power and authority.[d] He wrote courteous letters to urge the immediate descent of Frederick.[e]

Tumults in Austria detained the Emperor; stormy weather his bride. Æneas Sylvius spent sixty weary days at Telamona.[f] At length, on the same day, the Emperor entered Florence, his bride Leghorn. They met at Sienna. Sienna thought it well to appear to be full of joy, was delighted with the urbanity and condescension of the Emperor, renounced her suspicions of Æneas, recalled all his kindred, some of whom, with other nobles, were in exile; and entreated the Bishop, whom the people now called the father of his country, to represent the City before the Pope.

The imperial cavalcade set off for Rome. As they descended the Ciminian hill, which overhangs Viterbo, the Emperor called Æneas to his side. "I shall live to see you Cardinal, I shall live to see you Pope." Æneas, with proper modesty, protested that he did not aspire to either of these perilous dignities. At Rome the marriage was solemnised by the Pope himself,[g] afterwards the coronation with great magnificence.[h] Æneas Sylvius made a speech for the Em-

March 16, 1452.

---

[d] "Si voluisset tantum possum ibat Ecclesia: cleri majestas omnis extinguebatur; nec tu hodie in hoc statu esses, in quo te videntes lætamur."— P. 191.

[e] The most full account of this affair, with the letter of Æneas to the Pope, is in the Hist. Frederic. III. apud Kollar, pp. 187 et seq.

[f] He whiled away his time by visiting the old Etrurian cities in the neighbourhood. Æneas had a remarkable, almost a premature, taste for antiquities and for the beauties of nature.

[g] Æneas Sylvius describes the whole at great length, p. 277 et seq.

[h] The cautious Pope had arrayed

peror. The day after, during an interview at which Æneas was present, the Emperor and the Pope communicated two extraordinary dreams.[1] The Emperor, the last time that the Cardinal of Bologna left Vienna, had dreamed that he was crowned not by a Roman, but by the Cardinal of Bologna. "It is the privilege," said the Pope, "of those set up to rule the people to have true dreams. I myself dreamed that my predecessor Eugenius, the night before his death, had arrayed me in the Pontifical dress and mitre, and placed me on the throne. Take thou my seat, I depart to St. Peter." The humble Thomas of Sarzana had not been without his ambition![k] The prediction of the Emperor as to the advancement of Æneas Sylvius, now on such amicable terms with the Pope, might have been expected to meet its own immediate accomplishment, as far as the Cardinalate. Æneas, however, received only a barren promise, which Pope Nicolas did not live to fulfil. But he returned to Germany Papal Ambassador and Legate to Bohemia, Silesia, Austria, Moravia, Styria, Carinthia, Carniola,—afterwards, at the Emperor's request, to Hungary. The Legatine character gave him great weight, he exercised it with his accustomed sagacity, and in perfect fidelity to Frederick. He was armed, as Legate, with Papal censures against all the enemies of Frederick. But these Austrian affairs belong not to our history.

Throughout Christendom, except in the narrow corner of Bohemia, Pope Nicolas V. ruled supreme. Yet even Nicolas V. was not secure against the inextinguishable turbulence of the Roman people. The republicanism

---

all the militia of the city, and occupied St. Angelo and the other strongholds with an imposing force to keep the peace.

[1] Muratori, sub ann.
[k] Vita Frederic., p. 296.

of the Crescentii, of Arnold of Brescia, of Brancaleone, of Rienzi, of Baroncelli, had still its champions and its martyrs. Stephen Porcaro was the last heir, till very modern times, of this dangerous and undying race. Stephen Porcaro was of equestrian family, of powerful and kindling eloquence. On the death of Eugenius (Eugenius himself had been driven from Rome by popular insurrection) Porcaro had urged the rising of the people, the proclamation of the Republic.[m] Pope Nicolas, anxious to conciliate all orders, appointed the dangerous demagogue on a mission in the Roman territory. On his return Porcaro renewed his agitation. He boldly avowed his opinions, and almost announced himself as defender of the liberties of the Roman people. He was sent in honourable exile to Bologna, under the sole restraint that he should present himself every day before Bessarion, the Cardinal Legate. He returned secretly to Rome. A conspiracy had been organised in which the nephew of Porcaro took the lead. Stephen Porcaro harangued the conspirators, inveighed against the tyranny of the rulers, the arbitrary proscription, the banishment, even the execution, of Roman citizens. He declared that it was ignominious that the city which had ruled the world should be subject to the dominion of priests, who were women rather than men.[n] He would cast off for ever the degrading yoke. He had at his command three hundred hired soldiers. Four hundred noble Romans were ready to appear in arms.

---

[m] "Dicens omnem servitutem turpem, fœdissimam autem quæ presbyteris præstaretur, rogabatque Romanos, dum Cardinales clausi essent, aliquod auderet pro libertate."—Æneas Sylvius, V. Fred. III., p. 135.

[n] "Turpe esse dictitans eam orbem, quæ totum sibi subjecerit orbem, nunc sacerdotum imperio subjacere, quos rectius fœminas quam viros quisque appellaverit."—Æneas Sylvius, Europa, p. 450.

He appealed to their cupidity as to their patriotism: to-morrow they might be in possession of a million of gold pieces.° If the aims of Porcaro were noble, his immediate designs, the designs with which he was charged, and with seeming truth,° were those of the robber, the bloody and cowardly assassin.ⁱ The contemplated mode of insurrection had the further horror of impious sacrilege. The Pope and the Cardinals were to be surprised while solemnising the mass on the festival of the Epiphany. The Papal stables near the church were to be set on fire. In the tumult Porcaro was to appear in purple and with the ensigns of magistracy, to force or gain his way as a worshipper towards the altar. The Pope was to be seized; it was said that the chains were found, chains of gold, which had been displayed to the insurgents, which were to fetter his holy person,ʳ only, however, to be thrown into a dungeon as a hostage to compel his brother to surrender the Castle of St. Angelo. His after-fate was perhaps to be that of his brethren the Cardinals, who were to be massacred without mercy. The shaven crown was no longer to be an object of fear or respect in Rome.⁸ The insurgents had nicely calculated the amount of plunder: from the Palace of the Pope 200,000 florins; from the Sacred College, 200,000; from the merchants and public officers 200,000; from

---

° Zantfliet, Stephano Infessura, Platina.

ᵖ Vita Nicolai V., p. 128.

ⁱ Sismondi, true to his republican bias, raises Stephen Porcaro to a hero and a martyr; and while he perhaps exaggerates the cruelty of the Pope, hardly touches on its justification, the atrocity of the plot. When will Italian freedom forswear assassination as its first and favourite weapon?—1857.

It has done so, and Italy is free!— 1864.

ʳ "Ad colligandum alt præsulem, catenam auream secum attulit, a se jampridem paratam quam congregatis ostendit."—Æn. Syl. Europa, p. 460.

⁸ "Velle enim aiebat se id agere, ut æternum intra hæc mœnia capitis rasi dentes vereri non oporteret."— Leo Alberti.

the magazines and salt depôts 200,000; from the confiscated property of the enemies of the revolution 100,000.

The conspiracy was detected or betrayed.[1] The house where the conspirators assembled was surrounded with troops. Porcaro escaped, but was found next day, hidden by his sister in a chest. Sciarra Porcaro, the nephew, cut his way through the soldiers and fled. Many servants and quantities of arms were found in the house. The very day of his capture the bodies of Stephen Porcaro and nine of his accomplices were seen hanging from the battlements of the Castle of St. Angelo. They had in vain implored confession and the last sacrament. Many other executions followed. Two Canons of St. Peter's were involved in the plot: one was found innocent and released; the other fled to Damascus, where he remained till after the death of the Pope. Large rewards were offered for some who had escaped: one thousand ducats if produced alive, five hundred if dead. Some were allowed to be seized in Padua and Venice. The Cardinal of Metz interceded for Battista Persona; it was alleged that he was guiltless. The Pope promised mercy: whether on new evidence or not, he was hung the next morning: the indignant Cardinal left Rome. Jan. 7, A.D. 1453.

The Pope was bitterly mortified at this ingratitude of the Roman people for his mild government, the peace which they enjoyed, the wealth which had poured into the city, the magnificent embellishments of Rome. He became anxious and morose. Remorse for blood, if necessarily, too prodigally shed, would weigh heavily

---

[1] According to Stephano Infessura they attacked one hundred of the Pope's guards, and killed the Marescallo.

on a Pope who had shrunk from war as unchristian.* The famous architect Leo Alberti (employed, it is true, by Nicolas V. in his splendid designs for St. Peter's) describes the unexampled state of prosperity enjoyed under Nicolas, for which the conspirators would have made that cruel return. "The whole of Latium was at peace: the last thing to be expected was that any Roman could think to change the state of affairs for the better by a revolution. The domain of the Church was in a high state of cultivation: the city had become a city of gold through the Jubilee; the dignity of the citizens was respected: all reasonable petitions were granted at once by the Pontiff. There were no exactions, no new taxes. Justice was fairly administered. It was the whole care of the Pope to adorn the city." The more devout and the more wealthy were indignant at the design to plunder and massacre the foreigners whose profuse wealth enabled the Romans to live in ease and luxury; at the profanation of the Church by promiscuous slaughter, of the altar itself by blood; the total destruction of the Cardinals, the priesthood, of religion itself: the seizure of the Pope, whose feet distant potentates crowded to kiss on his sublime function of sacrifice; the dragging him forth, loaded with chains, perhaps his death! The calmest looked on the

---

* See in Collier (i. p. 672) the curious account of Porcaro's conspiracy given in England by the Pope's Nuncio Clement Vincentio: "It was drawn," said the Nuncio, "from the brothels and profligates of Rome." The Nuncio suggests a form of public thanksgiving for the Pope's deliverance, and intimates that a letter from the English clergy would be acceptable, denouncing Rome as degenerating to the licentiousness of old Babylon, and advising the Pope to leave the wicked city, and reside in some other country. The Nuncio and Collector was also to hint the expediency of a subsidy to enable the Pope to leave Rome and Italy. The form of prayer was issued, says Collier, but no more done.

suppression of the conspiracy and the almost total extirpation of the conspirators with satisfaction.*

Now came that event which, however foreseen by the few wiser prophetic spirits, burst on Europe and on Christendom with the stunning and appalling effect of absolute suddenness—the taking of Constantinople by the Turks. On no two European minds did this disaster work with more profound or more absorbing terror than on Pope Nicolas V. and Æneas Sylvius: nor could any one allege more sound reasons for that terror than the Pope and the Bishop of Sienna. Who could estimate better than Æneas, from his intimate knowledge of all the countries of Europe, of Italy, Germany, France, England, the extent of the danger which impended over the Latin world? Never since its earlier outburst might Mohammedanism seem so likely to subjugate if not to swallow up distracted and disunited Christendom, as under the Turks. By sea and land they were equally formidable. If Christendom should resist, on what frontier? All were menaced, all in danger. What city, what kingdom, would arrest the fierce, the perpetual invasion? From this period throughout the affairs of Germany (at Frankfort he preached a crusade) to the end of his Legatine power, of his Cardinalate, of his Papacy, of his life, this was the one absorbing thought, one passion, of Æneas Sylvius. The immediate advance of the victorious Mohammed through Hungary, Dalmatia, to the border, the centre of Italy, was stopped by a single fortress, Belgrade; by a preacher, John Capistrano; by a hero, John Huniades. But it was not till, above a century later, when Don John of Austria, at Lepanto,

May 29, A.D. 1453.

A.D. 1472.

---

* Leo Battista Alberti. Porcaria Conjuratio apud Muratori, xxv. p. 310.

by sea, and much later, John Sobieski, before Vienna, by land, broke the spell of Mohammedan conquest, that Europe or Christendom might repose in security.[7]

The death of Nicolas V. was hastened, it was said, by the taking of Constantinople. Grief, shame, fear worked on a constitution broken by the gout. But Nicolas V. foresaw not that in remote futurity the peaceful, not the warlike, consequences of the fall of Constantinople would be most fatal to the Popedom—that what was the glory of Nicolas V. would become among the foremost causes of the ruin of mediæval religion: that it would aid in shaking to the base, and in severing for ever the majestic unity of Latin Christianity.[s]

March 24, 1455.

---

[7] Compare Gibbon, ch. lxvii. xii. p. 162.

[s] I cannot refrain, though my History closes with Nicolas V., from subjoining a few sentences on the end of Æneas Sylvius Piccolomini.

On the death of Nicolas V., the Cardinal Bessarion, for learning, dignity, character, stood high above the whole College of Cardinals. The election had been almost declared in his favour. The Cardinal of Avignon was seized with indignation. "Would they have for a Pope a Greek, a recent proselyte, a man with a beard? Was the Latin Church fallen so low that it must have recourse to the Greeks?" The jealousy of the West was roused: a Spaniard, the first of the fatal house of Borgia, was raised to the Papal throne, Callistus III. Æneas was at Frankfort, pressing on reluctant Germany a crusade against the Turks. The Germans thought more of their contest with the Pope than of the security of Christendom. Frederick III. was urged to seize the opportunity of the election of a new Pope to assert the liberties of the Empire and of the German Church. Æneas averted the strife, and persuaded the Emperor that he had more to hope than fear from the Pope. He was sent with the congratulations of the Emperor to Callistus III. A promotion of Cardinals was expected. The name of Æneas was in all men's mouths. he received congratulations. The Pope named but three, one his nephew, Borgia, the future Alexander VI. Æneas was about to return to Germany, but his presence was needed in Italy: Sienna was besieged by James Piccinino: war threatened between the Pope and Alfonso King of Naples. Æneas, as ambassador to Naples, secured an honourable treaty. The Pope would not lose, and was obliged to reward the indispensable Æneas. He was created Cardinal of

Nicolas V. aspired to make Italy the domicile, Rome the capital, of letters and arts. As to letters, his was

Sienna (Dec. 1456).

So, without dishonour or ingratitude, Æneas Sylvius was released from the service of his Imperial master. The Cardinal must devote himself to the interests of the Church; the Italian to those of Italy. He need breathe no more the thick and heavy air of Germany.

A year and a half has passed, and Æneas Sylvius Piccolomini (Aug. 21, A.D. 1458) is Pope Pius II.

Few men of more consummate ability had sat on the throne of St. Peter; few men more disposed to maintain the Papal power to the height of its supremacy. He boldly, unreservedly, absolutely condemned the heretical tenets of Æneas Sylvius. He reproached the King of France for the audacious Pragmatic Sanction: it was not less sacrilegious, not less impious than the decrees of the Council of Basle. But Pius II. had the sagacity to know that the days of Innocent III. and Boniface VIII. were passed. He learnt by bitter experience that those, too, of Urban II. were gone by. It was not for want of exertion, or of eloquence far surpassing that which rapt the Council of Clermont to frenzy, that Pius II. did not array Christendom in a more politic, more justifiable crusade against advancing Mohammedanism. Even the colder Council of Mantua seemed to kindle to enthusiasm. Against the Turks Germany would furnish 42,000 men; Hungary, 20,000 horse, 20,000 foot; Burgundy, 6000. The Duke of Burgundy accepted the command. Even the Italian kingdoms, dukedoms, republics, consented to be assessed. The Prince of Este threw down 300,000 florins. Italy was to raise a great fleet; France and Spain promised aid.

The proclamation of the Universal League of Christendom might seem a signal for a general war throughout Christendom. The war of the Roses raged in England; all Germany was in arms, bent on civil strife; the French fleet set sail, not against the Turks, but against Naples; Piccinino and Malatesta renewed the war in the Roman territory; the Savelli were in insurrection in Rome.

Pope Pius was not satisfied with endeavouring to rouse all Christendom to a crusade against the Turks: he undertook a more Christian, if a more desperate enterprise, the conversion of the Sultan. He published a long elaborate address to Mahomet II. Throughout this singular document the tone is courteous, conciliatory, almost flattering; not till its close, denunciatory against the imposture of the Koran. "Nothing was wanting to make Mahomet the mightiest sovereign the world had ever seen, nothing but a little water for his baptism, and belief in the Gospel. The world would bow down before Mahomet the Christian Emperor." "The great Sultan is no careless Atheist, no Epicurean; he believes in God and in the Immortality of the soul. What has been the end of all great conquerors,— Semiramis, Hercules, Bacchus, Nebuchadnezzar, Cyrus, Alexander, Julius Cæsar, Attila, Tamerlane? They are

not the ostentatious patronage of a magnificent Sovereign; nor was it the sagacious policy which would enslave to the service of the Church that of which it might anticipate the dangerous rebellion. It was not the religion of authority seeking to make itself master of all which might hereafter either confirm or contest that authority. In Nicolas it was pure and genuine,

all burning in the flames of hell. Your law allows all to be saved by their own religion, except renegades from Islam; we maintain, on the contrary, that all who believe not our creed must be damned." From this dangerous argument the Pope proceeds to enlarge on the Christian as contrasted with the Mohammedan faith. However justly he might argue on Christianity, the stern predestinarians of Islam must have been surprised at finding themselves charged with supposing the world ruled by chance, not by Providence. There is much more strange lore on Mohammedan superstitions and Arabian priestcraft. The Turks were of a noble Scythian race: the Pope marvels that they can follow Egyptians and Arabians in their religion: Christianity had been a far more congenial faith.

How strangely, how nobly did Pius II., at the close of his life, redeem the weaknesses, the treachery, the inconsistency, the unblushing effrontery of self-interest of his earlier years. Pius II. was the only Pope who, in his deep and conscientious devotion, would imperil his own sacred person in the Crusade against the Turks, and engage in a war, if ever justifiable in a Pope, justifiable when the liberty,

the Christianity of Europe might seem on the hazard. At Ancona (A.D. 1463), amid the total desertion of the leaders pledged to the Holy War,— amid the host of common soldiers, murmuring that they had been paid only in Indulgences, in which they had ceased to trust, not in hard money; a host starving for want of sustenance, which the Pope, once the cool and politic statesman, now become a sanguine, enthusiastic old man, had not thought of providing.—Pius II. alone maintained his courage. As the faith of others waxed cold, his became more ardent. He offered with one of his Cardinals to embark and throw himself into Ragusa, threatened by the Turks. And this refined and accomplished man died, as Peter the Hermit or St. Bernard might have died. The faithful Cardinal of Pavia watched his last moments. The sight of the sails of the Venetian fleet had for a moment kindled up all his ardour, but made him feel more deeply his failing strength. The Cardinal has described his end with the touching simplicity of real affection and reverence. "'Pray for me, my son,' were his last words." His friends bewailed and honoured him as a martyr in the cause of Christianity.*

---

* Comment. Card. Papiensis, p. 356.

almost innate, love of letters. In his lowlier station the ambition, pride, pleasure, passion, avarice of Thomas of Sarzana had been the study, the collection, of books. In every country into which he followed the train of the Cardinal Legate, his object was the purchase of manuscripts or copies of them. The Cardinal di Santa Croce (Albergata) encouraged him by his munificence; but the Cardinal's munificence could not keep pace with the prodigality of his follower. In his affluence Thomas devoted all he possessed to the same end, as in his poverty his most anxious fear had been lest he should be compelled to part with his treasures. So great was his reputation, that when Cosmo de' Medici proposed to open the Library of St. Marco at Florence, endowed with the books of Nicolo Nicoli, Thomas of Sarzana was requested to furnish a plan for the arrangement and for the catalogue. This became the model adopted in the other great libraries—that of the Badia at Florence, that of the Count of Montefeltro at Urbino, of Alexander Sforza at Pesaro. No sooner was Nicolas Pope than he applied himself to the foundation of the Vatican Library. Five thousand volumes were speedily collected. The wondering age boasted that no such library had existed since the days of the Ptolemies.

The scholars of Italy flocked to Rome, each to receive his task from the generous Pope, who rewarded their labours with ample payment. He seemed determined to enrich the West with all which survived of Grecian literature. The fall of Constantinople, long threatened, had been preceded by the immigration of many learned Greeks. Some, as the Cardinal Bessarion, had been naturalised after the Council of Florence.[*] Franco,

---

[*] Compare Disquisitio de Nicolai V. Pont. Max. erga literas et literarios viros patrocinio. Ad calc. Vit. Nicol. V. a Dominico Georgio. Roma, 1742.

Germany, even England, the Byzantine Empire, Greece, had been ransacked by industrious agents for copies of all the Greek authors. No branch of letters was without its interpreters. Notwithstanding the bold writings of Laurentius Valla, who had already startled the world by his discovery of the fraud of Constantine's donation, he was entrusted with the translation of Herodotus and Thucydides. Poggio undertook the Cyropædia of Xenophon and Diodorus Siculus; Nicolas Perotto, Polybius. Guarino of Verona and George of Tiferna, Strabo, the latter, four books of Dion Prusæus, Pietro Candido, Appian.

Of the philosophers, Perotto sent out the Enchiridion of Epictetus; Theodore of Gaza some of the works of Theophrastus, and of Aristotle: George of Trebisond, the Laws of Plato. On George of Trebisond was imposed the more arduous task, the Almagest of Ptolemy. Lilius Ægidius contributed some of the works of the Alexandrian Philo. From Rinuccio of Arezzo came the Life and Fables of Æsop and the letters of Hippocrates; from John Aurispa, the Commentary of Hierocles on the golden verses of Pythagoras. Nicolas had an ardent desire to read the two great poems of Homer in Latin verse. They were only known by the prose version of Leontius Pilatus, executed under the care of Boccaccio. Philelpho, whom the Pope had received with eager cordiality, and bestowed on him, as a first gift, 500 golden ducats, relates, that just before his death, the Pope offered him a fine palace in Rome, and farms in the Roman territory, which would maintain his whole family in case and honour, and to deposit ten thousand pieces of gold, to be paid when he should have finished the Iliad and the Odyssey.[b]

---

[b] Epist. Philipp. quoted in the Disquisitio, p. 194. Æneas Sylvius says that a certain Horace of Rome was employed on the Iliad. Part of the

Nor were the Fathers of the Greek Church without due honour. Basil, the two Gregories, Cyril, the Evangelic Preparation of Eusebius by George of Trebisond, a new version of Dionysius the Areopagite, opened the theology of the Greeks to the inquiring West.[c]

There was not as yet any awful apprehension of impairing the sacred majesty of the Vulgate Bible. Manetti, a Florentine, in his day the most famous for his erudition, was authorised and urged to execute a new version of the whole Scriptures from the Hebrew and the Greek. He completed the Psalms from the Syriac, the whole New Testament, except perhaps the Acts of the Apostles.

Thus to Nicolas V., Italy, or rather Latin Christianity, mainly owes her age of learning, as well as its fatal consequence to Rome and to Latin Christianity, which in his honest ardour he would be the last to foresee. It was the splendid vision of Nicolas V. that this revival of letters, which in certain circles became almost a new religion, would not be the bondslave but the handmaid or willing minister of the old. Latin Christianity was to array itself in all the spoils of the ancient world, and so maintain as a natural result (there was nothing of policy in his thought), and with increasing and universal veneration, her dominion over the mind of man. The rebellion of Letters, and the effects of that rebellion, we must hereafter endeavour to explain.

But Rome under Nicolas V. was not to be the centre of letters alone, she was to resume her rank as the

---

first book in Latin verse, with a dedication to Nicolas V., is in the Vatican.

[c] Nicolas obtained a copy of the Commentaries of Chrysostom on St. Matthew, which had been so rare in the West, that Aquinas had said he would rather possess it than the city of Paris.

centre of Art, more especially of architectural magnificence. Rome was to be as of old the Lawgiver of Civilisation; pilgrims from all parts of the world, from curiosity, for business or from religion, were to bow down before the confessed supremacy of her splendid works.

Progress of human intellect.

The century from the death of Boniface VIII. to the accession of Martin V., during the Avignonese exile, and the Schism, had been a period of disaster, neglect, decay, ruin; of that slow creeping, crumbling ruin, which is perhaps more fatal to ancient cities than conflagration, usually limited in its ravages, or the irruption of barbarous enemies.[d] Martin V. had made some advances to the restoration of the financial prosperity of the Popedom; Eugenius IV. had reasserted the endangered spiritual supremacy. Both had paid some attention to the dilapidated churches, palaces, walls of the city. Under Nicolas V. Rome aspired to rise again at once to her strength and to her splendour. The Pope was to be a great Sovereign Prince, but above the Sovereign Prince he was to be the successor of St. Peter. Rome was to be at once the strong citadel, and the noblest sanctuary in the world, unassailable by her enemies both without and within from her fortifications; commanding the world to awe by the unrivalled majesty of her churches. The Jubilee had poured enormous wealth into the Treasury of the Pope; his ordinary revenues, both from the Papal territory and from Christendom at large, began to flow in with peace and with the revival of his authority. That wealth was all expended with the most liberal magnificence. Already had it dawned

---

[d] Read Petrarch's well-known letter—Gibbon. Bunsen and Platner. Roms Beschreibung.

upon the mind of Nicolas V. that the Cathedral of the Chief of the Apostles ought to rival, or to surpass all the churches in Christendom in vastness and majesty. It was to be entirely rebuilt from its foundations.* Julius II. and Leo X. did but accomplish the design of Nicolas V. Had Nicolas lived, Bramante and Michael Angelo might have been prematurely anticipated by Rosellini of Florence and Leo Battista Alberti. He had even erected an august and spacious Tribune, to be swept away with the rest of the building by his bolder and more ambitious successors. The mosaic pavement in the apse, begun by Nicolas V., was completed by Paul II., at the cost of more than 5000 pieces of gold.[f]

By the side, and under the shadow of this noblest of churches, the Supreme Pontiff was to have his most stately palace. The Lateran, and the Palace near S. Maria Maggiore, sumptuously restored by Nicolas V., were to bow before this more glorious edifice. The description may still be read of its spacious courts, its cool green gardens, its dashing fountains, its theatre, its hall for public ceremonies, for the conclave and the Pontifical coronation, the treasury, the library; this chamber, perhaps as dearest to the tastes of Nicolas, was the first part, if not the only part achieved. The Palace had its three stories for summer, for winter, and for spring, even to the offices and kitchens.[g] The Cardinals were to dwell around the Pope, if in less lofty, yet still in noble Palaces. The Vatican was to be the Capitol of the Capital of Christendom. The whole

---

* Georgio, in his Life of Nicolas V., says (p. 180). "Basilicam vero S. Petri Principis Apostolorum a fundamentis magnifice inchoare et perficere meditabatur." In the Life of Manetti (Muratori, I. R. T.), vol. iii. is a long description of the plan of the church, and the design of the Pope. See also Bonanni Templi Vaticani Historia, c. xi., with the references.

f Georgio, p. 167.

g In Manetti's Life of Nicolas V.

Leonine city, which had too long lain almost open to the invading stranger, and was not safe from the turbulent Romans, was to expand in security as well as splendour around the residence of St. Peter and his successors. The bridge of St. Angelo was bordered with turrets for defence and ornament; the Castle of St. Angelo, the citadel which commanded the bridge, was strengthened by outward bulwarks, and by four towers at the corners, within laid out into halls and chambers. It was connected by strong walls with the Vatican; a huge tower began to rise, the commencement of formidable works of defence beyond the gardens of the Vatican. From the bridge of St. Angelo three broad streets, with open porticoes, and shops within them, were to radiate; the central one led direct to the portico of St. Peter's, before which Nicolas V. designed to set up the famous obelisk, which Sixtus V. at infinite cost, and with all the science of Fontana, hardly succeeded in placing on its base. The street to the left ran along the Tiber; that to the right, to the Vatican and the Palatine Gate.

Nor did the Pontiff design to expend all his munificence on St. Peter's and the Vatican. Decay, from violence or want of repair, had fallen on the forty churches called the Stations, visited by the more solemn processions, especially those which, with St. Peter's, made the more Holy Seven, the Lateran, S. Maria Maggiore, S. Stephen on Monte Celio, the Apostles', S. Paul and S. Lorenzo beyond the walls. All shared more or less in his restoring bounty. Three other churches, S. Maria beyond the Tiber, S. Theodore, S. Prassede were rebuilt; the Pantheon, now consecrated to the Virgin and all Saints, was covered with a roof of lead.

The Pontiff would secure the city from foreign foes, who for centuries, either through the feuds, the perfidy, or the turbulence of the Romans themselves, or from their own ambition or hostility, had desolated the city. In the whole circuit, from the Porta Flumentana to the Pyramid of Cestius, and so all round the city, the walls were strengthened, towers erected, fosses deepened. The Capitol was restored to its ancient strength and solidity. In order to convey his building materials to the city, perhaps provisions, he cleansed the channel of the Anio; he repaired the stately aqueduct which brought the Acqua Vergine to the Fountain of Trevi. He restored the Milvian bridge.

The munificence of Nicolas confined not itself to Rome. Everywhere in the Roman territory rose churches, castles, public edifices. Already the splendid church of S. Francis, at Assisi, wanted repair: Nicolas built a church dedicated to S. Francis, at his favoured town of Fabriano; one at Gualdo in Umbria, to S. Benedict. Among his princely works was a castle at Fabriano, great buildings at Centumcellæ, the walls of Civita Castellana, a citadel at Narni, with bulwarks and deep fosses; another at Civita Vecchia; baths near Viterbo; buildings for ornament and for defence at Spoleto.[h]

The younger Arts, Sculpture and Painting, began under his auspices still further to improve. Fra Angelico painted at Rome at the special command or request of Nicolas V.

Nicolas V., on his deathbed, communicated to the

[h] On the astonishment and admiration excited by the buildings of Nicolas V., read the passages of Æneas Sylvius, Vit. Frederic. III. "Quantum vero animo hic valeret, et quam vastus sit ejus animus, ejus ædificia monstrant, quo nemo aut magnificentius aut celerius aut splendidius quam ipse ædificavit. Nam turres et muri par eum constructi nulli priscorum arte vel magnitudine cedunt."—P. 138. "Namque at priscorum Cæsarum moles totius urbis structura superat, sic ædificia Nicolai Papæ, quicquid ubique emet moderni laboris excellunt."—P. 282. The Emperor Frederick, himself an excellent architect, stood in amazement.

Cardinals, who stood around in respectful sorrow, his last Will and Testament. This solemn appeal, as it were, to God and man, after a copious and minute confession of faith, turned to his architectural works. These holy and worldly edifices he had raised not from ambition, from pride, from vain-glory, or for the perpetuation of his name, but for two great ends, the maintenance of the authority of the Church of Rome, and her more commanding dignity above all Christian people, as well as her security against lawless persecution. The majesty of such sacred imperishable monuments profoundly impresses the mind of man with the perpetuity, the eternity of religion. As to the secular buildings, the walls, towers, citadels, he recounts the dangers, the persecutions of Popes from early days; Popes insulted, Popes dethroned, Popes imprisoned, Popes banished, Popes murdered, from Eugenius II. through all the darker ages, down to the conspiracy of Stephen Porcaro against himself. These were his motives for the conception and execution of so many sumptuous and so solid edifices. He proceeds to that sad burthen on his weary soul, the taking of Constantinople. He boasts with some, but surely blameless pride, of the peace of Italy; he had restrained, allayed, appeased the fierce wars among all the Princes and all the Republics.[1]

Nor does he speak with less satisfaction or delight of his own labours in the cause of Letters; the purchase of books, the copying of manuscripts, the encouragement of scholars; he appeals to the personal knowledge of the Cardinals, to the world, even to higher judgement,

---

[1] "Bella ipsa, quibus undique frementibus jampridem tota bino Italia vexabatur, ita compescuimus, ita denique sedavimus, ut omnes Principes, Respublicas, et Italos Populos ad maximam concordiam summamque pacem induceremus."

on his acquisition and his employment of the wealth of the Pontificate: "all these and every other kind of treasure were not accumulated by avarice, not by simony, not by largesses, not by parsimony, as ye know; but only through the grace of the most merciful Creator, the peace of the Church, and the perpetual tranquillity of my Pontificate."[k]

Thus in Nicolas V. closed one great age of the Papacy. In Nicolas the Sovereign Italian Prince and the Pontiff met in serene and amicable dignity; he had no temptation to found a princely family. But before long the Pontiff was to be lost in the Sovereign Prince. Nor was it less evident that the exclusive dominion of Latin Christianity was drawing to a close, though nearly a century might elapse before the final secession of Teutonic Christianity, and the great permanent division of Christendom. Each successive Pontificate might seem determined to advance, to hasten that still slow but inevitable revolution; the audacious nepotism of Sixtus IV., the wickedness of Alexander VI., which defy palliation; the wars of Julius II., with the hoary Pope at the head of ferocious armies; the political intrigues and disasters of Clement VII.

[k] "Hæc omnia pleraque alia divitiarum et gazarum genera nobis non ex avaritiâ, non ex simoniâ, non ex largitionibus, non ex parsimoniâ ut scitis, sed ex divinâ duntaxat benignissimi Creatoris gratiâ, et ex pace Ecclesiasticâ perpetuâque Pontificatus nostri tranquillitate provenisse non dubitamus."—Ibid. Manetti seems to assert that this long testament was read by the dying Pope. The improbability of this throws no doubt on its authenticity.

END OF VOL. VIII.

LONDON:
PRINTED BY WILLIAM CLOWES AND SONS, STAMFORD STREET
AND CHARING CROSS.

www.ingramcontent.com/pod-product-compliance
Lightning Source LLC
Chambersburg PA
CBHW021426300426
44114CB00010B/668